The Event

The Event

LITERATURE AND THEORY **ILAI ROWNER**

University of Nebraska Press
Lincoln and London

© 2015 by the Board of Regents of the University of Nebraska.
All rights reserved. Manufactured in the United States of America. ∞
Library of Congress Cataloging-in-Publication Data
Rowner, Ilai.
The event: literature and theory / Ilai Rowner.
pages cm
Includes bibliographical references and index.
ISBN 978-0-8032-4585-3 (hardback)
ISBN 978-0-8032-8648-1 (epub)
ISBN 978-0-8032-8649-8 (mobi)
ISBN 978-0-8032-8650-4 (pdf).
1. Literature—Philosophy. I. Title.
PN45.R64 2015
809—dc23
2014024696
Set in Minion Pro, Franklin Gothic,
and Century by Lindsey Auten.
Designed by Karla Johnson.

Contents

	Preface	vii
	Acknowledgments	xv
1.	Introduction: Historical Event, Narrative Event, Literary Event	1
2.	INTERMEZZO: The Cave in Homer's *Odyssey* and the Café in Marguerite Duras's *Moderato Cantabile*	45

PART ONE: THEORY

3.	Martin Heidegger: The Event of Appropriation	57
4.	Maurice Blanchot: The Event of Dying	71
5.	Jacques Derrida: The Non-Advent of the Event	96
6.	Gilles Deleuze: The Becoming of the Event	122

PART TWO: LITERATURE

7.	Toward a Theory of Literary Events: Conceptions and Principles	161
8.	AIR RAID ONE: Marcel Proust's *Time Regained*	177
9.	Writing Corporeally: A Vital Move	191

10. AIR RAID TWO:
    Louis-Ferdinand Céline's
    Fable for Another Time — 209

11. AIR RAID THREE:
    T. S. Eliot's "Little Gidding"
    from *Four Quartets* — 227

12. Conclusion: Being Is in the
    Hands of the Event — 239

    Notes — 241

    Bibliography — 281

    Index — 295

Preface

This book is based on research I carried out in French literature and theory. It examines a key concept within contemporary literary studies by asking the following question: What is the literary event, and how is it possible to think about it? The term *event*, which has troubled the minds of major thinkers and scholars in very different domains (from historiography through performance art to analytical philosophy), allows us to follow the emergence of a theoretical approach that evolved in Continental thought after World War II and thus to look at the philosophical conditions of literary thinking at one of its most innovative pinnacles, at the apex of classical modernism and at its point of transition into what has since become known as postmodernism.

What I have tried to present here is an effort part scholarly and part creative to formulate a contemporary poetics, which I name, perhaps roughly, a theory of literary events. I wanted to ponder by means of this concept whether there is a moment that is unique to literature, even if only ideally, a moment that testifies to its creative value. And so the question that preoccupied me was not a historical or sociopolitical one in the sense currently common in cultural studies. This thinking about the literary event is not situated in a particular economic, technological, or ideological field and does not manifest itself as a set of empirical findings regarding a distinctive literary corpus. In this book the event is studied as a phenomenological-ontological concept that enables us to examine the art of literature as a necessary appeal of creativity. Here the event is considered neither as an occurrence in the world (historical facts, breaking news) nor as a representative or narrative incident in a novel or short story. The literary event cannot be reduced either to an extralinguistic reality or to its existence inside the linguistic realm. One of the major efforts of this book is to construct the event as a dynamic in-between entity, a liminal movement that blends the unknown factors of a happening with the vivid performance of linguistic creation.

Binding together being and language means that the event is generally felt in literature as an outburst, a moment of rupture and change, as an elusive action and an irresistible force of otherness, thereby situating a singular conception of literary creativity in relation to crisis and defining the importance of literature as *a compound of crisis*: a crisis that puts to the test any settled value of truth, a crisis of representation, a crisis of language itself, a crisis that concerns the destiny of the one who produces the work as well as the identity of the work produced.

Questioning the concept of the event enables us to examine in depth the violence of precisely this crisis. It allows us to open up the intensive temporal segment of the crisis insofar as it is a crucial factor, real as well as symbolic, in the becoming of the work of art. In this sense the event is both the motive that brings this crisis into existence and the concrete place of its realization; it is the evidence of the unfolding of the crisis in the text and by the text, and it is the abstract catalyst that makes the text possible.

It would be an impossible and hence superfluous task to distinguish between an event that is meaningful and one that is without value. Since the advent of psychoanalysis we know that an event may occur in the banal contact with the most basic object. Modern literature bears this out again and again: the texture of a stone or the roots of a tree in Sartre's *Nausea*, the passing look at the Ballast Office clock in the first version of Joyce's *A Portrait of the Artist as a Young Man*, or even the mere clanking of a spoon against a plate in Proust's *Time Regained* arouse unexpected and intense inner stirrings, aesthetically as well as existentially. And so the main problematic the event poses to literature is caught under the question not of "What?" but of "How?" How can the literary event be defined? How is it possible to study the literary event not by determining its absolute essence but by drawing the conditions and principles for the examination of literary moments that stab and wound, moments in which it is felt that the work "cries out" while it is taken to the very limits of its ability and in which the creative energy of one detail outdoes that of the whole? And thus the questions "What is the event?" and "What is the literary event?," which guide part 1 of this book, change in part 2 into "How do we construct from its very roots a thinking of the event of literature?" That is to say, what are the conceptual tools and moves by means of which the literary event in all its complexity can be thought of—an event that connects the novelty of the work of language with the incomprehensible appearance and experience of being?

A clear illustration of what the term *literary event* refers to can be achieved by means of a short analysis of the Lord Chandos letter, written by the Viennese poet Hugo Von Hofmannsthal.[1] This short piece offers a fictional letter, supposedly written in the seventeenth century, which describes the story of an intellectual who loses his faith in the work of art, gives up all his literary activity, and wraps himself in a great silence: "the literary works which I am supposed to have ahead of me are separated from me by a gulf as unbridgeable as the ones behind me. And those I hesitate to call my own, so unfamiliar do they seem. . . . In brief, this is my case: I have completely lost the ability to think or speak coherently about anything at all."[2]

The event of the letter unfolds in two moments. The first of these is the collapse of the certainties that until then supported Lord Chandos's competencies and artistic projects. The second is a kind of inverted vision in which a new artistic destiny suddenly is revealed, demanding a poetics as yet unformulated. The first moment describes the crumbling of the hitherto firm values on which man's world rested. Chandos has to chide his little daughter and demonstrate "to her the necessity of always being truthful," but words and ideas are suddenly all jumbled inside him; the sentence becomes confused before he can speak it; his face pales in consternation, and as he experiences a kind of nervous breakdown he leaves his daughter, slamming the door behind him. "Everything came to pieces, the pieces broke into more pieces, and nothing could be encompassed by one idea. Isolated words swam about me; they turned into eyes that stared at me and into which I had to stare back, dizzying whirlpools which spun around and around and led into the void."[3]

The first moment of the literary event imposes a caesura on Chandos; the second introduces an exceptional transformation and constitutes the letter's climax. Having decided to withdraw from human society and to leave the very pinnacles of the human spirit, Chandos feels close to the silent simplicity of things—"a harrow left in a field, a dog in the sun, a shabby churchyard"—and then one day, near his farm, he experiences a kind of epiphany. In his mind's eye appears the horrible scene of rats dying in a cellar: "It was all there. The cool and musty cellar air, full of the sharp, sweetish smell of the poison, and the shrilling of the death cries echoing against mildewed walls. Those convulsed clumps of powerlessness, those desperations colliding with one another in confusion. The frantic search for ways out. The cold glares of fury when two meet at a blocked crevice."[4]

The scene is so vividly described that it might not have been only imagined; perhaps this was a denied real perception, since Chandos himself has just ordered to have rat poison scattered in the cellar: "A mother was there, whose dying young thrashed about her. But she was not looking at those in their death agonies, or at the unyielding stone walls, but off into space, or through space into the infinite, and gnashing her teeth as she looked! If there was a slave standing near Niobe in helpless fright as she turned to stone, he must have gone through what I went through when the soul of this beast I saw within me bared its teeth to its dreadful fate."[5]

The literary event of Hofmannsthal's letter actually bears out how literary style simultaneously captures and generates imperceptible movements of being that remain senseless. The work of writing obeys the law of the event and at the same time presents the intensity of images and bodies that take part in it. This letter offers a simple model of thinking the event of literature. It indicates how the "becoming" of literature constitutes itself as onto-poetic change in the world. The language of the old world is replaced by the appearance of being as a new artistic experience and image: the liminal status of animal suffering, the insignificant disaster of rats, their contortions and screams—all these justify the work itself.

Still, to be more precise, this is just the beginning of the analysis of the literary event of the Lord Chandos letter, for it must be argued with greater acuity what, here, constitutes the internal becoming of the event. Why, for instance, does the event come to pass between two looks exchanged between parents and children: the father who is unable to reprove his daughter, and the mother rat who holds on to her dying young while her gaze travels into infinity? The human father and the animal mother are both unable to shield their children from the collapse of consciousness and from the terrible disaster of the present. The father covers his face and flees into loneliness and the open terrain, while the inferior creature surprisingly reveals motherly sensibilities, opens her face upward to a prohibited sight that is revealed through this gaze (very much like Andromache clinging to her executed son in Euripides's play *The Women of Troy*).

Moreover, what is the mouth's grimace that links, on the one hand, the expelled father, whose words crumble in his mouth "like rotten mushrooms," with, on the other, the mother rat, her jaw contracted, "gnashing her teeth," an animal noise that arises from the mouth of the earth, lacking any concept and meaning, but which appears as both proclamation and dread of the world: "when the soul of this beast I saw within me bared its teeth to its dreadful fate." What is it about the "corporeality of the event" that unites the human condition, Chandos and his daughter, with the mildewed, poisonous reeking cellar and the shrieks of dying rats? What is it about the corporeality that is expressed through the opened eyelids and the spasmodic jaw? How does a boundless immanent movement come to take place through these body parts, causing the distinction between inner and outer feeling to fade: "I feel a blissful and utterly eternal interplay in me and around me, and amid the to-and-fro there is nothing into which I cannot merge."[6]

The eyes in this letter want to see things as they are, to be exposed to things in their exemplary muteness: no longer to look with words, not to look in words, and in this way to escape the terror of the words' own gaze since they turned into a type of illusory divinity—"a garden full of eyeless statuary." Similarly, words are chewed and disintegrate inside the mouth due to an inexplicable uneasiness, "an inexplicable uneasiness in even pronouncing the words 'spirit,' 'soul,' or 'body.'" Words are voided of meaning and dissolve in the mouth; stutter and speechlessness transform into stasis and silence. Worse, tongue itself becomes teeth, resulting in a maw stripped of its sense, the convulsion of an unintelligible animal, teeth that gnaw away at the world's expanse like the naked expression of being a body once and for all: the raw testimony of the body's horror and of its vulnerability.

In this manner, the terrible fate of animality that Lord Chandos witnesses "through space into the infinite" becomes a new creative object, a call for impossible invention out of crisis, creation brought about by the event itself beyond any possibility of books and beyond the limits of writing, creation that Chandos feels in the silence he imposes on himself or in unmediated outbursts of which it cannot be known how they will find expression. This is the real aspect of becoming, a reality that must be cast in the aesthetic and ethical direction that Gilles Deleuze outlines toward the end of the twentieth century: "every man who suffers is a piece of meat. Meat is the common zone of man and the beast . . . a zone of indiscernibility more profound than any sentimental identification: the man who suffers is a beast. The beast that suffers is a man. This is the reality of becoming."[7]

In this short example from Hofmannsthal, in this compound that comes about between the literary text and the inexplicable forces of the event, *corporeality* appears as an important dimension making a vital project out of literary creation. Here I am not thinking of literary representations of the body or the way the writer's body creates his language, but of the effort to reveal the impersonal corporeality of the event itself.

The literary text is a wonderful laboratory for looking into the event's corporeality, into the material or carnal skeleton that establishes the event as historical or narrative fact. In the context of modern painting, Deleuze discusses the need to make the "head" emerge from beneath the "face," to make emerge the crude dimension of the figure from civilization's depiction of the face, that is, from the camouflage of a sociohistorical identity; in a similar way the corporeality of the event must be taken out of the historical or narrative facts, the words and image from which it was made must reveal the emergence of its raw becoming. This is what a reading of Hofmannsthal must attempt to achieve: through tongue and teeth, the poison in the cellar and the open spaces, the animal's spasms and man's stutter, one has to find the fundamental intensity out of which the event emerges, both as a phenomenon that partakes from the real and as a virtual phenomenon that is subject to inexhaustible transformation. What we must consider in this book is the ambiguous celebration of the *corporeality of the event* in the literary text. Does what distinguishes the literary event inhere in the fact that the fictive poetics of literature leads to what does not happen within the happening, that is, strives toward what is always different, always imperceptible in the comprehensible circumstances themselves, what has not yet been experienced as such within the known confines of the event. Doesn't the literary demand an incorporeal realm that arises from and within the degree zero of corporeality itself?

The structure of this book is quite simple. To provide a background to my argument, the introduction discusses the differences between the historical event, narrative event, and literary event. I examine in the introductory chapter why the literary event cannot be reduced to the conventional use of the event in historiography and in narratology, and, therefore, needs to be thought of in philosophical terms. Next, part 1 discusses the theoretical features of the event as they relate to the work of Heidegger, Blanchot, Derrida, and Deleuze. Part 2 considers how thinking of the event may contribute to understanding the literary writing by sketching some practical principles toward a reading of the event in literature. Following especially in Deleuze's footsteps, I propose later on a vital critical approach that inquires into the relations between image and real, between the actual and virtual of the corporeal dimension of the event in literature. Here perhaps lies the importance of this book: its attempt to understand how the event's corporeality weaves being and language together in an un-happening modality of happening.

The discussion of literature becomes more specific when I examine a series of events, namely, air raids on European capitals during the two world wars as they are portrayed in several literary works. The violence and the astonishment of these events yield a fertile ground for observing how creativity bursts out of an experience in which not only being-in-the-world but the very possibility of writing are put to the test. My analysis of these events in literature aims to connect with the slow formation of theoretical thought in the book, and more than that, to stir and startle that thought; it begins from theory and makes a fast escape in order to reveal the singular force of the writings of Marcel Proust, Louis-Ferdinand Céline, and T. S. Eliot. So, I hope, it will also be possible to read these analyses as independent units.

The chapters on Proust, Céline, and Eliot join an *intermezzo* chapter in which the entire project can be understood in a figurative way: the Cyclops's cave in the *Odyssey* transforms into a café in Marguerite Duras's *Moderato Cantabile*, the very place in which the most primitive corporeal reality already intermeshes with the manifold alterities of the incorporeal image.

Acknowledgments

I would like to express my sincere gratitude to mentors, friends, and colleagues: Julia Kristeva, Rachel Albeck-Gidron, Mirjam Hadar, Lindsay Citerman, Michal Ben Naftali, Michael Gluzman, Ruth Amossy, Nadine Kuperty-Zur, Orly Lubin, Galili Shahar, Avi Sagi, Eyal Zisser, Lars Iyer, Niall Lucy, Martin Rueff, Tiphaine Samyault, Yisrael Levin, Amotz Giladi, Lilach Nethanel, and Eshel Rowner.

Research scholarships and generous funding provided by Université Paris Diderot–Paris 7, Tel Aviv University, Bar-Ilan University, the research group ADARR, the Kipp Center, and the Porter Institute for Poetics and Semiotics at Tel Aviv University, as well as the Embassy of France in Israel, made the writing of this book possible.

I wish to thank the editors at the University of Nebraska Press and especially Kristen Elias Rowley for her great dedication and care in bringing out this work.

1

Introduction
Historical Event, Narrative Event, Literary Event

The central objective of this book is to reconsider the concept of the *event* from a philosophical vantage point, and with special reference to the literary text. Through the study of Heidegger, Blanchot, Derrida, and Deleuze, this book will suggest a method of thinking about the event of the literary work, both by examining the fundamental question of the literary creation and by providing the conditions for a different approach to literary criticism. The term *event* will be defined here as any irregular occurrence, real or fictional, that has effectively and obviously come about. At the same time, it is in the very substance of the event to comprise an unknown element that is imperceptible and inappropriable.[1] At the foundation of this book lies the supposition that literature, as an art of language and as an act of fiction, essentially relates to the problem of the event and is precisely concerned with the event's dimension of inexhaustibility, to the *eventness* of the event, which simultaneously is the condition for its concrete occurrence and projects its ideal inconceivability.

What is literature's approach to the event? How does literature produce and give testimony to events? How must we define literature with regard to the singular moment of an irregular event? This study will suggest that the way the act of writing deals with the event, and specifically with the elusive element of happening-in-process, reveals the creative energy of the work of literature, namely, the work's production of new movements of writing and new imaginative combinations based on intensive configurations of living sensations.

Expressing the meaning of the event is not the aim of literature, especially not where such meaning would purport to be proof of a scientific order of knowledge or of a social episteme and practices. On the contrary, literary writing will be defined by reference to the *senseless* moment of the event. Literature relies on the particular moment when a failing of sense occurs as the result of rupture, a momentary excess or lack of sense where there is no longer a settled and presupposed experience in the world and conventional rules for creation are absent.

It is true that any event, even the most implausible, might have a name, a ground from which it becomes actual and a new horizon that it inaugurates. The event can relate to a specific theme and *topos*. Sometimes it narratively joins other events through the configuration of a plot or through poetry's metaphorical and symbolic relation. At other times, literary inquiry is required to borrow tools from other domains (philosophy, psychoanalysis, politics) for literature to create itself anew and to evolve its own path. However, in all these cases, the singularity of the literary discourse depends not on what we know or understand through poetic or historical interpretations, but rather on the undefined feeling of an *eventness* that does not have any literal expression or *telos*.

A sign that unexpectedly appears or a blow that suddenly hits—it is through violent disturbance, astonishing irruption and disruption, or confusion between image and reality that the event incessantly acts on the literary work as a call for absolute creation in which the reverberation of writing and reading must obstinately persist. The event stamps itself on the literary work as an entity of fascination or anxiety. A happening that remains nameless forces itself on the work through these passions. The work of literature, as both writing and reading, becomes then the making of the event itself: the more one engages with the event's unprecedented order, surrendering to unheard ambiguous language and sensations, the more the work becomes "the offspring of the event," to borrow Deleuze's beautiful expression.[2]

The writer, and perhaps even before the writer, the reader, must be reborn through the work of literature. The one who is engaged in the work has to experience "a sort of leaping in place [*saut sur place*] of the whole body," to become the offspring of the event not by revealing the objective facts or by unfolding the entirety of what actually happened.[3] It may be more accurate to say that the experience of literature must pull us into an involuntary metamorphosis that follows *the un-happening within the happening.*

This does not mean that the aim of artistic creation is to reach stillness within perpetual motion, in T. S. Eliot's words.⁴ Nor does it mean that literature must reach the pure void, the ideal gratuity of fictional reverie, or inversely that it is its task to decipher the law of any confused daylight accident. Here the un-happening is the dazzling reality of the happening itself. The absolute surprise and striking appearance of the event affect the writing and constitute the energetic vitality of a great fictional work, not only as an exigency of reorganization and recovery of sense, as Ricoeur believes, but first and foremost as the risk and promise of the event's senselessness.⁵ As Lyotard puts it: "The modern is a feeling for the event as such, impromptu, imminent, urgent, disarming knowledge and even consciousness. The event is an absolute performative: it happens. Fashion [la mode] is affirmed by the desire to be the event."⁶

The event may well open the way to what is singular in literature. It may be that at the heart of every event there is a hiatus of ignorance that makes for the terrifying and beautiful gift of literature. But, to begin with, a preliminary conceptual examination must be observed, which asks again: How can we define the literary event? Is it the event of the text or the events that are narrated in the text? Is it the historical events that the text refers to or the symbolic event itself that affects the course of history? The literary text is inhabited by multiple series of events; literature narrates fictitious events and refers to historical or mythic events. The term *event* presents a line of action; it supposes that movement in time and change occur. It is a sequence of acts and facts, a transmutation or a passage between two different states. The event therefore is the most fundamental element of any narrative structure and the kernel of all historical understanding.

To be more precise, we must examine the conventional use of the term *event* both in the writing of history and in narrative theory. This is our first concern: to examine how the act of literary writing considers the substance of the event differently from historiography and narratology. How does this new notion of the event define the work of literature differently from the manner in which it is defined by the narrative intelligence of history and the fictional structure of plot? How does the literary writing of the event differ from the writing experience of historiography and from the narrative composition of plot?

The Historical Event

In *Time and Narrative I*, Ricoeur is preoccupied by what he defines as the circle between time and narrative, or the circular exchange between temporal experience and narrative configuration. His thesis is that time can be humanly grasped only when it is arranged by a narrative intelligence: it is only when we articulate time in a story that it becomes historical. This assertion remains valid if we consider it from the opposite perspective: history attains meaning only as a result of the insertion of time into the narrative. Since the narrative's meaning becomes realizable through its temporal characteristics, no historical knowledge stands absolutely free from narrative intelligibility.

In his extensive discussion of the indirect relation between history and narrative, Ricoeur turns his attention to the event as an intersection between the ontological happening within the course of time and its epistemological function in the intelligible reconstruction created by historical discourse. He assumes that the historical event has the following qualities:[7]

a. History privileges the event that has effectively taken place in the past.
b. The event relates necessarily to the human actor either as its author or victim.
c. The event brings about change.
d. Unlike a universal law, the event is conventionally conceived as unrepeatable and singular.
e. The event is contingent and not necessary.
f. The event is a deviation from the norm rather than a construction model.

How effective are these qualities when applied in the methodological research of historiography? Bensa and Fassin roughly distinguish between three moments in the writing of history with regard to the status of the event.⁸ The first is that of traditional positivist history, which considers the event as the main object of its research, resulting in a history of wars and revolutions, great events and heroes. Ricoeur's assumptions can be literally observed here, insofar as historians have classically described the event as a decisive temporal leap that changes the political order. The second moment appears as historiography approaches the methods of the social sciences. The Annales School, and particularly Braudel, criticizes the privilege historiography gives to the event's sudden emergence and its immediate influence on the individual by inversely suggesting a "total history" that touches upon multiple domains of knowledge (economic, geographic, spiritual) and is based on collective "conjunctures" occurring in the temporal extension of the *longue durée*, the long term. Regarding the third moment, Bensa and Fassin mention Pierre Nora's article "The Return of the Event": here, the meaning of the event is no longer a matter of the importance of the happening itself but a question of social production by mass communication. In this moment, historiography must address itself to the present time, the state of affairs in the modern democracy, where the event is one symptom that reveals how current discursive practices produce and establish what happens in time.

Ricoeur focuses on the split between historicity as perceived by the Annales School and historical positivism. As he apprehends the critique of the Annales and their disillusionment with positivist reconstitutions of the past, he demonstrates first that the way history writing conceives of the event influences both the method of inquiry into and the comprehension of the past, and next that even the historical method that rejects the event cannot, however, absolutely avoid it. History cannot be without events. Even if the Annalistes defend a critical inquiry that rejects the event as the core of the historical narrative, because the event inaugurates "a history of short, sharp, nervous vibrations," they admit other models of quasi-events and conjunctures that contribute to the development of a new historical structure, of an "anonymous history, working in the depths, and most often silent."⁹

On this same matter, Paul Veyne observes that the Annales, while presenting an eventless historiography and setting aside the "battles and treaties," opens historiography to new "nonevents": "what is not an event are those events not yet hailed as such: The history of terrors, of *mentalités*, of madness, or of the search for security across the ages. We shall therefore call the nonevent that historicity of which as such we are not yet aware."[10]

Ricoeur explains moreover how this contestation of the traditional event affects the narrative intelligence of history. The event now becomes a variable that participates in heterogeneous temporalities, in contradictory chronologies, and in the diverse rhythms of different realms of life. However, the *longue durée* method and the scientific discourse of the Annales remain compatible with the narrative model of *discordant concordance* that Ricoeur develops from the Aristotelian concept of *muthos*. "The facts only exist in and through plots," Ricoeur writes, quoting Veyne. The event is not only what happens but precisely what could be told, what may assume order in spite of its relative disorder.

The non-chronological, eventless history of the Annales School allows Ricoeur to extend the conception of *muthos* beyond the familiar poetic genres of plot. Dissimulating any relation to the order of the story and yet preserving analogically narrative categories, the new historicism affirms paradoxically that the *muthos* can be stretched into a hermeneutical model of discordant concordance. This "synthesis of the heterogeneous" underlies all acts of historical understanding. According to Ricoeur, it thus furnishes an explanation of the transformation from the divergent experience of happening in time and the convergence of the constituted events through the discursive transmission of history.[11]

What happens in the course of this transformation? Ricoeur distinguishes three stages in which this *chrono-logos* of *muthos* is activated through historical elaboration. He calls the text of the *muthos* the result of an act of "configuration" that mediates between the "prefiguration" of the real experience in time and the operation of "refiguration" that applies to the reception of the text as a historical discourse. With these three steps Ricoeur conceives of a major theory of narrative intelligence, showing how the story continually participates in the reconstruction of sense and asserting its supremacy over the temporal disorder of the event.

The act of prefiguration reveals the pre-understanding of the world that allows the passage from physical occurrence to historical narrative; it displays the meaningful destination of the event and its intelligible elements that reveal history's capacity of being told. Configuration is the composition of the historical narrative itself in which the unity of the *muthos* both protects the discordance of the event and endows it with newly settled sense. Finally, refiguration is where the historical event becomes the cultural property of a society of readers and writers. The textual configuration provides a certain explanation of the prefigured occurrence, and thus it is available to be refigured by the understanding and interpretation of the circle of people who share the same discourse.[12]

Although Ricoeur does not restrict his hermeneutic model of narrative only to history, he finds in the narrative traces of historiography a privileged ground that makes the transformation of the event into a unit of sense effectively visible. In doing so, he points to some of the important motivations and premises of the historical understanding of the event. Reading Aron and Marrou, he writes: "If historians are implicated in historical knowing, they cannot propose the impossible task for themselves of re-actualizing the past. . . . [I]f this lived past were accessible to us, it would not be so as an object of knowledge. For, when it was present, this past was like our present, confused, multiform, and unintelligible. Instead, history aims at knowledge, an organized vision, established upon chains of causal or teleological relations, on the basis of meaning and values."[13]

Later, and more specifically on the problem of event, he quotes Veyne: "History is the description of what is specific, that is, understandable, in human events." As much as history looks for purposes, reasons, and chances, the organization of the historical plot will follow a logic of probability that is allowed "freely to slice up the field of events."[14]

All these observations withdraw from the scientific positivism of history: The past cannot have a truthful existence, but only a sort of Kantian postulated reality. The past cannot be accessible as it was effectuated in the present, since its retrospective re-cognition already introduces the construction of a certain order. Yet, historiography strives for a certain "factual story" of the past; it remains faithful to the project of understanding the past and of culling meaning from it. Paradoxically, it is only through an organized vision that the event can open itself to such historical knowledge and that the historian can find certain rules and necessities in it.

This methodological conflict between historical doubt and trust is one of the major motivations of Gadamer's hermeneutics. Heideggerian more than Kantian, Gadamer strives to unfold the condition and disposition from which our understanding of the past arises. He suggests approaching the problem of the past event by using the term *experience* (*Erfahrung*).[15] He mainly contests Hegel's historical assumption, which demands definitive knowledge of past experience instead of having relatively open access to it. Hegel traces a historical progression of knowledge acquisition, based on the dialectical process whereby the universal takes possession of the particular. While Hegel finds a necessary seat for the validity of the universal consciousness of history in unpredictable experience, to acknowledge what is *true* within the particular experience, historical consciousness must nevertheless overcome the particular by means of the general, rediscovering itself and thus reestablishing the coherent cognition of its becoming through the difference of the event.

Gadamer demonstrates how Hegelianism leads to a scientific conception of history that claims to objectively reflect the particularity of the experience. But since in this method object and consciousness maintain a complete identity, Hegelian universalism eventually only confirms its own presuppositions in its encounter with experience. Instead of arguing how unpredictable experience defines negativity as the constitutive movement of meaning beyond its own site, Gadamer indicates how the negativity encountered in every new experience resists all laws of science. This resistance of experience is precisely the foundation of a hermeneutic historicity shorn of scientific pretensions; it is both what makes possible the mutual openness of past and present, and at the same time what sets the limits of this openness.

Gadamer understands that being open to the particularity of the past means recognizing what is new in a specific event. The new relates both to the limited situation of the past event and to the comprehensive situation of the present. The mutual openness between past and present is limited by the historical situation, which, according to Gadamer, expresses in a more existential sense the recognition of human finitude. Thus, every operation of historical hermeneutics must first take into account human finitude, which Gadamer calls "historically effected consciousness," in contrast to the timeless illusion of an objective consciousness.

It is only when we take into consideration human finitude, when we assume the temporariness and uncertainty of human insight as our discrete destiny, that we are guided by our historical situation. "Genuine experience is experience of one's own historicity," writes Gadamer.[16] This is why the questions we direct at the past and our capacity to hear how the past questions us first and foremost come to expose our own cultural inheritance and traditional expectations.

Hence Gadamer vacillates between the need to expand historical understanding and to suspend whatever it is that falsifies understanding. On the one hand, we must acquire an openness to new experience, finding what is irreducible in the past event through an infinite dialogue between present and past. On the other hand, openness *to* past experience is possible only due to an openness *of* the experience itself. We can question the past only in the very mode by which everything that is handed down to us presents itself to us, by means of the elements the present has in common with the past, through a common language and a common tradition that welcome understanding and yet undermine understanding due to the necessary confusion of times.

Collecting and reviving a rich assemblage of relative viewpoints is a necessary condition of hermeneutical historicity, yet it is also insufficient. It must be accompanied by a critical separation that supervises the reciprocities between present and past. This is where Gadamer legitimates a "temporal distance" which he argues is required to prevent the illusory confusion of present with past and, at the same time, needed as a touchstone for present judgment of the past. Even if Gadamer calls for open processes of understanding rather than definitive knowledge of the past, this regulative filter of "historical distance" shows that the ongoing formation of understanding has to step back from experience in order to observe its particular intimacy with that experience. Only through detachment from the past can we distinguish our true attachments from our false ones and distinguish what advances understanding from what leads to misunderstanding.[17]

Hermeneutic historicity refuses to scientifically master the astonishment and the unpredictability of the event, yet it does demand to *understand* the event. It does not merely attest to it as a "manifestation of life," as Dilthey would have it, but strives for its "true meaning," to confirm or to refute our expectations of sense.[18] Understanding the historical event means suggesting a specific reconstitution of its sense, even if we are aware that the involvement of the historian's subjectivity is undeniable, even if we know that the written text is a constructed discourse cut off from the living experience and that causality is a conventional order produced by human abstraction, and not inherent in things themselves.

Gadamer's temporal distance, Ricoeur's narrative hermeneutics, Aron, Marrou, Veyne—they all point in the same direction: although historical knowledge and method are scientifically questionable, historiography remains faithful to the pre-evaluation of what makes sense in the event and of how the event is subject to a larger unity of sense.

This view breeds many problems. First, one can ask about the source of the event's sense: Should we look for it within the happening itself or does it depend on the historian's point of view? (Gadamer). Second, we notice that the sense of the event is malleable: either it generates out of itself a meaningful destination or it takes on a new sense deriving from its context and imposed once we have enough hindsight (Ricoeur). Third, and more generally, we might doubt whether the very claim that the event has a sense actually only masks its singularity: the historical instauration of order simply means the cancellation of the event's irregularity, unpredictability, and contingency.

It is with this last problem that my main disagreement with the historical view lies. Ricoeur would likely agree that historiography does not cancel the event but rather forms an ethical suspension of it. He would say that discontinuity is a necessary component of continuity, that with the benefit of delay the historian fills the event with practical and essential insights in order to gain a grip on its anarchic aspects.[19]

In this same manner, Gadamer's temporal distance defends a critical perception of the irrationality of the event without obliterating it by rationality. But even then, does the historical discourse remain blind to the very *eventness* of the event, namely, to its vacant rupture and its excessive movement? Sense-making's commitment to truthfulness always leaves us with a hiatus between what we want to understand and what must be understood, between the historian's questioning and the credibility of the historical document.

The event is never neutral in historical writing. The neutrality of its very happening may in fact *absolutely not* be what history affirms to be an event. Historiography vacillates between a praxis of reproduction and a praxis of production, between the recognition that the living past refuses to be an object of knowledge and the profound care for the evocation of the past. In this wavering, the unmeasured event wears the mask of measure and name, of *followability* and probability, dissimulating perhaps that not even one event takes place in history at all.

By way of contrast with the notion of "temporal distance" or "historical distance" in the context of historiography, I would like to suggest a "fictive distance" for literature. If "historical distance" is necessary for the disinterested observation of the event, "fictive distance" emphasizes from the start that the literary text needs to have an interest that exceeds the event's sense. While "historical distance" is a quantitative temporal measure that is associated with understanding, "fictive distance" is a qualitative measure presupposing that there is always something in the event that cannot be said or known.

Gadamer argues that historical distance is not an abyss over which the historian builds a bridge with the sole intention of reviving the past from oblivion. This distance must be respected: it indicates that the advantage of the historical discourse evolves beyond the happening event. This abyss is not a weakness; on the contrary, it is where the productive historical dialogue begins: the effective consequences of the event become visible and the historian's questions gain shape and complexity.

"Fictive distance" suggests other discursive operations and other images of *eventness*. The event does not exist beyond a temporal distance, but a "fictive distance" is inherent to the event itself. The writer must not step back to acquire a panoramic view over the event. In fact, the writer must be carried away by the event, involuntarily delivering him- or herself to its blinding light in order to perceive secretly that which diverges from what can be acknowledged. Proust's sensible signs of the truthful reality of the work offer a good example of this. "Fictive distance" defines the event differently, not as a settled instant deformation within the historical construction of time but rather as an uncontrolled happening that unties its very movement away from all historical propositions. In other words, rather than being situated independently before the act of writing, the event of literature necessarily depends on the creativity of writing.

In a well-known passage of the *Poetics*, Aristotle already affirmed that the role of the poet differs from that of the historian to the extent that the potential event differs from what has actually taken place. But it is not only the different status of the event that is at stake in this comparison. Blanchot, who was among other literary thinkers an essentialist theoretician, demonstrates that the language which literature "speaks" is absolutely different from the language of history.[20] In this sense, the distinction between "historical distance" and "fictive distance" expands both Aristotle's and Blanchot's ideas by focusing on the motivation and position of writing vis-à-vis the event. It is the different manner of writing, expressing, attesting, or narrating that creates the different experience of the event. It is a matter of a different kind of attention and emphasis that tries to avoid the formal separation between the real and the fictive, between particular and general, or between prose and poetry.

If history could be called the art of the event's sense, then literature would be the artistic effort of the event's non-sense. If history demands *what exactly has taken place* in a given moment of the past, literary inquiry aspires for *the non-place of the taking place:* what is there in the event that does not reveal itself exactly in the happening.

The past event is the thematic object of a historicity that stamps writing with the authority of constative speech. Representing the facts consecutively is exactly what this aspect of discourse does, along with the task of describing extended impressions and formulating their present interest. Literature, in contrast, has no interest in the undeniable fact of the event; it is precisely the unknown movement of the happening that affects literature's performative language and its manner of speech.

The traditional gaps between subjective and objective, construction and reconstruction are insufficient when speaking of the difference between literature and history. There is historical research that is subjectively constructed and, vice versa, novels that pretend to objectively reconstruct a certain reality. The difference with history stems more precisely from the fact that literature does not have to cross a temporal distance but only a fictive distance; literature is not subordinate to an object in time, but only to the image and sensation of the written movement that brings about the "other time" in time, as Blanchot would have it. When the words of literature acknowledge fictive distance, this means that they penetrate the womb of images and sensations of the event, the corporeal invention of the event.

Thus the reconstruction of an experience in literature does not take place separately from the process of the writing experience itself. The effect of reality in the literary text depends inevitably on the movement of the work itself, in such a way that there is no longer a clear distinction between "real" and "textual," between "before" and "after," or between "outside" and "inside." Writing or reading the work of literature consists of creating the presence of an event that simultaneously escapes full presentation. But the writing and reading of literature do not only proceed as the movement in which the event takes place and becomes an actual experience. In the realm of literature there is a constant call for the event to come, where the unmeasured disorder of the event is invited to overflow in order to regenerate the creativity of the work. Penetrating the "fictive distance" thus renders writing as the event itself, leading one toward the beginning of the event, the promise of reaching both its singularity and its transformative energy without ever arriving. This is what Blanchot tells us when he writes that "the nature of narrative is no way foretold, when one sees in it the true account of an exceptional event, which took place and which one could try to report. Narrative is not the relating of an event but this event itself, the approach of this event, the place where it is called on to unfold, an event still to come, by the magnetic power of which the narrative itself can hope to come true."[21]

The Narrative Event

The term *event* is fundamentally bound to the concept of plot in narrative theory.[22] Tomashevsky already employed the word *plot* (*syuzhet*) to describe the orderly sequence of events "presented in the work."[23] More recently, Jurij Lotman has written: "We take an event to mean the smallest indivisible unit of plot construction."[24] Gérard Genette, in *Figures III*, before proceeding with his structural terminology and method, also uses the term *event*—either as the content, or as the discourse, or as the act of telling itself—to define the narrative (*récit*) as the principal object of narratology.[25]

The common narrative structure of the plot can be defined either as a narrative unit of one or more events or as the succession of events that composes a narrative relation. Either the plot encompasses the sum total of a sequence of events, such as Ulysses's returning home in the *Odyssey*, or the plot builds itself gradually from the progression and accumulation of different events, as it happens remarkably in the first chapters of the *Iliad*.

Through the study of Aristotle's *Poetics*, Ricoeur attributes the characteristics of *chronological* and *non-chronological* to these two models of plot: "The former [the chronological] constitutes the episodic dimension of narrative. It characterizes the story insofar as it is made up of events. The second is the configurational dimension properly speaking, thanks to which the plot transforms the event into a story."[26] The chronological nature of a plot is also a question of perspective, of whether we observe the action of an event from outside or inside the plot. Chronological organization would be the superimposed theme of one sequence of events, while non-chronological organization composes the plot from the juxtaposition of diverse events.

But whether chronological or non-chronological, the event is no longer a singular and closed occurrence. Thus Ricoeur argues that the idea of *narrativity* presupposes the openness of the event beyond its isolation, an openness that enables meaningful organization with other events and to gain sense from the event's contribution to the whole. While the plot reduces the event to a larger unit of sense, narratology recognizes that the more singular the event appears, the more chance it has to become the object of a story. From Aristotle to Barthes, narrative theory relates the challenge of the event to the description of its importance in the plot: what makes an event so important, more prominent than other events, that it becomes engaged with a narrative operation? How must narrative analysis take the meaning of the event into consideration? What are the conditional terms enabling understanding of the function and the hierarchy of narrative events? From a general perspective, these questions trigger two different lines of explanation: a mimetic-cultural explanation that transcends the literary text, and a structural explanation whose reasons and instruments are in the text itself.

In a long chapter on the event, Lotman recognizes that the cultural semantic field determines whether an act is insignificant or essential. Naturally, a certain worldview is sensitive to certain forms of occurrences, locating their content and comparing their different values. Lotman quotes Tolstoy, for example, who writes that the melody of a poor street musician is a greater object of writing than the events communicated in the newspapers and in history books. Gogol emphasizes social rank and profession instead of romantic sentimentality. Both testify to having a hierarchy of events that assumes a singular relationship to the world. In this perspective, Lotman understands that a change in the cultural codes at a given historical moment causes the same narrative situation to appear twisted. The task of literature is to inaugurate new writing events that create new perceptions: to value the insignificant, to reveal the unheard-of as a new source of inspiration, or to bring to light the detail that defamiliarizes the most common is the driving force of the historical evolution of literature.[27]

Structural narratology, however, brackets the cultural dimension in order to focus on the internal rules and the deep structure of the text itself. In this sense, Greimas, Todorov, and Barthes conceive of a narrative grammar that fundamentally extends from the structure of the grammatical phrase with every category of the proposition corresponding to a larger unit of discourse. The articulation between subject, verb, and object of the phrase structures the integration of the elements in the narrative: the protagonist, the action, and the desired object. "A narrative is a long sentence," writes Barthes, "just as every constative sentence is in a way the rough outline of a short narrative."[28]

action (48a). In the tragedy, for instance, the characters' ethical and mythical nobility renders possible the universality of tragic essence over and beyond the particular disaster. In terms of *mimesis*, the fact that the action designates human confrontation is necessitated both for the sake of the credibility of the work and for its moral or psychological value.

As concerns narrative composition, Aristotle illustrates the crucial importance in tragedy of action over and beyond character. He sagaciously perceives that the *muthos*, the organization of acts into one system, is open to include a given incident mainly because of the content it supplies to the unity of action of the whole. That is to say: even if a certain incident carries psychological information or allows for dramatic description it should be rejected unless it serves the action. "An indeterminately large number of things happen to any one person, not all of which constitute a unity; likewise a single individual performs many actions, and they do not make up a single action" (51a). And later: "when he [Homer] composed the *Odyssey* he did not include everything which happened to Odysseus. . . . [T]he occurrence of . . . these events did not make the occurrence of the other necessary or probable" (51a).[34] In Aristotle's narrative model, the event has meaning only as a narrated act that contributes to the order of the adventure. The *muthos* has to construct itself upon the succession of distinct sections that forms an organic unity of action: the action has been completed (*téléias*) for long enough (*megethos*) and constitutes a sum total (*holes*) (50b). "The structure of the various sections of the events must be such that the transposition or removal of any one section dislocates and changes the whole" (51a).[35] In other words, the poet never allows for chance to decide: in composing the plot, the poet must remove all accidental circumstance that does not agree with the "probability" and the "necessity" that organize the logic of the action. Hence the plot that does not abide by the coherence of its logic and that exposes a succession of acts lacking narrative reason is poetically condemned as an "episodic plot" or as "simple action" (51b; Ch. X).[36] "To make up a plot," writes Ricoeur, "is already to make the intelligible spring from the accidental, the universal from the singular, the necessary or the probable from the episodic."[37]

But this is not all. Something curious must be noted: the complicated model of *muthos*, as opposed to the simple episodic succession, encompasses a greater type of event. Paradoxically, the more the action remains attached to its internal logic, the more intensely guided it will be by a reversal (*metabole; metabasis*) as a result of which the sense of the action will turn upside down. Similar to Barthes and Todorov, who distinguish exceptional action from iterative states of affairs, the nucleus event from the cloud of manifest acts, Aristotle's narrative theory constructs the continuous sequence of incidents on a single, subversive, discontinuous happening.

Thus, the organization of episodes must be controlled by the logic of the plot, the order of actions should respond to an internal causality rather than simply following the chronology of one act after another (52a). Surprisingly however, this logic of the plot is governed by the major threat of what Aristotle calls the *peripeteia*: a transformation in the order of the action, a catastrophe that violently changes the fortune of the characters from good to bad, from success to failure (51a; 52b).

The logic of the plot is paradoxically based on its own undermining through the reversal of the *peripeteia*. The order of the plot emerges from a moment of disorder. This reversal risks breaking the plot's coherence and continuity, but at the same time it stirs up the great effects of *pathos* and causes the emergence of "recognition," which then is responsible for leading into the "denouement" and the "catharsis" of the *muthos*. Of course, the event of the *peripeteia* provides a clear and visible justification to the series of acts that the poetic composition imitates. However, the sudden crisis that it exposes sometimes appears more momentous than the plot itself and thus is liable to obliterate the constructed unity of the work of art.

In this intersection between excess and moderation, Aristotle chooses to restrain the inordinate consequences of the myth and to control compassion and terror by means of reason. Although *peripeteia* seemingly runs counter to the expected course of events, its astonishment cannot be the effect of pure chance, as is the case, for example, with the sudden intervention of the *deus ex machina*. The *pathos* that issues from the unpredictable *peripeteia* is meaningful only if it is stealthily rooted in the narrative plan, "as if for a purpose [comme à dessein]" (52a 1–10).[38] The daunting calamity has to respect the internal necessity and probability of the composition (52a). In this way, tragedy steers the error-afflicted situation toward purification and the feeling of terror toward recognition.

In this sense, Ricoeur observes, "The art of composition consists in making this discordance appear concordant.... The discordant overthrows the concordant in life, but not in tragic art.... By including the discordant in the concordant, the plot includes the affecting within the intelligible.... [P]athos is one ingredient of the imitating or representing of praxis."[39]

Aristotle understands perfectly well that it is only by way of the concordant thread of the plot that *peripeteia*'s discordance can be fully integrated, namely, by presenting a paradoxical fusion through which the aroused perplexity opens out into a greater lucidity and the tragic error calls forth the restoration of truth. Thus, the violent pathos becomes indispensable in the learning of human ethics and aesthetics, the contingent becomes necessary, the most intensely subjective becomes a cultural object, and the exposition of art celebrates the continuity of the human spirit over death.

At a first glance, Lotman's theory of the event appears to be a modern interpretation and expansion of Aristotle's *peripeteia*.[40] But a closer look shows that Lotman's proposal, on the contrary, may be seen to hide the seeds of an anti-narrative conception of the event that brings it closer to the present approach.

In contrast with the logic of Aristotle's necessity and probability, Lotman argues that not only has pure chance an important place in the plot, but the improbable event is indeed the necessary essence of the plot. The more possible it seems that an occurrence may not have occurred, the more intense and deeply informative the perplexity appears: "An event is that which did occur, though it could also not have occurred. The less probability that a given event will take place..., the higher the rank of that event on the plot scale."[41]

Lotman argues that the improbable event is usually due to a violation of a prohibition, a transgression of an explicit limit. While this violation implies the very possibility of a text to have a plot, the idea of violation already presupposes an existent layer that is "plot-less," claims Lotman, an iterative, dominant semantic structure with a fixed boundary. As a rule, the plot, which is constituted on a model of violation, is secondary to the foundation of a normative and plot-less state of affairs. This state of affairs is always constructed from binary values arranged in a distinct spatial organization (*topos*): rich against poor, native versus stranger, orthodox and heretical, friend and enemy.

In other words, the concept of plot establishes itself on the static nature of a plot-less world. The violation of a forbidden boundary or limit creates plot and negates the normative *topos*, although this plot-less primary order is indispensable if the transgression is to occur, as it provides the basic development of the plot with elementary information and meaning. Lotman summarizes this circular conception of the event by means of an ambiguous phrase: "A text that possesses plot is built on the foundation of the plot-less text as its negation."[42]

For Lotman this phrase simply means that the plot is the expansion of an event that asserts the "plot-less" *topos* through negation: "the movement of the plot, the *event*, is the crossing of that forbidden border which the plot-less structure establishes.... Therefore a plot can always be reduced to a basic episode." Examples are the episode of Orpheus's descent to the land of the dead, Romeo and Juliet breaking the hostility between their families, and Titus's wish, against Roman law, to marry a foreigner, Berenice.

Still, it seems that this difficult phrase opens itself to a different understanding with far-reaching consequences. Insofar as the dialectical reading cannot imagine a transgression without the reestablishment of the law, the "revolutionary element" of the event must be considered as a literary entity in its own right. Instead of merely reducing the event to the idea of plot that affirms the plot-less image of the world by destabilizing it, the question must be asked, how the negation of the event affirms its own liminality, as if it was so to speak a *plot-less image of plot*.[43]

Since the event is effectively a transformation or an interruption, Lotman unintentionally gives the impression that the event might form a kind of plot-less plot. That is to say, the event, in this case, is specifically the power from which the plot appears without plot, since basically it is the absolute negation of every spatial order and every worldly image. Lotman himself admits: "An event is that which did occur, though it could also not have occurred. The less probability that a given event will take place . . . , the higher the rank of that event on the plot scale." To take further this ambiguity in Lotman's formulation, I would like to argue that the event is the "non-place" of the work, or the "non-act" of the plot. It is the non-act that cannot be reduced to the series of acts of the *muthos* and, at the same time, that which cannot be felt without the composition of acts itself.

In comparison to narratology, in which the meaning of a given occurrence is summarized by the narrative elements it has in the layout of the story, a theory of the literary event must strive to conceive of the event in its own right, without relation to the narrative course of the plot. If narratology mainly observes the structural or mimetic organization of different facts, a critical theory of the literary event should examine the elements that diverge from the structure of the plot in such a way that the discourse of the literary event is not forced to pass through the construction of the work as a whole.

The general idea of *emplotment* embraces the unpredictable energy of the event to such an extent that the event takes form. Controlling and regulating the most temporary and arbitrary by situating it in a gradual progression allows the work to enjoy both the vital disorder and the clear order of an impersonal sense. The main event of the work holds information that is elementary for the narrative: the semantic field and the common motifs of a specific realm, the evident functions of an experience, and the sum total of a theme. On a different approach, the suspension of the anecdotal continuity would set the wild forces of the event free from the plot's progression and bring back its independence as an obstacle to the plot. If any one of the events that hides in the core of the plot is examined with care, this may reveal an irreducible immensity and thus the possibility that the plot as such can then be questioned or even prevented. The ungraspable turbulence of the event retains the plot-less image of plot, holds the enigmatic seeds that entail both the need to tell and the end of all tales. A theory of literary events must suggest a different strategy of reading and different striving for the creativity of literature. The boundless elements that resist the narrative pattern demonstrate that the event is not a finite happening fixed in the text. Every occurrence the reader observes in the text of literature, particularly if it is an occurrence that affirms a solid improbability, one whose proper law is the pure desire of violation, implies an instinct that comes from outside the text, as if the text comprises a formless variable that eludes technical signification, an uncontrollable impulse that is essentially foreign to the linguistic order.

What exactly is this variable that brings a non-linguistic impulse into the text? How does one name this instinct that marks the "unhappening" within an intelligible happening? To a certain degree, the text obviously is a mimetic activity, transposing external reference into the meaningful order of semantic signs and symbolic figures. Using the terms of *prefiguration* and *refiguration*, Ricoeur argues that even the most innovative writer applies a pre-understanding of the world that is shared with the re-understanding of the reader.[44] Already, conducting his structural analysis, Barthes finds that beyond the narrative function, the text contains other informative factors such as social and physiological "indices," atmospheric connotations, or even descriptive "reality effects" that seem to be justified merely by way of creating a pure referential illusion that attests to a concrete presence.[45] Finally, stylistic analysis, issuing from Benveniste's linguistics of the statement (*enonciation*), continues this line by revealing that textual elements (i.e., the use of person, aspectual verb patterns, demonstrative articles or spatial and temporal deictics) express the conditional situation of the discourse and the subjective production of sense in order to construct a particular image of the world.[46]

These few examples offer a solid explanation of the extraneous variables that affect the text. But they only ensure a textual model in which the book is an image of the world, as Deleuze and Guattari argue, an axiom that the text attests to, or represents, mainly *what* is happening outside of the text, as if "book" and "world" were two different spheres that analogically reflect one another.[47] Instead, the intensive "book-world" bond, the incompatible encounter between experience and expression, emphasizes *how* the fact that something is happening keeps on affecting the text by its refusal to be totally appropriated, and *in what way* the forces of the happening change both the manner of writing and the shape of a vision. The *theory of the literary event* begins its analysis by finding these traces of impossible appropriation, of the as-yet-unformed datum of knowledge and style, the moments in which the work is submitted to the vivid movement of event that affirms itself not as an image of the world but as a revolution without image.

Blanchot writes: "The work always means: not knowing that art exists already, not knowing that there is already a world."[48] The event of literature begins with this very act of ignoring, with the intelligent creativity that retains its ardent ignorance, the intelligent creativity which is the potentiality that this ignoring presupposes. The literary text certainly follows a fascination with the world, devouring its details and appropriating its wholeness, yet there is an expropriated element that constantly infiltrates the textual fabric: the event is a real action only as a call for a world to come. We must look for the momentary disruption in a stable situation; we must be ready for the slight aberration of every presupposition, signification, and denotation in order to gain some impression of the violence of the being of becoming. The event is the violence of the being of becoming, following Nietzsche's and Deleuze's thinking, and in contrast to Hegel's becoming of being.[49] The event is the becoming-surprise, Nancy writes, the being of what happens, the *that* itself of the *that-it-happens*, "the *that* there is, the *that* without which there would be nothing."[50]

This is not new. In the last half century, literary critical theory obstinately approaches this undeclared outside that agitates within the text. Barthes defines *style* as a biological voice that holds the corporeal secret of the writer. Meschonnic posits *rhythm* as the key term of anthropological, ethical, and poetic implications of the subject in the discourse. Kristeva elaborates a psychoanalytical explanation of the *prelinguistic semiotic impulses* that permeate the symbolic order within the language of modern poetics.[51] Blanchot speaks of the misleading source of the imaginary, the *neuter*, that assigns literature the ontological task of depriving the subject of self and the real of sense. All these major projects give different names to the Dionysian aspect of creativity, different descriptions of an unconscious that calls forth renovation from crisis, different accounts of a generative function that elicit the plural and infinite movement from the fixed and finite ground of the text.

Following this tradition, my argument consists of examining these break-out moments in which the work reaches its limit. These moments are not necessarily the great episodes of the work; they may even be of a secondary and local importance. In this sense, whether it is done in terms of cultural mimetic preference or those of narrative categories, the hierarchical evaluation of different events is not the concern of this analysis. The event I'm looking for could have the form of "a moment of rage," "a suffocating trial, impossible" ("un moment de rage, une épreuve suffocante, impossible") such as those that haunt Bataille;[52] the "undefinable movements" and "rapid sensations" that attract Nathalie Sarraute, or a banal detail, an "insignificant incident," un "*événement faible*"[53] of the type that catches Barthes's or Robbe-Grillet's attention. What really matters here is the level to which the event retains its enigmatic force with the aim to unfold the deviation of its construction. What really matters is not the declarative statement of the event but rather the way the ontological, psychological, or ethical information it carries remains partially undeclared. Semiconductor and semi-misleader, the nonlinguistic experience must become the "being of the text," as Genette would put it, for it cannot be perceived unless it yokes itself to the experience of the written movement of style.[54]

If the *eventness* of the event is a factor that goes beyond the text, while being dependent on the text all the same, this leads us to dwell midways between "life" and "writing." *Event analysis* focuses on the articulation between what is roughly and commonly distinguished as "experience" versus "expression." The objective of this proposal is to follow, as closely as possible, the singular tension that is at work in the happening. I will ask, for example, how the "*that* it happens" becomes involved in the dynamic of composition, how inversely the growing imaginary effort of the words implies an adventure of new corporeal sensations, interfering with the living effect and outcome of those who are involved in the process of writing and reading.

Hence the question "How does the event singularly construct itself?" does not point either to the representative order of *emplotment* or to the internal economy of the textual production of sense. The *theory of the literary event* is certainly indebted to the achievements of past theorizations. It cannot avoid using their terminology. And yet the move it would like to suggest must remain cautious, unsatisfied, first with regard to the mimetic references of the text, both cultural and historical, and second as concerns the semiotic functioning of the linguistic sign which rejects any supposed naive transparency of the text. On the one hand, every realistic aspiration eventually meets the convention of what is considered to be real. But to admit, on the other hand, that any "effect of the real" is a mere textual illusion, that is, to submit the entire experience of literature to the immanence of linguistic and narrative structure, is tantamount to impoverishing the real impulse that ontologically affirms that the invention of literature exceeds all regulative mechanisms of representation.

The Literary Event: An Ontological Question

In his story "Emma Zunz," Borges comments on the event: "The most solemn of events are outside time—whether because in the most solemn of events the immediate past is severed, as it were, from the future or because the elements that compose those events seem not to be consecutive."[55] Witold Gombrowicz calls this impression "the very boundary of chance and non-chance" in his book *Cosmos*, where the line of writing becomes the amazement itself of this same temporal disorder: "All this within time that was reverberating like a gong, filled to the brim, cascade, vortex, swarm, cloud, the Milky Way, dust, sounds, events, this and that etc., etc., etc."[56] This fascination or anxiety—this "gong" within or outside time, or what Marguerite Duras calls this "empty gong"[57]—is wonderfully expressed by Robert Musil, who wishes to articulate the terror of the un-happening of the event.[58] This fear is also described by one of Henry James's characters as an urgent but unknown danger, as the "beast" that haunts him, as a mystery in the face of which he can only avow: "I don't know that, you see. I don't focus it. I can't name it. I only know I'm exposed."[59] The one who is always locked in combat with this "something that comes from outside, with something unaccountable, that looks like fate," as Alfred Döblin writes in *Berlin Alexanderplatz*, may eventually be given to understand "how it all came about," but only in the end.[60]

A reverberating gong, an unaccountable something, a frightened un-happening, a state of suspense and affliction—each of these enigmatic experiences of the event requires an interrogation that transcends the closed realms of history of literature, generic classification, or traditional poetics, and yet the central argument of this book is that the event's dazzling reality and compelled amazement may constitute the energetic vitality of all stylistically great fictional works.

From the outset, it is necessary to state that the literary event cannot be reduced to mere extralinguistic occurrence or textual-narrative incident, to the *mimesis* of history, or to a *poiesis* of plot. It must, rather, be an adventure toward the *un-happening within the happening*, engaging the art of words to explore the non-place within the taking place, encompassing an unknown factor that is responsible for the irregularity of the happening and which answers the demand for a singular linguistic creation.

The question of the literary event thus leads us to seek premises that go beyond the aesthetic, beyond the formal exercise and historical institution of literature. Unlike the general conception of the historical or the narrative event, the definition of the literary event suggested here must confront a farther-reaching questioning that concerns the destination of thinking itself and the expressions of the becoming of being in modern thinking.[61]

Indeed, any theory of literature is fundamentally based on a broadest philosophical or ideological stratum, and any literary criticism constructs itself on epistemological choices. Since Barthes's defense of the "Nouvelle Critique" in France, we know that even a critical approach that pretends to be scientifically objective is not innocent as it seems.[62] I believe that the present study of the literary event must not deny this; it must underscore the importance of putting literary criticism on solid philosophical ground, determining conceptual principles and tools that may open the plural horizons of theory and at the same time stimulating the desire to illuminate literary texts from a different viewpoint, while preserving their singularity and their manifold components.

Thus, an insight into the literary event is better gained from a philosophical perspective, that is, a phenomenological perspective of ontology that clarifies what in the happening binds being and language together. Heidegger's later writings and the various responses to his thinking in France grappled directly with this same problem:

how to define a generative and un-achieved conception of the event in which being exposes itself through a singular experience that entails linguistic invention. This idealistic notion of a dynamic event of being allows us to head toward a critical ground of thinking that is not limited to a punctual theoretical realm or discipline, as opposed to recent articles published in France on this same topic.[63] A radical contestation of the very conditions of thinking, it includes the nature of the literary creation as a questioning of the possibility itself of language and experience.

It is necessary to embark on a preliminary reading in order to trace a philosophical archaeology of the significance of the event with special reference to the literary text. The writings of Heidegger, Blanchot, Derrida, and Deleuze seem crucial, not only because of their respective conceptual engagement with this specific matter, but also because of the key role each attributes to the act of writing as such, particularly in modern literature that challenges the classical logos. Their ontological phenomenology, their hermeneutics and poststructural accomplishments, pave the way for contemporary thinkers such as Badiou and Romano to develop their own philosophy of event as well as for the present research to suggest a new literary-critical discourse on the event.

Heidegger's late writings establish the conditions for the ontological priority of the event. Heidegger's concept of *Ereignis*, usually translated as the "event of appropriation," is linked with the *ontological difference* between Being and beings.[64] In this sense, Heidegger considers *Ereignis*, unlike its common German use, as not merely an occurrence in the world: "'event' is not simply occurrence, but that which makes any occurrence possible."[65] *Ereignis* does not refer to beings that *are* in the world: as an ontological event, it is better caught under the impersonal "It" that conveys the possible giving of the world.[66] *Ereignis* relates to the process by which Being *gives* itself to beings, manifests itself before our eyes, and speaks itself through language by a twofold movement of concealment and disclosure. Simultaneously, *Ereignis* names the ongoing process, as long as man and Being belong to each other, in which man attains proper identity and presence. In other words, Being as an "event of appropriation" is neither the infinite permanent presence nor the dialectical becoming of a total conception of history. It is, rather the non-predetermined historical destination of a transformable visibility and language. This uncanny emergence of Being, the way it comes into view and appeals through language, is the foundation of human destiny insofar as destiny is understood as the being of difference itself. In other words, the human possibility of having a proper place and historical understanding is due to man's engagement in a relation with Being. This ontological difference between man and Being that makes possible appearance and understanding can paradoxically be established only because there is a respective gathering and hermeneutic convergence between the divergences.

Heidegger reserves an important place for the question of language and poetry. To begin with, the event of Being beckons, or makes an appeal, through the act of human speech. Language is man's peculiar way, insofar as he is conscious of his finitude, of exposing himself to Being. Furthermore, Heidegger argues that language is what constitutes the very possibility of bringing man into existence at the moment where the conventional function of language puts itself into question by etymologically and poetically revealing its source.[67] Thus in poetry Heidegger finds a "pure language" that questions its own origin of sound and light, that is, the infrastructure of visibility and hearing. Poetry is the "primal form of building," the road toward man's own sense, preserving his historical inheritance and rearticulating his unique position between heaven and earth.[68] As the language of poetry, therefore, is "the basic capacity for human dwelling," it idealistically offers mortals a grounding in their being.[69]

In Blanchot's essays, the event becomes the prerogative of the work of literature and the destiny of the writer and reader. The event occurs only to the one who is involved with the work of art: the one who experiences the "disappearance of language" and the "resemblance" of the image. Blanchot's own expression "To live an event as an image" ("Vivre un événement en image") and his notion of realizing a world in the "supreme and silent disappearance" of language imply the ontological necessity of literature. Thus the event can only be apprehended or realized from a particular artistic attitude and through a particular artistic practice. That "something like literature exists" means that there is a principle of illusoriness that penetrates Being, a fictitious wandering that detaches the subject from itself and unmoors the reality of stable sense.[70]

Heidegger's conception of the event locates a man's dwelling where language speaks purely, in poetry. Blanchot, by contrast, follows Mallarmé's and Kafka's modern project of surrender to the "trial of the other night" where the literary experience becomes a dizzying homelessness; here, approaching is at the same time a distancing, and the attraction of the beyond only accentuates the force of indifference. The irregular nature of the event is not that of mystic epiphany or catastrophe. It is a necessary process of ceaseless dissimulation that appears when literature confronts the impossible. This movement erodes language's ability to understand, conceive, or perceive. It separates the writer from his or her work inserting the voice of a vacant neutrality in which nothing occurs except "the idle profundity of being" ("la profondeur désoeuvrée de l'être").[71]

In this same manner, Levinas describes the contrast between Blanchot and Heidegger: "Already in Heidegger, art, beyond all esthetic meaning, made the 'truth of being' shine forth, but it shared that ability with other forms of existence. Blanchot sees art's vocation as exclusive. But above all, writing does not lead to the truth of being. One might say that it leads to the errancy of being—to being as a place of going astray, to the uninhabitable."[72]

The work of literature brings the impossible event into the "world's daylight," Blanchot would have said. Among its different designations as the neuter, the outside, white space, or ceaseless murmur, Blanchot also dedicates the question of dying (*mourir*) to this subversive absence. To die, in this sense, is not the affirmation of the writer's spiritual strength as he or she faces nothingness and thus the subjective horizon of the impossible. Dying as an ongoing process, on the contrary, is the trace of the "non-place" and the "non-identity" that incessantly *un-happens* and is therefore *absent from* the work. Letting the language of the impossible speak is for Blanchot the assignment of modern literature as an art that no longer serves human causes or mirrors man's face, having become the event of the writer's incessant dying, having become, that is, what he or she cannot know or write. The event, in other words, is the affirmation of the being of the work as such, that is, of the work qua work: the open horizon of a temporal and spatial metamorphosis, a "degree zero" of an impersonal entity that is the *other* of any entity, and hence of a sense that is the *other* of any sense. "The work always means: not knowing that art exists already, not knowing that there is already a world."[73]

Derrida takes Heidegger's and Blanchot's thoughts about the event further. He elaborates Heidegger's event of appropriation by means of a more radical conception of difference by thinking of the event as an encounter of "expropriation." Here the event is no longer an analogical gathering together of separate entities, and thus, as one no longer extends itself to the other as a gift, there is no proper identity and dwelling in face of the other. The ex-appropriation marks the *absolute alterity* of the encounter in which there are no agreed boundaries of Being, there is no Logos, between proper self and other. Derrida's model of event refers to a kind of "disparate" that itself *"holds together,"* a heterogeneous and dissymmetrical binding without agreement.[74] As such, the event accentuates the singularity of a clash occurring for the first and last time, an unexpected irruption or invasion of an occurrence that is radically open to the chance and venture embodied by the coming of the impossible.

Derrida explains: "Although the experience of an event, the mode according to which it affects us, calls for a movement of appropriation . . . there is no event worthy of its name except insofar as this appropriation *falters* at some border or frontier. A frontier, however, with neither front nor confrontation, one that incomprehension does not run into head on since it does not take the form of a solid front: it escapes, remains evasive, open, undecided, indeterminable. Whence the unappropriability."[75]

At this point Derrida joins Blanchot's aspiration of the impossible event as a sort of negative transcendence, an expropriation that conditions any proper self, an Outside that is always already part of the very intimacy of being "at home."[76] According to Derrida, this impossible aspect of what effectively takes place defines the "eventfulness" or the "eventness" of the event: "The event's eventfulness depends on this experience of the impossible."[77] In other words, its impossibility is the singular movement that the event demands to make in order to conceive of its possible experience and language. But this movement comes about only through a process of suspension and repetition which already manifests itself as different from the event. In other words, any—perceptually or linguistically—possible appropriation of the event is necessarily a different reappearance of the event as other; for this Derrida uses the term *iterability* or the neologism *hauntology*. The possible impression and expression of the event are already separate from its impossibility. This is why Derrida paradoxically claims that the surprise and the striking violence of the event are essentially un-experienced experience or unaccomplished accomplishment. At the heart of any event there is an aporia that can be experienced only as a terrible non-arrival, as that which fails to come about and therefore realizes itself through modalities of continuous mourning and an endless call: "Come!"

This understanding guides Derrida's strategy of reading and interpretation as well as his ethical critique of the important political events of his time. He explores the way in which new technologies represent these events and thus offers new grounds for thinking. As part of this elaboration he defines the conditions and consequences of the ghostly vision of *hauntology* that questions the ontology of presence. In its place he suggests a concept of historicity based on a series of singular and exemplary events that cannot happen unless they continuously repeat themselves through the technical manipulations of image and writing. In this sense, he elaborates a temporality marked by the past future tense, by traumatic corporeal experience, and by the revealing of the generative alterity of texts.

Literature for Derrida is a "writing event," a textual performance that neither comes after the event (constative speech) nor engenders the event so that it may confirm the presence of the speaker and addressee (performative speech). Instead, he defines the writing event of literature as the absolute experience of precariousness, wherein "the movement of its inscription is the very possibility of its effacement."[78] Literature emerges not only from the other voice of impersonality, from the fictitious image and arbitrary inscription that contests the referential condition of truthful presence and personal testimony—it always incorporates the possible disappearance of language itself.[79]

Understanding literature as an erratic discourse whose order is disobedience and whose law is the absolute other may lead to the endless effacement of the "event without event," an event where "this coming implicates in and of itself the coming back."[80] Inversely, engaging in the unspeakable substance of the event creates an endless, ecstatic aspiration for the "new" as what is always still to come, for the impossible interruption that holds the promise of invention, which is where the event finally begins or ends.

After Heidegger, Blanchot, and Derrida, Deleuze offers an ontological consideration of the event that is rooted in a different philosophical tradition. Referring to the Stoics, Spinoza, Nietzsche, Bergson, and Foucault, Deleuze's ontology leans on three principles: immanence, multiplicity, and differentiation. Deleuze perceives Being as a chaotic surface or *physis* that does not submit to a transcendent intelligence or to a transcendentally evident condition of recognition. Being is, rather, a plane of immanence on which the movement of differentiation generates itself from itself as infinite multiplicity. From this perspective, Deleuze defines the event as the productive articulation between the creation of sense and real substantive movement. "The plane of immanence has two facets as Thought and as Nature, as *Nous* and as *Physis*."[81] The event is the active frontier at which the matter of substance and the force of thinking converge by enacting their unstable divergence.

In contrast to Aristotle's unity of Being which has multiple senses, and unlike Heidegger's ontological difference, which is restricted to hermeneutic agreement, Deleuze's Being is uniquely spoken as the very act of differentiation: "Being is said in a single and same sense of everything of which it is said, but that of which it is said differs; it is said of difference itself."[82] In other words, for Deleuze the "plane of immanence" is founded in pure difference, an arbitrary contingency that affirms itself only through the event of an actualization. The event is, thus, a real occurrence as well as an ideal process that brings into existence *singularities* and *multiplicities* that exceed any inference from a potential whole. The immanence of the event is, therefore, an infinite flow within the finite and real happening, a finite infinity that does not correspond, for example, to the incarnation of the divine or to the way the Idea protects the representation of the whole. Deleuze's event resembles the non-image of the underlying unconscious, the violent and elusive movement of an impersonal and pre-individual entity that undermines the real as it breaks out from beneath or "from behind the back" and creates an ongoing dissymmetrical interaction between the series of sense and things, language and life.

Deleuze prefers to characterize the event in terms of *virtual* and *actual*, both dimensions of the real, in contrast to Blanchot's and Derrida's *impossible-possible*. This conceptual shift is one of Deleuze's major contributions to the ontological question of the event. According to this new terminology, the actualization associated with any historical state of affairs is accompanied by an ahistorical virtualization that reveals the generative power of the real. The virtual is inseparable from the actual, though it continually introduces degrees of dissimilarity that intensively transform the actualization into a pure act of differentiation.

Deleuze then borrows Nietzsche's concept of "becoming," thus translating Blanchot's "Outside" and Derrida's "absolute other" and, as such, accentuating the real but virtual flow that passes *through* and *between* any actual matter of fact. The becoming of the event does not correspond simply to what happens; instead, it refers to an element *within* the happening that resists any settled organization into a state of affairs. As such, Blanchot's incessant *dying* and Derrida's *hauntology* evolve, in Deleuze's writing, into a vital and ahistorical project of becoming. The vanishing neutrality or the aporia of un-experienced experience is, in Deleuze's view, the tendency of the forces of life to flee and overflow a specific situation. Deleuze's interest in extra-philosophical realms such as art, anthropology, psychoanalysis, and biological phenomena reflects only the singular enactment, that is, the factual corporeality in which becoming launches itself as pure mutation, deviation, and multiplicity. Inversely, going outside the tradition and territory of philosophy allows the ontology of becoming to diagnose "what is new in an existing being, . . . [and to] sense the creation of a mode of existence," and, as such, to reinvent a vigorous philosophy: a new language, a new territory, new modes of existence that resist and set free the life that man imprisons.[83]

The creation of literature and writing fascinates Deleuze as a virtual creativity of sense that stems from the complex intersection of the actual with the undeniable force of life. Literary writing emanates directly from reality and simultaneously goes beyond it to question any established order of the real. Deleuze might be said to seek in literature the restless creation in which the event affirms its double face as both a singular linguistic assemblage and a real distribution of things, intensively confounding or combining the senseless corporeality of things with the incorporeal sense of language, a signifier without a clear signified and vice versa.[84]

In other words, the work of literature is a privileged ground for exposing the actualization (*effectuation*) of the event: the historical circumstances, the corporeal experience, or the fictional force of extraordinary incidents. The horror of war, the moment of death, the intimate wound or weakness traverse and affect the act of writing as the immediate testimony of living bodies. Yet Deleuze also believes that literature must uncover the impersonal power of the event in order to be born as the offspring of the event's becoming. Only when writing succeeds in extricating the forces of life from a private experience or from an actual situation can it produce a counter-actualization (*counter-effectuation*) of the event. The writer who exposes her- or himself to this internal transformation imposed by the horror of war, the moment of death, or the intimate wound or weakness inversely embodies the event's forces and language by inventing new machineries of sense and new individuations of life. "Willing the event" is Deleuze's formulation of the Stoics' *amor fati* and of Nietzsche's "eternal return."[85] "Willing the event" is the moment at which the work of literature affirms multiplicity: the secret point at which the stylistic expression is no longer subjective and life's adventures become an impersonal singularity. "A man, a woman, a beast, a stomach" become, in the experiment of writing, degrees of intensity, unique combinations of sensations and perceptions, a geography of lines and connections in constant change, proliferating and resonating with one another, for as long as becoming passes through bodies and words.

Blanchot's aspiration toward homelessness and un-sensed being, Derrida's impossible experience, and Deleuze's immanent multiplicity contradict other philosophical projects of the event, such as those of Badiou, Romano, and Juranville. Since it closely follows the former ontological and poststructural line, and adopts, in particular, Deleuze's ahistorical becoming, this study puts aside Juranville's historical definition of the event, Romano's subjective hermeneutics of the *advenant*, and Badiou's rehabilitation of the truth with respect to the evental site (*site evenementiel*). These thinkers' writings require a long examination that goes beyond the corpus of this study. Nevertheless, let us have a brief look at these alternative approaches to the event with respect to the foregoing analysis.

Alain Juranville looks for the key to the true knowledge of historical existence in the event. He designates Christ's sacrifice as the primordial event and the true act of Revolution as the terminal event of humanity. These two momentums—Christ's sacrifice and the act of Revolution—point to a universal Religion. Juranville accuses Deleuze and Derrida of remaining philosophically abstract and pagan, having neglected to justify the objective sense of the event. For Juranville, Derrida perceives knowledge as merely false knowledge, while Deleuze fails to speak of "the terminal historical event towards which [philosophy] itself is headed (justice, Revolution), nothing, *a fortiori*, of the primordial historical event for which there would be the sacrifice of Christ."[86]

Claude Romano speaks of the conditions of rupture and the re-beginning of the event.[87] He posits "the evential [evenemential] *uncondition*" of all history in contrast with a contextual historicity; the latter explains in advance the *inner*-worldly (*intra-mondaine*) causality of a fact (*evenementiel*).[88] But Romano insists on conjugating "the phenomenology of the event" into a "hermeneutics of the *advenant*," a new subjectivity he essentially defines as "the one *to whom* something can happen."[89] In other words, the only dimensions from which the pure event (*l'événementia*l) becomes visible is in the process of subjectivization of the *advenant* in which he or she, the *advenant*, him- or herself, becomes a being capable of experience and self-understanding. In this sense, Romano certainly continues Heidegger's approach to Being through *Dasein*,[90] and he even joins Derrida's affirmation: "[T]he event ought above all to *happen* to someone, to some living being who is thus is *affected* by it, consciously or unconsciously. No event without *experience*."[91] Unlike Derrida, however, Romano remains attached to a comprehensive mode of the *advenant*'s *historial* experience and sense to come. Unlike for Deleuze, Romano's event becomes the birthplace for a new subjectivity, not for the non-subjective violence that affirms multiplicity. Romano does not consider the event as an impersonal and pre-individual site of forces, that is, as a transformable foundation of collective assemblages that incongruously resonate actual bodies and virtual ideas.

Badiou's ontology of the event presents complex and subtle differences from Deleuze's and therefore requires a more detailed observation than this brief discussion warrants.[92] In principle, Badiou rejects the vital virtuality of Deleuze's event and claims, on the contrary, that there are only *actual situations* in which the event is the un-presented void. The event, for Badiou, is the "One" extended to an *evental site*, and hence to "a multiple being-on-the-edge-of-the-void," which remains in a state of absence within the situation. However, it is this fact of the event proceeding from the void that constitutes the source of truth on the basis of a miracle that is not present in the situation in which it is presented.

At this point Badiou locates our task of finding the actual inscription of the *undecidable* truth in order to name it and follow it "faithfully." Insofar as the truth is the "oblivion of oblivion," actual forms of truth cannot be situated in the world but only in the forgetfulness of time itself. That is to say, for instance, in the real experience of "révolutions (politiques), des passions (amoureuses), des inventions (scientifiques) et des créations (artistiques)."[93]

The Singularity of the Literary Event

The opening sections of this book elaborate a concept of the event in an ontological order of thinking that binds together the experience of being and the possibility of language. This perspective conceives of the literary act as necessarily implicated in the irregular emergence of the event. Thus, according to Heidegger, poetry is the condition of man's belonging to the event of Being. Blanchot and Derrida, each in his own way, understands literature as an illusory founding of difference that exposes being not as a dwelling but rather as an erratic wandering. As for Deleuze, the effort of writing aims to extract the becoming of things and thus renders literature one of the creative realizations of intensive events.

Heidegger, Blanchot, Derrida, and Deleuze offer theoretical premises for a literary approach to the event, while also leaving room for the concrete technical articulation of the event in the work of literature. Philosophy often remains alien to the textual functioning of the literary work, its practical instruments and ideals. This is why this research is dedicated to finding a method of thinking aimed to expose the singularity of the literary event within the realm of literary theory. Not only does the concept of the event allow for an essential questioning of the work of literature; it also offers particular instruments for a critical analysis of literary fragments and passages that have not yet been apprehended in this way. Thinking of the event does not merely provide new instruments to speculatively reconsider literature as an art and as a discourse; in chapter 7 of this book I am offering principles and conceptions that pave the way for a theory of literary events.

The first set of principles of the theory of literary events is the attention given to irregular moments in the work. A radical moment must be extracted from the text so as to examine its construction: the singular manner in which a happening engenders interaction between artistic materials and real living forces. The starting point of this critical approach is this unstable boundary between the production of poetic-fictional manipulations and the imposed real forces. This dynamic combination defines the speed and power of the event's creative energy.

This close reading of a selected moment must be accompanied by the suspension of declarative knowledge and judgment, by the suspension of reference to narrative structure and sociohistorical signs of representation. Let the work express the impersonal creative energy required by the event—in other words, the message of the plot, the biography of the writer, and the political reality in which the work has been conceived or received must be set aside. Attentive reading immerses itself in the particular movement of the work, conscious that something is always in the process of being made, as if the finite-writing is still *a l'état vivant*, awaiting the infinite involvement of the reader.

The second set of principles of the theory of literary events is the understanding that the singular happening which passes across the unstable boundary of language and the real can never be reduced to a coherent structure. The event reveals neither *what there is* in the work of art nor the *dominant* element in it, or in an artistic movement or an aesthetic epoch. Nor is the event a structure whose underlying organization must be uncovered. Rather, it is an irreducible disarray, a dissymmetrical multiplicity in the face of which, surprised, one asks, What is happening here? What has happened that seems unbearable? How does the work make this happen? The event is, therefore, a figure of a mystery that astonishes more than calling for a scientific solution.

This troubled astonishment results in the third set of principles of the theory of literary events. The literary work usually testifies to a fantastic or historically extraordinary occurrence, but what is more important is the way in which the work produces constant virtual change. The question "What is happening in the work?" certainly does not refer to the event's perceptible theme. In fact., the question concerns a theme that reveals a perceptible secret, an infinite form of secrecy that produces, in the movement of language, the becoming of the happening itself. In other words, the theory of literary events examines the reemergence of the erratic entity which is *the eventness itself* or the *being of becoming* of the event. As such, this critical act suggests that we perceive the literary traces of the proliferation of the event by locating its "plot-less deviation" and "fictitious distance." What occurs in a singular moment of the work must consequently be approached through a different type of questioning, an interrogation aimed at discovering what does not happen in the happening or at the non-place of what is taking place.

This last question leads us back to where I started. Unlike the historical occurrence or the narrative unit, the singularity of the literary approach to the event can be summarized as the poetic and fictional adventure towards *the un-happening within the happening*. Paradoxically, the unknown element of the literary event is also the *that* itself of the *that-it-happens*; to quote Nancy again, it is "the *that* without which there would be nothing."[94] While the event retains its enigmatic force, the literary work, from its side, provides its creative deviation. No longer having the status of declared historical occurrence or of a narrative unit in a system, the event is, instead, the tension of the undeclared boundary between living forces and modes of expression. It emerges in the work as a nonlinguistic "being of becoming" that ties itself to the equivocal movement of style and composition. In this respect, I have previously shown how Heidegger, Blanchot, and Deleuze conceive of the literary act as implying the irregular emergence of the event, and thus it could be said, conversely, that they consider how the ontological entity—this moving boundary or this neutral outside—penetrates the textual happening.

From a modernist perspective, and following Deleuze's notion of immanence, this ontological entity may be named *the corporeal* to denote the ontological intersection at which the un-happening agitates the happening. Literature is where the *corporeality of the event* offers itself in all its ambiguity. On the one hand, the corporeal is the rudimentary condition of happening; it provides the raw material of the event and thus is *necessary* to any creative work of writing. On the other hand, the corporeality of the event resists symbolic action; the corporeal remains irreducible to any linguistic proposition and, as a result, consists in the virtual power of un-happening. Constantly present yet inexhaustible, urgent but insatiable, the corporeality of the event endows the words with living expression while remaining alien to the textual economy. Intensively vital but always senseless, the corporeal attaches to the imaginary act of literature both the primitive basis of the real and the becoming of fictitious impersonal *uncertainty*.

The twofold nature of the corporeal as the un-happening modality of happening can be apprehended either in transcendent or in immanent terms. The transcendent direction emphasizes the absolute other that acts on the event: essentially the impossible experience or the ungraspable that is always about to occur, that which incessantly does not come about ("ce qui ne cesse pas de ne pas arriver"). The other, immanent, manner of thinking insists, instead, that the event distinguishably takes place. Any real state of affairs enfolds among or between its declared elements, an undetermined movement of flight. Roughly speaking, Blanchot's and Derrida's transcendence points at the un-accomplished of any accomplishment, and this is why they categorically perceive of the act of literature as a *dying corporeality*. Deleuze's immanence has it, on the contrary, that the un-accomplished is also a real—albeit virtual—accomplishment: "There are thus two accomplishments, which are like [i.e., which take the form of] actualization [effectuation] and counter-actualization [contre-effectuation]."[95] This is why Deleuze defends literature's process of *living corporeality*.

From a transcendental angle, the dying corporeality of literature becomes, according to Derrida, the survival speech of *auto*bio-thanato*graphy*: "*from* my death, *from* the place and *from* the taking-place, better yet, from the *having-taken-place*, already, of my death."[96] From Deleuze, by contrast, the living corporeality of literature can be apprehended as follows: "Syntax is the set of necessary detours that are created in each case to reveal the life in things."[97] It is through art and literature, for Derrida and Blanchot, that a terminology of shadowy present-absence, of "night bodies" and different states of death, emerges. Deleuze, by contrast, glorifies the living decomposition in literature, the hybridity and animality, the written infliction of the wound, the will for the event to occur by a sensible capturing of multiple "affects" and "percepts."

Choosing not to take a Blanchotian, Derridean *dying move,* I suggest in chapter 9 of this book that we conceive of the event as consisting of a Deleuzian *vital move*, that is to say, the process by which the corporeal becomes a principle of vitality that necessarily conditions and singularizes the event of literature. For the event's un-happening to burst out, the work of literature must penetrate into the living corporeality of the event, spreading its unpredictable violence, its infinite movement and senseless inscription. The poetic and fictional experience of literature strives to extract the life energy of the event, imbuing the linguistic texture with the inner dynamic of the declared change and, as such, becoming a type of incorporeal incarnation of the event itself.

Proust's and Céline's air-raid episodes serve as good examples for the theory of literary events as vital move. At a first glance these intense moments in *Time Regained* and *Fable for Another Time* are ostensibly historical accounts of the bombardment of Paris during the World War I and World War II, respectively. The recognizable theme of the sky pouring fire adds to the political situation an additional religious sense of *force majeure*, apocalyptic retribution and the horror of the new technologies of destruction. But this historically and thematically narrative situation is complicated by a perverted ahistorical desire that acts on the writing. We see this both in Proust's orgiastic utopia of homosexual sadomasochism during the air raid and in Céline's air raid, which occurs during the scene of the sexual seduction of the narrator's wife by his best friend.

The above-mentioned living corporeality, defined here as the vital move of the literary events, holds the key to a historical manifestation of the events and, at the same time, to an ahistorical latency that remains undefined, though obviously striking. In terms of the corporeal construction of these events, the vital move must look for the substantial disposition of bodies and for the way these bodies are distributed in an impersonal relation of forces. In Proust's case, the event is displayed in the disjunctive synthesis of the war series (the dark city, the bombardment) and the brothel series (Charlus chained, the flogging); in Céline's case, the event reveals the conflict between Ferdinand and Jules, between the political, collective treason and the private, carnal treachery.

But something else in the body of the event—the living corporeality of the event—renders both the actual state of affairs and the virtual power (*puissance*) that continuously produce new levels of images and new modes of existence. This is what I call *writing corporeally*, the moment where the corporeal is the condition for the textual image to acquire an impersonal expression of life, precisely due to the imaginative mistranslation of the corporeal. This is the moment when the corporeal not only constitutes the undeniable fact of the happening, it is also the abyssal becoming that relaunches the dissimilitude of the event: the deviation and multiplicity that operate within the happening all at once.

In this sense, Proust's air-raid event cannot be summarized by either the bombing of the dark city of Paris-Pompeii-Sodom or the new figure of Prometheus, the Baron De Charlus's sacrifice to the "pure matter" of sexual transgression. The key to the singularity of this event is the need to juxtapose these two series of violations, to synchronize the different "violent inscriptions" and "violated bodies" by noting *the incompatible* throb *between the lashings of the whip and the falling of the bombs*. These rhythmic pulses, juxtaposing and superimposing the strikes, substituting and blending the floggings with the blasts, actualize the non-presence of the corporeal violation. This is also how the virtual *becoming of the event* appears both as necessary trial and as ongoing metamorphosis.

Céline's air raid also responds to another logic, which is that of neither a historical war report nor an anecdote of an indecent sexual encounter. Céline produces a corporeal mise-en-scène of a struggle between inclusion and exclusion. Surrounded by the threat of the bomber planes and the excitement of the crowd, Ferdinand and Jules ostensibly fight over Lili, while in reality they struggle for the possession of legitimate artistic power. Whoever succeeds in sexually penetrating Lili will determine the order of art, the order of the "good hole," banishing the other, the outlaw, the excluded one, who must fall into the "other hole" of prison. This is when *the virtual becoming of* Céline's *event* strikes: the moment when we perceive that the sirens in this war do not warn against the bombs, but instead point to a different danger. The alarms signal Ferdinand's expulsion from the hole, indeed, announce his exclusion from primitive protection and it indicates that eventually explosion will well up from underground: from an enormous gutter that overflows the whole of Paris, as indeed happens at the end of the novel. A corporeal explosion accompanies this cosmic inversion, a centrifugal force of self-destitution, dizziness, nausea, and vomiting. Ferdinand's "expelled" sentences are no longer either collective or private; he succeeds in transporting himself deliriously into *infinity*, going beyond both human corporeality and language. He himself becomes the fascination and the apocalyptic storm of war as he offers a material utopia of animality and an abstract evaporation into music.

Proust's bombardment exposes members of the aristocracy as they engage in a utopic vision of Sodom in a male brothel, while in Céline's constitutes an apocalyptic moment when everything is destroyed, everything becomes subject to treason: the most intimate relations as well as the political and artistic. T. S. Eliot's London Blitz, by contrast, featuring in "Little Gidding," is where the poet meets the ghost of a dead master. The dead man's spirit comes to guide the poet and to bring consolation in these times of calamity by pointing out a timeless dimension within them. The tongue of fire that is the dead man's wisdom, as opposed to the tongue of fire spat by the fighter plane, allows Eliot to create a fundamentally monistic poetic composition: this fire purifies and annihilates at one and the same time. The Heraclitean fire, constitutive force of this world, generates itself as the perpetual difference between destruction and creation, even though it remains identical and one. From this perspective, one can also describe the meditative movement of Eliot's poetry: the one and the same forces itself on itself as if to extract from itself the unknown motion of difference. In Eliot, willing the event is tantamount to donning the poisoned shirt of fate and to learn exposing oneself to the inevitable peal of fire—not to fear the message of the bomber—in order then to take one's place on the arbitrary frontier between happening and non-happening, and between life and death. In this manner, Eliot calls one to experience the blind spot of the event when the fire turns over within itself, burning and distilling simultaneously until the present surrenders its metaphysical knot between terror and beauty.

2

INTERMEZZO

The Cave in Homer's *Odyssey* and the Café in Marguerite Duras's *Moderato Cantabile*

> "*L'Odyssée* devenue leur tombeau."
> Maurice Blanchot, *Le livre à venir*

The absolute sign of strangeness that marks the violent encounter between Odysseus and Polyphemus in the Cyclops's cave is perhaps the essence of the *Odyssey*. The dreadful moment when Odysseus and his men fall prey to the dark trap of the cave and the end of the journey home appears inevitable is also the moment when the entire exploration—throughout the sail and even later in Phaeacia's hall and in Ithaca—is subsumed under the title of "no-body."[1]

Between Odysseus and Polyphemus, no common ground is possible. They are strangers who must destroy one another, abolish the other in his infinite capacity to threaten one's self-identity, and thus to survive.

The failure in peaceful foreign relations is not due to the lawless, savage nature of the monster, as Odysseus, the cosmopolitan passenger, gods-fearing Odysseus, judges. While he carries a gift as an offering of hospitality, he senses danger from the outset, expecting the worst, and in doing so he contributes to the cultural clash. He and his civilized friends, even if they do not abuse hospitality by partaking of the Cyclops's goat cheese, nevertheless invade his solitude, surprising him at home like thieves who come to plunder other men. Why else would the Cyclops lose his temper? He is a milkman, not a hunter; why all of a sudden does he become an impulsive and cruel carnivore? At this point, there being no escape and no definitive boundaries between the rivals, the enclosed cave affirms that a death sentence underlies any rudimentary encounter with the other: "the monster's cave you thought would be your death."[2]

Now, the cave becomes a sort of furnace: Odysseus and his men, the

Cyclops and his flock, none of them retain an independent substantive presence. They cling to one another, and this imbroglio gradually gives birth to "the body of the event." They weave, unpredictably, a new texture of forces, waves of corporeal sensation and flashing images. Such are the terrified gestures in the cave, the jolting noises, the broken bodies on the ground, accentuating the speed and power of the happening. Observe the panic as it scuttles in the deepest dark, the glaring eye that exposes the intruders in the blaze of fire. Listen to the crashing boulder and the monster's rumbling voice. Beyond moral judgment and psychological difference—between Odysseus's cunning and the Cyclops's cruelty—beyond the foreground plot with its verbal exchange and action, it is in the writing of the corporeal motions and positions that urgency and danger present themselves. The inchoate experience of the corporeal is where the event emerges violently, incomprehensibly surprising, opening a threshold to the immensity of the living instant and to the deviation itself of the plotless image.

Hence, only paralyzed astonishment testifies to the lurching, lunging of Polyphemus, the hulk's abrupt hands that scoop two men at once: "rapping them on the ground . . . their brains gushed out all over, soaked the floor—and ripping them limb from limb to fix his meal."[3] How can writing encounter this primitive condition of absolute corporeality: grabbing, knocking, and devouring? How can writing define its creative capacity once the event inscribes itself unconcealed on the bodies? What is the language of the nocturnal cave, the language of the breathtaking stroke and evident horror, when the drunken giant vomits out the wine all mixed with human flesh, or when the gouging of the one-eye comes with fire, blood, and smoke: "till blood came boiling up around that smoking shaft and the hot blast singed his brow and eyelids round the core and the broiling eyeball burst—."[4]

Exposing these corporeal qualities and extracting them from the continuity of the story shows that the event really happened: it has effectively taken place. Two nights separate the day they penetrate the cave from the day of their ensuing flight. Six warriors, friends of Odysseus, are devoured alive. As for the Cyclops, from now on, accompanied by his animals, he will have to bear his ignorance and blindness. Casualty and death prove that the encounter indeed has taken place in space and time; yet the writing implies one consequence that is left unmeasured. One cannot pass by the fact that the name "Nobody" arises as the embodiment of this struggle and puts into question whether the event has happened at all.

"Nobody—that's my name," Odysseus says to the Cyclops. This is not a simple pun, not the triumph of human irony over the beast, nor the comedian's illusion or the magician's sleight of hand striving to convince us to circumvent the law of tragedy. Rather, this is the point at which literature assumes that the dreadful actualization of the body enfolds the secret-made-visible of no-body. If there is a sudden change from horror to laughter it is not only because paradigmatically the situation reverses, as Odysseus indeed leads astray and makes a fool of his enemy: it is because there is a shadow of doubt whether no-body has suffered and no-body has inflicted the damage, whether no-one narrates the event and nothing eventually occurs at the core of the real happening.

Retrospectively, Odysseus claims that this illusory logic of fiction is a kind of brilliant idea that comes to solve the situation according to its wish; The name of "no-body" (*outis*) is a calculated trick (*metis*) that transforms the trap of reality into an artificial theater where everyone plays a role, as, for example, in the second part of *Don Quixote*. However, one cannot but see that the fictitious sign of "no-body" stems from the proximity of the imminent danger, from the risky play with wine and murder. The incorporeal "no-body" is attached to the absolute corporeality of the event. First, Odysseus calls himself "no-body" by way of a last chance to escape his own fear; "no-body" later becomes Polyphemus's drunken pronouncement, and, finally, it is the inverted judgment of the other Cyclopes outside the cave.

"No-body" appears as the sign of Odysseus's impending death; it signals Polyphemus's drunken madness and the intervention of the third party—the other Cyclopes—who, from the outside, disprove the possibility of the event. The sign of no-body as the unknown side of the *body of the event* traverses the entire scene as a floating signifier. "I'm Nobody," says Odysseus facing the Cyclops's gullet. "Nobody's killing me now," Polyphemus howls with pain. "If Nobody is attacking you, then you are alone, and you clearly don't know what you are talking about," the other Cyclopes respond outside the sealed cave.

The absolute corporeality of the event literally envelops the corporeality of no-body. There seems to be an inversion here, following three metamorphoses, three incarnations, so to speak, of the impersonal "no-body," an inversion that not only destabilizes but also neutralizes the actual balance of power. Odysseus becomes the total stranger, the one without face who is present without being there, already escaped or already dead. Under the influence of the wine, Polyphemus becomes subject to his own shadows and phantoms. Perhaps he is dreaming of the old heroic prophecy, while digesting the appetizer made up of the spineless concrete visitors. The introduction of deep sleep and later the eye wound, the blindness, all this joins the Cyclopes' final statement that *something else* has happened inside. The source of violence and pain appears undefined once they ascertain the solitude of Polyphemus; it may be madness or illness or "a plague sent here by mighty Zeus."

This inversion does not mean that nothing has happened at all, but rather that something else emanates from the cave's walls and reenters it as the counter-image of the event. The incarnation of "no-body" in the cave bodies forth the equivocal image of the event, thus suspending the actual happening by introducing a virtual difference into it. In other words, the image does not mirror what is present in the cave; instead, it produces a necessary deformation of the evident confrontation, a split or a change in which any corporeal gesture doubles itself into plural variations and versions. Who is it? Where is it? What exactly is happening? Why and how?

By inserting a doubt of un-happening through the work of literary fiction, the image of "no-body" neutralizes, without canceling, the struggle between Odysseus and Polyphemus. The inscription of "strangeness" is no longer local or personal—it rather affirms the problem of the event as such, namely, the fact that an un-happening inhabits the real happening, that there is a random virtuality that acts within the actual occurrence: the most concrete is the most inconceivable.

Revealing this force of contingency at the heart of happening, interfering with the unaccomplished variable of the accomplished facts: this is literature's task with regard to the event. This is how literature produces events and testifies to the movement of their happening. The erratic sign of "no-body" does not merely indicate the evanescent lightness of any fatal encounter, the free work of fiction that shields from the real violence, by reassuring, for instance, that Odysseus and the one-eyed giant are just a story, no more than a tale. Instead, "no-body" encapsulates the abyss of taking-place itself, the strange wonder and resistance implied by any sense of surprise that reveals the way an event is pregnant—so to speak—with other events and other languages, other bodies and other images. As such, the real but uncertain body of "no-body" is not only the personal condition for Odysseus's flight; it also figures forth how the singular actualization of the event is precisely and simultaneously the means by which the event becomes impersonal, subject to other possibilities, mutations, or variations that can inhabit it.

If the corporeality of the event is compared to the nocturnal cave in which the primitive struggle occurs, "no-body" is the *eventness* dimension of the event, the incorporeal through which the cave opens up to the light. This opening is necessarily a mistranslation, a point of dissimilitude that divides the present occurrence into a variable past and future. The Cyclops suddenly remembers the ancient prophecy in which a giant he believed to be like him came to deprive him of his sight, while Odysseus is free now to become the survivor and the cursed one, the poet and the future hero of his own epic narration.

The dark cave of the Cyclops transforms into a modern café in the small industrial port of Marguerite Duras's novel *Moderato Cantabile*. The struggle for survival between Odysseus's heroic cunning and lawless monstrosity becomes the shared decision of an anonymous couple to surrender to the impossibility of desire. A shooting has recently occurred in this café, a woman has been murdered. The desperate act of a lover interrupts the monotony of small-town life: "What was that? ... Something happened ... No, it's nothing."[5] A shout of despair penetrates the repetitive and disciplined piano lesson of a young boy and causes his mother to abandon her regular "moderate singing" in favor of what she needs and cannot have.

A new ritual begins here for this un-avowed mother: different steps and a different music lead her to seek *that unbearable "Thing"* in the resonance of the fatal encounter, the murder or suicide. Thus, she begins spinning around the event's enchanted core. Duras's bare language reduces this move to a twofold action of striving to "come over" there, to "attain," in order, then, to "know" and to "realize"— not a specific object or understanding, but rather the making of the action itself. This woman trembles: returning to the café to find out what has happened to the other couple who drank from love and death, this is also an inverted effort. The more she approaches, the less she knows what is going on in herself, and thus she feels incapable of attaining and realizing the event. A man is waiting there for her, a solitary stranger sitting at the edge of the bar, *idling the hours away*, far from everyday duties. He is sitting there as if he was her medium, he seduces her with a jug of wine so as together to reexperience the orgiastic mystery through the ceremony of speech.

She asks that the man tell her about the dead woman: "But please tell me, how did she come to realize that that was what she wanted from him, how did she know so clearly what she wanted him to do?" So the man replies: "I imagine that one day," he said, "one morning at dawn she suddenly knew what she wanted [desirait] him to do. Everything became so clear for her that she told him what she wanted [quel serait son désir]."[6] Then again she asks: "You think it was she who first brought it up, who first dared mention it, and that then they talked about it together as they talked about other things?" "I don't know any more about it than you do. Maybe they only talked about it once, maybe every day. How will we ever know? But somehow they both reached exactly the same stage, three days ago, where they no longer knew what they were doing."[7]

Duras's direct speech seems simple and bare, naively and completely exposed. The speakers obsessively repeat the same verbs, but insist on leaving them open by omitting nouns and objects. The grammatical articles insinuate what is crucial and obvious but suspend it as unnamable. This effect produces a growing tension that blurs the distinction between the present couple and the absent couple. Do the words transmit the voice of an absent third and fourth party, or do they express the speakers' own desire?

Suffused with a ghostly voice, the dialogue becomes revelatory: it transgresses the formal limits between the speakers, as the presence between them erotically affirms itself with all its force. Alternatively, the talk becomes sorcery, Eros inhabiting Thanatos: abstract communication that *conjures up* the necessary apparition of another presence through the living bodies.

While Odysseus invents the name of "no-body" to set himself free from the sealed cave, Duras's technique of "free direct speech" takes the opposite direction as she looks for a breach to enter into the cave of the event, in order to enact the primitive law of its corporeality. This is where the event engenders a *becoming* in the literary work: every reconstructed detail that points back to what has happened between the first couple advances the encounter of the new couple. This latter couple, Anne and Chauvin, incarnates the former only to be detached from it and thus to reveal their own particular dis-incarnation.

The event is not an intrigue that literature must concretely clarify or decipher. As the walls of the cave remain sealed, Anne and Chauvin do not claim to shed light on the shadows. Inversely, they apply the art of divination; like an actor through whom the fictitious assumes a real body, they evoke spirits. One may say that by directing their gaze toward the *shining* of the event, Anne and Chauvin become its *troubled amazement*, its living fire or running silhouette. They randomly extricate the virtual image from the actual event; they seek to immerse themselves in the trembling through which the fictitious germinates buds of other realities, other languages and corporealities to come.

The more Anne and Chauvin follow the deterministic road of death that catches the first couple, the more they achieve their own imaginary triumph. The sign of marvel touches them both: while death strikes the first couple, Anne and Chauvin are tormented by "another hunger." A nuptials of gunfire separated the first couple: "One night they pace back and forth in their rooms, like caged animals, not knowing what's happening to them"; "he couldn't make up his mind, couldn't decide whether he wanted her alive or dead"; "then the time came when he thought he could no longer touch her except to . . ."[8] Anne and Chauvin's separation, by contrast and inversely, is achieved by an act of lovemaking, a distant and clandestine longing for touch that involves the excitement of nature itself.

The exceptional moment of chapter 7 in *Moderato Cantabile* is where the immensity of a fragment overflows the literary work as a whole. The actual body of the event now enacts the virtual power of metamorphosis, the *energy of life* bursts forth with all its violence, and the literary work becomes vital in the broadest sense. Physical touch does not reduce the lovers to a *danse macabre*; instead, the touch stays present as a melancholic promise drawing the lovers into a sort of "mating flight" that animates the entire space between them, inside the house and outdoors, the entire town, both sea and sky. A silent fervor attaching to all objects and all senses, a fever leading all and everything astray, following the secret agreement between Anne's drunkenness inside the house and Chauvin's wandering in the streets. The wind on the shore, the perfume of magnolias, the mouth and the withered flower, the half-eaten salmon and the duck on the table, all transform into one single name and into an unrepressed confession.

> Anne Desbaresdes keeps on drinking. Tonight the champagne has the annihilating taste of the unknown lips of the man outside in the street.... Again she runs her finger through the blond disorder of her hair. The circles under her eyes are deeper than before. Tonight she cried. By now the moon has risen above the town, and above the man lying on the beach [sur le corps d'un homme alongé au bord de la mer].... The meaningless shapes of the magnolias caress the eyes of the solitary man. Once again Anne Desbaresdes takes her glass, which has just been refilled, and drinks. Unlike the others, its warmth fires her witch's loins. Her breasts, heavy on either side of the heavy flower, suffer from its sudden collapse and hurt her. Her mouth, filled with wine, encompasses a name she does not speak. All this is accomplished in painful silence [cet événement silencieux lui brise les reins].⁹

This is how the fictitious language of literature meets the open injunction of the event itself. When the literary work pays attention to the imperceptible gestures in the informative description, when it captures frustration overflowing as the wine touches the lips and the scent of flowers undresses the body, the language of fiction introduces a new dimension of happening into the declared situation. The creative vocation of the event triumphs when language governs the represented spatiality and temporality according to its own specific necessity. The stylistic performance and composition bring about the intensive relationship between Anne and Chauvin by juxtaposing their separated desires in the instantaneous continuity of the written sequence. This technique allows the reader to perceive how the realized connection is also a strong expectation, how one body grows out of another's distance. The work becomes an inspired road, an unknown road leading toward an actualization that has already occurred within its own movement. The affirmation of the event's un-accomplishment is already inscribed in the achievement of the writing, between the composed sensations and the unpredictable combinations of words-images.

Enfolded in the body of the event, the sign of "no-body" brought an additional darkness from outside into the Cyclops's cave and hollowed out the mortal struggle. Duras wishes, on the contrary, for the cave to remain full and sealed, but for this to happen it has to reveal itself to the daylight. Odysseus points out that the event has effectively happened, that nevertheless it folds something else into this happening that allows for acknowledgment and narration. Anne enjoins this nobody to react, not to provide her with a possible narration yielded by the struggle, but rather to embody the real but uncertain corporeal law of the event.

The literary creation does not dissipate when one finishes reading and closes the book. Like ancient drawings on the walls of a cave, the text remains alive as long as one can reexperience the event that binds image together with the ontological body. In this perspective, the question is not whether the event in the cave has happened or whether the image succeeds in representing the un-representable happening. It is rather a question of tension: in what way does the incorporeal image stem from the corporeal horror in the Cyclops myth? In what way does Duras's imaginary become immersed in the primitive scene to infuse new corporeal pulsation into the writing? This is how the event creates itself through the text while the text releases new power and speed from the event.

PART ONE THEORY

3

Martin Heidegger
The Event of Appropriation

This theoretical inquiry into the concept of the *event* starts with Heidegger's thinking about *das Ereignis*, usually translated as "event of appropriation," by means of which he elaborates a philosophy of Being as event.[1] Indeed, Heidegger offers an important source in the study of the event insofar as it is considered not as a simple happening in the world but rather as that which makes any happening possible. The priority Heidegger assigns this term casts a new light on some acute traditional problems concerning the conception of time and presence, the identity of things, human being, and the essence of language. These reconsiderations radically changed Continental philosophy by opening a path of direct influence on French philosophy and literature through the work of Levinas, Blanchot, and Derrida, as well as touching more indirectly on Foucault and Deleuze. The phenomenological ontology of *Ereignis* will serve us as the foundation for a conceptual genealogy of the event after World War II. Heidegger reveals elementary problems and perspectives, not to say central arguments and metaphors, that will allow us to approach and observe the concept of the event in its contemporary form.

An Enigmatic Term

In his later thought, the concept of *Ereignis* is an essential concept in Heidegger's ontology. From his essay "The Origin of the Work of Art" and the first articles on Hölderlin's poetry in the late 1930s, the question of Being is linked to this enigmatic term, which allows us to think of the emergence and the becoming of *what is there* through a changing relationship between differences, as a constellation of differences. *Ereignis* is the process by which Heidegger defines the interplay of different ontological properties in their belonging and coming together. In this process, nothing is self-determined a priori and nothing stands in and of itself as it would in a monadology. *Ereignis* is the movement by which any particular element of thinking draws its proper nature from the encounter with another element and from their mutual relationship: they are "extended as a gift, one to the other."[2] No element has any property in and of itself: it is therefore the effect or the result of the ontological event of relationship. *Ereignis* names the primary and generative event of plurivocity which provides the disclosure of Being and in which the human being who thinks through language finds its historical openness to Being. As such, *Ereignis* is a movement of differentiation and simultaneously the way the differences are maintained together, conferring a property to what has been dislocated.[3]

The concept of *Ereignis* is extremely obscure. When one reads Heidegger's writing, the enigma of the term is apparent. While it is obvious that this fundamental concept deeply concerns thinking, it is inaccessible to sensory perception or logical understanding. Heidegger writes in 1957, in *Identity and Difference*: "The words *event of appropriation*, . . . should now speak as a key term in the service of thinking. As such a key term, it can no more be translated than the Greek *Logos* or the Chinese *Tao*."[4] We must therefore enter into what we call the "event of appropriation," says Heidegger, while as a term that guides us crucially on the path of thinking it is nevertheless untranslatably hermetic. A few years later, in 1962, in *On Time and Being*, Heidegger develops the same difficulty: "the sole purpose of this lecture was to bring before our eyes Being itself as the *event of Appropriation*."[5] In the same breath, however, he argues that "we can never place Appropriation in front of us."[6] The impasse of the concept remains. Heidegger claims to bring before our eyes that which can never be placed in front of us. "Appropriation must after all 'be' something." He continues: "However: Appropriation neither *is*, nor *is* Appropriation *there*."[7]

The impossible definition of this concept does not release us from the obligation of questioning its sense; on the contrary, the task becomes imperative. Similar statements concerning the definition of Being can be found at the beginning of *Being and Time*: "The indefinability of Being does not eliminate the question of its meaning; it demands that we look that question in the face."[8]

Event Rather Than Ground

In an illuminating essay, Philippe Verstraeten also observes the difficulty of defining *Ereignis* in itself.[9] He notes that Heidegger's writings develop the concept of *Ereignis* in the context of different relationships. Thus, *Identity and Difference* concerns *Ereigns* in view of human being and Being; *On Time and Being* raises the term *Ereignis* by dealing with the temporality of Being, and similarly, *On the Way to Language* develops the concept of *Ereignis* as the belonging of human being (*Dasein*) to language. *Ereignis* is therefore an abstract term that withdraws by granting the combination of diverse ontological dimensions which, in return, prevents this process from having a settled regulation and definitive direction.

In fact, the categorical definition of *Ereignis* lacks any sense whatsoever unless it follows a historically experienced turn in the work of thinking Being. The event of appropriation names the movement *by which* and *in which* Being allows to be thought in itself. *Ereignis* is the term Heidegger assigns to the twofold movement of Being, disclosing itself by way of concealment, as it yields itself to beings. *Ereignis* cannot be thought in terms of "is-ness"—as it still occurs in the terminology of *Being and Time* in which Being is particularly considered from *Dasein*'s existential openness—but requires the impersonal "it" that gives Being; Being *is* not, but *there is*, in French *il y a*, in German *Es gibt*, which literally means "it gives"; an "it" that gives presence, as long as "it" remains undefined, on condition that it is never given as it is.[10]

Dismantling and overcoming the foundations of metaphysics became a major project in Heidegger's later thought.[11] Unlike the ontological, empirical, or transcendental premises of metaphysics, *Ereignis* suggests what is left unthought by metaphysics, an original ground for thinking (*Urgrund*) that consists in a "leaping" clear of all grounding and into the "abyss" (*Abgrund*) of indetermination. Rather than reestablishing a safe seat for thinking, the abyss, following Schelling, constitutes human liberty and sovereignty by granting access to what Heidegger names, after Rilke, *the open*, that is, an origin lacking both a primordial and an ulterior principle, where human language and thought renounce the conditions for either objectifying or subjectifying the world, renounce self-appropriation and rational representation, and thus, by leaping beyond categorical boundaries, are flung into danger.

This leap into the "abyss" or into the "open" assumes no ground of thought. It is the thinker's venture precisely to enter the realm of empty nothingness or boundless indetermination, so as to both remain "securely in the venture" and to maintain the questioning of thought.[12] In so doing the thinker experiences the movement of *Ereignis* itself, that is, the vibration and force of the relationship that brings the ontological dimensions together. From a topological conception, *Ereignis* "is an event rather than a ground," writes Bruns.[13] It is an open event, a leap into the Open, which conditions the possibility of thought and the evolving possibility of a new thought. In this sense, Heidegger warns us that *Ereignis* should not be considered in its common German use, namely, as a simple occurrence that happens in the world. It is not a present occurrence that somehow eludes the categories of metaphysics and logic, but rather the ungrounded process that conditions the possibility of any event, namely and principally, the way Being makes "world" possible and the way human being has access to the call of Being. "The term event of appropriation here no longer means what we would otherwise call a happening, an occurrence," he writes; "'event' is not simply occurrence, but that which makes any occurrence possible."[14]

In what terms does Heidegger describe how "that which makes any occurrence possible" proceeds? I will limit myself to the exploration of two main points in the next two sections:

1. The question of time. *Ereignis* provides an explanation for the "coming into view" of the present by opening the concept of presence to its absent dimensions and thus inaugurating a subversive temporality of repetition and becoming.
2. The question of language. Here Heidegger deals with the notion of the human relationship to Being and the status of poetry as the construction of men and women's historical consciousness in the world.

On the Way to Appearance

Ereignis is at the core of the phenomenological ontological question of the concealed and revealed unfolding (*déploiment*) of the appearance, which is to say, it generates not only the way a phenomenon is discovered and shows itself in the present but also the way the presence itself is given. *Ereignis* names the very movement of becoming placed before the eyes (*Er-äugen*), the emergence of manifestation that is connected with the noun *Auge* (eye) and is consequently related to what becomes visible, and to what comes into the light. Claude Romano clarifies: "*Ereignis* is therefore that which makes something like Being possible and, more precisely, it is that from which Being itself can be shown and appear (come into view, according to the root of *Er-äugen*) *as event*.... *Ereignis* is the 'condition' for the manifestation of Being as event."[15] Romano quotes, moreover, from Heidegger's French translator François Fédier: "*Ereignis* must be understood as the movement which leads to visibility, makes a view possible, makes appear, and thus makes a standing-out.... *Ereignis* does not name an event, *but that which makes way for an event*: the appearing that takes place first of all ... so that an event can appear."[16]

But the appearance of something can be considered only in terms of the movement of self-division. What seems a present phenomenon is not as simple as it appears to be: its manifestation and our perception of it depend upon the necessary conditions of self-difference. Heidegger announces that one who looks for the process of *Ereignis* dwells in the twofold movement in which withdrawal into the invisible is the origin of all possible visibility. Absence is then introduced into the realm of presence. The appearance into the light occludes the initial germ of clarity, and as such it promises a future possibility of happening that is present only in the form of absence.[17]

The deployment of the appearance entails a change in the way presence is regularly conceived. Now presence is no longer a stable term based on having its roots in the present. The traditional identification of presence with the present represents time as a spatial succession of stable points in the "now." The present, in this order, is not only an instant that is distinct from both past and future but also that which permits measuring the no-longer-now of the past and the not-yet-now of the future. The present dominates the presences of both past and future, and as a result, the presence of the past still concerns us, and the possibility of the future has already begun.[18]

The notion of *Ereignis*, by contrast, reveals a new conception of presence in which absence is active: "It . . . names a presence of absence."[19] This absence releases time from being represented as a successive line of fixed now-points whose gap can always be calculated in terms of numbers and their difference measured in the light of sameness.[20] Now presence becomes the continual division of the present by what has already been and what is still to come.[21] Thus the intervention in the present of past and future absence reveals the unaccomplished presence of that which is coming into view. The present is open to receiving the status of transmutation. Heidegger distinguishes, in this sense, between the notion of presence (*Anwesenheit*) and that of presencing (*Anwesen*), the latter is related to the interplay of time's three dimensions and to their convergent opening as a fourth dimension.[22]

Absence is what creates movement in presence. Consideration of past and future in the present enables a dynamic conception of the present. Now, the ontological presence is understood as that which approaches the present while restraining itself from being completely in the present. The undeclared presence of the past and the unpredictable presence of the future bring about appearance as difference: the act of appearing is the becoming of the future as other; it is the repetition of the past as something other than what it once was.

In light of the tension between past, present, and future, absence as a mode of presence opens up and reveals what is unknown within appearing as such. The past and the future are the absent extensions of the present. What has been denied in the past and what will be withheld in the future are given as absence in the process of appearing.[23] The *denied* past constitutes the appearance as a different *repetition* of the past. The *withholding* of the future projects the appearance as a different *becoming*. This twofold *holding back* provokes a transformation. Becoming and repeating are the movements that yield appearance. Repetition is what guarantees the *possibility* of appearing, while becoming is what delivers the *change* of appearing. Repetition and becoming both ensure and change the appearance. Repetition and becoming are unaccomplished presence that constantly grants and deforms the appearance as the present manifests itself as a ceaseless happening.

This vision of the absence of presence becomes part of the motion of the hermeneutic circle: a continual circular motion between repeating and becoming where any act of inquiry is both the continuation of what has already begun and a striving toward an end that already exists in the beginning. In other words, the appearance is the starting point at which the circle finishes. The path of thinking aims to reach what has been there from the start. Heidegger's task remains therefore to critically elucidate the motion of the circle itself: not to overcome the circle, but rather to obstinately try to leap into it, asking how to reach an unprecedented gaze from which the arrival to where we started appears as if we were there for the first time.[24] T. S. Eliot writes similarly: "We shall not cease from exploration / And the end of all our exploring / Will be to arrive where we started / And know the place for the first time."[25]

To choose the path of repetition, or that of becoming, means, according to Heidegger, to flatten the movement of the circle, because these two directions are finally the same: "Origin always comes to meet us from the future."[26] The "Protestant" return to the absent source of appearance reveals and releases new meanings here and now. Inversely, what emerges does so as the promise of "the earliest hour of mourning," as long as the expected future suspends itself.

Repetition leads not only to a methodical return to what is denied from and by appearance but also to a new conception of the historicity of thought. This is the sense in which Heidegger returns, for example, to study the pre-Socratic sources of metaphysics. Revisiting the tradition of philosophy by interpreting other thinkers' works allows him to develop not only a new philosophical method but also new questions that are not yet found in the tradition.[27] In order to criticize the metaphysical tradition, Heidegger tries, for example, to find what metaphysics basically ignores. He affirms that metaphysics tends to ignore *historicity* and particularly the different ways in which Being shows itself and transforms itself throughout history.[28] Reverting to the source of metaphysics allows Heidegger subsequently to locate, on the contrary, the historical representation of Being throughout metaphysics: "as the *hen*, the unifying unique One, as the *logos*, the gathering that preserves the All, as *idea, ousia, energia, substantia, actualitas, perceptio, monad*, as objectivity, as the being posited of self-positing in the sense of the will of reason, of love, of the spirit, of power, as the will to will in the eternal recurrence of the same."[29] By conducting a historiology, an archaeology of Being, Heidegger critically reverses the premises of metaphysics in order to continue to trace the open becoming of the historicity of thinking. Returning to the concealed source of Being means also to bring to light the manifold appearances of Being. Each effort to expose the showing of Being constitutes a historical epoch. The showing of Being within the process of *Ereignis* takes the shape of a historical transformation, in which the claim of Being must be heard through thought as language. The appearance of history is, therefore, a claim of transformation, a "sudden epochal transformation which cannot be plotted out in advance."[30] Heidegger is bound to the philosophical tradition only with the intention to move toward an as yet immature thought. He writes: "Each man is in each instance in dialogue with his forebears, and perhaps even more and in a more hidden manner with those who will come after him."[31]

It is exactly with reference to this question that Agamben demonstrates the particularity of Heidegger's conception of historicity with regard to Hegel's speculative historical dialectic. According to Hegel, historical appearance is included in the spirit's movement toward its fulfillment and toward its absolute return to itself. Heidegger's historical transmission remains open, so to speak, since the source of destiny, Being as *Ereignis*, withdraws from any historical destination. The form of destination is now detached from the contents of destiny. The historical transformation remains a secret that transmits only the act of change. Every historical transmission can now experience the *untransmissible* that conditions it. The untransmissible transmits itself through every transmission. The historical transformation is not stipulated by way of progress or coherence but only by the fact that there is and must be transformation. Taking account of the groundless and the untransmissible aspects of *Ereignis* leads Agamben to observe Heidegger's own end of history, yet compared with Hegel the historical spirit, here, does not achieve fulfillment; on the contrary, history releases itself into a conception of infinity: "the absence of destiny and ground is thus transformed into an in-finite destiny and ground."[32]

The Vibration of Language

"It is usual to think of appropriation (*Aneignung*) as an act of possessive individualism," writes Bruns.[33] Normally, appropriation designates a subjective act of taking ownership. What was strange and different becomes familiar and proper through the act of appropriation. The subject names and objectifies; as a result of the linguistic act things become present to him, appear as his own production and are subsumed in his own continuity.

Heidegger suggests thinking differently of the essence of appropriation, as an event in which the subject no longer owns the appropriated object, succeeding thus to establish it qua property, at a secure distance from the world. The event of appropriation, according to Heidegger, restores the subject back to the world, removing him from the position of passive spectator into the activity of being a participant. One should recall in this regard Heidegger's lecture on the principle of identity in which every entity is no longer "itself the same," "the same for itself," or "the unity with itself,"[34] but stems, by "losing those qualities with which metaphysics has endowed" it, from the event of appropriation.[35] Thus, Bruns explains, the event of appropriation now does not feature "as a subjective act of appropriation, but as an event in which we are caught up-appropriated, if you like, or say expropriated: no longer self-determining but taken out of ourselves and put into play."[36]

The essence of language changes necessarily as a result of this "play." Heidegger starts by conceiving of language as a central channel through which the relationship of human and Being becomes manifest. Language is the human being's peculiar way, insofar as he is consciousness of his finitude, to expose himself to Being. The claim of Being passes through language; by the faculty of language, Being conditions the historical framework of human being. Human, in return, is the being that thinks with language and thus causes Being to appear different. Being and human being therefore belong to one another and dwell within this gathering mainly through language. Their respective essence is grasped through language as the "self-vibration" of *Ereignis*. "For language is the most delicate and thus the most susceptible vibration holding everything within the suspended structure of the appropriation."[37]

According to Heidegger, language makes visible the relationship between human being and Being. Language "places before the eyes" how human beings and Being reach each other. The etymological link between *Sagen* (saying) and *Zeigen* (showing) confirms that Being's dispatch of visibility is idealistically connected to verbal emission, which is to say that language demands an act of understanding like an illuminating light.[38] Heidegger believes that the unity of Being operates as a hermeneutic convergence between various dimensions of sense and expression.[39] In the same manner that humans receive and perceive the disclosing light of Being (*Blicken*; *Blitzen*), they should remain open to hearing and pronouncing the claim of Being through the act of language. The way a human being perceives and hears the announcement of Being determines the appearance of Being itself and applies furthermore to a man or a woman's regard for and understanding of his or her proper essence and destiny.[40]

Heidegger conceives of the essence of language in an unusual manner. Language is not the property of a human being; rather, a human being speaks only by virtue of responding to the appeal of Being: "It is language that first brings man about, brings him into existence . . . man would be bespoken by language."[41] The words a human being speaks testify first and foremost to the relationship between Being and human beings. Being comes into the present by appointing a necessary announcement, but its message appears only through the articulation and the sounding of human speech. A human being is able to speak only by first listening to the *saying* of Being, and his or her listening determines his or her speech as a response to the Being of language.[42]

The twofold movement whereby present appearance covers and uncovers corresponds directly to the twofold movement of being on the way to language. By responding to Being, a human being's speech holds its message and transforms it into a human understanding that allows the latter eventually to come to his own self and to acquire a proper self from its extension into Being. Language is thus a mediator through which the event of appropriation between human beings and Being occurs. However, Heidegger's need to create a new language that purely thinks what remains universally unthought makes language an event in its own right.

In this sense, Heidegger distinguishes between Being's original language (*Sage*) and human speech (*Sprache*) in order to reveal language's own nature. With these terms he determines how the language of Being emerges through human speech only as the unsayable hearing that makes possible every saying (as the unspoken which resides in every spoken word). He writes: "What remains unsaid is the noiseless voice of Being, which 'speaks' in every word to which we attend."[43]

The unsaid is neither the simple negation of human saying nor the full and potential reservoir from which we draw every partial utterance. The unsaid is that which allows for the showing—rather than the saying—in human speech. The original language of Being remains unsaid in human speech by showing the manner in which language points at itself. It remains unsaid, since it designates nothing beyond the spoken word except the process of saying the word itself. In every word enounced, the unsaid hints, suggests something, beckons us, and shows "at least one trait" of the possible constitution of language. It is, thus, as if the sounding word could simultaneously hear and reveal the silence and murmur by which language comes to say through the human being. In its discharge, human speech both shows and conceals the regression of the word back into itself, and thereby the retracing of speech toward the source of language.

The path back toward the source of speech follows the pure nature of language: here "language speaks," announces Heidegger, and our task is to "speak about speech qua speech," to hear the proper speaking of language through our speech.[44]

This idea is illustrated by five lines from Samuel Beckett's last poem, "What Is the Word" (1988) (though Beckett certainly holds a different artistic vision).[45] The unspeakable that undermines any word produces a unique, stammered music that retraces the way language constructs itself:

> [. . .]
> this—
> what is the word—
> this this—
> this this here—
> all this this here—
> [. . .]

Heidegger would not consider this impossibility of language as a negative experience of being in the world. On the contrary, it is only through this poetic deformation that one can inquire how language "brings man about, bring him into existence," that is to say, how language provides us with a place and destination, how it provides a ground for thinking, displays an appearance, awakening and renewing the presence of other things and, consequently, how it brings all separate beings together in its abiding realm.[46]

Heidegger finds in poetry a privileged ground for apprehending how the original language of Being conveys itself in humans' words: "What is spoken purely is the poem."[47] The creativity of poetry becomes effective whenever the order of words and the order of things do not coincide perfectly. This is when language reveals a difference in which the reflection of the unsaid is experienced as it is. The unsaid brings along a danger: it puts the existence of the human into doubt. This, however, is exactly why poetic creation must confront this danger, namely, to allow the unsaid resound purely and thereby to show the active process of language.[48] This urges poetry to overcome the limits of thinking and to open itself to the intimacy of the world. Through the works of Hölderlin, Rilke, Trakl, and George, poets who question the essence of poetry and the poet's vocation, Heidegger elaborates modes of expression of the unsaid that play an important role in bringing to light the original language.

In his essay on Stefan George's poem "Words," Heidegger discusses two kinds of poetic work. The first is characterized by the joyful work of naming: the word gains power over things by naming them, preserving them even when the things themselves have disappeared, and thus it instills a confidence between words and world. The second type of poem conveys, by contrast, the renouncement of poetic power at the moment when the action of naming exhausts itself and present things as a result disappear. At this stage, "the relation to the word must also undergo a transformation."[49] In the second poem, the task of the words is no longer to designate what *are* the present things as if the world was a determined and stable ground, made to be objectified and possessed by man. Now, instead, words must revert to their own secret, preserving this secret and perceiving in its void the resistance of things to being possessed. So long as words remain ambiguous, things lack too and hence the air of danger or mourning of poets in a "destitute time."[50] But this negation is only the threshold to a fundamental affirmation. The fall into the abyss between words and things leads to a new recognition in which words are stripped of comprehensive expression and designation to reveal the very foundation of language: here things, as well, are called into their intimacy, and this enhances their being and their own "thingness" beyond their usual name, utility, and representation.[51]

Heidegger defines poetry as the essence of all art, in the sense that poetry embodies the pure activity of founding the event of the present in language. The poet realizes and preserves this act of founding; his or her vocation is therefore to be the guardian of Being and the messenger of the original language. Poetry transmits into human speech the not-transmitted which is responsible for any transmission. Only when language questions its founding, as does poetry, by revealing the roots of language while celebrating the new creation of the present, does it testify to the nature of human being. Indeed, then it guarantees and makes possible the establishment of the historical ground and being of humans in the world:[52] "Poetry is what first brings man onto the earth, making him belong to it, and thus brings him into dwelling."[53]

As the internal laboratory of language, poetry offers humans "the primal form of building," "the basic capacity for human dwelling."[54] Not only does the act of poetizing constitute the possibility of having any relation at all to the world, but language determines the particular structure of thinking in place and time. In this sense, language has a teleological responsibility: it offers the basic instruments by which humans are capable to measure their specific position between heaven and earth along with their situatedness in time. But the development of technical instruments and tools does not coincide with the nature of language itself. This is why language will be no more than the disposition to set up a dwelling. As far as it endows mortals with a primary dwelling in their Being, Heidegger defines language as "the house of Being,"[55] which appropriates human beings as an immanent call for making existence possible.[56]

A Constellation of Differences: The Analogy

Two axes of difference, self-division and relationship, compose the event of appropriation. Perhaps the act of appropriation can be defined, as Heidegger suggests, as the relationship that sustains all other relations.[57] This definition corresponds also to the meaning of *analogy*: the congruence between relations that organizes differences without abolishing them.[58] Appropriation ensures the encounter of human being with Being in their difference: their mutual belonging emerges from their difference, and it is the unity of their assembly that simultaneously motivates their own particular difference. Heidegger cannot conceive of difference without a process of gathering. He interlaces association with dislocation, the tendency toward integration with the need for dispersion.

In an interview about Heidegger, Derrida develops this interrogation even further: "The problem is to know whether it is possible to think of *Versammlung* (gathering) by including, integrating and assimilating in it the game of difference, of dislocation and of dissociation; or whether it is only insofar as there is an irreducible risk of dispersion, of secrecy, dissemination, that the *Versammlung* can enounce itself."[59] After Heidegger, Blanchot, Derrida, and Deleuze attempt to move forward and to think the event as pure difference, as an "event of *ex*propriation" that is dominated by neither Logos nor Being. To think "a difference which does not let itself be gathered" ("une différence qui ne se laisse pas rassembler"): this is what Derrida suggests will sharpen the thinking of the event.[60]

4

Maurice Blanchot
The Event of Dying

While Heidegger takes a general ontological perspective, Blanchot deals with the question of the event as an interrogation that mainly concerns the being of literature. Language is no longer the channel through which Being and man come to belong to one another; the fictive essence of language according to Blanchot deprives the subject of self and robs the real of sense. If Heidegger regards poetry as a truthful principle that is the source and foundation of man's dwelling, Blanchot assigns it an illusory principle that affects both the experience of the writer and the written work itself. Thus *the event of the literary work* suggests the inessential essence of the imaginary as the main exigency for modern creation and thinking, an epistemological turn regarding which Foucault asserts: "it is now so necessary to think through fiction—while in the past it was a matter of thinking the truth."[1]

If "Something Like Literature Exists," What Does This Imply about Being?

"Let us try to investigate with more precision what happens to us because 'we have art,'" asks Blanchot in *The Space of Literature*.[2] "What is the result of the fact that we have literature? What is implied about being if one states that 'something like literature exists'?"[3] This is perhaps the principal question of Blanchot's thinking. The question is not only what it means that we experience "something like literature," nor indeed that there is "something like literature" in our world, but rather what happens to us because of this being the case, that is to say: What happens to the world because of literature?

The formulation of Blanchot's question proposes a course of action, a mode of activity that appears with literature and results from it. Blanchot does not doubt how we know that there is literature or, eventually, what in fact *is* literature. He suggests that literature *is*, that something like "fiction" or like the "imaginary" takes place as such. Sometimes it seems "we have literature," he says, sometimes literature places itself before us, sometimes we follows its exigency, its appeal and expectation. If literature takes place essentially as an event of images and as a movement of words, what does this mode of existence imply? What exactly happens within the existence of literature? And what eventually happens to us as a result of this occurrence? These questions are not part of an aesthetical, political, or theological approach. Blanchot indicates furthermore that literature implies being, namely, that the question of literature is an ontological one. Yet, what does he mean with "being," and what does it mean that the work of literature relates to this question?[4]

In several sequences of chapter 7 of *The Space of Literature*, Blanchot sketches an "imprecise outline" ("un schéma grossier")[5] of different historical moments of artistic practice and understanding. Having started out as the language and icons of the gods, the work of art subsequently came to serve political and aesthetic aims, before becoming a figure in and of itself and "a work which *is*, and nothing more" ("une œuvre qui soit—et rien de plus").[6]

Initially, art is the sign of what transcends human capacity: as such it is related to religious ritual and sacrificial ceremonies, to the will and wisdom of the gods. The gods present themselves through the work of art, since art appears to be out of human time and beyond measure and mastery. Art does not serve human purposes in any immediate way, nor is it an efficient activity: it enfolds a kind of mystery and ecstasy. Art realizes humans' necessary appeal to absolute powers and constitutes their interaction with these. In this regard the poet transmits a message to the community, but the latter hears only "the sacred, not the poem" ("C'est le sacré qu'entendent les hommes, non le poème").[7]

When man becomes present to himself and the gods lose both their necessity and their reality, art appears as the work of man. Everything in art now is a human sign and the history of man's own activity. Authenticity refers to what is made by man and for man. Art serves "humanism" in two fundamental ways: by offering man and woman real instruments of self-recognition and self-performance, and by expressing human beings' pure essence as part of its practice. Art, then, is manifest as an object forged by useful actions and possessing general values, while simultaneously, in its most particular qualities, art conveys through its matter a useless passion that exposes the condition of the soul. The more subjective and particular art grows, the more objective and general it becomes. "The more this self becomes deep, insatiable, and empty, the more powerful is the advance of the human will, which already . . . has posed the world as a set of objects that can be produced and are destined to usefulness."[8] In this condition, poetry is no longer a sacred language or an autonomous work of beauty; it refers to and reveals, above all, the authentic life of the poet. The artist takes the place that has become vacant due to the absence of the gods; he personifies and embodies his own art, and consequently he represents Universal Man aesthetically and politically.

To these first two moments Blanchot opposes another artistic essence. Here art is no longer engaged in the service of either the sacred or the human. Art is no longer subordinate to any powers other than itself. All its instruments and significations draw toward its own singular "experience" and "space." In this case, Blanchot argues that art is not even "art for art's sake," but only what it *is*: a new research, a tacit concern, a question difficult to grasp, "where what counts is no longer the artist or active labor or any of the values upon which the world is built or even any of the other values upon which formerly the beyond opened."[9]

In this new artistic moment, the affirmation of what art *is* passes through the negation of what art *is for*, what it *is utilized for*. This is why Blanchot describes art by means of negative definitions: he determines the qualities of the work by what art is not. A work of art is not personal, but impersonal; it is not finished, but always unfinished. The work cannot be measured in terms of historical time, it cannot appear in the real present but it opens a path into the presence of the unreal, into the presence of absence. "The impossible is its task" ("l'impossible qui est sa tâche")—not the protection of the possible.[10] Its light shines from the darkness, and the writer himself has no power over his own work; he is dispossessed by it, "his name is erased and his memory fades" ("le nom s'efface et la mémoire s'éteint").[11]

Yet the use of negation here must be met with suspicion.[12] At this point negation is not opposed to affirmation; on the contrary, negation, here, is only the concealed affirmation of the being of the work. This negation exhibits only the dissimulated appearance of the work.[13] Indeed, any affirmation as such would immediately fall into a teleological conception; any affirmation would render the work as the object and purpose of either humans or the gods. It would, as a consequence, always be pointing at what exists beyond the work of art itself.

The path toward knowing the literary work is always ambiguous. We can only know what the literary work *is* through the concealment of negation. If we affirm, for instance, that a work is im-personal, un-finished, im-possible, and so on, these definitions merely represent a truthful disguise of something else. In other words, the very discourse of this artistic moment risks falling into an unfathomable vertigo, in the form of either infinite paradox or the tautologous definition of the undefined.

Still, is it possible to reflect on this ambiguous movement in Blanchot's thought? How are we to apprehend this ambiguity in light of Blanchot's first questions "What is the result of the fact that we have literature?" What happens when the work *is*, and nothing more?

It is only now, in relation to this third moment, that Blanchot can discuss literature in terms of the "event." Only when literature refers to nothing beyond what it is can the event of literature be comprehended as *is*, without being either the event of the gods or the event of man. For even if one perceives the presence of the gods in the poem, the gods disappear in the materiality of language: through the filtering of a word's image and rhythm, the gods are dispossessed of their power.[14] Even if we may state that the poem is a human endeavor, the heart of the poem is, nevertheless, what always slips out of man's or woman's hands; it is an unrecognized voice in him or in her, the language of what he or she is unable to speak, the space of words that is never where it is.[15]

Thus, we begin to approach the event of the literary work only when we direct ourselves at those elements that relate neither to man or gods because they are always on the other side, behind or outside both the divine order and the historical-cultural circumstances. The event of the poem begins when man and gods, conscience and truth, vanish. The event of the work always escapes both man and gods, hiding from their significant and serious grasp, even if, in the act of dissimulation, man and gods are given a certain face and name.

Blanchot does not renounce the effort of giving literature a certain essence and necessity. However, pure artistic nature can be affirmed only as being *essentially inessential.* This contradiction is Blanchot's main proclamation: When writers or readers approach the region of literature, when they experience the very movement of literature, they reach the threshold at which negation only dissimulates affirmation, where light emanates from the darkness, another time happens within time, and another universe conquers their reality.[16] To quote Blanchot, the one who belongs to the work risks "not just his life, not only the world where he dwells, but his essence, his right to truth, and, even more, his right to death."[17]

By admitting that literature is necessary neither to life nor to man nor to the world, one begins, according to Blanchot, to grasp its fascination and danger. When, in vigorous doubt, one asks, How is it that literature is always other than it is? Why does it always escape categorization? Why does literature always dwell in the distance and what is the nature of the signals it sends from this distance? Only once one concedes that it runs counter to life's reason, to man's values, and to the order of the world, the essence of literature begins to offer itself as both burden and promise. Now the essence of literature begins to impose itself and to be experienced as an endless wandering guided by error and disappearance. In this sense, the event of literature begins only when one gives oneself over to the danger and promise of error and disappearance.

Blanchot concludes:

> the more the world is affirmed as the future and the broad daylight of truth, where everything will have value, bear meaning, where the whole will be achieved under the mastery of man and for his use, the more it seems that art must descend toward that point where nothing has meaning yet, the more it matters that art maintain the movement, the insecurity and the grief of that which escapes every grasp and all ends. The artist and the poet seem to have

received this mission: to call us obstinately back to error, to turn us toward that space where everything we propose, everything we have acquired, everything we are, all that opens upon the earth and in the sky, returns to insignificance, and where what approaches is the nonserious and the nontrue, as if perhaps thence sprang the source of all authenticity.[18]

The Event of the Work

I will focus on two aspects of Blanchot's study of the event by exposing two main problems, each linked to one of his books and the respective myths that are central to them. In *The Space of Literature*, Orpheus's descent into the Underworld introduces the first interrogation of the event: What happens to the writer at the point of the literary event? In *The Book to Come*, the analysis of Ulysses's encounter with the song of the Sirens opens another question: How does the event affect the possibility of the narrative (*récit*) as a principle of literary writing?

Greek mythology, as it features in Blanchot's method, cannot be understood to serve as mere illustration of a conceptual argument. The use of the myths of Orpheus and the Sirens, both originary fables of occidental aesthetics, displays a strategy of thinking that rejects logical sense and discursive truth. The encounter with the extraordinary, the essential promise and peril in the face of the unknown, poses the most exacting question to literature. In these myths, literature directly confronts the land of death, the image and voice of the unbearable, the challenge of insanity and ruse. From this perspective, myth constitutes a concretization of the event of literature as an excessive experience and occurrence, and shows for all to see that its truth cannot be grasped rationally. The truth of a myth can only be apprehended within the elusive movement of inspiration and fascination. This is why Blanchot, in his rendering of these myths, suspends their conclusion and their traditional moral, as if to convey the depth of terror and charm purely as they are: the enigmatic instant in which to see is to become blind, approaching is always distancing, absence is presence, and neglect calls forth attraction.

Blanchot does exactly what he says.[19] By adapting the myth to his critical language, he keeps us in constant doubt whether the moment of Orpheus's gaze, the moment of the Sirens' song, has already occurred, whether the enchanted voice and the eye blink have happened at all, whether they will ever reveal themselves completely. The event of the work is not a truth to know but a movement to feel. Perhaps the event gives itself over entirely in Orpheus's gaze and the Sirens' song. The problem is that Blanchot's writing repeats and comments on these moments to the extent that the text only covers exactly what Orpheus sees and Ulysses hears: a pure void, a silent language, the depth and shadow of the elemental, a song that is always to come.[20] What exactly is the unspeakable and the unsituated event of the work that may suggest that Orpheus and Ulysses have seen and heard nothing at all? In wandering and orbiting around, we make the illusory movement that Blanchot wants us to comprehend—leaving comprehension behind while never having reached it in the first place.[21]

Orpheus's Gaze

Orpheus goes down into the Underworld to find Eurydice. With the genius of his musical powers, he enters the land of death and convinces Hades to restore Eurydice to life. Hades agrees on one condition: as he makes his way back toward the light, Orpheus must never turn around to make sure of Eurydice's presence behind him. Orpheus fails the test, breaks the interdiction, and turns only to see Eurydice falling down, vanishing like a shadow in the night. The myth ends tragically. Orpheus becomes insane: despair and death put an end to the glory of art.

The well-known structure of the myth and its solid poetic symbols allow Blanchot to intervene directly where its secret refuses to be elucidated. The myth of Orpheus becomes the privileged ground for creating a new poetic movement, or at least the ground from which the force of this movement can be assessed. He achieves this by extracting from its mystery a new image of "origin," an image that might invert the commonly received understanding of the myth and therefore contemporary poetic research in general.[22]

Where does Blanchot locate the event of the work in this myth? Why does it appear specifically with this last gaze of Orpheus, namely, at the instant of Orpheus's failure? Indeed, Blanchot begins by hesitating as to the nature of Orpheus's step into the night of the Underworld: the transgression is evident, the challenge is extremely dangerous, the fascination of the song and the image of Eurydice have already passed to the other side of life, subverting the order of the world by going beyond mortal nature. But according to Blanchot, this "first night" does not yet convey a modern artistic concern. This is precisely because the night of the Underworld remains, in Blanchot's terminology, "the essential night" of art, a "holy night," that is, the night in front of which art displays its own power and influence as Orpheus succeeds to render Hades sensible to his demand by the realization of his talent.

Indeed, by challenging the reality of the human condition, this "holy night" is where art finds its source and exposes its strength: creating fictions and possible worlds, transforming reality into image and ideas, naming and stirring up the darkest emotions of the soul, revivifying invisible memories and yearnings.[23] As long as this "holy night" of art dominates, the "other night," that is, the veritable subversive night, does not take place.[24] The writer will have to risk not only his life and artistic skill, but he will also have to lose all certainty in and of the work. In this perspective, the event of the work is not the moment in which the writer makes the impossible possible by the force of his performance; it is the moment in which the writer fails, gives up Eurydice, renounces his own achievements, and flings himself "outside," beyond the protection of the work and beyond his own competence, toward the immense threshold of the impossible. It is this leap out of positive knowledge and reflective thinking that Blanchot calls the event of the work: the expressive failure of the writer and the passage through which the truthful essence of art becomes empty and insignificant.

This is what Blanchot finds in the moment of Orpheus's last gaze. Everything turns over after this un-seen return: Eurydice disappears in the blink of an eye, instead of regaining shining figure and form in the light of day. Orpheus loses hold of Eurydice, his song and music; he is left to see only the growing distance that separates Eurydice from him. The "essential night" which so far enveloped the poem with charm and mastery is suddenly voided.

How, then, does Blanchot interpret Orpheus's failure? How does this event achieve a decisive shift in our understanding of the work of art? Paradoxically, what is referred to here as "event" concerns mainly the physical ruin of the poetic instant: a new mode of *inspiration* for the writer and a new *image* of the work. At the very moment that Eurydice vanishes from Orpheus's sight and as the writer is predestined to irredeemable collapse, the work of art affirms itself. By refusing to belong to the writer, the work of art forces the writer to sacrifice an impossible gift.[25] The writer is isolated, set apart from the work. The event now takes place through this overpowering contact which causes to split it from the writer. The event proceeds through this irreducible distance in a double process: while the work affirms itself as *spectral*, the writer is caught within the *movement of dying* (*mourir*).

"Writing begins with Orpheus's gaze," writes Blanchot, "but in order to descend toward this instant, Orpheus has to possess the power of art already."[26] The activity of art does not begin with Orpheus's gaze; the power of art exists already before this. What begins with Orpheus's gaze is rather the affirmation of the disappearance of art: the erratic activity of absence in which Blanchot locates the ultimate signs of the being itself of the work. "The poet, by the fact that he speaks poetically, disappears into this language and becomes the very disappearance that is accomplished in language, the only initiator and principle: the source."[27]

What exactly is Blanchot's conception of the "being of the work"? Unlike Heidegger, Blanchot does not suggest that Being itself is constituted through the work of art or that the work of art opens itself to the claim of Being. Blanchot's "being of the work" is not the moment in which a human being arrives to find an authentic place to dwell, nor is it the original foundation of her or his identity, nor indeed the sensible recognition in which a man or woman understands him- or herself as being in existence, with and among other things and creatures in the world.[28] On the contrary, Blanchot elaborates his own conception of the being of literature from Mallarmé's experience of poetry. Heidegger's commentary on Hölderlin's verse "poetically man dwells," and the essence of language, which for the philosopher inheres in poetry as "the basic capacity for human dwelling," are far from Mallarmé's preoccupation with the poetical space and *séjour*. Blanchot makes the difference with Heidegger explicit: "For Mallarmé, what the poets build, space-abyss and foundation of language—is what does not remain, and the authentic dwelling is not the shelter where man is preserved, but has to do with pitfall, with perdition and the chasm, and with that 'memorable crisis' that alone allows one to reach the moving void, place where the creative task begins."[29]

As the pure language that questions the human capacity of speech, the being of the work of art, and of poetry in particular, no longer determines the meaning of man or the way in which language truthfully "brings man about, brings him into existence." Mallarmé, by contrast, is troubled as he faces the "fictitious" truth of the work of art. The realm of literature begins when language deviates from the common possibility of mutual understanding, when the image and sound of the word are detached from the robust evidence of the thing and when an unrecognizable neutral voice hollows out the conventional elaboration of writing.

In Mallarmé, Blanchot recognizes the fact that any act of writing presents an abyssal lack (*la perdition et le gouffre*) in which the writer can no longer confirm his or her own speech and is only able to erase the presence of the world and destabilize the accomplishment of its existence.[30] "Mallarmé taught us that the word is the manifest non-existence of what it designates," writes Foucault in "The Thought from Outside."[31] Blanchot himself adds: "Words, we know, have the power to make things disappear, to make them appear as things that have vanished. . . . But words, having the power to make things 'arise' at the heart of their absence—words which are masters of this absence—also have the power to disappear in it themselves."[32] Mallarmé is troubled not only due to literature's ability to make things absent but also because of its ability to evoke things *from* absence. Literature realizes things "in a supreme and silent disappearance," creating a world of "phantoms" that is completely unlike the world of things themselves.[33]

That is why, when something like literature takes place, it is not *existence* or the fact of belonging to *reality* that is at stake, or even the need to deny reality or escape from it into a pure and autonomous sphere. It is rather *unreality* that is at issue here: the *unreal* as an original movement of the work of art and literature: "When he names the essential . . . it always relates to something that has for foundation only the acknowledged and affirmed unreality of fiction."[34]

The being of the work must be studied precisely in this primary movement of *unreality* in which the work cannot be located and the writer is authentically dispossessed of a habitat. In this perspective, Blanchot argues that the transformation of the real into image and language's act of disappearance is not conveyed through the word as an isolated expressive unit, but rather emerges in the poetic articulation between words, when the words disappear too, dragged along in the rhythmic movement of evaporating sounds and vanishing shadows.

The disappearance of the real in language is accompanied by the disappearance of language itself. According to Blanchot, the poetic inheritance of Mallarmé does not claim to establish a perpetual and truthful universe of words that remains unaffected by the ephemeral history or reality. The space of the poem does not reveal the pure color of the words, but rather their reflection and refractions in an infinite degree of shades. What is left of the words in the poem is their sensible articulation, the pure mobility of their relation (music). This is why Blanchot sees in Mallarmé's conception of the poem not only the harbinger of a new artistic space and time, of a new artistic enterprise and necessity, but mainly the advent of an original or neutral language, an "impersonal murmur" that conveys the way literature questions its being.

Indeed, Mallarmé's new conception of the poem, and his paradoxical aspiration to write an absolute "Book" made of silent absence—perhaps like Flaubert wishes to write a "book about nothing"—indicate a new space that is "nowhere wherever it is," a fictional temporality without stable presence[35] or an inauguration of art that is always still to come.[36] But these are all different aspects of the same incessant movement of otherness and difference that Blanchot defines as the "terrible rumor of absence," the "initial rumor" or the "wandering language" that is at the core of literature.[37] In this region, language has become "the idle profundity of being, the domain where the word becomes being but does not signify and does not reveal."[38]

Much as we experience the incessant rumble produced by technologies of mass communications or the ongoing roar of the big city, Blanchot suggests that the literary event is an essential exigency of our being modern, because it approaches the ideal error of *fiction* and *simulacrum*. Exposing the constant act of disappearance, dissimulation, or unreality, literature has to deal with the overwhelming quest for what is always other, other than it is, other than one is able to write, an otherness that not only denies itself but also affirms itself by negation.[39]

In face of this "initial murmur," the modern work of literature must risk its center and achievement, must give itself over to disparity, discordance, and roaming: "On the day when this wandering language imposes itself, we will witness a distinctive disturbance of all the books: a reconquest, by this wandering language, of the works that had for an instant mastered it and that are always more or less its accomplishment, for it is their secret." The task of the writer, then, is "an entirely different one . . . that of entering, more than anyone else, into a relationship of intimacy with the initial rumor. It is at that price alone that he can silence it, and hear it in this silence, then express it, after having transformed it."[40]

With the idea of the "initial murmur" or the "idleness [désoeuvrement] of being," we get a clearer view of the ambiguity of Blanchot's interpretation of Orpheus's failure. Eurydice is released, she appears in her disappearance, she is present in absence like an *anonymous shade or specter* representing the return to the chaotic furnace.[41] Simultaneously, the writer loses the possibility of achieving the work. Renouncing possession of his work, he must wander without name and memory, without the protection of truth; writing becomes an infinite separation whose right to conclude and to die has become exhausted: it is a perpetual homelessness of writing without writing. The writer, here, cannot free himself from his destiny; he can no longer offer his work to the immortal temple of human memory. He must instead enter the ceaseless vertigo *of dying* (*mourir*).

What exactly does this mean: the movement of "dying whereby the right to die is exhausted"? In what sense does the writer face an incessant experience of dying? A look at this process of "dying" will allow us to understand what happens concretely in the event of literature.

The Movement of Dying

Blanchot contests both classicism's aspiration toward objectivity and the subjective authenticity of the romantic approach. Pretending to be the result of the author's impersonal detachment, classicism, according to Blanchot, in fact serves its undeclared political interests, confirming the values and forms of the dominant social class by representing the nature of all mankind with the ideas and orders of a constructed objectivity. Romantic subjectivity, by contrast, positions the work as merely secondary to the personality of the author; the work is the realization of a preexistent gift and the fulfillment of an "inborn" talent that expresses the author's spiritual liberty.

Contesting the authenticity of romantic *inspiration* and classical *impersonality* alike, Blanchot finds in the work of some eminent writers, such as Hölderlin, Mallarmé, Kafka, and Rilke, the momentum with which these terms are turned upside down. Paradoxically, these writers' experiences lend them the authority to speak of lack of inspiration and the impossibility of impersonality. Here, the proper name of the author is neither the sign of romantic genius nor the essence of detachment: rather, it points at the hero of the void, who is the site of an expressive encounter with the force of absence. Thus, Blanchot suggests a new image of writing which is not only an experience that amounts to the loss of any authority or right but also connotes the great patience and desire of the one who imposes silence by sacrificing himself to the impossible and as such elaborates its unique tone in the work.[42]

Henceforth, the sign of inspiration is to be the lack of inspiration.[43] The work is the road toward inspiration, and not inversely: inspiration leading toward the work. For Blanchot's part, this inspiration marks the refusal of inspiration, the writer's fascination in facing this refusal or the attraction that results from this neglect. This work toward inspiration varies from one writer to another. It may reveal itself as an impossible expression, as an instant of insanity, of irremediable finitude, or as a collapse of thinking. Inspiration has the illusory truth of a painful symptom: a great fervor of fear or fatigue, a mixture of hallucination and perception which in turn imposes interruption and transmutation in the work, through the intrusion of incessant murmur or virtual inertia. An example is Roland Barthes's grief on the death of his mother, which becomes the condition for writing a novel, a new language, *Vita Nova*, which Barthes eventually never wrote.[44]

In the same manner, the literary work's demand for impersonality, for Blanchot, is not the same as the search of objective representation as it has been expressed ever since the classical epic poem and tragedy all the way until the realistic novel.[45] The impersonal no longer endeavors to meet the challenge of embracing the world of knowledge as much and as best as possible with the aim to create a total work that contains and preserves the entire universe in an organized image. From now on, the demand for impersonality purports that we be carried out of the world of knowledge, beyond human judgment, to where not even a possible imagination or dream offers protection. Impersonal writing, in this sense, must inhabit the voice of the unknown, not simply represent what undermines the decisive order of a conscience; it must give real space to the void and anonymity of the unknown, a space where no one can speak or testify for her- or himself and where there is no certainty whether in fact anything is happening at all.

It is through achieving impersonality, Blanchot suggests, that the work of literature makes the crucial passage from the sphere of "I" to the sphere of the third-person singular neuter, "It," *Il* in French; from the accomplished time of the present to the iterative time of the unaccomplished. Impersonality opens a literary space in which there is no identification and no present occurrence. No one in this space is able to say "I," and nothing can be designated as accomplished. Writing emerges otherwise and from elsewhere, like a neutral voice, as we witness for example in Beckett's *L'innommable*, or like an undefined vision, as in Robbe-Grillet's *La jalousie*, or in an iterative mode of time, as in Duras's *Hiroshima mon amour*, which oscillates "peu à peu quoique austitôt," between "awaiting and oblivion."[46]

Blanchot believes that this lack of inspiration and impersonality concerns a singular experience of death, a singular death dispossessing the writer of his right to die. The writer who follows the impersonal confronts its most difficult consequence as death as such. But this singular death can no longer be experienced as personal and as an effective end in the present. Death is no longer the essential trial through which the writer affirms his personality. It is no longer the moment in which the writer confirms his authentic identity in light of what negates his life and meaning. Writing has stopped being stimulated by the promise either to "die properly" (to be able to die with dignity, wise like the stoic or with honor like the romantic) or to survive beyond death.[47] It is now a work of ceaseless death, not the last and final beat; it has become the suspension of the moment in which nothing can be experienced and no one is able to affirm his or her own identity. For Blanchot, the writer dies continuously while incessantly experiencing the impossibility of dying, for dying is the event of the writer who becomes nobody and for whom nothing has ever happened.[48]

Blanchot suggests that we understand the activity of death in writing in terms of its double aspect: "there is one death which circulates in the language of possibility, of liberty, which has for its furthest horizon the freedom to die and the capacity to take mortal risks; and there is its double, which is ungraspable. It is what I cannot grasp, what is not linked to *me* by any relation of any sort. It is that which never comes and toward which I do not direct myself."[49]

Death has a double face: it is both possible and impossible. Death comes to me, to me only, it is my own death; it emanates from my body as an inevitable possibility: as the illness of my body, as the risk I have taken or the accident in which I have been involved. But at the same time, death happens without me; death destroys my ability to assert either that something happens to me or that it has ever happened at all. I can never experience my own death, only perhaps as part of the process of my alteration and transformation into the image of myself.

When Blanchot says that traditionally a "writer writes to be able to die," he means that the writer's work appropriates the impossibility of death by making it intelligible, possible to grasp. Death strikes every day, we are surrounded by its natural evidence even if its appearances are usually unpredictable. Those who remain alive dominate the absence created by death by making it present, giving it real space and sense, wrapping it in cultural ceremonies and historical memories that affirm the particularity of life now that it appears temporary. Writing, in this sense, is an authentic way of appropriating death, granting death a unique essence and truth. It is the project of becoming mortal, of admitting the destiny of being mortal, and in doing so, of succeeding "to shelter something from death" (Blanchot quotes from Gide's

Journal, July 27, 1922). Literature that confronts death attaches itself, therefore, to the very idea of the universal progress of humanity. The writer becomes a historical exemplum, and the work contributes an immortal body to the accomplishment of the spirit.[50]

When a "writer writes to be able to die," he uses literature to serve his human qualities and powers. In doing so he reduces the impossibility of death to the urgent interests of his personal experience and present situation. But there is another side to death that is essentially irreducible and ungraspable. This is neutral and unaccomplished death, which is the impossible source, so to speak, of any real death—impossible, because it escapes in essence from its very happening.[51]

It is for this paradoxical death that Blanchot reserves the notion of the interminable event of *dying*. This death is not the end of the writer's life but rather the impossible demand that the writer must confront in face of the *being* of the work itself. The task of literature is to reveal the movement of this dying, since the autonomous unreality of the work exposes an un-happening event that happens to anyone and no one in particular: the sheer movement of words.

Indeed, Blanchot argues that "the writer must die to be able to write." Writing, for him, is by definition writing from death or from the infinity of dying and not at all with a view to life. Perhaps the transformation imposed on life by words shows how reality appears differingly through disappearance, how the work of art, when it has the power of a fictitious voice, replaces the human voice. In this sense, writing is never the death of the writer himself, but the suspension of his death and his survival, a sort of vacuum or interval within life in which the words are revenants from the afterlife. This is why Blanchot and later Derrida endow the writer with the incessant unexperienced experience of his death, "the instant of my death henceforth always in abeyance" ("l'instant de ma mort désormais toujours en instance").[52]

This empty interval of dying thus dominates writing. Dying constitutes the trial of the "modern" vocation of writing. Dying occurs at the very moment when the one who writes expropriates death, surrenders to the being of literature, abandons the objective of existence for the sake of the naked movement of literature which belongs to essentially no one and cannot even be summed up by a poetic or artistic agenda (formalism, symbolism, etc.). Dying is the secret concern, however meaningless and nameless, by which the writer removes his imprint from nothingness, in order to be carried away by the impossible and unaccomplished death that fictitious truth reveals.

Although writing as an act of dying may begin naturally with the appropriation of the visible effect of death, where the unknown acquires a possible face, name, and experience, it can only strive toward the point of dying "by means of skill, savoir faire, effort, the certitudes which the world takes for granted, and yet this point [this point of dying] has nothing to do with such means; it is a stranger to the world, it remains foreign to all achievement and constantly ruins all deliberate action."[53]

Even if literature evokes death through the writer's skill and by giving death a present identity, the event of dying by contrast appears completely foreign and indifferent to all the deliberate actions of writing. In facing impossible and unaccomplished death, writing encounters a radical reversal: from comprising the extreme power of the writer's achievement, the confrontation with death now becomes a no-place that bears no relation to him.[54] Writing becomes a second writing, so to speak, produced by the other hand that does not write. The words no longer body forth the unknown: instead, they maintain its concealment and expose its disappearance. The dying of the writer occurs where words seem to betray, when the writer loses his grip on things and becomes foreign to his own life. However, with this desertion, other voices also appear, a radical invasion that exposes the work to the absence of its own foundation: this is the affirmation of an "outside," of "white space," of a "mad murmur," the domination of a neutral speech that is always illusive, substituting an "objectless fascination" for any human passion.[55]

Dying is not only a negative act that dismisses the writer from his power; the event of dying is also the affirmative emergence of what is wholly indifferent to the writer. Dying is the "beast in the jungle" whose imperceptible, imponderable immensity the writer foresees in every familiar speech, the "irreducible other" that the writer cannot remember to render or to tell, for it concerns the horror and the laughter of oblivion.

This is why the writer can never attain death absolutely, although he must always reach for it. But while literature can never fully express death, it is through death that it reveals what is excluded from its speech and what remains inexpressible. The writer must die to be able to write. And therefore it is "inevitable, but inaccessible; certain, but ungraspable."[56] Dying is always relevant and always there, and yet it cannot be realized.

Indeed, the ceaseless movement of dying inaugurates an obscure guideline for literature. Blanchot's specific analyses of literary works and experiences present concrete approaches to this radical reversal of dying: Mallarmé's *Igitur* and *Un coup de dés*, Rilke's long silence between *Malte Laurids Brigge* and the *Duino Elegies*, Proust's early abandoning of *Jean Santeuil*, Hölderlin's insanity, *Lord Chandos* of Hofmannstahl, Artaud's collapse of thought, the unaccomplished incest in Musil, or Breton's automatic writing. Among many others, these examples offer tangible expressions of the anonymous necessity and struggle imposed by the force of dying.

Emphasizing at times processes of writing (expression) and then again mental experiences (content), Blanchot's literary criticism strives to pinpoint the reversal from which a strange absence takes root. In these readings he locates and examines the specific moment in which the work begins to undermine itself. He follows the movement with which the writer becomes anonymous, the movement of the writer's never-ending attempt to approach this point of reversal in which the absence of dying imposes a singular expression. However, since dying can expose itself only as unaccomplished, Blanchot argues that the writer does not cease to die or never finishes dying.

The event of dying changes the writing experience in terms of time, identity, and space. The repetition that marks unaccomplished temporality destroys the simple possibility of accomplishing writing in the present. The writer's loss of the power to identify and testify to him- or herself by employing the first-person singular entails that writing now confronts an unspeakable language that addresses no one and reveals nothing. Finally, the point of departure for this writing is no longer constituted by the ways of the world and reality, but rather by a type of unreal "outside" that shows how all things lose any use and meaning, in favor of shades and specters that come back not as the reflected image of reality but through the different appearance of the void.[57]

This is the challenge of the event of literature that the writer must confront. Something occurs in literature by which the writer suffers irreversible exile, beyond all territory and away from any present. Since the language with which he creates becomes constantly "foreign," he no longer has the possibility of recognizing his own experience. The writer is set apart from his work. The work is not a place, a "world" in which he takes refuge or eventually claims his right to be by producing sense and knowledge. Interpreting the work from the author's perspective by considering either his mastery or his weakness ignores the specific source and material of the work, namely, the relation of the image to Being. "We must, then, try to grasp again in the literary work the place where language is still a relationship without power, a language of naked relation, foreign to all mastery and all servitude."[58]

The Song of the Sirens: The Event and the Narrative (*Récit*)

Orpheus's gaze presents the event of the writer's dying as the new trajectory of fiction, when he sets free the movement of writing by giving himself up to the anonymous voice of the work. Ulysses's encounter with the sirens shows the inverse example of a possible approach at narrating the impossible by ingeniously transforming the extraordinary into a comprehensible narrative.

Orpheus turns back to witness the gap between the writer and the work. With the voice of the Sirens, however, Blanchot elaborates on another myth of origins in order to show the act of writing as it technically bypasses this distance by the realization of a narrative. As he turns his attention to the myth of the Sirens, Blanchot puts aside the failure of the writer and focuses on the accomplished writing itself. He asks: How does the unaccomplished event of literature present itself in the accomplished writing? How does Ulysses's fascination in facing the Sirens both condition the possibility of writing a narrative and put it at risk?

What is the song of the Sirens? Why does Blanchot find in it the original image of the being of literature? What is so extraordinary in this song that Blanchot recognizes in it the fascination of the event of the work? At the beginning of *The Book to Come*, Blanchot offers several descriptions of the nature of this song: in the wilderness of the sea, this song was nothing like the truthful source of all songs; it was only the illusory hint that beckons toward an end, the promise of a feasible crossing of the distance toward the joyful source of the song. Meant to enchant the sailors, Blanchot says, the song was not simply extraordinarily beautiful; indeed, it may have been the most common song, but it was sung in the most alien voice, evoking the "inhuman" that inheres in every human voice, thereby prompting the sailors to betray themselves, to lose themselves in the greatest desire.

This song was no more than a movement toward the beginning of the song; it was no more than the real song suggesting the beatitude of the marvelous beyond. This is why Blanchot argues that reaching the truthful source of the song was impossible. Not only because the mother-region of music was closed forming the only silent point bereft of music; not only because the source of the song had a faint presence regarding which the sailors felt as if they were leaving it behind and yet never reaching its destination; but principally because the nonexistence of the Sirens was their real power of attraction. The song of the Sirens was impossible because nobody could bear witness to it: the sailors could not experience it without being shipwrecked, without dying. Hence Blanchot concludes by conceiving of the Sirens' voice as a song without song, a song of the abyss and of silence, a nonexistent song that offers the promise of existence and the power of its lacking dimension: "music, in this region of source and origin, had itself disappeared more completely than in any other place in the world: sea where, ears blocked, the living sank, and where the Sirens, as proof of their good will, had also, one day, to disappear."[59]

Ulysses was the first and the last sailor who enjoyed this region of song while remaining alive. Using technical ruses and the wisdom of foresight, he reduced the dignity of the unreal song of the Sirens to a discredited and immoral temptation. Revealing the secret of their mysterious song, the Sirens took on corporeal existence: a visible appearance, a voice that could be heard, and a body that could be exploited and appropriated. Blanchot describes this metamorphosis remarkably: Ulysses loses his hearing as he hears the unspeakable, and in proud acknowledgment of his deafness he digs a spoken grave for the Sirens in the *Odyssey*.

Thus, by telling the un-experienced experience of the event, Ulysses transforms the immediate danger of the song into the inoffensive adventure of the narrative. The accomplished navigation of Ulysses becomes Homer's narrative, reasonable and sufficiently calm to recount, in the name of Ulysses: the insanity and distortion he has suffered in face of the source of literature. Of course, the encounter with the source of literature can only be told after the event, after its danger has passed and by turning away from its dazzling attraction. Still, without this encounter, the promise of the charming and horrifying navigation of literature cannot be heard. And so the impossible song of the Sirens is indispensable for the telling of any narrative: "That is not an allegory. There is an obscure struggle underway between any narrative and the encounter with the Sirens."[60]

The myth of the Sirens leads Blanchot to discuss different literary genres, to define the novel as opposed to the narrative (*récit*), though not by the formal means of conventional definition, but rather by reference to these genres' internal qualities, as if it concerned different navigations of literature and different adventures of writing. The narrative begins where the novel ends: It is true that what Blanchot calls a narrative can also exist in novels, in novellas, or maybe even in poetry. Yet, even if it belongs to a novel, a narrative is an entirely different experience of the encounter with the Sirens. The distinction between novel and narrative resides in the reaction to the encounter with the Sirens, to the ontological event of literature, that is. The novel stretches the distracted navigation toward the point of the encounter while the narrative is the absolute navigation of the encounter itself.

The novel has the quality of the inconstant work of man, replete with the rich explorations and the multiple objects of knowledge on offer in the limited human world. It has no pretension of disrupting the human condition by striving toward a determined destination or by reaching a decisive end. On the contrary, the novel finds its pleasure and melancholy in the accessible diversity of the world; it presents the irony and despair of time-bound indecisions and coincidences. Blanchot argues that the contemporary novel is perhaps the most pleasant and reader-friendly genre, because "distraction [divertissement] is its profound song," because through its protracted and dispersed movement the novel refuses and forgets the extraordinary encounter with the source of literature in favor of ordinary preoccupation and play.

As opposed to the novel, the narrative is devoted to the absolute encounter with the source of literature. The narrative does not only narrate an exceptional occurrence, something that has already taken place; it is the movement itself toward this occurrence. Indeed, Blanchot admits that usually there is no difference in the actual telling or recounting of a narrative or a novel: the difference is rather that the narrative is wholly dedicated to a decisive destination and determined end. It is haunted by one single and overwhelming episode, because the exceptional occurrence is only the threshold to the secret pull of the Sirens' song; that is, the exceptional occurrence is only the breach that opens out directly into the impossible event of the work of literature.

The narrative is the place in which the possibility of telling becomes the struggle with the impossible event of literature. Telling an occurrence that is unusual, that holds an unknown truth, only constitutes the initial movement toward narrating.[61] This is why Blanchot affirms that the narrative's narration cannot be understood simply as an account of what has already occurred; this would miss the essence of the narrative. Narrating the narrative is the very movement of happening in which the impossible event may possibly take place, because beyond the limits of the narrative the event has no reality, while within the narrative there is nothing left to tell once its secret is yielded.

As a fundamental experience of writing, the narrative of Ulysses would be the never-ending navigation toward the inaccessibility of the song. The narrative pretends only to tell the fascination of the song, while the song itself refuses to assume a stable presence, either before the narrative or after the narrative. One may well wonder whether the song exists at all. The song remains silent within the expression of its fascination; what remains from the extraordinary encounter is only the heroic struggle or the effort of the made journey, but never the song itself.

This is exactly what Blanchot notes: as long as the narrative welcomes the song, the song dissipates and affirms its unreality. But also, inversely, once the narrative becomes engaged in the encounter, it reaches its limits: now it contains an immensity that cannot be contained; it hears the song in its deafness. Even if the narrative covers the enchantment of the Sirens with regular words, their song continues to affect every trace of the writing. Even when the narrative succeeds in bypassing the impossible event of literature, the dissimulated presence of the event essentially interferes with the narrative performance, luring like a secret attraction, opening a distant new horizon and adding to the pressure of the narrative's exceptionality. Much as the Sirens' song is only the starting point toward the source of the song, the event is no more than the narrative's movement toward the event.

Blanchot argues that any narrative must encounter the fictitious truth of the Sirens, because their song is the demand itself of narration and the limit of its creation; it is what generates both the necessity and the impossibility to tell. The song is the promise itself of having the rudimentary power of writing, and through it the realization of the narration takes the form of what cannot be written. Into the *techne* of art, the Sirens insert an "impossible" variable, a source beyond control that conditions and enables the artistic work on the one hand while on the other constituting that work as a "yearning," for it will never be capable of containing: its empty, elusive, absent origin. Now, Homer comprises the unexperienced moment of death of Ulysses: The *Odyssey* covers the abyssal voice of the Sirens, and in doing so the narrative reveals its own movement toward itself, toward its disappearance in the production of the imaginary reality: "That is one of the strange qualities, or should we say one of the aims, of narration. It 'relates' only itself, and at the same time as this relation occurs, it produces what it recounts, what is possible as an account only if it actualizes what happens in this account, for then it possesses the point or the framework where the reality that the narrative 'describes' can endlessly join with its reality as narrative, can guarantee it and find in it its guarantee."[62]

This experience of narration in view of the event suggests a new temporality for the literary work. As long as Blanchot contests the peaceful separation between the event that happens and the work of writing, the narrative emphasizes the odd temporality of its nature. The narrative neither simply narrates a past experience nor projects itself as a future possible world without ever being affected expressively, without questioning its own verbal actions and techniques of imaging. In other words, the narrative does not subordinate itself to historical reliability and regularity; it does not transparently transmit the temporal mode of succession and progression of historical circumstances. On the contrary, Blanchot defines the narrative in light of an undefined event that cannot be located either before or after the narrative and therefore disrupts the temporality of literature. This temporally inaccessible event dominates the movement of the entire narrative until its effect invades the very performance of the work. Now, the texture of the narrative takes on the ambiguous temporality of the event: possible writing is the approach toward writing's encounter with the impossible—and *simultaneously* it is what necessarily results from the exigency of the impossible.

This ambiguity has a great effect on the realization of the literary work. The event is not before or after the narration; it is present in each instance of the narrative as a suspension and as a digression between "what is about to happen" and "what has already happened." This is why the present of the narrative as it was composed, from Flaubert and James up to Borges and Gombrowicz, captures the danger of the unpredictable. Inevitably, writing produces an exceptional breach in the ordinary observation of time, an exceptional penetration that relates to no present time and that even undermines each present instant that it seems to inhabit.[63]

Blanchot's conception of literature not only denies the idea of representation but undermines every possibility of presentation, because for Blanchot its very movement consists in transforming the real into the imaginary, the world of knowledge into the other world of image, that is, the reasonable into the chasm of hallucination.[64]

Blanchot claims that the event imposes a metamorphosis: When writing is under the influence of the impossible, every element of the narrative undergoes the metamorphosis of fiction. The style of writing, the time and space of the work, the writer himself, and perhaps the reader, too, fall prey to the horror of this transformation that Blanchot renders in condensed form when he refers to the passage—"little by little although right away"—to the non-world of images.

The act of giving oneself over to the image does not enjoy the protection of the unreal. On the contrary, the suspension of the real introduces violent alteration. The image does not present a stable resemblance against which the difference from reality can be measured; word does not simply replace thing. Instead, the image of literature is an affirmation in the modality of suggestion, of "maybe," of "it may have been," that is the modality of fictional hypothesis.[65] This could be the peculiar force of literature: by affirming the irreducible alterity of its image, literature offers an unaccomplished presence that gives birth to an entirely new present; it is a qualitative novelty, resonating Ezra Pound's "Make it new!," which always remains new, always reemerges in its innovation.

In this perspective, the critical task of "a theory of literary events" would be to locate a decisive encounter with the imaginary in the work at hand. It would be necessary to examine the extent to which the work delivers itself to the becoming-imagined of the real, and to observe how this power of alteration affects the writer and the process of writing—as Barthes would say, the writer's obligation to enter into a difficult relationship with his or her own language.[66] The quality of the inventive content or the freedom of fantasy offered in the incredible worlds of fiction are not the issue. At stake is precisely the way in which the fascinating attraction of that *otherworld* questions the possibility of speaking and narrating. How does writing discover what refuses to be discovered? How does the unexperienced event come into view through the elusive movement of language? While the narrative has perhaps reduced the fatal song of the Sirens to an inoffensive literary experience, the search for the song of the Sirens in the literary work never reaches its end and continues demanding to meet the impossible.

5

Jacques Derrida
The Non-Advent of the Event

Derrida is evidently a Blanchotian philosopher. While continuing to affirm Heidegger's influence, he radicalizes, through Levinas, the thought of *difference* in order to methodologically establish the condition for a "science of the singular." Here, the thinking of the event and its challenge to modern existence must first of all takes the shape of a concrete and dramatic *performance* of writing: to write in the limits and in the margins of thinking so that the making of the work itself testifies to the subversive powers at play when the grounds of thinking come under question. Indeed, Heidegger and Blanchot can be seen to have done the same, but in Derrida it is taken further: by bringing to bear historical context, generic conventions, and technical praxis, the process of his writing makes for an experience that registers the unpredictable appearance of the event, its traumatic corporeal symptoms, and the resulting transformation of thinking away from the traditional logic of metaphysical premises through a close deconstructive dialogue with that thinking.

The concept of the event can be found throughout Derrida's work. Starting from the influence of the structural and phenomenological perspective, the event is already thought in "Signature, Event, Context" published in *Margins of Philosophy*. Later, the books dedicated to Ponge, Celan, and Blanchot associate the absolute invention of the event with the discursive creativity of literature as the intimate concern of the other, as a desacralized discourse that transmits by inverting the liberal tradition and the value of speech itself in the historical context of the foundation and becoming of democracies. Finally, the political writings after the Gulf War and 9/11 concretize this abstract thinking into social and psychoanalytical phenomena, taking account of the new technologies of representation, the current progress of science, and strategies of power.

The Im-possible Event

In 1997 Derrida was invited to Montreal to participate in a seminar on the conceptual problem of the event. Following the title of this encounter, "Is Saying the Event Possible?," Derrida questions the very possibility of experiencing the event and of "saying" the event as it happens.[1] He asks whether there is a way—because there is a real necessity—to experience the un-experienced action of the event or to express the possible im-possibility of its articulation. Methodologically speaking, Derrida suggests developing a new experience of language in order to perceive and make visible in vivo the transformation caused by the event. He demands that the event be discussed in terms of impossibility: "We should speak here of the im-possible event, an im-possible that is not merely impossible, that is not merely the opposite of possible, that is also the condition or chance of the possible. An im-possible that is the very experience of the possible. This means transforming the conception, or the experience, or the saying of the experience of the possible and the impossible ."[2]

This conceptual interrogation begins under the sign of the impossible. If there is an event, it is impossible: the event is the impossible aspect of what is effectively taking place. In Derrida's language, the impossible is not simply a negative opposite. The impossible affords the chance to undergo the imposed transformation so as to follow the possible condition of the event's experience and speech.[3]

Why does Derrida define the event as impossible? Why does the experience of the impossible condition the "eventfulness" or the "eventness" of the event?[4] In what sense can one apprehend the elements that remain both unsaid and prohibited (*inter-dit*)—that make up the event? The recording of this seminar in Montreal in 1997 and, a few years later, the book deriving from the interview dedicated to the events in New York City on September 11, 2001, offer two meaningful speech-acts in which Derrida debates how crucial it is to ask about the nature of the event today in the political atmosphere at the turn of the century.[5] On these occasions he once more illuminates some definitions of the event and suggests how its impossible characteristics stimulate the movement of thinking toward a possible appropriation. Let us enumerate some points on which Derrida bases his discussion.

1. The event is by definition an absolute surprise; it cannot be anticipated and is essentially un-planned. It is an interruption, a deviation from the expected progress of historical causality. When everything is predictable, nothing happens. The event is, therefore, exceptional, singular, and unprecedented.[6]
2. The event attacks all horizons of expectation. It hits and shocks the subject affected and leaves him unprotected. It appears and proceeds at maximal speed[7] as if it had descended on the subject from on high: "The event as event, as absolute surprise, must fall on me. Why? Because if it doesn't fall on me, it means that I see it coming, that there's a horizon of expectation.... The event can only seem to me to be impossible before it occurs [arriver]."[8]
3. What is taking place calls forth a movement of *appropriation* (*Ereignis*) that involves a fundamental *ex-appropriation* (*Enteignis*). That the event is unpredictable puts to the test any capacity of understanding. The event is *that which* one does not understand; it opens and reveals itself as a phenomenon of inappropriability (*inappropriablité*), as that which both resists and challenges the need to comprehend. Incomprehension here not only marks the difficulty to recognize or identify but also names the failure to grasp, to contain, and to embrace what is coming about. Therefore it is impossible to make the event one's own or to reach a compromise with it. "Although the experience of an event, the mode according to which it affects us, calls for a movement of appropriation ... there is no event worthy of its name except insofar as this appropriation *falters* at some border or frontier. A frontier, however, with neither front nor confrontation, one that incomprehension does not run into head on since it does not take the form of a solid front: it escapes, remains evasive, open, undecided, indeterminable. Whence the unappropriability."[9]
4. The pure singularity of the event exposes the subject to the limit of appropriation, and thus to the encounter with the other. The event shows how the infinite difference of the other subverts and recedes, orders and disappears, reveals itself absolutely and obliquely. In-

sofar as the other invades one's own home, overflows one's harbor, fascinates and transforms with all its force, the subject reacts by refusing to welcome this alterity, since he is not prepared or not ready to do so. In this case, the presence of the other is irreducible but at the same time equivocal, threatening, and deceptive;[10] the exchange with it, therefore, can be established only by a deprivation of one's own property.

5. The event imposes a language that does not belong to the order of knowing. It exceeds all pre-established and pre-dictable notions. This pure singularity goes beyond all essence, truth, or law. Derrida writes: "The saying [of the event] remains or should remain disarmed, utterly disarmed by this very impossibility."[11] Yet this lack of language, this ignorance or deficiency in "saying" the event, must not lead to a closure: it should be followed by fundamental affirmation and ceaseless questioning. Affirmation and questioning are more like primary attitudes that invite and accept the impossible aspect of the event. Both are open to the chance and to the threat of the event. Both consist of an approaching and undergoing of it. The affirmation is the unspoken willingness or readiness to welcome the unknown, to change and so to engage the act of language with the sharp insistence of questioning.

6. This leads to one of Derrida's most interesting insights about the repetition of the event's singularity. Having said that the event itself never makes a full appearance and that it cannot be appropriated in its totality, Derrida argues that the event takes the infinite form of secrecy, a secrecy that "haunts" any possible experience as a spectral return. He goes on to state that the unpredictable event cannot be apprehended or accepted unless it appears to be repeated. The absolute singularity of the event emerges only within the impression of a repetition, as that which is coming back and yet is still to come. The event causes a duplication in which the new already has the aspect of a *revenant*: "It is new. The coming is absolutely new. But the novelty of this coming implicates in and of itself the coming back."[12]

The impossible haunts the possible experience as a ghostly appearance and a ghostly speech by introducing a process of "spectrality" or "iterability."[13] These key terms in Derrida's work designate a process in which a phenomenon repeats itself by taking a different appearance. This is a process of repetition in which the return of the same differs from itself, thus showing that the power of difference is at the heart of the very notion of identity.

In this context, the fact that the novelty of the event surpasses all established instruments of thinking implies that one can only face the event paradoxically by facing backward. In this momentary vacuum of deferral and difference it is not only the testimonial process that comes into question; the technical appropriation by images and words testifies to the event by already changing it, repeating its symptoms and reminders in a different semiotic system and revoking the past differently. In this iterative time, the event as such also upsets any stable notion of happening in time, namely, by raising the possibility that the event does not take place in the present and has indeed no presence at all.[14]

The points I have just presented are conveyed again on a third occasion in this same period, at a conference held at the French National Library in Paris in January 2001. Here, Derrida presents a description that divides the drama of the event into several sites of action: (a) the event is the manner in which a singular occurrence emerges and manifests itself; (b) it suggests a subjective experience or disposition that responds to this singularity; and (c) the event is a matter of language and testimony:

> [W]hat happens ought to keep, so we think, some nonprogrammable and therefore incalculable singularity. An event worthy of the name ought not, so we think, to give in or be reduced to repetition. To respond to its name, the event ought above all to *happen* to someone, to some living being who is thus is *affected* by it, consciously or unconsciously. No event without *experience* . . . . It is difficult, however, to conceive of a living being *to* whom or *through* whom something happens without an affection getting *inscribed* in a sensible, aesthetic manner right on some body or some organic matter. . . . Perhaps another thinking is heralded here. . . . a thinking that has not yet thought what it must think, namely, thought, namely, what is given to be thought with the name

"thought," beyond knowledge, theory, philosophy, literature, the fine arts—and even technics.[15]

Following this quotation, it is necessary to explore the above-mentioned sites of action little by little and one by one in order to clarify not only what Derrida writes about the event but also how this concept offers new possibilities of creating and thinking. How, moreover, does it introduce new critical horizons: a "science of ghosts," a "science of the singular," a "science of chance," a "science of writing" (*Grammatologie*), a science without science.

The "Thing" That Happens

In *Parages* (1986), a book dedicated to Blanchot's fiction, Derrida distinguishes between the core of the event as the "Thing" (*la Chose*) and the accidents and impressions that are immediately attributed to it. At first sight, the event understood as "the thing itself" can be compared to the traditional Aristotelian conception of general essence, as opposed to particular accident, or to Kant's *noumenon* versus *phenomenon*. The event itself as "thing," says Derrida, never happens: it is the thing to which accidents happen; it is not that which physically appears, but rather the condition for any appearance. "Perhaps *chose* has always designated, in philosophy, that which does not come about [*n'arrive pas*]. Things come about, but *la Chose*, in its determination as *hupokeimenon* or *res*, is the substance to which 'accidents" happen and to which predicates attach, but which cannot itself be the accident or predicate of something else. *La chose n'arrive pas à autre chose*. *La chose*, when defined as the *hupokeimenon*, is that to which the *sumbebekos* or accident happens, but which, being a thing, *chose*, does not happen, does not come about."[16]

This definition of the event effectively uses the traditional conception of the thing, but only with the need to de-purify it.[17] When Derrida names the elusive presence of the event the "Thing" instead of referring to the self-identical permanence of Substance or Idea, he suggests the inauguration of a different *logos*. Unlike the truthful presence of the Idea, which remains eternally unforgettable insofar as *logos* resists all absence and oblivion, the event is a pure Idea as long as it remains impure, that is, as long as its truth is neither categorical nor self-identical.

In other words, the event questions the foundations of *logos* itself, as well as the steps of logic and the truth to which they purport to lead. When one is thrown into an occurring situation dominated by an unidentified "thing," not only is the potentiality of one's fore-understanding or one's involvement in the world destabilized, but, even more so, the very possibility of the world itself collapses. Although one does not know yet what is happening, one knows the event is there as the suspension of all concepts; one knows that one must accept the event's effect as a strong intuition without a concept.[18]

The event imposes a crisis of naming. This crisis features explicitly in Derrida's text on 9/11, where he notes that the attempt to repeat and to cling to the designation and images of the "terrorist attack" amounts to an actual dissimulation of the horror and its dazzling. Thus, regarding, for instance, the television coverage of the event, he observes a verbal redundancy that only conceals and denies the powerlessness of language, that only demonstrates the attempt to restore control, to reassure the mind and eventually to cover up the unspoken perplexity in the face of that which cannot have a name.[19]

Naming the eventness of the event as the im-possible "thing" gives a name to the horror that attacks the possibility of the common name itself. The "thing" remains open, embodying infinite names and effacing each and every one of them. Yet this infinity and anonymity is neither divine nor abstract. Derrida declares that the event emerges concretely within an absolute proximity and singularity.[20] The problem is that the very concreteness of the event only lays bare its concealment, as with Zeus and Semele, where full exposure to the brightness of the event imposes blindness. Hence, the "thing" does not refer to a local problem of denomination or designation within a defined context. It questions the taking-place itself, the context itself, the very possibility of the place and time, of happening.[21]

This relation between excessive concreteness and lack of testimony explains why Derrida considers the *eventness* as the "thing" that arrives without arriving, as what takes place without having a place. This twofold direction of the event, advancing and withdrawing at once, is an important heritage Derrida takes from Heidegger. Reading Blanchot leads Derrida furthermore to define this "non-advent of the event" as necessarily "terrible."[22] The event arrives as a terrible thing, because it bears the frightening aspect of no-thing. "Here, *la Chose* is 'terrible' because in its very not-happening it happens (comes about) to the 'Come,' in its *pas de chose* [no thing, thingly step, thingly "not"]."²³

The event is not only a terrible no-thing; in this last quote the French word *pas* adds a further paradoxical or labyrinthine element. In *Parages*, Derrida extends Blanchot's elaboration of the twofold sense of the word *pas*, which can be interpreted here as both step and stop, or as Leavey translates it, "*P*ace Not(s)," in order to reopen this "strange proceeding" of advancing and blocking the way at one and the same time, of moving by digression insofar as the step creates and annuls itself, along with the path and the aim.

This is the new logical step Derrida wishes to carry out with Blanchot—somewhat like a Beckettian walking that embraces and neutralizes all directions, moving forward toward backward in the same spot—this "de-distancing" which leads to the step-beyond and to the no-beyond at once. "In order that 'I am truly in the beyond, if the beyond is that which admits of no beyond [*pas d'au-delà*],' the pace [*le pas*] that carries me there must clear itself [*se franchisse*], annul in preserving the beyond."²⁴ As such, the event as the no/pace beyond impels the subject at each and every moment, while remaining beyond the subject's reach.²⁵

One of Derrida's achievements consists in bringing to bear Heidegger's and Blanchot's abstract notion of aporia through concrete ethical and political consideration. Using empirical terms to comment on 9/11 and the Gulf War,²⁶ Derrida suggests distinguishing between the raw fact of the event and the constructed "impression" that we gain from it, between the "thing" of the happening itself and the production of impressions, whether it is the spontaneous reaction of an eyewitness or the controlled interpretation of it. He observes that the corporeal event of war is totally unlike the event constructed by the media. There is an abyssal difference between the event that happens in the eyes of victims and the event that lives through the simulacra of images, the interference of technology, and the reappropriation of information.²⁷

The image of a victim differs from the victim himself. It is the dead, not their image, who testify to the "thing" of the event. On the one hand, each death is singular and thus marks the war's really having taken place, says Derrida, in response to Baudrillard's claim, in *The Gulf War Did Not Take Place*, that television reporting cancels the real experience of the war. Each wound traces an undeniable reality that exceeds any simulacrum and possibility of virtualization. But how, on the other hand, do the dead testify to the above-mentioned *non-happening* of what happens? Is there a contradiction here between the undeniable fact of the event and the "thing" that takes place as no-thing?

In the Montreal seminar (1997), Derrida offers a vague solution to this question: "I'd say that we must ceaselessly analyze the mechanisms of what I've just dubbed trans-information or reappropriation, the becoming-simulacrum or becoming-televisual of events, analyze them in politico-historical terms, without forgetting, if possible, that an event took place that cannot under any circumstance be reduced to its analysis, an event that cannot be reduced to any saying. It's the unsayable: the dead, *for example*, the dead."[28] The existence of the victims is proof not only that the event has taken place but also that the extreme violence cannot be reduced to any impression and knowledgeable statement: "It's the unsayable: the dead, *for example*, the dead."

In other words, though the victims were fully exposed to the historical event, only their silent corpses now show the no-where and the no-time of eventness. Thus, in pointing at the victims' corpses, Derrida defines the "singularity" and "exemplarity" of the event: the one who is totally caught up in the event cannot testify to its coming, other than through the inanimate and stupefied gaze. "At the instant death, the impossible, will become possible as impossible."[29] The event imprints its absolute trace on the dead, those who by definition escape the work of mourning, as the eventness itself remains prohibited (*interdit*) and unsayable (*indicible*).

The war or disaster must then be analyzed from the point of view of the victim's corpse. In this sense, the presence of the dead body is not the partial realization of the *idea* of war—there is no self-identity of war—but rather the self-concealment of the *singular and exemplary event* of war. It is in the expression of the dead victim's face that the "thing" appears as no-thing; it is in the reflection of his eyes that the affirmation of the "terrible" shines.[30] From this perspective, the impossible event is not a simple part of the whole unit of history, for it is basically the interruption of all possible experience and what eludes all work of memory.

But this is not all. Even if this unmeasured temporal segment cannot be reduced to fit in the regular course of history, Derrida says that the "thing" of the event gives form to the "impression" we have of it, and this "impression" must be analyzed through a political and historical prism. This suggests that the "thing" of the event is already subject to the possible technics of multiple description and diverse imagery. As long as the "thing" does not limit itself to a concrete present realization, it stimulates the desire and indeed the necessity of having an accessible version of and reaction to the event. Nevertheless, there is no simple continuity or hierarchy between "thing" and "impression." The "thing" informs the "impression" only insofar as it remains secret, while the impression invents the image of the event over and beyond any recognizable source.

Again, the point of view of the dead shows why, on the one hand, the "thing" of the event cannot be appropriated, and why, on the other hand, the "impression" of the event can testify only in the realm of simulacra. Thus is subverted any relation between origin and copy, between source and imitation, presence and representation. The dead body presents an intersection: the path to the *impossible singularity* of the event passes through the *possible simulacra* of the event. The former points to an un-experienced experience; the latter refer to discursive practices and imagery that can be found anytime and everywhere. The first testifies to a spatial encounter dominated by a strong prohibition; the second, obsessed by this prohibition, creates ceaseless repetition and difference, temporal suspension and temporal renewal or survival.[31]

At this intersection, the logic of *iterability* or *spectrality* comes into play. This differential structure displays, as mentioned earlier, a series of repetitions in which *alterity* inhabits the same. In other words, we are already confronted with *incessant difference*, namely, that the impression can be considered only and always outside of the happening itself. In a similar vein, our encounter is already with a *repeated trace* of the event that is translated into different languages, transposed into diverse empirical contexts and domains, and that reappears from the future as the phantom of the past: "The missing of the archive, the ghost, the phantom—that's the future."[32]

The Science of the Singular:
The Emergence of the Event as Other

Derrida argues that the law of the event remains unspeakable, as the trace it leaves on the body is absolute in a manner that is reminiscent of the law machine in Kafka's *Penal Colony*. Yet there are accessible impressions of the event that already present its simulacra; there are accessible impacts of the event that continue multiplying and concealing its *secret*, as if the origin of the event was always already metaphorical. What exactly does it mean to testify to a secret? asks Derrida in *Demeure* (1998).[33] Does the secret apply to that which refuses all testimony, or to the absence of attestation itself? How can we engage in the secret while the secret disengages us once we try to reveal it? How can we attest on behalf of one whose experience lacks speech and remains prohibited (*interdite*)? Can we know the secret of the dead or the prisoner, the child or the animal, without losing it? How can we share the speechless without betraying it?[34]

All these questions point to the emergence of the event as "other." Whether the event is completely other or whether the other comes with the event as absent attestation, the indecipherable secret of alterity is that which orders and traverses any possible experience of the event. Engaging in the secret and disengaging from the secret are not voluntary actions; both emanate from the injunction of the other, and this is an injunction to which one has to submit.

What is the coming of the other, such that it demands absolute submission? Derrida defines the other as something that is always improper, always inappropriate, always announces itself as different from itself, like Proteus, the mythological god of the sea who constantly changed shape and face. In this sense, the other is not a problem one can resolve or avoid, nor is it a foreigner, someone or something outlandish, someone or something that can be either properly included in or excluded from the homeland. The other brings eternal trouble: it is neither within nor without, and while it has already happened, it is still to come. The other announces itself as unclassifiable, as unbalanced, always excessive and at fault, always both desirable and unbearable. I cannot choose the other; I cannot define myself in light of the other. On the contrary, the other haunts me, observes me, delivers an injunction that concerns only me. This is why the emergence of the event as other is necessarily an *emergency*, a real, suddenly emerging threat, a claim on my attention and my response.

In *Signesponge* (1975), a lecture dedicated to the poetry of Francis Ponge, Derrida observes the other in Ponge's poetry of things. Orange, oyster, bread, candle, table, sponge—when these articles become written as poems, they stop being trivial objects. Ponge's things are neither objects nor subjects; they are other-things. Unlike objects, the poet can neither use nor subdue them. Unlike subjects, the poet cannot exchange and negotiate with them. When the poet asks how orange, oyster, or bread inscribes its particular being on the writing, he hears their idiom remaining mute, he hears how they are steeped in foreign language, and paradoxically, he recognizes the absolute demand of poetry. In other words, it is precisely because things resist appropriation or communication, because of their indifferent, patient silence, that they demand we write the estrangement of the most banal.

> Thus the thing would be the other, the other-thing which gives me an order or addresses an impossible, intransigent, insatiable demand to me, without an exchange and without a transaction, without a possible contract. Without a word, without speaking to me, it addresses itself to me, to me alone in my irreplaceable singularity, in my solitude as well. I owe to the thing an absolute respect which no general law would mediate: the law of the thing is singularity and difference as well. An infinite debt ties me to it, a duty without funds or foundation. I shall never acquit myself of it. Thus the thing is not an object; it cannot become one.[35]

Poetry is not a matter of allowing things to speak purely, by themselves and without human intervention, for being fundamentally *other*, things do not speak and thus any intention or attempt to name them or assign them a language betrays them. Things do not speak; they beckon, they appear in the modality of "to come," they are constantly in the coming of the event as *other*. Things do not speak: they haunt; like a void secret, they haunt the poet.

Thus the poet stands before the thing owing an ineffable and infinite debt, a secular transposition of the sacred original sin. The other-thing demands to follow unknown rules and un(pre)dictable language, each time assigning the challenge of creating and acting according to a singular law that, no sooner than assigned, is immediately transgressed. The impossible contract between the poet's proper signature and the signature of the other-thing is what Derrida calls the "countersignature" or "the event of signature," an event of writing in which come together the attraction and the distance between poet, thing, and emergent signature of their encounter in a poem.

This description is reminiscent of Heidegger's essay on Stefan George's poem "Words." Heidegger conceives of a poetic language that releases the thing from its name in favor of its intimate matter and appearance in the world. This fundamental language does not represent the thing but makes it possible to show and to convey the thing in its difference. Nevertheless, for Heidegger the thought of difference only occurs in a constellation marked by belonging-together. He cannot consider the difference of a thing unless it participates in an *event of appropriation*, a process through which difference becomes the principle of identity and through which the *thingness* of the thing receives a proper place.

In a long interview about Heidegger, Derrida mentions his debt to the German philosopher while insisting on certain reservations and divergences regarding the conceptions of *event*, *difference*, and the *other*.

> "What I said about the event does not easily correspond to Heidegger. I am on the side of dislocation, of dispersion, of dissemination. . . . the conflict; he [Heidegger] thinks of it as that which gathers together the adversaries, as that which keeps together the opposite poles; I think of a difference which does not even keep together the differences [différents]. . . . I'm trying to think a difference which does not let itself be gathered"; and later on: "I'm resisting it from the side of what does not allow gathering—alas! Alas and not, by the way, because the fact of resistance to gathering can be experienced as an anxiety, sadness and loss—dislocation, dissemination, the being-not-at-home, etc.—is nevertheless a chance. The chance of encounter, of justice, of absolute alterity. . . . and, inversely [in Heidegger], on the side of gathering, of Logos or of

Being, of course the chance of gathering exists, but certainly also a certain non-encounter, a certain blindness to the other, a certain annulment of the event, a certain pure non-eventfulness. This would be the debate."[36]

Derrida suggests avoiding the critical analysis of the event by means of the modality of "appropriation" and considering it by a differential structure that escapes all possible movement of gathering and admits the necessity of absolute alterity. Inversely, he suggests reversing *Ereignis* (appropriation) by a process of "expropriation" (*Enteignis*).[37] With this term, Derrida describes another relation to the other in which difference is not a secondary emanation from the logic of the proper. In an effort to go beyond the strict opposition in which the proper either excludes or includes the other, Derrida conceives of the other as a force both threatening and constituting the experience of appropriation: ex-appropriation accentuates the action of difference within the process of appropriation. Here difference not only reveals the limited nature of comprehension or containment in the process of appropriation but also releases and preserves the alterity expropriated. Difference calls for transformation of the proper, leaves the proper open to the excess of the other in order to meet the other as other. Finally, in the process of ex-appropriation the proper loses its centrality, disseminates itself as a "multiple configuration of mastery without mastery," and becomes dependent on the coming of the other.[38]

In his lecture on Ponge, Derrida declares that the event of expropriation is the only "fabula" in which the thing as other can offer itself completely as prohibited (*interdit*).[39] He proposes to name this event *Ereignis in abyss*, since the encounter between the poet and the thing as other can take place only within the passage and the transformation of an abyss.

The abyss already plays an important role for Heidegger when he wishes to think without the metaphysical concepts.[40] For Derrida, the abyss becomes the only ground on which the other shows itself without being appropriated, the only ground on which the other undermines the proper, and, consequently, the only ground on which the encounter relies not on a movement of gathering together but on the irreducible difference that maintains all elements in their heterogeneity as a disparate compound.

The event of expropriation thus takes place in the abyss that attracts and repulses the elements in their divergence. We saw earlier that there is no true exchange, true compromise, or gathering between the poet and the other-thing, as they are basically heterogeneous.[41] Lacking a common denominator, this antinomy becomes a constant tension between disjoint elements or an abrupt arbitrary clash. One reaches the other yet remains different; the other haunts the proper yet remains inaccessible; every step toward transcendence includes the negation of the step itself. Any incursion into the realm of the other implies the flight of the other.

One can illustrate this encounter as if the abyss sets into motion a play of mirrors. Derrida speaks in this sense of *mise en abyme*, an abyssal mirror in which we do not see the reflections of a proper self in different degrees and frames, but rather the reflections of the abyss that sheds its pale light on in-appropriable deformations and inversions of that which cannot be recognized.[42] We look at the abyssal play of mirrors without identifying our own presence: all we see is a series of alterations without presence. The abyss stages a play of absent identities: colored lights turn into shades of gray, the image vanishes into the void. "No *opposition* is more pertinent between the near and the far, no identity either.... It can approach *as other*, in its phenomenon as other [*phénomène d'autre*], only in distancing itself and can *appear* in its far of infinite alterity only in drawing nearer [*se rapprocher*]."[43]

In this vision of the abyssal encounter, there is no longer a proper place in contrast to the place of the other. There are no agreed-upon boundaries, no more frontiers to be protected or surpassed. There are no general or sacred laws that we must respect. There is neither a beginning to "becoming other" nor an end to the injunction of the other. There is only the fundamental solitude of the abyss, the labyrinth of the abyss, a passage that holds a disappearance, an approaching that is a distancing, an undecided step of suspension or digression, a call for what never arrives, and the arrival that we never attain.

But in thinking this abyssal encounter, does Derrida run the risk of considering a type of event that never actually happens? By insisting on the coming of the irreducible other, does he end up with a notion of event in which everything stays in endless suspension, an ever-growing anticipation and tension, a notion of encounter-without-encounter in which he stumbles at the very same place he criticized with relation to Heidegger: the place in which no real encounter with the other ever occurs?

This modality of the non-advent of the event can be discussed in relation to two critical efforts of thought. First, following Heidegger's *Ereignis*, the event is not simply an occurrence, but that which makes any occurrence possible.[44] The event consists first of observing what does not occur manifestly although making the occurrence possible. This in a way refers directly to the principal act of deconstruction: The event is exactly what remains concealed in the happening, what comes without coming and thus comes back as pure novelty, provoking the future from either the excess or the lack of the past occurrence, like the mind that constantly reverts to and simultaneously interrupts the stream that always already overflows experience itself. Second, from an opposite angle, Blanchot shows that when the impossible finally happens, it necessarily fails to occur. This is why we radically experience the event as a constant mourning *of* the impossible and as a call *for* or appeal *to* the impossible. Derrida describes this grief and this appeal in the face of the impossible as an experience of passion, an experience he names in the whispered anticipation "Come," a paradoxical anticipation in which one exposes oneself to what one does not see coming—the passion of the event itself that is both a determinate demand and an open invitation for the absolute other to come.[45] "Come" because, as Blanchot puts it, the extraordinary begins merely where everything ceases: "What is extraordinary begins at the moment *I stop*. But I am no longer able to speak of it" ("L'extraordinaire commence au moment où je m'arrête. Mais je ne suis plus maître d'en parler").[46]

The Other in the Literary Text

Following Blanchot, Derrida defines writing, and particularly the language of literature, as the task and aspiration of the impossible. As opposed to oral speech, which manifests itself through an identified and present speaker, and which has been traditionally seen to incarnate a particular manifestation of truth itself, thus revoking the original Word, writing is the realm in which the absolute other appears unconditionally. The evocation of the other already occurs in the presence as such of any written trace, and it becomes even more visible in the specific modes of poetic and literary language, where writing in principle subverts all discursive boundaries and sources of speech, because polysemy and the heterogeneous degrees of illegibility prevent the reduction of the written text to a single unit of meaning, intention, or referential context.

Derrida quotes the words of Paul Celan: "the *wholly other* thus comes to open the thought of the poem to some thing or sake (*Sache*: 'in eines Anderen Sache zu sprechen . . . in eines *ganz Anderen* Sache'), whose otherness must not contradict, but ally itself with, by expropriating it, the 'ownmost sake' just in question."[47] The injunction of the other proclaims itself as the source of concern and of the thing (*Sache*) in the poetry of Ponge and Celan, or as the most secret encounter in the narratives of Blanchot (*La folie du jour; Death Sentence; The Instant of My Death*).

The project of Derrida's literary criticism consists therefore in asking how the singular law of the other leaves its traces in every writing experience. How does the other impose itself on the writing? What is the counter-signature of the other that marks the text, and how can we find the password to the unspoken coming of the other? In this manner, Derrida closely and attentively follows the logic of "the *Pace*-not (s)" (*Pas*) and "Come" (*Viens*), of the "Arrêt" and "Living-on" (*Sur-Vivance*) in *Parages*, the book on Blanchot. He finds Celan's secret password in the Hebrew word *Shibboleth*, which applies both to the inscription of the date in the poem and the idiomatic event between plural idioms. Finally, he analyzes the sPonge-towel of Francis Ponge as a peculiar object of writing that blends the proper and the improper signature without distinction.[48]

The effect of alterity or otherness in the literary text testifies to both the singularity and the exemplarity of the event at stake. In principle, each literary event follows a singular law; each event, insofar as it is irreplaceable, takes place for the first and last time. But this singular event also leaves an exemplary trace.[49] Alterity cannot simply be equated with the presence of the occurrence; it is also what constitutes the vehicle by which the event is transformed into an impersonal text. The writing of the singular, which characterizes, for example, the traumatic testimony of the political horrors of the twentieth century, also provokes a repetitive exemplarity, effacing the historical occurrence itself, since it is able to give rise to an unnamable force, "to a work that depends without depending on this very event."[50]

Exemplarity in this case does not mean an objective law or fixed pattern. The condition of legibility of a particular event of writing does not depend on a general knowledge or on accepted codes of truth. The idea of pure translation (of a pure signified)[51] from one language to another or from one experience to another also implies the effacement of the singularity of the other in language and the abolishment of the signifying (*signifiant*) structure of the trace itself. In contrast, Derrida believes that the exemplarity of the event follows a strategy of translation that extracts the legibility from the illegible aspects of the singular: from the textual creations of disruption, inconsistency, delay, ambiguity, hesitation, tangles, and so forth. The force of a text emanates from the untranslatable aspects of language and experience, which he calls *remainders* (*restance*) or *residues* (*restes*), among other concepts that simultaneously re-mark the event and demarcate (*démarque*) what escapes the event. Thus, the singularity of the event becomes exemplary within a text only if it resists full understanding and appropriation, only if it releases semantic or semiotic *residues*, and if it brings about a process of *iterability* or *spectrality*.

The exemplarity of a text invites readers to attend a singular event that they have not experienced themselves. However, readers are able to experience it only through misunderstanding, or rather, through mistranslation; that is to say, only if the event generally comprises mistranslations and generates mistranslations. The exemplarity of a written trace, or of a reading of written trace, is not a simple communication and re-presentation of an absent event that has already taken place. Exemplarity "is not a continuous modification of presence," but rather the rupture in presence manifested in the structure of the trace.[52] It does not matter whether the situation is present or absent; the written trace already marks the repetitive act of rupture by the deferred/differed signifier that directs itself to another signifier and as such transforms the event into other. Writing shows how the event is already altered through the symbolic technics of language, already involved in a different time and place, and already evoking different impressions and judgments. In other words, exemplarity is also the transgression of the singular law of the event. It is "the unsayable: the dead, *for example*, the dead."[53] The very anonymous and neutral aspects of exemplarity, its uncomprehending comprehension, enable the opening of the written event to other series of events, reassembling other lived experiences and finally provoking the creation of other works of art.[54]

The Trauma

The need to conceive of the event as *irreducible other* may run counter to the event's effect in the present. The immediate corporeal experience of those who are exposed to the event puts into question Derrida's need to conceive of the event as that which comes up without coming. Derrida's philosophical project of breaking with the metaphysics of presence by studying the consequences of *différance* may appear incompatible with the conception of a unique and undeniable event. It seems that one of Derrida's fundamental challenges is the difficulty of reconciling the unpredictability of *a single taking place* with the *technical* repetition and difference of its *exemplary inscription*.

"It would be a matter of thinking an event that is undeniable but without pure presence," Derrida formulates the difficulty in the earlier-mentioned conference at the French National Library in January 2001.[55] But again, if the event necessarily affects someone's body and leaves a mark on it, how can one argue that there is no pure presence of the event and that the event takes place without having a place?

Earlier I mentioned the dead as the evident rupture of a happening that remains nevertheless silent and prohibited. Those who were lost or have disappeared (*les disparus*) do not experience the event of their death, although they were fully exposed to its happening. Victims are the only witnesses who escape from the possible inscription of the event, returning therefore and haunting the historical memory from the coming future as *revenants*.

On other occasions, Derrida speaks of the event's corporeal experience as the work of mourning, of traumatism or symptomatology.[56]

These designations are important to the present analysis of the event, since they openly announce a tendency, absent in Blanchot and Heidegger, to tie the problem of the event to psychoanalytic concepts. The notion of trauma allows us to think of what comes to light no longer in phenomenological terms of perception and appearance but rather with reference to the implication of desire in the experience.[57] This process of trauma questions furthermore why there should be certain features of the event that repeat themselves until they individualize the perception of a subject.

Derrida does not mention trauma only to describe major events and to distinguish them from everyday life. Trauma reveals itself wherever alterity affects desire: it can occur anywhere, even at a pleasant moment, even in the middle of the most ordinary act.[58] From the point of view of corporeal experience, the concept of trauma designates the modality of "eventness" that is constantly at work in the organic mechanism. This modality obliterates the separation between the corporeal act and the happening, for the event not only affects or endangers someone's experience; the mental projection of a threat, a strong feeling of strangeness, too, could through the repetition of a primitive scene from the past, cause a flood of unconscious *phantasms* and impulsive excitations within the ordinary.

Derrida understands, however, that using the notion of trauma with reference to everyday situations exhausts and blurs the term's force. Therefore, he conceives of the trauma as the corporeal test (*l'épreuve*) of the event. The trauma puts human experience to the test by imprinting on the body the event's process of ex-appropriation (*inappropriabilité*).

Beyond its positive psychological meaning, Derrida argues that the trauma exceeds the memory's reproduction of a past occurrence and admits the necessity of another temporality that rejects the chronological order: an anachrony or untimeliness, "this sort of non-contemporaneity of present time with itself."[59] According to Derrida, trauma does not simply refer to a present repetition of a past and accomplished event; it emanates from the coming future, inflicting the terrible threat that the worst is still to come. "We are talking about a trauma, and thus an event, whose temporality proceeds neither from the now that is present nor from the present that is past but from an im-presentable to come [à venir]. A weapon wounds and leaves forever open an unconscious scar; but this weapon is terrifying because it comes from the to-come, from the future, a future so radically to come that it resists even the grammar of the future anterior."[60]

The burning wound troubles not because of the confrontation with the past but because of the immeasurable terror of the coming future, in the same manner as Barthes avows, after Winnicott, his fear from a collapse that has occurred.[61] The chronological development of causality in which the present of the past causes and creates a predictable future is undermined by a time that is out of joint, by the traumatic time of un-present. Usually, Derrida attaches this event's temporality to the French past future tense, which denotes "what will already have taken place."[62] This modality of time does not suggest that there was no present experience in the past, but rather that the time past was experienced as unaccomplished yet.

The event engraves a present and undeniable wound upon the body, yet at the heart of trauma there is neither "before" nor "after" the event that has taken place. There is only a double and illusory state of survival and suspension of the terrible that is still to come. Trauma speaks from the body, from the open wound, as the Greek word denotes in itself, and not from the "objective" course and discourse of history; it speaks in the mode of the symptom. Here also, the claim of a corporeal symptom is undeniable: one cannot ignore this most distant proximity of the body, this self-alteration. But the symptom offers an empty message; its manifestation is already part of a process of compulsive repetition and of the displacement of that which refuses to be deciphered. Symptomatology never rises to a stable sense of language; its message is equivocal because it does not reveal the source of the sender, perhaps it does not link to a sender at all, and therefore causes uncontrolled effects on the body, a psychosomatic language that overflows all personal understanding and striving for coherency.

Trauma shows that both the violence and the chance of the event are not played out yet; however, at the same time, trauma evokes another misleading experience in which the unknown future cannot be appropriated or accepted unless it seems to be repeated as if it were already played out. We endure the approaching terror or promise by turning our face, by looking backward to what, without our knowledge, already began happening in the past. Following Freud[63] more than Nietzsche or Deleuze but still not very far from understanding the "eternal return" as a selective repetition of what differs, the trauma according to Derrida offers a model of a temporal event without present. Trauma comes from a radical, un-present future, although we are already submitting to the consequences of the past wound.

Whether trauma consists in the repetition of the unaccomplished, denying and suspending the event in presence, or whether the traumatic event is the accomplished repetition of what has been always denied and suspended, Derrida's concern has shifted away from the Aristotelian distinction between history and fiction, and the question of whether the event really happened or only remains a possibility if the event is true or false, credible or not. Derrida seeks a mode of writing-event in which fictitious and real, or serious and hilarious, can no longer be distinguished.[64] The writing-event is the act neither of revealing what has really happened nor of anticipating what will shortly come to pass. Nor does writing consist of creating fictional events that are limited to the work of literature. Derrida's question is how the writer experiences the language of the trauma and how writing becomes a traumatic exercise. How then the traumatic experiences lead the writer to evolve a style that not only articulates or makes an event, not only represents or presents an event, but in which, given the important role of alterity, the event is real only if it is a reverberate fear and passion of the fictitious as well.

The Writing of the Event

Beginning with the article on "Signature, Event, Context" in *Margins of Philosophy*, Derrida uses the terminology of Austin's philosophy of speech acts.[65] Austin distinguishes mainly between constative and performative utterances. The *constative* refers to a verbal description of a situation that is external to the utterance itself and precedes it. The *performative*, however, is an utterance that effects or produces a situation without necessarily depending on an external or previous referent. The constative consists in relating or reporting an accomplished event, whereas the performative creates an event itself while performing it. "There's an utterance that is called *constative*, a theoretical speech that consists in saying what is, describing or noting what is, and there's an utterance that is called *performative* and that does in speaking. For instance, when I make a promise, I'm not saying an event. I'm producing it by my commitment. . . . It's a speech-event, a saying-event."[66]

These terms may be very effective for the theory of literature. On the one hand, the constative follows the logic of representation: the short story or novel narrates a fact that happens in a place and time that are not necessarily related to the act of writing. On the other hand, the performative points to the logic of presentation, in which the work of literature produces an event in the very process of textual writing. The event itself is thus immanent to the act of writing and does not exist outside the style and narrative mode. Performative writing describes the event at the same time that it traces itself. The constative act of writing is always secondary, indicating, clarifying or interpreting what has already occurred.

In relation to the history of literature, these linguistic terms return to the old aesthetic debate between mimesis and "art for art's sake." They are indeed useful to the taxonomy of genres, distinguishing the historical novel or memoirs from pure fiction, characterizing different literary projects between political and social realism and the modernist stream of consciousness or the *nouveau roman*.

For Derrida, the writing of the event is neither constative nor performative. Indeed, these linguistic acts are necessarily part of the writing event, but they do not correspond to the experience and work of trauma; they both fail to register the "thing" of the event and the iterability of its linguistic inscription. The constative is a cognitive "saying" that describes or interprets, organizing the diverse conjunctures a posteriori without having been directly exposed to them, and thus it manipulates them through the distance of time. "The saying of knowledge regarding the event lacks, in a certain manner a priori, the event's singularity simply because it comes after and it loses the singularity in generality."[67] When constative writing deviates from the impersonal sense of giving account or reporting, it becomes involved in the event and becomes a performative act that transforms and produces other events.[68]

The performative is certainly a "saying-event." Austin was the first to demonstrate its operation in specific social contexts, where language acts and serves as confession, apology, promise, or threat. Yet, Austin's pragmatism remains attached to the logic of communication and institutional regulations in which the utterance is necessarily related to the first person in the present and must be pronounced correctly in order to be successful.[69] The speech act is effective and valid only if a living, conscious person pronounces it, testifying to a unique present and incorporating a repetitive convention of a specific procedure, saying "I do," "I confess," "I judge you," "I'm warning you," "I baptize you," and so forth.

Yet, according to Derrida, this combination of the uniqueness of the present and repetitive rituality cannot act as a pure "writing-event." The performative fundamentally relies on a positive ground of predictable happenings and a programmed repetition of the same. The authoritative assurance of the speaker and the fixed process of the ceremony neutralize the event that the saying has pretended to enact.[70] On the contrary, Derrida argues that the performative is a "saying-event" only if it detaches itself from the demonstration of its presence and the conventionality of its context. The saying event becomes unpredictable and other only when its action exposes the speaker to failure and the ceremony to the risk of collapse. "It is often said, quite rightly, that a performative utterance produces the event of which it speaks. But one should also know that wherever there is some performative, that is, in the strict and Austinian sense of the term, the mastery in the first-person present of an 'I can,' 'I may' guaranteed and legitimated by conventions, well, then, all pure eventness is neutralized, muffled, suspended. What happens, by definition, what comes about in an unforeseeable and singular manner, couldn't care less about the performative."[71]

In what does the writing event differ from the performative "saying-event"? What does it mean to concretely expose the writing event to the risk of collapse and failure? In what sense does writing consist of a performed act without presence and without defined context? I will limit my answer to a few brief points.

Above all, it is a question of dissociating the exercise and experience of writing from the linguistic conditions of communication and speech.[72] According to Derrida, the very function of the written trace signalizes the absolute absence of both sender and receiver. Writing, particularly literary writing, must not be understood as a more complex or more expansive version of an expressive and informative message, coming from the writer's present toward the present of the reader. Instead, writing is the force that breaks with reference to a specific context and presence, introducing a play of irreducible difference that is responsible for maintaining the text open, transformable, undefined, and expropriated.

Through the acts of encoding and naming, writing is able to invoke the absence of a past present and to protect presence from the possibility of an absent future. However, the conception of the trace as *difference* goes beyond all relative modification or restoration of a combined presence and absence. The trace is not an objective and permanent encoding of an author's experience, but it is already a re-marking that de-marcates itself, acting in different linguistic economies, playing with different structures and contexts. This conception calls for a philosophy of writing that admits the confrontation between the minimal capacity of repetitive legibility and the absolute void of sense, the canceling of all present occurrences.

From this perspective, only the textual mark that avoids the representation of the constative and the presentation of the performative creates a writing event. Only when the textual mark detaches from a present context by refusing to have any original and pure referent and by coming to bring about the possibility of infinite references, only then it shows the creative force of its own act. The re-mark de-marcates itself by necessity, referring to another written trace while appearing other in the movement of difference. Writing then becomes a saying-event without presence: a saying-event without a saying. This summarizes the creative task and the political task Derrida assigns to the writing of literature: it reveals an intention that does not know itself, exposing nobody's testimony,[73] describing, as it does, the imaginative and sensible passion of un-experienced experiences while yet remaining legible and translatable by others who have not participated in it.

This is the risk of collapse and failure that the writing event must confront. Literature bears in its work the total disappearance of humanity, the total disappearance of the manuscript itself, while all the time conscious that it has no presence outside that realm.[74] Narrating from the prohibition (*interdiction*) to narrate, from "the instant of death," Derrida risks conceiving of the writing event as that which never happens; it is precisely the linguistic and experiential *remainder* that can never be appropriated and which consequently dominates the entire work, as in the writing of Mallarmé, Kafka, and Joyce.

As long as the writer exposes himself to danger, forcing alterity to sign in the absence of his signature or allowing the other to come without agreement, the work might be affected by a *non-advent* that imposes the return of its *remainder*. Perhaps it is possible to locate the writing event in a specific moment (e.g., the moment Dante or Ulysses faints in his religious exploration or universal wandering).[75] Perhaps there are contradictory elements that remain secret in the work and will eventually undermine its entire structure. Perhaps the work is the cause and concern of the event itself, performing a verbal subversion (like Melville's Bartleby's statement), performing a saying that does not know itself: the impossibility of narrating an experience that becomes present only through the necessity of narrating it.[76] Perhaps, moreover, the process of writing constitutes the event itself, the "science of specters" in which the only happening is the passage itself from the real constative or performative writing to the pure imaginary and fictional. Like the Sirens' song in the *Odyssey* or the white whale's appearance in *Moby Dick*, this transformation cannot be experienced, although it is the condition of all written experience. Derrida's writing-event could, then, be captured by Foucault's words on Blanchot:

> this discourse outside what it says, is an incessant advance toward that whose absolutely finespun light has never received language.... [F]rom the moment discourse ceases to follow the slope of self-interiorizing thought and, addressing the very being of language, returns thought to the outside; from that moment, in a single stroke, it becomes a meticulous narration of experiences, encounters, and improbable signs—language about the outside of all language, speech about the invisible side of words.... a listening less to what is articulated in language than to the void circulating between its words, to the murmur that is forever taking it a part.[77]

6

Gilles Deleuze
The Becoming of the Event

The return to the ontological questions of philosophy and their renewal is Gilles Deleuze's most pressing project. It is his philosophical priority to refuse any transcendent ideas or transcendental conditions; instead, he tends to examine the vital forces of an immanent structure. Using the term "plane of immanence," Deleuze suggests that thinking relates to the surface of a concrete reality that it absolutely does not transcend. Thinking does not merely depend on real experience: like a pre-Socratic sage of nature, Deleuze claims that the force of thinking, its astonishment and creativity, consists of the material movement of Being, as if reality forces itself to think within us.[1]

Deleuze draws the plane of immanence as an infinite, fluid surface that renders possible an ontological conception of endless mutation and multiplicity. There is nothing beyond this surface; it is a transmuting whole: it creates itself as multiplicity and with the same movement provides its own sense. No superior power dominates or controls this immanent surface. There is no pure intelligence, a higher sphere that vertically organizes the circulation of life in universal categories or that distributes matter in stable forms. Nor is there a closed transcendental laboratory of consciousness that appropriates the world according to pure conditions of recognition or a phenomenological demand for intentionality.[2]

"When immanence is no longer immanent to something other than itself it is possible to think of a plane of immanence."[3] Deleuze argues with Guattari in *What Is Philosophy?* that the construction of an immanent substance is necessarily related to a pre- or non-philosophical intuition; it does not correspond to the foundation of a fixed system of reasoning.⁴ The idea of the infinite is required neither to confirm nor to justify the philosophical system from above or from below, but it inheres in the surface itself as an unfixed chaotic element. If philosophy is the exercise of thinking, then to think is to confront this chaos and to ponder from this non-philosophical intuition of chaos, accepting that the chaotic metastases are always there, not only as indispensable "boundaries" and "holes" within the construction of *physis* and *noûs* but also as the internal motives that engender them both, as "that which cannot be thought and yet must be thought."⁵

Furthermore, Deleuze conceives of the plane of immanence as if it were spreading within and out of chaos. He imagines this plane like a colander or filter, one that does not simply extricate order from disorder but is placed upon this disorder, as streams of chaos continuously pass through the gaps and cracks, destabilizing the entire edifice. Chaos forces thought to re-create itself infinitely. Thinking must renounce its own principles and established models in order to remain open to the fluidity of chaos.

This conception can be illustrated by Deleuze's critique of the philosophical premises of "good sense" and "common sense," both traditional principles that reduce chaotic diversity to a dogmatic image of thought.⁶ "Good sense" determines the order of a correct direction; all movement is reduced to an image of stability in which we can locate a fixed point from which to foresee a regulated progression that drains the diverse directions into one dominant direction. In the same way, "common sense" postulates a shared and complete faculty that unifies the diverse faculties in order to form normal and identifiable beings. "Common sense" defines permanent and reflected syntheses that allow the placement of any phenomenon as a distinct "subject" in front of an "object," as a "self" in the "world."

Deleuze shows furthermore how the agreement between "good sense" and "common sense"—between the correct direction of the ordinary and the synthesis aimed at the identification of the same—refers necessarily and purely to the notion of "God." The idea of God puts everything in order: God is indeed the origin or the end, the supreme principle of identity and the outcome of all directions. "In this complementarity of good sense and common sense, the alliance between the self, the world, and God is sealed—God being the final outcome of directions and the supreme principle of identities."[7]

Deleuze's project of immanence rejects these presuppositions of universality and rationality by claiming that they only cover the natural *doxa* with the philosophical clothes of concepts. The principle of identity and the regulation of truthful method bind singular experiences and faculties to a mechanical disciplinary procedure that oppresses thinking and reconfirms the dogmatic representation of identified subject and formal object.

By contrast, there is nothing regular or permanent in a thinking that remains open to the unformed constructivism imposed by chaos. A philosophy of immanence must be free of the outline of pure subject or represented object, permanent world or transcendent God. Instead, thinking must expose itself to the multiplicity of an active and actual series of events, that is, to the singular elements that constantly appear in the novelty of variously composed events. Thinking must stem from the becoming of events and from the singular elements that are constantly redistributed within them.

Refusing to follow the transcendent tendency of Platonism and even declaring a readiness, after Nietzsche, to admit the need for reversing its metaphysical heritage, Deleuze does not submit the real to the hierarchical duality between the Idea and its copy, between the intelligible and the sensible, the permanent and the ephemeral. Inversely, it is only when the real has the status of simulacrum, which, first, contests the resemblance between the world of essences and the world of appearances, and, second, interrupts the derivation of the plurality of phenomena from the one original source of Being, that one can consider an ontology based on multiplicity.[8]

Precisely because the dissimilitude of the simulacrum inserts internal difference into the real, Being can be pronounced of one surface of chaos that affirms multiplicity. Only when the affirmation of Being derives from the infinite force of divergence does the sense of events and *singularities* escape all imposed categorical order, thus becoming unpredictable. When the only repetition of Being is what differs, the event and its singular components produce constantly new "machineries of sense."[9]

Whether the real constructs itself on the force and image of simulacrum, or things and entities constantly create new compositions of sense, the question remains: How to formulate a project of constructivism? If things and bodies, events and singularities are naturally in a state of constant mutation, how can we generate a general sense of the world and an ontological understanding, before jumping to the conclusion of an infinite relativism? In what manner can a more open and plural construction of thinking reverse and renew the relation between the giving of sense and the real? Or, to use Deleuze's words, how is it possible to conceive of a plane of immanence based on the "magical formula" *pluralism = monism*?[10]

Deleuze understands that an ontology of immanence must interrogate the giving of sense without separating it from the matter of *physis*. He argues that "the image of thought" cannot dominate the real by means of logic; sense does not derive from an absolute principle, from a potential reservoir, or an origin. A phenomenon's source of sense does not exist beyond the phenomenon itself, as the higher sense or the profound sense of sense. On the contrary, the giving of sense must stem from the unintelligibility of the real, from the pure becoming of the real that has neither a defined direction nor a possible unity. The giving of sense is therefore immanent to the surface of the phenomenon; it arises as an "effect" of the phenomenon. But sense results from the real phenomenon only if it traces the latter's divergent limit. Not only can sense not coincide with the phenomenon, but it is what undoes the possibility of the phenomenon's absolute signification, what measures the gaps in the coherent state of being in order to maintain the phenomenon in a state of incessant becoming and productivity.

"It is thus pleasing that there resounds today the news that sense is never a principle or an origin, but that it is produced. It is not something to discover, to restore, and to re-employ; it is something to produce by a new machinery. It belongs to no height or depth, but rather to a surface effect, being inseparable from the surface which is its proper dimension."[11]

"In every respect, truth is a matter of production, not of adequation. It is a matter of genitality, not of innateness or reminiscence. We cannot accept that the grounded remains the same as it was before, the same as when it was not grounded, when it has not passed the test of grounding.... To ground is to metamorphose."[12]

Between Sense and Real

It is by means of the concept of the event that Deleuze examines the relation between the emergence of sense and the becoming of the real. In *The Logic of Sense* he develops the event mainly from the philosophy of the Stoics. Using the Stoical distinction between the corporeal state of things and incorporeal linguistic propositions, Deleuze develops a philosophical model ignored by Platonism's metaphysics that presupposes a different interaction between logic and physics, between a dynamic idealism of the real and a theory of expression and sense.

Located in the center of this construction, the event has three main functions: first, it comes to mark *difference* as the mode of articulation between the creation of sense and the becoming of the real; second, it affirms the *immanence* of sense and the real within the one plane of Being; and third, it creates from this immanent intensity the metamorphosis of the real and the unpredictable *multiplicity* of sense. Differentiation, immanence, and multiplicity, then, are the roles of the event that Deleuze develops, roles that are effective only if they do not form a presupposed image of thinking.

Quoting Bréhier, Deleuze defines the ontological construction of the Stoics by distinguishing two main series of being, or "two planes of being."[13] The *corporeal series*, on the one hand, corresponds to any actual property, substance, or "state of things"; it applies also to any substantial force and action, cause and energy. A man is a body that is seated on the body of a chair: here a corporeal encounter already takes place. Everything within this corporeal space has physical particles. The universe is thus populated by encounters and corporeal combinations, according to the mutual tension between bodies. The *incorporeal series*, on the other hand, refers to linguistic propositions or expressions.[14] These have no real status of being, only a "manner of being." Deleuze remarks that the incorporeal results from corporeal encounters and has a semi-autonomous status of being the effect of the bodies. Deleuze emphasizes, however, that this "effect" must not be considered in terms of causality, but rather as an optical effect or sound effect that already differs from the bodies. The incorporeal is no longer a quality of the state of things. It pertains instead to the realm of language, which acts infinitely on the surface of bodies as the image of their manifestation, signification, or designation.[15]

Between these two series of being, there is a third entity. Deleuze suggests calling "event" the interaction between language and bodies, corporeal and incorporeal, words and things.[16] The event stands between these series as their mutual boundary. It is a third entity that has to enable and maintain the *immanent transition* between the two, between the sense that arises as an effect from the bodies' encounter and the force of language as the "extra-being" that affects the surface. There is no stable procedure of happening that makes the series match once and for all. No proper laws of representation can be installed between words and things. The unstable interaction between the series of being guarantees their difference, thus creating an active boundary that makes them converge in their divergence. This is what Deleuze defines as the event of "disjunctive synthesis": the becoming of the real manipulates the production of sense; the sense stems from the situation of the bodies and continues to exert influence on the bodies without ever blending with them completely, because the sense produced imposes dissimilitude on the real.[17] "*Sense is both the expressible or the expressed of the proposition, and the attribute of the state of affairs*. It turns one side toward things and one side toward propositions. But it does not merge with the proposition which expresses it any more than with the state of affairs or the quality which the proposition denotes. . . . It is in this sense that it is an 'event': *on the condition that the event is not confused with its spatio-temporal realization in a state of affairs*. We will not ask therefore what is the sense of the event: the event is sense itself. The event belongs essentially to language; it has an essential relationship to language. But language is what is said of things."[18]

Deleuze situates the event at the intersection of two ontological dimensions: the one leads to a theory of sense, while the other seeks a way to consider the becoming of the real. "Everything happens at the boundary between things and propositions" without being reduced to the realm of either the one or the other.[19] The event never amounts to a specific meaning of a certain proposition or to an actual state of affairs. It is, rather, the process of the emergence of sense through linguistic propositions and through the spatiotemporal realization of things. For example, when literary works breathe new life into the figurative entity of a place—Duras's "Hiroshima" or "Nevers," Proust's "Illiers—Combray" or "Florence," Borges's "Buenos Aires"—naming is effectively produced by the presence of the place, but it is already a phantasmagoric image emerging from a compilation of linguistic performances that transforms the place into something else; an image that "displaces" the place.

The concept of the event presupposes a new principle of production that generates both the possibility of sense and the becoming of the real. The event has a double face: it concerns and affects both the series of things and the series of words. This is true on one imperative condition: that the event never pertains totally to either one of these series. This implies that the production of sense never fits into the meaning of a single or general proposition while the intensity of becoming is never completely reduced to an actual state of things.[20] As for Deleuze, he offers a concrete example of this idea when he finds in Nietzsche's writing a new philosophical discourse that exposes a complex intersection between unavoidable corporeal experience and the stylistic endeavor to make new sense. The event in this example is both Nietzsche's suffering and distress and his poetic aphorisms that subvert the traditional propositions of philosophy. However, in Deleuze's terminology the event remains effective only if it does not reduce itself to either Nietzsche's personal existence or his authorial intentions and objectives. The event must remain open to the tentative connection between language and reality, where the power of life and the work's expressive capacity inspire one another and thus make a vivid plea for sense and adventure. "Nietzsche has at his disposal a method of his own invention. We should not be satisfied with either biography or bibliography; we must reach a secret point where the anecdote of life and the aphorism of thought amount to one and the same thing."[21] Only then does the event become a principle of production, a machine of new expressions and diverse corporeal effects: a "Dionysian sense-producing machine" that passes through both individuals and societies and can be used by all manner of political visions, life experiences, or cultural ideals.[22]

It is the function of the event to make the two series of being converge in their divergence. Between the corporeal and the incorporeal, between language and the real, the event unfolds itself as "disjunctive synthesis." The conjugation of the series is achieved by an element of *difference* and a kind of "relation without relation." The event is the active boundary between the series, which first intensifies their communication, so that sense becomes manifest together with the movement of the real, and, second, brings about incessant ramifications and transformations of *singularities* that are redistributed within each one of the series.[23] The immanent surface is thus this type of realization of infinite events between dissymmetric series.

Beyond Structuralism

Deleuze compares the event between the series of being to the idea of the structure. He follows in this respect the structuralist turn,[24] analyzes its procedures as well as the new possibilities it opens to contemporary thinking in diverse fields of research. He moreover evokes the work of thinkers such as Lévi-Strauss, Foucault, Lacan, and Althusser, for whom the sense of a phenomenon is produced in the circulation and combination between different elements of the structure.

Deleuze emphasizes the novelty of structuralism, the plurality and instability that mark the structural machine, and contrasts this with historical positivist approaches, existential humanism, transcendental phenomenology, or any essentializing tendency. Yet, he argues, the risk of structuralism consists in assuming the structure as a primary condition of the singularity of the elements themselves. When this is the case, the distribution of the elements becomes methodically static and preconceived; structure then transcends the plane of immanence, merely organizing chaos rather than also being destabilized by it.

From this perspective, *The Logic of Sense* is a wonderful example of poststructural critique.[25] Deleuze does not emphasize the *strength* of the structural bounds but rather the *force* yielded by the structure's circulation. The structure promises a formal method through which the humanities might acquire quasi-scientific validity. It has no fixed center other than its own relative circulation. It is true that the circulation between respective positions generates the structural production of sense. Still, it is only when circulation overcomes its relativity and explores its absolute power that the need to efface the centrality of the structure itself also arises. The very conception of circulation, which first made it theoretically possible to advance to the procedure of structuralism, now demands the undoing of the structure itself. The process of differentiation that renders possible the communication between several elements cannot be limited to distinct positions, respective relations, and schematic consequences of combinations. All measured boundaries must be abolished in order to avoid imposing transcendent structure on singular elements. The work of thinking must be exposed to the danger of an absolute circulation in which there is no landmark other than the unsettled element of difference. This difference has neither beginning nor end; it simply undermines all closure and coherence. It renders possible the communication between diverse structures, and it is responsible for bringing in new elements from other fields and for reaffirming the change of the old ones. Accordingly, difference can never occupy the role of a center, because it has neither stable location nor proper content, and in this sense it transforms the structure into an open assemblage (*agencement*).

This is where Deleuze's redefinition of structuralism joins Blanchot and Derrida, who devoted their thought to the neutral and erratic entity that exposes relative circulation to interminable motion and drags the formal structure into a groundless abyss. Yet the differences between Blanchot, Derrida, and Deleuze are easy to observe. Derrida and Blanchot tend to focus on the priority of *absolute alterity* and the elusive step of thinking toward the "outside." Each emphasizes the impossible experience of an illusory transcendence: appearance can only affirm itself by way of disappearance; the present can only accomplish itself in the realm of absence or through the act of *différance*. This is why their writing is a constant effort of dissemination, a dizzy wandering toward the uninhabitable. What they offer finally is only the expressive encounter with this void or this "other night," the act of mourning and calling out, the persistent need for a re-beginning and the idle fatigue of an unaccomplished event.

Deleuze's consideration of the unstable and vacant element of circulation offers a different perspective. The chaotic factor that undoes the formal structure enables the affirmation of the overflowing and vital plane of immanence. In contrast to Blanchot and Derrida, Deleuze does not look for the absent and abyssal aspects of what remains ungraspable, but acknowledges neutral and absolute circulation as a principle of production that releases the singular forces of the elements and provides multiple redistributions within the series: "This is the principle of the emission of singularities."[26] Deleuze's vision of the event is much more corporeal and concrete; it is not an abstract un-accomplished event, but a composition of tangible forces, contiguously concentrated in the unstable boundary or limit that passes between and through the two series. This is why—to return to the Stoical model—what matters in the event, what as said associates the series of language with the series of things, is not the hermetic lacuna and the empty act of difference, but the variable element of difference which is the indispensable condition for conceiving a plane of immanence multi-populated by singular cases of sense production and corporeal encounters.

Having expanded the circumference of the structure, Deleuze suggests comparing the action of the event to a paradoxical act. Beyond the structural model, the event interlaces the series and forms a problematic tie, similar to the equivocality of paradox. Quoting, for instance, the paradox of Chrysippus—"If you say something, it passes through your lips; so, if you say "chariot," a chariot passes through your lips"[27]— Deleuze points out a junction at which things and words have no stable designated reference or ideal meaning, but on the contrary are constantly manipulated by the paradoxical construction, creating multiple possibilities of sense and states of things. The paradoxical construction of sense deviates from the logical conditions of truth or falsehood. In fact, the paradox absolutely exhausts this alternative, because its truth is confounded by a treacherously contradictory statement. The impossibility of submitting the paradoxical construction to logical analysis does not simply highlight the inversion of sense or the lack of sense, as in Camus's philosophy of the absurd. Instead, Deleuze affirms that the paradox produces an accumulation of sense precisely because it challenges the conditions of meaning. Thus it would be reductive to claim that paradox lacks any sense at all; it is the power of talking nonsense that gives paradox the creativity of unheard-of sense.[28]

Let us remember that Deleuze is quick to acknowledge that if one considers the action of the event as a paradoxical entity, this must be accompanied by abandoning the priority of logical writing and rational judgment. The paradoxical statement still maintains a certain tension with logic: it engages in ironic play, makes puns, contests the conditions of meaning, and reverses the distinctive values of truth and false, good and bad. This is why Deleuze observes in the literary work, especially in modern fiction, a more profound and inherent modality of the event, an active state of *nonsense* that does not reach for speculative problems and solutions, but rather questions immediately, as it is, the boundary between the real and the expression of sense.[29]

The writing of the Israeli poet Hezy Leskly offers goods examples of this. Deleuze would probably have laughed out loud reading the fifth poem of the cycle, "Hebrew Lesson":

> Once the word becomes body
> And the body opens its mouth
> To say the word from which
> It was made—
> I will embrace this body
> And put it, at my side, to bed.[30]

Beyond the discourse of paradox, the creative power of nonsense interlaces in fiction with a particular composition of sensations and living experiences. In this regard, Badiou notes admirably that one of Deleuze's most striking moods and philosophical tonalities is an unconditional acceptance that the production of a sense of the real affirms itself beyond all judicial human points of view—beyond all objective designation, subjective manifestation, or ideal meaning—and that accordingly even the destruction of a war or an incomprehensible disaster are effective events in which non-sense is a real construction of sense. "This is a trait of Deleuze that I particularly appreciate: a sort of unwavering love for the world as it is, a love that, beyond optimism and pessimism alike, signifies that it is always futile, always falling short of thought as such, to *judge* the world."[31]

This letting the world speak as it is (*tel qu'il est*) does not begin with Deleuze. The search for the entity that creates the becoming of things and the production of sense without rising above or beyond them as the sense of sense or as the sense of things could easily join the phenomenological motto of "returning to things themselves." In this same vein, Renaud Barbaras recently wrote: "Returning to things themselves takes the form of a contact with Being prior to the separation between the pre-theoretical world and idealizations" ("le retour aux choses mêmes prend la forme d'un contact avec l'Être avant la séparation du monde préthéorique et des idealizations").[32] However, a major difference between phenomenology and the ontology of the event is that Being, according to the latter, is certainly not an original ante-predicative state, but an active principle of production that takes place within the dissymmetric series, so much so that it cannot be defined without reference to their actual *singularities*. Hence, Deleuze rejects both the phenomenological naïveté of letting things speak for themselves (avoiding unavoidable mediation) and the imposed structural relation between things, which cuts reality according to a prior logic of mediation and fails thus to register their singular activity and sense.

In what terms, then, is it possible to conceive of the event that occurs both in the corporeal series of things and the incorporeal series of words? How does the event allow the singularities of the series to affirm themselves without organizing them from above or below? How does Deleuze determine the event as an immanent circulation that infinitely subdivides the series? The opening part of *The Logic of Sense* qualifies the event both as inherent to each one of the series and constantly passing from one to the other. "It is both word=x and thing=x. Since it belongs simultaneously to both series, it has two sides. But the sides are never balanced, joined together or paired off, because the paradoxical element is always in disequilibrium in relation to itself. . . . [I]t is at once excess and lack, empty square and supernumerary object, a place without an occupant and an occupant without a place, 'floating signifier' and floated signified, esoteric word and exoteric thing, white word and black object."[33]

Thus, Deleuze defines the event as an equivocal, random (*aléatoire*), and variable entity: an entity bereft of place or a place bereft of entity, a signified that has no signifier or a signifier that does not signify. By means of these qualities Deleuze succeeds in assuming that every linguistic expression and every corporeal state already contains the variable power of event that produces it, even if these series do not reveal any conceptual meaning or designate any clear state of things.

This is where the novelty of Deleuze's question of Being manifests itself. While making words and things converge, the event exposes the striving for sense and the formless movement of generation. While making the sense of the expression appear and stirring the becoming in the state of things, the actual manifestation of language and things only maintains the event in a state of virtuality. The event is thus a new ontological conception only when the possibility of sense is created by an act of nonsense—only when, similarly, the realization of an actual state of things diverges from the virtual power that brings it into existence.

This new ontological conception of the event not only gives priority to the singular phenomenon; it also suggests that every singular phenomenon is generated by an impersonal sense/real-making machine. The series of being are not only the "actual" presentation of a certain phenomenon, subject or object; they are at the same time the incessant compositions that virtually produce what is singular.

Again Deleuze takes inspiration from Nietzsche, and this allows him to consider the concept of "singularities" both as impersonal and pre-individual, simultaneously virtual and actual, having both sense and nonsense. In this way he avoids the traditional opposition of general and particular, collective and individual, universal and personal, the infinite supremeness of Being and the superior finiteness of the subject. Hence, the concept of singularities forms the core of the new conception of *élan vital* or *will to power*: "This is something neither individual nor personal, but rather singular. Being not an undifferentiated abyss, it leaps from one singularity to another . . . (except that there is no longer any subject), it is not man or God, and even less man in the place of God. The subject is this free, anonymous, and nomadic singularity which traverses men as well as plants and animals independently of the matter of their individuation and the form of their personality."[34] Deleuze presents us with an elaboration of a transcendental philosophy without the coherence of a subjective consciousness, or with a wild empiricism without the coherent synthesis of experience: all we have are disparate elements in a chaotic machine of individuation.

Sense and Nonsense

Deleuze's plane of immanence is rooted in groundless chaos, and this challenges the traditional alternative between Being and non-Being: either the philosopher chooses to constitute Being as an absolute order, or like a mystic or poet he lets chaos speak: "*either* an undifferentiated ground, a groundlessness, formless nonbeing, or an abyss without differences and without properties, *or* a supremely individuated Being and an intensely personalized Form. Without this Being or this Form, you will have only chaos."[35]

Deleuze refuses to exclude chaos from the thinking of Being; instead, borrowing the term *chaosmos* from Joyce, he suggests considering Being as one surface of chaos.[36] This allows him to confront the unpredictable and the unintelligible sense of the real. Chaos becomes active in the project of releasing the real experience from the conceptual conditions of thinking. It reveals the act of nonsense that spreads out the present singularities without imposing formal categorization on them and before classifying them in a certain organization.

Nonsense, then, is neither simply nor logically the opposite of sense. It is, inversely, the productive movement toward sense. Like the variable and paradoxical elements, nonsense remains neutral in order to engender the very possibility of the production of sense. Having no sense of its own, nonsense purely resists the absence of sense; it is the virtual entity that yields sense without corresponding to any concrete meaning and without referring to an accomplished state of affairs. "Nonsense is that which has no sense, and that which, as such and as it enacts the donation of sense, is opposed to the absence of sense. This is what we must understand by '*nonsense*.'"[37]

The internal neutrality and productivity of nonsense fundamentally assert the three conditions of Deleuze's event: multiplicity, differentiation and immanence.

Multiplicity: because nonsense has no sense of its own, it is the condition of the infinite circulation of the series. The sense produced is always an intermediate moment in the course of the multiple movements of production. In this perspective, the creation of a concrete meaning or the realization of a state of affairs is merely the unstable actualization that supposes the production of nonsense with which it is infused.

Differentiation: in this manner Deleuze contests the hermeneutic circle, in which relative meaning always derives from the ideal or universal presumption of understanding that conditions it.[38] Instead, the making of sense by nonsense accentuates the process of dissimilitude in which sense emerges. Now sense no longer resembles what makes it possible; it neither finds its justification within an original fore-sense, nor does it refer to an a priori category. Now sense only expresses the internal *enactment* of Being itself, the power of generation or the dynamic movement *for* sense.

Immanence: while the act of nonsense exposes the One and chaotic movement of Being, its violence is also that which makes the two series of being necessarily heterogeneous. The event affirms the immanent surface through language and things by stretching their joint and unstable boundary.[39] The nonsense of the event is the entity that displaces the movement of Being through the different productions of language and things. Hence the one plane of immanence is no more than the necessary foundation of pure multiplicity and chance (*hasard*). Immanence is thus an infinite "disjunctive synthesis," the concrete substantive production of sense without sense, and the vital power of generation and individuation of any species and organism.

This ontological foundation, which emphasizes the production of nonsense, leads Deleuze, in later works, to progressively abandon the term *sense*, which impedes a direct approach to the unpredictable and unintelligible articulation between expression in language and the becoming of the real. His creative psychoanalytical approach, his critical theories of art and literature, his encyclopedic networks and cultural geographies are all experimental analyses that concretely develop this philosophical effort. The nonsense of *The Logic of Sense* and the effort in *Difference and Repetition* to give birth once more to the sensible within sense, formulated as the "Being of the sensible" or as a "transcendental-empiricism"—all this leads the way to Deleuze's next works.

In *Anti-Oedipus*, Deleuze and Guattari create the "desiring machine" as the immanent principle of production, the production of production that floods all categorical or idealistic expression of sense by distributing the flow of desire in the sphere of reality. Later, in the introduction of *A Thousand Plateaus*, they suggest substituting the term *function* (*faire*) for *signification*. This critical demand informs the entire book; instead of asking what a text means ("Qu'est-ce que ça veut dire?"), it poses the following question: How does it work? ("Comment ça marche?")—not only from a formal semiotic perspective, namely, how the text produces its own sense, but more specifically inquiring how the text creates its movements and gestures, together with what other external cultural practices, signs and assemblages. Or in other words: How does writing constitute a complicated simultaneous articulation of life and expression, a "rhizome of bookworld" instead of a book-image of the world? Finally, with Deleuze's book on Francis Bacon, which carries the subtitle *The Logic of Sensation*, the rejection of the notion of "sense" is completed.

Virtual and Actual

Suspending the meaningful results of thinking in favor of the productive movement of nonsense exposes the procedure by which the plane of immanence speaks itself as pure multiplicity.[40] Being-as-event can be compared to an internal laboratory of production that shapes and creates, personifies and individualizes both the emergence of a phenomenon and the light of language that brings the phenomenon to consciousness. This conception might well be taken to correspond to Heidegger's ontology of *Ereignis*. According to Heidegger, *Ereignis* is the primary process that projects the order of Being through language and shows how appearance is given through perception. Yet this correlation between Heidegger and Deleuze is not as simple as it seems. Deleuze takes the idea of the event into completely different directions.

Badiou argues that Deleuze attaches great importance to the shift Heidegger made from phenomenological intentionality to the concealed-unconcealed ambiguity of ontology. But Heidegger comes to a halt somewhere in the middle of this movement when he restricts the unity of Being to the hermeneutic convergence between its visible and linguistic ontological dimensions. Language "places before the eyes" the way toward understanding, just as the light of Being "speaks" as the possibility of perception. The etymological link between *Sagen* (saying) and *Zeigen* (showing) sustains this analogical relation.[41] Heidegger, writes Badiou, "refolds and closes up all the separations, the differentiations without resemblances, and the unresolved divergences that alone *prove* the equality and neutrality of the One." Deleuze, by contrast, is closer to Nietzsche's and Foucault's lines of thinking and radicalizes the struggle and the dissimilitude between the diverse productions of Being. Badiou defines his ontological strategy as follows: "one has to explain that the 'non-relation is still a relation, and even a relation of a deeper sort.'"[42] Heidegger's event of Being is offered as a gift to thinking, while Deleuze's always does violence to thinking.

It is true that Heidegger already propounds Being's power of differentiation. The complete withdrawal of Being back into the absent source of possibility is the force that allows realized beings to reach out differently according to their historical situation. But Heidegger's ontological difference does not correspond to the model of disjunctive synthesis and to the event that emerges between heterogeneous series. According to Deleuze, Being ceases to act as an ideal condition for the production of sense, even if it grants sense by withdrawing itself completely from beings. Instead, the differentiation of Being affirms itself only through the real actualization of beings. Deleuze, more than Heidegger, succeeds in removing the emphasis from the potential production of sense and its similar application within the actual phenomenon, toward a concrete study of specific cases whose sense, as internal event of difference, must be gleaned above all from the material realization in which they have taken place.[43]

There is no production of sense before the actual realization of the phenomenon; the production of sense must respect the priority of the actual and take into account the complex economy and process that singularize it. Barthes's semiological analysis of fashion or cooking is a concrete example of a method that also follows this insight. Merleau-Ponty, even earlier, is highly preoccupied by the importance of the actual, giving priority to the concrete experience in which the subject's corporeal perception manifests its particular involvement in the world. The priority of the sensible leads to a specific approach to expression. Merleau-Ponty believes that expression of the sensible precedes the general ideas of thought. This assumption is abundantly manifest in artistic creation; the experience of a written style or of a certain gesture in painting is what creates both the subject of perception and the object perceived, reaffirming their interwovenness. Thus, the expressive gesture is not the temporary "clothing" of thought but what stimulates thought. Sensible expression is what leads thought to create and find new horizons of sense, in the same way as great writers, whose unique style consolidates their signature and program, "begin a book without knowing exactly what they are going to put into it."[44]

Deleuze's priority of the actual detaches more completely than Merleau-Ponty from the horizon of possibilities. Deleuze's philosophy is highly engaged by the actuality and singularity of the specific case. Yet the analysis of specific works of art, Deleuze's interest in theoretical models or historical situations, does not cause him to address them merely as the individual and cultural phenomena they constitute. The specific cases only form particular thresholds to the power of generation that brings them into existence. As we have already noticed, however, this ontological laboratory of production does not possess the status of a general potentiality or ideal possibility: *it is only the affirmation of the differentiation that takes place in the singular case as such*. The event is only the differentiation that passes through the actual, namely, the ontological aspect of its unpredictable becoming.

In this sense, Deleuze's analyses cannot be reduced to the historical or aesthetic facts themselves. The facts only provide the raw material and the framework in which the event activates the differentiation of the actual. To continue this argument, Deleuze has to deal with two principal tasks: he must situate *differentiation* in reality itself, and he must affirm that the differentiation of the real is pure, that is to say, not subordinate to the logic of identity and resemblance. In order to achieve this, Deleuze borrows the terms *actual* and *virtual* from Bergson.[45] These terms not only express the real dimension of Being by emphasizing their own indistinct difference under the rule of reality; Deleuze also uses them to disprove the traditional separation between the possibility of existence and existence itself.

The term *possible* enables the concept of existence by circumventing real existence itself. Like the concept of a given object, the possible holds the totality of its characteristics; therefore the movement of realization has absolutely no effect on the object. From this perspective, the possible projects itself onto all actual realizations; it conditions in advance all the ways in which the object comes into existence. This is why the individual and temporal characteristics of the real add nothing to the image of the concept; traditionally, the real is even excluded as the subordinate copy of the concept. In this way, the real and the possible reflect one another in a stable manner that confirms both their identity and representation: the realization resembles the possible, and the possible provides an image of the real.

Within this relation of identical resemblance, the differentiation of the real amounts only to the limitation and incarnation of the possible. What differs is only a secondary state that reconfirms the ideal image of identity and similitude. Deleuze refuses to accept this consequence by showing that the actualization of the real is already affected by a virtual movement of differentiation.[46] In contrast to the hierarchical subordination of the possible, the *virtual* is not separate from the real, it does not hover above the real, it has total reality being virtual, and as such it is the part of the simulacrum that always renders the actualization different. Deleuze defines the virtual as the simulacrum of the actual. Taking account of the ambiguous quality of dissimilarity and of the re-duplication of the simulacrum, the virtual introduces into any actual situation a movement of divergence and re-duplication (dividing or redoubling) that reveals the novelty and the creativity of the real. "The actualisation of the virtual, on the contrary, always takes place by difference, divergence or differenciation. Actualisation breaks with resemblance as a process no less than it does with identity as a principle. Actual terms never resemble the virtualities they incarnate. In this sense, actualisation or differenciation is always a genuine creation."[47] Traditionally, reference to the real from the abstract and conceptual image of the possible can only be made by organizing and confirming its description from the outside. The simulacrum of the virtual, on the contrary, accentuates the immanent productivity of the real. The virtual conditions the actual by engendering it with the repetitive movement of pure difference, the ramification and contingent process of the dynamic production of actualization.

Let us again remember that the virtual production of the actual is not an unquestionable a priori. If the virtual creates the actual, it is necessarily a chaotic and non-philosophical foundation, and yet it has a real effect: it yields the actual in the same way that non-sense yields sense. The virtual and the actual dwell together in the plane of immanence. One does not come before or after the other, they coexist as in a broken mirror, with the permanent tension between the disparate images maintaining their indistinct dependence: the virtual does not exist outside the actual, although it necessarily creates the actual. "From virtuals we descend to actual states of affairs, and from states of affairs we ascend to virtuals, without being able to isolate one from the other."[48]

The Becoming of the Event

Every movement of actualization is also an effect of virtualization. Yet still, we can reach the virtual only by first considering the actual condition of things. The actual concrete matter of fact guarantees the reality of the virtual, but the task of thinking consists in extricating *virtualities* from the actualities.

What, then, does it mean to extricate virtualities from the actualities? In *What Is Philosophy?* there is a clear description of this problem.[49] Studying Péguy's work *Clio*, Deleuze argues that the event is not the historical fact that takes place in the course of time. The event eludes, more precisely, the course of history by including a nonhistorical element that removes it out from the graspable or knowable present.

Deleuze assigns the concept *becoming* to the virtual differentiation that operates between event and historical fact. The term *event* does not denote what has factually happened, but points at the virtual region in which a constant immanent flow of becoming affects the historical present. This flow is real enough to make history happen, yet it never reduces itself to a concrete place and time.

Deleuze's definition of *becoming* is elusive. He continuously reminds us that becoming must be defined as a function of its historical conditions even if it interferes with the course of history by way of rupture and change. However, becoming cannot be understood by means of a historical logic. Becoming does not show, for instance, that which exists in the event and is to come about in history. Its happening never concretely indicates the convergence of a real future evolution with a speculative ideological goal. Deleuze insists that becoming is not simply a nonhistorical withdrawal that prepares for the next periodical shifts or that foresees the new cultural tendencies: "becoming-revolutionary," in this sense, never points to the future of the revolution or to its historical utopia. "Becoming-woman," another expression of Deleuze's, does not necessarily concern the fate of women's social status in a specific place and time, and sometimes, indeed, it does not concern women at all.

"Nothing happens there, but everything becomes.... Nothing happens there, and yet everything changes."[50] Becoming goes unnoticed: nothing seems to happen in history, yet something within the event deviates from the regular course of history and makes everything appear differently. Perhaps becoming signifies the deviation itself, a deviation whose direction one cannot know, a constant mutation that is imperceptible because it always comes both after preestablished knowledge and before knowledge establishes itself anew. Just as Blanchot's imaginary remains irreducible to any present time, and just as Derrida's event is both singular and exemplary (taking place for the first and last time yet displacing itself in other moments and contexts), Deleuze's becoming acts on the present as the never-ending production of the new, both untimely and occurring now. Like an arrow propelled from an unknown world, from terra incognita, becoming is the vertiginous force that qualifies the event out of history and tears history out of itself.

Thus, through the virtual action of becoming, the event overflows its harbor in the present. It does not correspond simply to what happens; the event refers to something *within* the happening. It contains an element of timeless immensity, an outside-within; it is the non-actual rupture within actuality, yet without its deviation and mutation, history cannot come about. "This is what we call the Event, or the part that eludes its own actualization in everything that happens. The event is not the state of affairs. It is actualized in a state of affairs, in a body, in a lived, but it has a shadowy and secret part that is continually subtracted from or added to its actualization: in contrast with the state of affairs, it neither begins nor ends but has gained or kept the infinite movement to which it gives consistency."[51]

This is precisely where extricating virtualities from the actualities becomes an ethical ambition, not just an ontological one.[52] Not only the production of sense is entailed by the becoming of the real; a mode of life, too, is required, a project of resistance and vitality. "Willing the event" is the phrase in which Deleuze captures this ambition: accepting the event that overwhelms you, feeling neither resentment nor resignation, desiring for it to occur. One must extricate the event from the factual state of affairs in which it takes place, extricate the becoming of any present happening in order for the subject itself to become the "offspring of the event" and to impose violently the impersonal reality of thinking.[53]

Deleuze offers Joë Bousquet's literary work as an exemplary case. The injury he sustains in the World War I leads him to write: "My wound existed before me, I was born to embody it."[54] Deleuze argues that Bousquet, here, does not express the unfortunate determinism of fate but his need for dignity in the face of what happens. The injury that paralyzes Bousquet's body came from the outside; before being incorporated, it existed regardless of whom it would touch. However, impersonal as injury may be, it meets the flesh that it harms. Once the injury is embodied, the personal struggle to endure and to bear it creates the event anew as if the injury originates in the body itself. In this sense, willing the event means being worthy of what happens, to deserve your circumstances not only by accepting them but also by creating from them, to make them repeat as if you were both the cause of their realization and the offspring reborn from their becoming.

This should not inversely be taken to mean that one should master the accidental, making it absolutely personal, seeing it merely as a individual acquisition, to be controlled and prepared for. The efficacy and the determination of science and technology may exemplify such an attitude, expanding as they do human ability and improving human achievement by finding ways of overcoming the obstacles toward a positive goal. According to this attitude, the circumstances are recast to deserve you; the personality only glorifies its reasons, always returns to itself by way of itself, and consequently remains unmoved and unaffected by the course of things.

Deleuze's attitude is quite different. "Willing the event" means to be sensibly affected by the accidents that befall one without succumbing to them: accepting war, wound, or death while simultaneously enduring and resisting their reality. Deleuze argues that Bousquet succeeds in experiencing his wound because he reaches the splendor of becoming within his personal suffering. Bousquet embodies the event of the wound because he has heard the claim of the wound, the *other* language of the wound, and has carried the wound to the point at which it reverses and opposes all injuries. This is how Deleuze interprets the Stoical moral of *amor fati*: it is to let oneself be pulled along by the unknown and impersonal truth of the event, to extricate the virtual sense of the event from the actual state of things.[55] This is achieved neither through imitation nor by reproduction of the lived and personal accident, but by revealing within the accidental the becoming of will and thinking. One must put pressure on the personal accident until it attains the point of pure affirmation, a point at which war returns and turns against itself and resists the full horror of war. Through the example of Bousquet, *amor fati* means to say yes to the vitality of war and to the passion of death in a manner that opposes all victimhood: "Taking the complaint and rage to the point that they are turned against what happens so as to set up the event, to isolate it, to extract it in the living concept."[56]

Aspects of Becoming: Language, Temporality, Spatiality

Because it preoccupies itself with extricating the virtualities from the actualities, philosophy has the concrete task of identifying and diagnosing the "becomings" in each present happening.[57] Thus, the ethical order of the event is bound to the ontology of becoming. The concept of becoming not only refers to the constant movement of real differentiation; it also poses the living body before the question of the capacity of its vitality and creativity. Following Spinoza and Nietzsche, the ethical order of becoming is opposed to the "doctrine of judgment." This ethics does not oppress the living by means of an image they should incarnate, but forms itself within and through the composition of forces that continually construct the existence of the body.

In his final book, *Essays Critical and Clinical*, Deleuze announces clearly that moral judgment, established on fixed and higher values, cannot apprehend "what is new in an existing being, nor even sense the creation of a mode of existence."[58] Inversely, the ethical motivation of becoming violates all stable organization: it sets free the gestures and desires that are foreign to the organic unity of a body, and emphasizes the qualities and associations that subvert the coherence of consciousness. This is why Deleuze observes that the creativity of thinking inevitably entails a fragile health, a mental or physical crack, precisely because of the exposure to the vivid enthusiasm and speed of becoming.[59]

In principle, a writer's or a philosopher's becoming gives birth to sense by maintaining the immanent corporeality of nonsense. The creativity of language and style does not only yield a different psychic and epistemic vision; it is also the work of new compositions of living experience and corporeality. Deleuze, thus, says about Beckett that his great artistic achievement can be summarized by the fact that his exhaustion of language "does not occur without a certain physiological exhaustion."[60] The becoming of a writer is not tantamount to acquiring symbolic authority through his or her work: first and foremost, writing is the absolute metamorphosis the event imposes on the writer: "becoming-animal," "becoming-woman," "becoming-child," or even "becoming-imperceptible."[61] This alteration essentially comes to upset the personal state of affairs; it is a radical change that must engage the condition of thinking and will, and therefore the fate of experience itself (*amor fati*).

This is what Deleuze expresses when he states, after Nietzsche, that the philosopher, like the writer and artist, has to be "the medical physician of civilization": precisely because his health is so fragile. The importance of this weakness, however, does not reside in personal neurosis and illness. It is, rather, the expression of an uncontainable exposure that marks the body with a profound inadequacy vis-à-vis the established civilization: "because they have seen something in life that is too much for anyone, too much for themselves, and that has put on them the quiet mark of death. But this something is also the source or breath that supports them through the illnesses of the lived (what Nietzsche called health)."[62]

Once again it should be noticed that becoming does not assign a specific idealist utopia to the work of art or to philosophy. Even when Deleuze writes that both artist and philosopher call for a land and people that are missing,[63] even then the task of becoming does not adhere to a political vision without being first of all implicated in an adventure of health, that is to say, in the singular enterprise of setting free the life that man imprisons through and within body and consciousness. The medical vocation of the philosophical or artistic creation approaches the virtual power of life without having any actual or historical accomplishment other than the creativity of resistance itself.

This means that the political engagement of philosophy and literature does not have to assign a future revolutionary solution to the oppression of the *doxa*; it concerns, above all, the critical revelation of the complexities of micro-politics in the present. This is what Deleuze calls, among many expressions, "the becoming minor" of body and writing, "an entire world of unconscious micropercepts, unconscious affects, fine segmentations," which is already active in the concrete state of affairs and therefore must be exposed.[64] This is the critical project of health for Deleuze: it is necessary to invent new styles, new lands, new modes of existence that are the result of both the real and singular becoming of one's own events as well as constituting the resistance to one's own historical and actual situation.

Perhaps this is what Deleuze means when he speaks of the complex knot between the singular (pre-individual) and the impersonal aspects of becoming. The fact that the event simultaneously awaits and precedes us, and yet does not exist beyond our own embodiment, demands the elaboration of new linguistic horizons, temporal and spatial perspectives. Hence, events are told in a language of "impersonal singularities." The temporality of the event is crossed by a double direction: what has already not yet occurred. Also, the spatiality of the event indicates an outside that is contained inside: the impersonal limit bursts into an intensive assemblage of singular forces. The rest of this chapter briefly develops three aspects of the philosophy of event according to Deleuze: the style of writing, the untimely, and the composition of forces.

Language

The event involves a linguistic transformation, a new language that simultaneously opposes the logic of the predicative proposition and appeals for new conditions of thinking. Thus the event is written in a language of "impersonal singularities" that are neither private nor collective, neither particular nor general, neither individual nor universal. Deleuze suggests formulating this association between the singular and the impersonal by imagining a new grammatical person, a "fourth-person singular" or "third person of the infinitive." In doing so, he follows Heidegger, Levinas, and Blanchot in asserting the priority of the neutral third-person "it" or the French *on*.

If the event refers to a subject, this is not a psychological, linguistic, or conceptual subject. The event deprives the subject of a stable identity, of an inner self that, like the closed unity of the ego, forms the center of experience. The event, moreover, gets rid of the copula *is* that endows the subject with the status of source of actions or property of attributes. The subject of the event refers to the neutrality of "it," as in the impersonal expression "it is raining" or Blanchot's concept of dying (*on meurt*). Resonating the style of Heidegger, Deleuze would say that the event *is not*, but *there is* (*Il y a*) an event; in the same manner, he writes elsewhere: "We will not ask therefore what is the sense of the event: the event is sense itself."[65]

But Deleuze suggests stretching this semiotic terminology even further by adding more elements to the neutrality of "it": the singularity of the indefinite article (*a* child, *an* animal, *a* tree, etc.), the impersonal activity of verbs in the infinitive (to love, to die, to eat, to speak, etc.), and, finally, "free" indirect discourse that bears out how, linguistically, the event is necessarily an assemblage of utterances.

To put it briefly, *the indefinite article* defines the singularity of the event. We normally generalize to form universal concepts referring to preexisting prototypes, species, or subjects using the definite article: *the* child, *the* animal, *the* tree. Conversely, the indefinite article individuates in relationship to a situation: When we say "*a* child was beaten" or "*an* animal hurt," the subject is continually constituted by the impersonal event in which it is involved and thus singularizes it. The event, therefore, necessarily exceeds the child's or the animal's own conceptual center and undermines its stable identity.[66]

Verbs, in their infinitive form, express the impersonality of the event. Possessing infinite power and unlimited activity, an infinitive neutralizes any form of conjugation, on the basis of a specific time, aspect, or person. To love, to die, to eat, to speak, or better yet, using the gerund: loving, dying, eating, speaking: the infinitive marks the measureless intrinsic continuity of the event from which measured conjugations are derived. In contrast with the predicative proposition, the verb is no longer related to the subject. Now, the event creates both subject and object, to the extent, at least, that they are actively involved in the corporeal encounter in which the event is taking place.

Free indirect discourse shows that every event is an assemblage. This discursive mode expresses the multiple voices, different impressions, and sensations that blend into one voice. The question is no longer "Who speaks?" The subject of the statement is no longer relevant when the discourse becomes a composition of plural registers, semantic fields, and idioms. Foucault's order of discourse teaches that even private events are collective. The technique of free indirect discourse not only explains how the private actually functions as collective utterance (Flaubert, for example, uses this technique to blur the narrative distinctions between objective and subjective voices, character and narrator, optic impression and imaginative expression); it also emphasizes the particularity of human language, that is, the capacity of human language to evoke, transmit, and twist things one has not personally experienced, not seen in person. Free and indirect, this mode of discourse is thus an actual image of the event that renders language possible: it blends the unique present occurrence with the independent words of plural speakers, with perceptions and insights from other places and times.

This discursive mode of the event is similar to Blanchot's being of language, to the incessantly wandering murmur that Blanchot develops from Mallarmé's inheritance and from modern literature (see, e.g., Blanchot's chapter on Beckett's *The Unnamable*). From quite a different perspective, the notion of free indirect discourse could also clarify the process Heidegger has in mind when he speaks of the inheritance of language that assigns *Dasein*, as opposed to animal being, a historical identity.[67] The Deleuzian vision of language, however, seeks neither the non-essential essence of fiction, the "zero degree of literature," nor the original testimony of human identity. This discourse only signifies the becoming of the event, the creativity of the one fulgurous and vital energy that is multiplicity.

Thus Deleuze is fascinated by the particular becomings of those writers who create new compositions and styles. He examines not only the practical process of their writing but also how in the work, the imperceptible flash of becoming appeals: Artaud's *body without organs*, Proust's spider style, Melville's or Hofmannsthal's becoming-animal, Kleist's turbulence, Woolf's *hecceitas*, Kafka's becoming-minor, Bousquet's wound, Lawrence's desire, or Fitzgerald's crack-up. These are only a few examples of how Deleuze's literary criticism locates and creates conceptual-personae of events.[68]

For a more precise idea on Deleuze's criticism, the essay titled "The Exhausted" explains well how everything in Beckett's work is exhausted except exhaustion itself, which becomes, on the contrary, its own creative vehicle.[69] Beckett's creation becomes un-exhausted exactly by virtue of being a compound of many exhausted figures (suffering from both physical and psychic fatigue). Deleuze concludes that the conceptual-persona of the exhausted is not simply a despairing representation of the human condition but rather affirms the operation of *difference* itself: giving birth to new languages (literary writing, spatial-movement, image, voice, and music) in diverse mediums such as theater, cinema, literature, and works for radio and television. The conceptual-persona of the exhausted becomes thus a specific event in which the singular assemblage of the corporeal and the incorporeal puts becoming into action.

Regarding Deleuze's literary criticism, Jacques Rancière argues that Deleuze analyses the process of writing by finding condensed symbols or fables that are immediate expressions of the writing's singular thought: "showing that operation [of literary writing] most often signifies, in Deleuze, focusing the analysis on the figure of an operator."[70] These operators, however, are not characters who are privileged "to the detriment of action," Rancière suggests; nor are they simply manipulations of representations, something that, paradoxically, has the effect of breaking off from the logic of representation in favor of the pure operation of language. These symbolic figures or conceptual personae are cases of multiplicity: indistinctly they disarrange language and world, displaying how becoming stimulates both the deviation of expression and the necessity for new sensible content to the extent that they actually become inseparable.

Finally, the language of event reaches its pinnacle with Deleuze's concept of "style." With this concept Deleuze generally describes the act of differentiation in writing.[71] With "style," Deleuze names all modern aspirations to break off with rhetorical embellishment, namely, those procedures of "non-style" through which language tends toward its ungrammatical limit, toward its dissolution in silence or music; the creation of foreign language within a dominant language, subverting the mother tongue's conventions; the urge to follow the multiple voices and phantoms that populate the writer's solitude; allowing the sentence to grow from the "middle," from the stammering hesitations and articulations of the syntax or from the rhythm of and between the sentences. These procedures are effective only when the linguistic material is imposed by corporeal forces coming from "outside." What a story tells or what a sentence says does not amount to the sense of the event; instead, the event haunts the entire work of language by producing singular and impersonal sensations whose name the writer does not know.

Temporality
The definition of the event as both singular and impersonal raises the issue of temporality. If we argue that the becoming of the event awaits us and precedes us, and yet does not exist apart from our embodiment, we are faced with a paradoxical aspect of time that points into opposite directions simultaneously: what has already occurred has not actually occurred yet. The real and singular accomplishment of the event is what renders the event unaccomplished, already forgotten in the past and yet to come in the future.

In *The Logic of Sense*, Deleuze sets two formal conditions for thinking about time. The first, *Chronos*, corresponds to the historical and chronological temporality of bodies; the present governs this time, while future and past are only secondarily conceived on the basis of the present, as memory and expectation, as acquired experience and anticipation. The second, *Aion*, corresponds to the time of the event. The priority of the present, which is in essence a corporeal tense, is abolished by the double direction of the incorporeal tenses, namely, past and future. What has already happened and what will happen causes the present to divide infinitely into unmeasured time through which the pure passage of becoming is transmitted.[72]

The beginning of this study showed that the distinction between the time of the event and the time of history, between *Aion* and *Chronos*, already exists in Heidegger's *On Time and Being*. Like Deleuze's prioritizing of the present in historical time, Heidegger observes the metaphysical link between *presence* and *the present*. As a distinct instant between two abysses, the present instant provides the acknowledged presence of what happens now as well as the possibility of measuring the presence of past and future, as if time were laid out across a stable spatial schema. This notion of time, *Chronos*, allows conceiving of mobility through immobility. Opposing this conception, Heidegger prescribes a critical approach that enables one to conceive of the very happening of "what is coming to be present" by emphasizing the activity of absence in presence. "We shall find in absence—be it what has been or what is to come—a manner of presencing [Anwesen] and approaching which by no means coincides with presencing in the sense of the immediate present [Gegenwart]."[73]

Extending Heidegger's ideas, Gadamer elaborates a historical hermeneutics that mainly criticizes the objective methods of nineteenth-century historicism.[74] He suggests locating absent elements in presence, namely, within the "prejudices" that condition the act of understanding in the present. Revealing these prejudices allows one to perceive the traditional belonging of one's own consciousness and cultural embeddedness and, thus, to put to the test the possibility of understanding: both what creates its interest in the past and what prevents it from reliably observing the past.

The examination of one's own prejudices, the preconceptual beliefs and judgments that condition one's thought, renders the infinite junctions between present and past accessible: through prejudices the past speaks in the present, and through prejudices the present reaches out to the past. However, even if there is a mutual dependence between present and past, as there is between presence and absence, Gadamer remains attached to the timeline of history, to the basic grid of what comes before and after. Even if Gadamer demands opening up the singular experience of the past without restoring or objectively mastering it, the horizons of past and present fuse, pointing merely to the future conception of a *possible variation*. In contrast, the time of event essentially breaks away from the realm of possibility, introducing absence into the present, just as impossible novelty invades the possible.

With clearly different motivations, Blanchot and Derrida both radicalize Heidegger's thought by emphasizing literature's and fiction's deviation from historical understanding. With Derrida's *hauntology* and Blanchot's *image event*, with the temporal understanding of *traumatism* and *dying*, ambiguous temporality displays the extent to which there is an "opening up which gives all presencing [Anwesen] into the open."[75] In this context, time can be understood by contradictory expressions: "the presence of absence," "presence without present," "taking place without having a place," the future perfect tense of "the already-pastness of what is to come," and the future past tense of "what will already have taken place." All of these expressions testify to the need for undermining the historical modality that organizes, after the event, the continuity of what comes before and after. Literature turns upside down the objective pretensions of historical detachment, including the assurance of values and the sense of tradition. More than history, literature exposes the temporality of the event: how the event tears itself away from history by finding at its heart the immensity of a necessary contingency that unfolds the event's singular movement and sense.

Approaching Deleuze, Blanchot and Derrida, each in his different way, define this immensity by emphasizing the impossible and unaccomplished character of the event. They describe the event's fascination with the "negative" effects of survival and suspension, oblivion and waiting. Deleuze understands similarly that the temporality of the event appears in terms of pure and measureless *becoming*. However, rather than trying to determine the *ungraspable* and *interminable* as such, he attaches more importance to the possible effects of becoming by showing its productive involvement and multiplicity.

In fact, Deleuze succeeds in developing the temporality of the event by substituting the immanent articulation of the *virtual* and the *actual* in place of the abstract terms of *impossible* and *possible*, or of the separation between *unreal* and *real*. Pure and measureless "becoming," not in the sense of impossible but rather of virtual, resides actively in the actual state of things. Deleuze understands that the temporality of the event cannot be conceived beyond the limited and measured time of history, although it differs essentially from history.

In other words, the virtuality of the *Aion* conditions the actuality of *Chronos*. The power of becoming's differentiation constitutes the bodies' movement in the present: what is commonly expressed as historical period, daily news, political circumstances, social or personal change. Cultural episteme and semiotic regimes derive from the ontology of event. The temporality of the event remains impersonal, incorporeal *actualization* (*effectuation*), though the corporeal experience that embodies the event adds the *counter-actualization* (*contre-effectuation*) of a singular reality to becoming.

Yet virtual becoming constantly flees the actual movement of time. As the immanent principle of difference and multiplicity, becoming runs counter to the stability and regularity of the present whose course Deleuze attaches to the transcendent order, to the surveillance of self-identical omnipresence of the divine. At the same time however, Deleuze defines the time of the virtual as the time of the "becoming-insane," as the time of the labyrinth, "The period of time which is smaller than the smallest period of continuous time imaginable in one direction is also the longest time, longer than the longest unit of continuous time imaginable in all directions."[76] The time of *Aion*, as Benveniste described its Greek etymology of life's effectiveness and youth, contrasts with the fixed and eternal wholeness of *Chronos*.[77]

The conception of one directional linear progress, thus, gets disrupted. Virtual time undermines the actual by dividing it into two simultaneous opposite directions: the present is torn between the past and the future, between what has just happened and what is about to happen. In this manner the surface of the present discloses an entity without a place, a permanent instability, the pure becoming that Deleuze qualifies with the title "the untimely" (*l'intempesive*). The untimely is that which comes about both too early and too late; it is both ephemeral and a conservation of the past resulting from the repetition of difference itself, a time that is in-between time, meanwhile or meantime (*un entre-temps*), as Deleuze and Guattari put it in *What Is Philosophy?*[78] In this sense, time is always a view from a middle position, in which any moment is considered to be a continued variation of dispersed series, where the abrupt arrival of the new is also the pure possibility of duration.

Defining the temporality of the event, Deleuze mentions Nietzsche's *eternal return*, Mallarmé's *throw of the dice* (*un coup de dés*), and Bergson's *duration*. Along with the untimely, these are other keys for deciphering the secret of becoming: Nietzsche's conception of the eternal repetition of the ephemeral, that is, ephemeral eternity understood as the selective repetition of what differs; Mallarmé's necessary movement of contingency, the absolute book that is the pure exception taking the form of the rules of chance; and Bergson's heterogeneity that has no other purpose than creative fluidity itself.

Robbe-Grillet creates his literature in relation to this notion of time; his work with Alain Resnais's "Last Year in Marienbad" uses the classic theme of betrayal between a married woman and a foreign lover in an aristocratic castle, but this elementary content is suspended by an artistic complexity that envelops everything in a troubled mystery: we don't know whether the moment of the lovers' encounter has occurred last year, this year, or perhaps never at all. Was it in Marienbad, in Karlsbad, or elsewhere? Was the love affair real, or was it hallucinated by an obsessive mind? Was it a struggle between men for a woman, or perhaps a labyrinth of reflections between mythical sculptures, theater scenes, and a story within a story?

Barthes would have agreed that this ontological time reveals a new artistic and literary understanding based on eternal difference: every literary work is the infinite returning mark of difference, not of identity.[79] The creativity of pure contingency is the symbolic quality of the work that refers and reopens a former sequence of texts that now spreads by way of ruptures and deviations, and through these ramifications and combinations brings forth new sequences of texts to come. Finally, this is how the time of becoming receives a moving spatiality, like a cubist painting or an abstract painting lacking both stable figurative source as well as truth and center.[80]

Spatiality
The shifts in emphasis, the substitution—brought about by the event—of the real articulation of *virtual* and *actual* for the abstract terms of *impossible* and *possible*, all these demand a new conception of space. Deleuze defines the event's spatial activity as an internal limit. The spatiality of the event is always an edge, a boundary passing through incompatible entities such as human and animal, or through hetero-

geneous modalities such as vision and sound, affirming their power by expressing the difference marking their encounter. This incessant differentiation draws a disrupted line, so to speak, a "fleeing line" of limit. However, this limit does not usually mark that which transcends a certain entity or series; it is not what visibly separates the *outside* from the *inside* of a given entity or series. Instead, this limit marks what always flows in the "middle" and "between" the *distinguishable* states of the entity, what constitutes its own "region of *indistinguishability*" with an other entity, namely, the effects of *the outside* within.

The limit is what brings the outside inside, what blurs the distinction between outside and inside. At the beginning of *Essays Critical and Clinical*, for example, Deleuze describes the limit of language as the outside inside the realm of language, not as what is excluded from the realm of language: "The limit is not outside language, it is the outside of language. It is made up of visions and auditions that are not of language, but which language alone makes possible."[81]

Hence, so long as the event occupies real space *it is defined as the limit of outside* and *not as what is outside the limit*. Deleuze borrows the term *outside* from Blanchot and Foucault.[82] But he notices an essential difference between these thinkers regarding this issue regarding whether this limit of the outside is void or full, whether it points to an open externality or to an internal corporeality, to an expressive disappearance or rather to a resistant vitalism. Blanchot would probably say that the outside is the impossible that predestines without destination, while Foucault, from Deleuze's point of view, would argue that the outside is the real action that unceasingly actualizes new "virtualities."

Blanchot's concept of "outside" not only runs counter to the positive tendency of knowledge and to the subjective internality of thought; it presupposes, also, the affirmation of a vacant language in which the very possibility of a unity of presence and experience disperses and vanishes. This is how Foucault describes Blanchot's thought of outside: "When language arrives at its own edge, what it finds is not a positivity that contradicts it, but the void that will efface it. Into the void it must go, consenting to come undone in the rumbling, in the immediate negation of what it says, in a silence that is not the intimacy of a secret but a pure outside where words endlessly unravel."[83]

In contrast, Foucault's use of the term *outside* is inevitably inspired by Nietzsche.[84] If Blanchot's outside offers itself as an original "contestation that effaces," the recourse to Nietzsche allows conceiving of the outside as vital resistance within a "force field." "Foucault therefore discovers the element that comes from outside: force.... It was necessary to recover force, in the Nietzschean sense, or power, in the very particular sense of 'will to power,' to discover this outside as limit, the last point before Being folds."[85] Foucault relates the "outside" to the virtual element of "force." It is in the space of "outside" that Foucault locates Nietzsche's thinking regarding the source of combat, of strife, as the "relation of forces" and as the condition of its ability to affect every living thing.

Deleuze notes that Foucault attains a profound Heraclitism, a strategy of endless combat between forces, based upon a relation of "non-relation," taking place in "non-place."[86] This "non-relation" that attracts the opposing forces is exactly the influence of the outside. It is what comes into the force field from outside, what sends out new forces and what agitates the forces into being irreducible adversaries, irreconcilably one against the other.

At this stage, Deleuze joins Foucault, conceiving a strategy of event in which the forces at stake do not coincide: there is only the "fleeing line" that passes between them, enforcing communication by way of irreducible difference and struggle. Here, Deleuze insists again that the forces are virtual and that their function and matter differ from the concrete forms in which they are actualized in history. The tension between forces is necessarily part, for example, of war, of religious or economic antagonism. The becoming of the forces, however, differs from the history of ideas and institutions, from the political aims and instruments they subserve. The forces act autonomously; they are the physical action of the outside: "it is a physics of abstract action.... [I]t is a physics of primary or bare matter."[87]

Thus, the outside, as the spatiality of the event, is a limit or demarcation line that attracts forces and makes them meet. The outside is no longer the illusory sign that beckons from the distance, using Blanchot's imagery.[88] It is rather a fold in the surface, a fold that is flooded by virtual forces that are in constant agitation, and thus changing the actual state of affairs, inventing new redistributions of sensations and knowledge, multiplying the positions and elements of the combat.[89] The forces, like the concept of singularities, are pre-individual and impersonal; they pass through people and objects, they generate and compose them, and as they do so they affirm the "vitality" of the outside.

Indeed, Deleuze assigns this liminality of the outside the quality of life's resistance.[90] The essential function of the forces is to resist, to oppose, to enter into the movement of struggle. This combined struggle of divergent forces eventually affirms the fundamentally aggregated nature of the plane of immanence.[91] Thus, the struggling forces on the plane of immanence create a space consisting of multiple folds of events, broken segments and splits, contracted connections and fractures, secret passages and metamorphoses.

Deleuze teaches us that every event is a nexus of forces, a geography of forces. He offers a toolbox with the instruments that assist in tracing the topology or mapping of the forces: their connections and contiguities, their capacity and their rhythm, their "longitude" and "latitude." Furthermore, he invites interaction with the event: for each individual to enter and get lost in the labyrinth of the event, to continue redistributing the forces and to feel their sensations. There is, effectively, nothing to know in this philosophy: only to be caught within the vivid movement of the event, only to become the impassioned "offspring of the event."

Literature, then, becomes a creative laboratory of such geographies of abstract and bare matter: it brings the attraction of the event's disparate forces into existence. Deleuze does not introduce cases of literature only with the intention of confirming their singularity. He does so in an effort to find a singular expression of becoming, and to reveal its creativity: How, then, does becoming traverse the process of writing and affect the matter of writing within the one and whole plane of immanence?

Neither historical testimony of the particular experience nor the *logos* that detaches completely from the real by raising general concepts, literature is a significant activity of the virtual. In literature, Deleuze seeks a style of writing that is situated between physics and metaphysics, between "eating" and "speaking." Literature necessarily confounds expression and life, undermining all oppressive rules of speech and yet absolutely abandoning itself to the exigency of life's impulses.

In literature, the external aspect of the event, the outside, shines forth because in this linguistic operation the virtual forces are real enough to affect the corporeal while already being incorporeal and thus beyond the concrete body's destiny. Though they create different images of personal, lived experience, these forces make the real abstract and in this sense capable of affecting the very conditions of the experience. This is why, when Deleuze suggests thinking about art and literature, for instance, in *What Is Philosophy?* he demands that the "affect" and "percept" of the work be considered as pre-individual and impersonal expressions of becoming, yet absolutely not as the "affection" and "perception" of the personal experience of the represented characters or of the writer's psychology.[92]

Identifying the space of the event means that one has to examine how the work of literature sets up new compositions of forces and sensations that pass through the narrative's accidents and characters. The point is to expose how impersonal "life," not personal "lived" experience, enters and find itself caught in the matter of language. A final question would be: How, starting from the fold or limit, does writing become a singular act of thinking,[93] a creative act that generates a thinking within thinking? A thinking from "the outside, further away than any external world, is also closer than any internal world."[94]

PART TWO **LITERATURE**

7

Toward a Theory of Literary Events
Conceptions and Principles

What Is Literature?

What is literature? What is the being of literature? What is the *literariness* of literature? What happens as a result of the fact that we have literature? Is there a particular substance or essence of literature? Although answers to these questions are offered in diverse classical poetics, aesthetics, and modern textual theories, these fundamental questions remain enigmatic. What is literature as a discourse and as an art, as an aesthetic object and as a poetic experience?

Recently, Genette, after Aristotle and Kant, Jakobson and Sartre, Valéry and Blanchot, summarized this question by pointing at two general criteria, *fiction* and *diction*, that spell out the conditions under which a text, oral or written, as compared to other arts and other types of verbal discourse, "can be perceived as a 'literary work' or, more broadly, as a (verbal) object with an aesthetic function."[1]

Aristotle was the first to define *poiesis* with reference to a thematic criterion: a work is poetic only when language serves as mimetic vehicle for a fictive invention. The fact that it is written in verse or in prose does not assign any specificity to literature. What matters is that the process of composition enters the generalized sphere of fiction, which carries a basic sense of impersonal disinterestedness. This disinterestedness is responsible for evoking, according to Kant, the nonconceptual pleasure of aesthetic judgment, which is independent both from any pragmatic interest and from the preconditions of scientific objectivity and truthfulness.

To this essence of fictional content, Genette adds a formal poetical criterion. He demonstrates how German romanticism generates the idea that poetry expresses the genuine spirit and sensible openness of literature as opposed to the ordinary state of life and the prosaic gesture of communication. This idea of pure language that has its end in itself and that "operates the indissociable union of sound and sense" reaches its climax with Mallarmé and Valéry and passes through Russian formalism as well as through Heidegger, Blanchot, and even the French "adventure of writing" of the *nouveau roman* and the new essay in the last half century. Here, the emphasis shifts from represented action to linguistic action, from narrative layout to poetic function, from the impersonal intelligence of the *fabula* to the personal experience of an idyllic self and a social-realist surrounding. This is the formal essence Genette finds in the criterion of "diction": the idea of poetry retains the pure condition of literature as an art of language.[2]

These two essentialist traits can be very useful when we understand them in terms of creative qualities and not as the closed and formal bounds of the generic seal. When they are perceived as open qualities, that is, as fictional and poetic visions or efforts, their combination characterizes not only the most classic and ambitious literary creations, that is, the Greek *epos* and tragedy, but also free modern poetry, including the work of Hölderlin, Baudelaire and Mallarmé, T. S. Eliot and Allen Ginsberg, as well as the remarkable variety of the anti-epic modern novel, from Flaubert to Claude Simon and Marguerite Duras, without setting aside non-fictional and non-poetic genres.

One can generalize and distinguish three moments in which the history of literature articulates essences of poetic-fiction: (1) *the classic moment*, which is marked by the effort to establish objective conventions of fabrication, depending on the nature of the genre, the protagonists and the technical instruments of style and composition; (2) *the romantic moment*, in which the literary work is governed by the subjective experience of the "genius" and is perceived henceforth as genuine testimony of his particular originality and as the symbolic value expressing the progress of the human spirit; and (3) *the modern moment*, where literary creation abandons both objective convention and subjective representation in order to be led by the particular exigency of the text itself: impersonal but composing a singular and exceptional vision, necessary but inventing a new manner of writing.

When Flaubert foresees in 1852, "And so I think that the novel has only just been born: it awaits its Homer," he certainly testifies to the third moment, which takes place in his own era, changing the condition of articulation between fiction and poetry. When, in the very same year, he writes, "I envision a style . . . that would pierce your idea like a dagger," "style in itself being an absolute manner of seeing things,"[3] he certainly follows the pure poetic aspiration of the "book about nothing," the "Livre sur Rien,"[4] the dream of the total work that steps back from the world by creating its own need and its own end as required by style and composition.

This new autonomy of the work, however, is not hermetic, does not absolutely reject any external reference. It only shows that literary texts are not directly extracted from the traditional reservoir, subordinately derivative from reality, or simply yielded by an immediate connection with the actual discourse. Instead, the work of literature must create its own exceptional law, which requires new artistic forms and modes of writing in order to become the condition of an adventure as yet unknown. Thus, verbal manipulation is no longer a technical performance that follows and achieves the plan of the work. Style, to take Flaubert as a characteristic example, is the deviation from the norm, a deformation, out of joint, that supplies a new instrument of perception and enables a different mental and corporeal exploration. This is the *vivacity* of a writing that absorbs, embraces, and rearranges all historical and ethnographic studies in a single gesture; a writing that confronts scientific observations and mythical ideas syntagmatically. Style in this sense is a sort of ideology of "becoming-metaphor" as a vital source of experimentation.

This modern moment is also a sobering moment vis-à-vis the naive perception of the pure originality of the self. Flaubert writes in 1857: "the illusion (if there is one) comes, on the contrary, from the *impersonality* of the work. It is a principle of mine that a writer must not be his own theme."[5] At this point he is already aware of the fact that the living experience and the determined intentions invested in the sign—whether it is in the form of a romantic subjectivity or a sociohistorical identity—sprawl out of control by disappearing or by multiplying themselves in the diverse tones and phenomena of the work. In the modern moment, the mature or inspired "author" does not situate himself in regard to the work as though he is its unique originator. On the contrary, it is through the way he releases his mastery over words and things that the poetic-fictive work now puts his entire world to the test and forces him to transmute through a sensory and imaginary effort. The literary activity affirms its essence as neither plausible probability nor authentic interiority and deed, but rather as a new impersonal experience of words that takes the form of an impenetrable and transformative fascination, of universally proliferating encyclopedic concatenations and of a haunted sense of internalized otherness. Thus it discovers both physically and metaphysically what strikes everyone without ever belonging to anyone: the most intimate which is anonymous.

One can summarize the dramatic difference that governs the modern articulation of poetic fiction by reference to the invention of the *body*. The component that definitely changes, I believe, the common characteristics of the social-realist novel or subjective romantic poetry is the fact that they are henceforth wrapped in the necessary and nameless presence of the *corporeal*. Of course, the deformation and emptiness of the living body have become a theme in the writings of Kafka, Artaud, and Beckett, violent sexuality and dehiscence in the work of Céline, Bataille, and Guyotat. Already Mallarmé's and Valéry's observations on dance regard the dancers' movements as an invitation to a new poetic experience. Writing the figurative metamorphoses of dancer into knife, goblet, or flower, as well as writing the figurative decomposition of dying bodies at the cusp of existence and in the margins of contemporary society—these are both new creative preoccupations that involve constant stylistic experimentation until the excess, the silence, or the flesh of the words becomes the sensible experience of the work itself. Art in general, and literature in particular, thus emerges as a dying-living physical gesture, a living organism enfolded in the inertia of the work. It is surely in this sense that Paul Celan remarks at the beginning of "The Meridian" that art is an infertile marionette, "puppet-like ... without offspring."[6] More than the problems of death or of the spirit, which dominated the romantic and post-romantic tradition (Hegel, Nietzsche, Heidegger), the impersonality of the body seems to characterize the modern experience of fiction and its poetic investigation. The topic of the body discloses how fundamentally modern literature explores the degree zero of thinking: On the one hand, the corporeal attaches the creative necessity of style and image to the vital perception of the real, to the naked condition of having identity, world, and language. On the other hand, the language of the corporeal remains always imperceptible or in-appropriable. The most intimate exposure to the undeniable presence of life eludes all conscious symbolic interrogation or cultural discursive means. The body is non-symbolic in itself, yet it is certainly the surviving presence of the corporeal that afford necessity and vitality to all symbolic knowledge.

Along with the paradigm of the body, along with the term of "corporeality," it may well be possible to define a third principle to which any poetic-fictional representation must answer in order to gain modern creativity and commitment. If classic fiction has a mimetic aspiration and romantic poetry a formal one, I argue that it is through its dependency on the corporeal that modern work blends necessity with inventiveness. Constantly present yet inexhaustible, immediately urgent though insatiable, the corporeal is what infuses words with expressive essence while remaining foreign to the textual economy. Intensively vital and also meaningless, the corporeal attaches to the imaginary both the primitive stronghold of the real (or the irreversible law of the real) and the becoming of an impersonal fictive *uncertainty*. The most exaggerated lunacy and fantasy in modern literature are strongly rooted in the wounds and desire of an elementary state of survival. What I suggest inaugurating is an essentialism or a historicism of vitality: a vital move in which "what can be done or seen" depends on "what can never be otherwise"; a move in which the promise of the possible body, in the sense of the classical term of "possible world," is condemned to the single real body whose matter is unidentified and senseless. Valéry's *Monsieur Teste* is a perfect example of this: the conceptual and fictive figure of the absolute genius is, at the same time, the most regular person, Monsieur Teste, an anonymous man who is unable to pay sufficient attention to his own body, to his own corporeal suffering, although his intellectual exercise must begin exactly there.[7]

This modern invention of the corporeal in art and literature will be discussed here very briefly, although it deserves substantial examination. Merleau-Ponty's ontological phenomenology, for instance, and particularly the concept of "the flesh of the world" (*la chair du monde*), exemplifies the extension of man's body to the world's material content. "Our body ... is made of the same sensible tissue as that of the world" ("Notre corps ... est fait de la même étoffe sensible que le monde"), he writes, defining the aesthetic act through the study of Cezanne's painting or Claude Simon's writing as the evolving exercise and speech of this reciprocal sensibility between body and world. In Merleau-Ponty's later thought the phenomenological osmosis between the condition of reflection and the impersonal apparition of things in themselves becomes a "chiasm" made of flesh.[8] Another important corporeal approach is Kristeva's poetic and linguistic psychoanalysis. In her latest books on Proust and Colette, Kristeva traces different psychic-semiotic histories of the conjunction between sensations and words, impressions and expressions, which becomes both an image incarnate and a style composed of affects. "Writing is an interpretation of language and the world, style and flesh, which reveals the universe and bodies to her as an 'arabesque.'"[9]

Deleuze's ontology continues this effort of psychoanalysis and phenomenology. He returns to the Stoics with the purpose of defining the world as *physis*, constituted of corporeal encounters that are indirectly instrumental in yielding an incorporeal production of sense, sounds, and signs of language. Deleuze suggests calling the *event* the virtual limit that projects language from bodies and makes it act upon bodies. In other words, the event incessantly interweaves actual bodies with linguistic emission by underscoring the difference that makes them converge. Words and things are, in this sense, in an unstable relationship, an asymmetrical tension that is responsible for their becoming individuation. Unlike Heidegger's hermeneutic convergence or Merleau-Ponty's aesthetic phenomenology, Deleuze follows Foucault's view regarding the struggle between saying and perceiving: "What we see never resides in what we say."[10] This fundamental inadequacy, which is one of Foucault's methodological principles in the effort to uncover an epistemological archaeology, receives an ontological groundwork in Deleuze's notion of the event. Being is the elusive liminality that passes between bodies and language, *physis* and *nous*: it supposes a creative multiplicity of discursive production and applies to the multiplicity of bodies' becoming. In this sense, the text of literature is no longer perceived as the discursive investment of the subjective sensibility or as the forceful imposition of the object's presence. Neither the author's nor the thing's corporeality is responsible for *signing* the text: neither the duplicated reflection whereby the subject performs his objectified possibilities nor vice versa. Rather, it is a third entity, a movement of becoming that runs between subject and object in an autonomous direction that tends to deform both by dispersing them into an unstable network of corporeal forces, affects, and percepts, an unstable network that brings itself into existence in the text as other. The literary text, on this view, is not the simple inscription of this force field; it is rather where this corporeal disposition demands to elaborate itself through text. The *corporeal* constructs itself through the *resistance of writing*, not only because real action or passion does not easily transmute into semantic signs and symbolic figures in the linguistic texture, but even more because the act of writing is differential in itself and thus resists transparent representation or judicious recognition. In other words, the materiality of syntax and composition sharpens and reveals the combined forces of the corporeal, but it also invokes "mistranslations"[11] which are essentially imaginary and which transcend the immediacy of the corporeal by enjoying a state of *incorporeality*.

This onto-poetic vision of multiple combinations of corporeality expands itself through the creative laboratory of art as an unsettled machine of sense and as a sort of virtual life energy. This machine of sense and life-energy produces the text from its middle position between the body's urgent proximity and the neutral distance of words' ideal vibration. This is how we might define the specificity of literary discourse: literature has to touch the living corporeality of the ontological event, but it does so only by passing through the incorporeality of that which presents itself by absence, namely, the *word-image* or the *image between words*. Composing itself by means of an incorporeal *word-image* or *image between words*, literature becomes vital only when it succeeds in penetrating the corporeal disposition that beckons it; otherwise it will fall prey to the total abstraction either of a language that elusively vanishes like music or of the pure *logos* of the eternal Idea.

The corporeal, following the above-mentioned definition, is the raw there is *(il-y-a)* of life that eludes all linguistic operation. In this sense, the corporeal as the impossibility of all language runs counter to Hölderlin's and Heidegger's conception of language in its very being as that which makes possible human inheritance as such; Derrida puts this conception even more illuminatingly: "we inherit language in order to be able to bear witness to the fact that we are inheritors, that is to say, we inherit the possibility of inheriting."[12] If this is the case, then one might argue that as a rule we inherit our body without language or that essentially *we do not inherit our body*, taking into account the problem and risk this formulation presents with regard to biological heredity and genetic science. We do not inherit our body like we inherit language. In this view, we are non-inheritors in our very being, because the corporeal does not make it possible for us to inherit or to pass on through inheritance; instead, it makes inheritance uncertain and necessary by installing the irreducible law of what is incessantly there as the impossibility of inheriting.[13]

This is why a work of language cannot have the quality of "poetic-fictional literature" unless it strains to appropriate the corporeal as its in-appropriable necessity and uncertainty. While language is fundamentally historical, a historical work of testimony, the body is the abyssal present of history; the body produces the ahistorical event in history, extricating history from its own course, from its dis-course, and giving it a carnal necessity in return.[14] Considering that neither writer nor reader inherits his own empirical body, considering that each is condemned to the eternal solitude of his own living body, literature forces them not to find a substitute habitat in a spiritual body made of language, but rather to become the offspring of the event that passes between the corporeal and language: to inherit the senseless energy of the corporeal that acts on the work as language exceeds its own purpose and deforms all proprietary experience. Blanchot becomes Deleuze becomes Bousquet or Klossowski.[15]

A Theory of Literary Events: Nine Principles

Taking up Deleuze's conception of corporeality and the question it poses to modern literature, the main question of this study can now be finally raised: What precisely is the literary event, and how can we define it in its broadest sense? Placing the concept of the event as its central problem, this approach to literature attempts to examine the dynamic entity that pertains neither to the immanence of the text nor to what transcends the text. In this view, the event serves as a third position that makes it possible to observe and produce the articulation between the textual and the corporeal. The main critical process consists in following the happening, blending the poetic-fictional creation with the vitality of the corporeal. The event is the mutable thicket that combines the imaginary matter of art with the living reality of forces and impulses. The literary critique of the event essentially asks: What is it that singularly takes place between a given moment of verbal creation and the forces of life? What takes place between them that focuses our attention to an energy of becoming that accumulates and accelerates its necessary animation through an uncontrollable investment in the creative gesture?

This series of questions allows us to begin looking for and through the criticism of the event. Indeed, this is where we have to begin so as to gain full access to the literary happening. The theory of literary events looks for an in-between position as its *FIRST PRINCIPLE*. This unstable position between the textual and the corporeal launches the interpretative process from neither inside the work nor outside it, and it does so by revealing neither the narrative and poetic structure of the event nor the psychohistorical or sociohistorical signs of representation. It is not a question of an all-out denial of the acknowledgeable information and the anecdotal layout that appear in the course of reading. Paying attention to the protagonists' actions and passions and to the reconstruction of the moral conflict and lesson are important aspects of the literary experience, but one has to momentarily suspend these in order to prevent one's own presumptions from getting in the way of the openness of the encounter between the realm of language and the corporeal exigency.

Admittedly this is a somewhat naive, intuitive, or descriptive method. It supposes a phenomenological suspension as its *SECOND*

PRINCIPLE. The suspension of all general rules and judgment, all original intentions or ideological aims, all semantic and historical references, allows the reader to read closely and therefore to become directly involved in the singular movement of the work. What motivates this suspension is the reader's need to immerse her- or himself in the work's own language and images. It is, hence, the theory of literary events' THIRD PRINCIPLE to recognize the work's particular rhythm and mood and to penetrate the region that can be named the "temporature" or the "temporament" of the work. One has to focus on the way the work deeply strikes, before the work of interpretation starts conceptualizing or codifying its context. "I think we ought to read only the kind of books that wound and stab us," Kafka writes; "we need the books that affect us like a disaster, that grieve us deeply."[16] In this sense, each reading intervention bears out that there are primary creative elements in the work of art that exceed all conscious understanding on the part of both reader and writer. Each reading is singular insofar as it always again poses the question to what extent the work renews itself, what is the virtual capacity of the actual work to create itself "out of" its creator's protection and "out of" the finite reality in which it was conceived or is being received.[17] In other words, the work has a time of its own in which there is no stable present, but either a past in which it was already made or a future in which it is always about to be. These precisely are the qualitative seeds of the work's sense, and their multiplicity is merely a "disposition towards openness" that goes beyond any quantitative meaning suggested by different readers in various historical situations. As Barthes writes: "The work is not surrounded, designated, protected or directed by any situation, no practical life is there to tell us the meaning which should be given to it: its ambiguity is always pure."[18]

This intuition must be taken into consideration when choosing to focus on a *fragment* of the work. As a FOURTH PRINCIPLE, this act of criticism must pay attention to the particular passage it selects from the entire work. Like the attentive scrutiny of a detail of a painting or a photograph, microanalysis has to lift out a creative problem and present it as a singular case study of "plot-less deviation" and "fictional distance." What is at stake is not the entire structure of the work and the characters as its operative agents, but rather its outer limits, the moments in which its organization reaches its limit, touching upon an immensity that makes the part larger than the whole. Proust's detail of Vermeer's *petit pan de mur jaune* is a major example of this. Daniel Arasse's *Le détail* and the subtle observation of the punctum in Barthes's *Camera Lucida* both elaborate on the nature of the detail: "The detail which interests me is not, or at least is not strictly, intentional, and probably must not be so. . . . A detail overwhelms the entirety of my reading; it is an intense mutation of my interest, a fulguration. . . . This *some-thing* has triggered me, has provoked a tiny shock, a *satori*, the passage of a void. . . . [W]e must speak of an *intense immobility*: linked to a detail (to a detonator), an explosion makes a little star on the pane of the text or of the photograph."[19]

When the detail appears immediately and sharply and yet lacks both sign and name, it calls upon the reader to engage in the work's continuous production of sense. As such, the necessarily confounding vertigo of the detail (here the textual fragment) encounters the reader's free decision to choose and to interpret it in order to observe its "writerly" nature, as Barthes puts it. Similar to the musical interpretation of preexisting musical creation, the reading becomes a rewritten work on an earlier work. It consists of an active intervention in the textual fragment itself, quoting and improvising its own elements, which can eventually lead to the production of a different variation on the event, although here, in the case of the literary event, the variation develops on the basis of a missing theme, on a lacuna or hiatus. Hence, as scientifically problematic as it may seem, the FIFTH PRINCIPLE of this approach consists in abolishing the distance between object of study and mode of examination in order to be swept away by the work's call for creation that erupts in these moments of immensity. As long as the literary event haunts the reader, he bestows new figurative and linguistic variations on these *holes* and *edges* in the work, and thus the extent of the interpreter's involvement in the weaving of the event itself becomes manifest. As Blanchot writes: "It would seem, then, that to read is not to write the book again, but to allow the book to be: written—this time all by itself."[20] One may argue even nowadays, idealistically or indeed foolishly, that the literary event, while depending on the cultural realizations of textual transmission and exchange, has its own phantasmagorical destiny, its own rhythm of haunting those who read and write, as it divides or spreads itself, expanding in time before disappearing into oblivion.

These descriptions illustrate that the theoretical assumption of the literary event follows a modality of becoming that runs counter to a passive state of being that would be amenable to generalization. The necessary encounter between the linguistic and the corporeal does not amount to a permanent structure, but rather leads to a variable, dynamic relationship between incompatible elements: words and things, syntax and action, discourse and occurrence, language and bodies, style and life. Indispensably, the creative event feeds on both the one and the other, yet it will not wholly and exhaustively amount to either one of them. However, because the event is defined here as textual, the method of observation that seems adequate is a close analysis of the actual elements presented in the text. It is only through reference to the textual matter that something about the event's sequences and development can be said, before other data and knowledge become integrated with or imposed upon the act of criticism. In other words, the earlier-mentioned suspension of judgment (the second principle) can succeed only if one adopts the immanent developments of textual criticism itself. One can use Genette's narrative axes (order, duration, frequency, focalization, voice) to construct the implicit order of the event's mise-en-scène. One can have recourse to Spitzer's stylistic analysis in order to observe the recurrent syntactic deviations and consequently the expressive spiritual characteristics of the event. Following Richard's thematic networks, it is possible to expose the motifs that are activated and manifested in the event by way of a sensible experience of a specific being in the world, then to proceed with Greimas's semiotic square in order to discover the deep system of values that sustains the semantic field on the surface. Finally, there is Jakobson's *dominant*, that explains the importance of the event with regard to the work's most fundamental pattern.

These instruments of the structural theory of literature are helpful to scrutinize how sense is produced beyond what the text is literally saying. The structural progress effectively heightens the reader's awareness of the priority of the work's texture and construction. The immanent autonomy of the work not only detaches itself from the writer's conscious intention or the reader's comprehension but also somewhat reinvents both.[21] Nonetheless, it must be stressed that these structural premises are important only if they do not call forth an ultimate conclusion. In contrast with the function that Jakobson attributes to the *dominant*, the event is not a focal element that visibly "guarantees the integrity of the structure . . . not only in the poetic work of an individual artist and not only in the poetic canon . . . but also in the art of a given epoch, viewed as a particular whole."[22] This is where the SIXTH PRINCIPLE makes its entrance: the event is never a coherent structure that states "what there is" in the work of art. The event is not a structure whose deeper values and organization must be uncovered once and for all through an act of semiotic decoding, thereby holding out the promise of a universal groundwork for any unique realization. The event is not a structure on the basis of which it is possible to find, if not things as such, then still the dominant pattern of relations by which the work represents things in the world.

On the contrary, the event questions the understanding of literature by considering the work of art qua movement: not merely a stable universe inhabited by multiple realized occurrences, but rather a mutable universe produced by the contingency of series of events that blend into each other indeterminately. This dynamic vision squarely opposes the static formal understanding of "there is." It suggests examining the work of literature with the intuition that something is always in the process of being made, something is always in between the already-happened and the to-be-happening. From this point of view, the question to ask is not "what is there" but rather "what is happening" in the work of art. The analysis consists in opening the work to its own "living state" (*à l'état vivant*), following Valéry's expression, to observe what becomes when the work is in the making.[23]

It is somewhat obvious to define the literary event as a simple active state of affairs or as a measurable state of change that accomplishes itself in the process of the work, for the literary event certainly has a visible face, it involves an actual performance or a narrative fact, an unbearable revelation and encounter that memorably echoes the importance of the literary episode, as can be witnessed in, for instance, *The Beast in the Jungle*, *The Horla*, *The Zahir*, *Betrothal in St. Domingo*, *Danton's Death*, and *Khirbet Khizeh*. However, these fantastic or historical references can form an event only because they retain a claim to what is still left in a state of virtual change. I call this claim awkwardly "the secret of the being of becoming."

This leads to the SEVENTH PRINCIPLE, namely, that the literary event is a perceptible secret; it is defined here as an absolute though visible secret. "The unreadable is readable as unreadable," Derrida says in this regard, "the unreadable insofar as readable." The point is not to puzzle figuring out its *finite content*, but rather to be struck by its secret *infinite form*.[24] Writers who keep their promise do not reveal their secret in the work; they make a secret of their work, they keep secret, to paraphrase Jean Paulhan. Or, with Valéry again: "The best work keeps its secret as much as possible. It takes a long time before we even suspect it holds its secret" ("Le meilleure ouvrage est celui qui garde son secret le plus longtemps. Pendant longtemps on ne se doute même pas qu'il a son secret").[25]

Sometimes the secret of the event imposes itself as the unique law of the work, as one single extraordinary episode, as can be seen in the genre of the novella. At other times the secret reverberates everywhere to such an extent that it cannot be located anywhere in particular. In the modern novel, for example, the multiple contingent bodies and diverse textual strategies dissimulate the event's secret. "Diversion is its profound song . . . its refusals and its rich negligence," writes Blanchot of the law of the modern novel.[26]

The generic classifications or historical epochs of literature are irrelevant here. Whether it is classicism's concealment of the literary work's technical fabrication or modern alienation and estrangement that lift and thereby reveal its artistic mask, what truly matters is that the secret resists deciphering. Whether it is the transparency and the narrative illusion of prose, the persistent form of an exact prosody, or the free articulation of creative syntax, the secret must emerge as a problem with no solution. Surely one must take into account the generic conventions (the writer's techniques and tongue, his or her discursive modality and tonality), but what is truly at stake here is the moment in which the work of literature creates a burden that becomes inevitable and unbearable. Celan claims that art itself is a problem that can take various forms. The concept of the literary event leads us straight to a questioning of the singularity of the problem of the work and of the way this problem, its very oppressiveness, projects an energetic capacity, an ongoing shifting that eventually renders the finite text of literature as an infinite universe.

Hence, the literary event asks for a certain truth implicated in this textual universe, a truthful entity that, even if it supposes the participation of both writer and reader, is, as such, a symbolic composition of sensations and forces that transcends the grip of any human intention or understanding. Lucian Freud wants to create a painting that enchants like a dream. Blanchot would have said that the work enchants with an inhuman fascination, and Deleuze would argue that the work is singularly impersonal. The theory of literary events furnishes the corporeal ground from which to observe and specify this demand for an ontology of the imaginary. Its task consists in following the intensity of the literary text as precisely as possible by reconstructing from it a mythology of happenings: to draw new configurations of becomings that constantly redistribute the corporeal forces through the motion of style, the virtual living energy through the artistic striving for sense. The theory of literary events is a mythology of happenings that celebrates neither social narrative nor cultural patterns. This ceremony is nondiscursive, because the new configurations of becomings consist of onto-poetic situations that refuse all general archetypes or thematic conceptualizations. And this introduces the EIGHTH PRINCIPLE of the literary event: it involves a mythology of happenings that displays new configurations of becomings.

Indeed, as a perceptible secret, the event seems at a first glance to be a narrative or conceptual figure. The critical act begins by identifying visible stylistic operations or particular thematic characteristics. The event's stylistic or thematic surface cannot initially be avoided, but this only establishes the foundations of its discursive possibilities. Even if we choose to clearly situate the event within a concrete corpus of research, this methodic proposal still supposes that the eventness of the event surpasses its own legible circumference. The literary event refuses to limit itself to the mere representation of a theme or to the presentation of a technical operation. Derrida's reading of Valéry's "Qual Quelle" conducts the same act of refusal. Based on the concept of the *implex*, Derrida defines a theme that resists all thematizing, a *topos* that has no characteristic motifs and rhetoric. Derrida's following words on the implex also hold for the literary event: "the implex is a complex of the present always enveloping the nonpresent and the other present in the simple appearance of its pointed identity. It is the potentiality or rather the power, the dynamis. . . . [The implex] envelops the possible of what it is not yet, the virtual capacity of that which presently it is not in act."[27]

To summarize, it is the vocation of the theory of literary events to open radical moments of literary creation with the aim of exposing an interaction between linguistic manipulations and corporeal forces. This textual analysis initially seeks to re-create a written variation deriving from the real imaginary energy that the work both emits and receives in these moments. We must closely follow what occurs between the artistic material (*matériau*) and the corporeal temperament that traverses it, not in order to confirm the dominant structure of "what there is" in the work, but rather to bring about the reemergence of the event's perceptible secret. Thus we envision a new "mythology of happenings" that asks not simply what happens in the work of literature, but also what is *the un-happening within the happening*. Passing through the "fictive distance" and the "plotless deviation," the happening in the literary event depends crucially on the non-place of the taking place. Yet, paradoxical though this may seem, what does not happen within the happening establishes the corporeal condition of the event. And this, finally, is the NINTH PRINCIPLE of the theory of literary events (see chapter 9, "Writing Corporeally").

8

AIR RAID ONE
Marcel Proust's *Time Regained*

When Proust writes about the air raid on Paris in *Time Regained*, the great forces of war visibly engage in combat with the aberrant forces of desire.[1] In the night of the Great War the narrator unexpectedly observes the Baron de Charlus in a brothel among other eminent men, an honorable deputy and a priest, who pay soldiers to be their sexual objects. The dramatic political situation blends with the extreme pleasure that comes from breaking prohibition. The excitement brought about by the bombing, rather than its danger, inspires the respectable aristocracy with a stubborn inclination to precipitate the *terrible*. Ecstatically protected, the Parisian *mondanité* enacts its denied desire by risking the abolishment of all cultural foundations as it uniquely inscribes the disaster as Sodom, a contemporary utopia of paganism.

In this passage Proust produces a writing machine that integrates disparate elements, combining primitive corporeal necessities with mythical celebrations, cosmological fascinations that are also moral agitations. To put it briefly, here the event is not the fire shooting down from the sky or the bomb dropping on the dark city. The event is not exhausted by the historical moment that transforms the old manners of the world, not even when this impression is reinforced by the audacious and complexly criminal expressions of homosexuality, by the appearance of a new Prometheus attached to the hidden chains of desire. Sexual sadomasochism and illusory joy in the blacked-out city shine a new light on the decency of high society: "it is thanks to vice that virtue is able to live."[2]

The literary event is not simply the actual or narrated happening, though the event has already occurred there, passing through and between the meticulous accumulations of forces that participate in the process of Proust's writing. Indeed, following the thematic torsions, scaling the different discursive levels and taking the stylistic turns, we approach the beginning of the event that paradoxically has already made possible this momentarily singular force field combining lines of perversion, punishment, and love.[3] In other words, we have to look instead for the impulse or the fervor that permanently both organizes and disorganizes this text.

From where should we gain entrance to the literary event? What is the starting point from which we can seek access to the event? Using Heidegger's definition, the threshold of the event is the ontological happening that makes any occurrence possible. Derrida attaches the sign of the *im-possible* to the event's very condition of possibility: "The event's eventfulness depends on this experience of the impossible."[4] Deleuze would avoid the unattainable characteristics of the impossible by relocating the event in the virtual becoming that acts on actual bodies and that constantly passes between them while also being extricable from them.

These general assumptions can be translated into concrete literary critical exigencies. Following Heidegger, the hermeneutic claim calls us to suspect the visible surface of the text. Here the demand is to seek out the conditional process that makes the entire written situation possible, the double movement of covering and uncovering that, while allowing the situation to unfold, prevents it from becoming manifest, like Penelope's never-accomplished weaving. More precisely, we have to read between the lines to discover the mechanism of dissimulation that brings about a new understanding of artistic principles along with a new sensibility regarding the conditions of visibility of artistic phenomena. But this claim or suggestion does not differ from the basic act of textual criticism, which consists of idealism's revealing of spiritual sense or a symbolic, hidden mystery; deconstruction's teasing out conflicting logics between and within texts and subtexts; the implications of psychoanalysis's unconscious; the specific decoding of historical references; the structural examination of the semiotic production; and so forth.

However, Derrida's melancholic gift for the impossible enables the literary demand of the event to be formulated more precisely. To ask *what does not happen or cannot come to happen in the happening* practically means spying on the conditional element of the situation exactly at its limits. To search for what makes the entire situation possible, for the *that* itself of the *that-it-happens*, consists in being attentive to the situation's margins, to its boundaries. This is where the situation reaches its end, where the happening is close to disappearing, because at this point overwhelming surprise governs, the surprise of some "thing" that had to occur and at the same time could not have occurred. What we have to locate are the frontiers, the outposts, the exit gates, and the barriers from which the event arrives in order to let go of itself in the exact moment when it loses itself, in order to deliver itself by discovering its prison. This is explicitly clear in Proust's passage describing the air raid. For example, at the extreme moment where the narrator faces the new machine of war, as if caught in a struggle with a new god—at this moment the threat of the *terrible* thing occurs as no-thing:

> In an instant the streets became totally black. At moments only, an enemy aeroplane flying very low lit up the spot upon which it wished to drop a bomb. I set off, but very soon I was lost. I thought of that day when, on my way to La Raspelière, I had met an aeroplane and my horse had reared as at the apparition of a god. Now, I thought, it would be a different meeting—with the god of evil, who would kill me. I started to walk faster in order to escape, like a traveller pursued by a tidal wave; I groped my way round dark squares from which I could find no way out.[5]

Another place from which the theory of event may take root is a reflective passage in this extreme moment of *Time Regained* in which the Baron de Charlus, the modern Prometheus and the "last man of Pompeii," becomes the *non-writer* of the narrator-writer's book. This is not only because Charlus is the one who prophetically gives the name "Sodom" to the present situation of the war, understanding that the disaster *will already have taken place* and foreseeing the fire that is about to destroy both Body and City.[6] Charlus is the *non-writer* of the book no less because he lacks the writer's vocation. This then leaves him, all the same, the absolute other who haunts the writing, as he possesses the key to the violent emotion to which the writer aspires and tragically lacks.[7]

> I said to myself: "How unfortunate it is that M. de Charlus is not a novelist or a poet! Not merely so that he could describe what he sees, but because the position in which a Charlus finds himself with respect to desire causes scandals to spring up around him, and compels him to take life seriously, to load pleasure with a weight of emotion. He cannot get stuck in an ironical and superficial view of things because a current of pain is perpetually reawakened within him. Almost every time he makes a declaration of love he is violently snubbed, if he does not run the risk of being sent to prison."[8]

Deleuze's essential contribution to this critical move is the relocation of the liminal entity. Deleuze draws attention away from the perspective of negative transcendence toward an immanent affirmation—from the aporetic aspect in which the situation takes negative possession by becoming deprived of what is beyond it, toward the co-existent virtual action on the other side of the actual situation of things. Compared to the impossible, the virtual act of difference already inheres in the factual concrete happening. The actual is, so to speak, prior to the virtual, although, paradoxically, the difference of the virtual conditions the actual. What is at stake here is no longer the vanishing truth of the other but rather the other's real naked certainty, which cannot be thought out of the actual case, though it can never be completely reduced to its present disposition. This is what I meant earlier by asserting that the literary event already resides in the historical or narrative context in which Proust articulates the air raid and the brothel. Only now, with Deleuze, the event's characteristics of conditionality and liminality are enriched with the idea of the pure physics of becoming.

In terms of literature, what the critical reader has to pursue is the movement that passes through and between the distinct states of affairs. The becoming is therefore virtually already present, constantly attracting new forces and agitating old ones; it is this intensive movement that produces the specific force field. The becoming already occurred insofar as it presents itself as pure deviation and mutation, as the historical "non-place." It is real and imperative enough to maintain the struggle between live forces, but only if it presents itself as their "non-relation," as the undetermined entity that keeps them under the same fertile pressure.

This is exactly the mission of a theory that examines the literary event: to invent a figure and language for the text's becoming in order to be caught up by the event's violence and its creative vitality. What Deleuze teaches us is that the figure and language of the text's becoming can only be forged from the corporeality of the happening itself, as if the differentiation of pure deviation and mutation is inherent to the corporeal condition of the event. It may be better to say that differentiation works from beneath or behind (*en-deçà*) the impersonal distribution of the corporeal. Differentiation is the qualitative limit that traverses bodies and is responsible for their proper transformation once they enter into negotiation with other bodies. Hence, becoming winds itself in between; it is the ambivalent attraction between incompatible bodies. But what is more important is that in this irreconcilable encounter becoming spells out the "degree zero" of the event's surface, the "plan of immanence," in Deleuze's terms, of the event: it inaugurates the a-symbolic language of the corporeal and the inevitable vitality of that language for all fictive invention.

The process of entering the corporeality of the event in the case of the episode, in *Time Regained*, describing a sexual encounter during the World War I air raid consists of first observing that Proust establishes a structure of violence organized by the following recurrent positional functions: the violator, the violated, the act of violence itself, and the witness or onlooker. These functions are activated in two settings: (1) the war series: the German aircraft (violator), the dark city (violated), the dropped bomb (violence), and the stunned and frightened spectators; and (2) the brothel series (Jupien's house): the fake gigolo-soldier (violator), the chained Baron de Charlus (violated), the flogging (violence), and the narrator's voyeurism.

Classifying the series is only one part of the process. It is more important to observe what happens between the series that destabilizes the structural schema. This is exactly what the model of the "disjunctive synthesis" allows us to perceive in the singular conjunction between the series: the deafening shooting from the sky is apprehended to blend in with the rhythmic beatings in the clandestine brothel.

Deleuze's model of disjunctive synthesis effectively "guarantees, therefore, the convergence of the two series which it traverses, but precisely on the condition that it makes them endlessly diverge."[9] The "disjunctive synthesis" in this sense resembles Proust's conception of the analogy. This poetic figure is an unpredictable transformation of the world. Although it imposes a certain similarity between different orders, Proust's analogy remains open in such a way that it makes the world appear in the form of variable stylistic "rings." Like ever-expanding waves, these rings swallow multiple orders by accentuating the difference between them and by keeping their relations incommensurable.[10]

In traditional rhetoric, *analogy* refers to a similar relation that combines distinct orders of elements into a new, closed system. For instance, one conventional analogy is that of night falling at the end of the day as life ends in death, establishing an image of the world that is governed by a cyclical pattern. Here, on the contrary, the contiguity between the orders, their "region of indistinguishability," as Deleuze would have said, is not conceived as the harmony that confirms their respective identity. Dissonance, instead, bends them into an arbitrary clash defining them as an "a-symmetric de-territorialization," disorganizing them by expropriating their forces into the "re-territorialization" of a singular event.

Now that the two series of war and the brothel are established, we enter the event that occurs between them, following the becoming that causes them to converge. Now we can start to synchronize the strikes and blows that virtually condition these series, that is, to synchronize the beating of the whip with the dropping of the bombs. Metaphorically speaking, we have to compose a piece of music that uses both the bombardment of Paris and the lashing of the whip against the body of Charlus. The onto-poetic becoming that traverses these series is the becoming audible of their tremorous dissimilitude: how the blast turns into a flogging, how the whistle of devastation repeats itself as a shivering flagellation—how one replaces the other, deviates from the other, or fuses with the other, by superposition and juxtaposition.

Experiencing the creative power of Proust's event means, in this case, accepting the most skeletal foundation of the situation, following the motion that agitates the bodies, entering the encounter's pulsation in which one body imposes its force on the other, as the violator inscribes the violation on the violated body: the German aircraft on the exposed city and the lashing of the whip on the back of Charlus. It is through this reduction of the situation to its corporeal skeleton that the event then acts on the testimonial comprehension of Marcel, the narrator, who remains stunned and fascinated by the voyeuristic spectacle while testifying to the incomprehensible comprehension of what he sees.

The synchronic strikes first lead the reader to perceive how the text traverses the two series, of the bombardment and of the sexual encounter. Each strike acts like a pump, its rhythmic contraction and expansion gather and redistribute images and motifs, allusions and hypotheses that transform the respective singularity of the series by accentuating their tension.[11] Here are some junctions that occur in this process and that simultaneously produce a new machinery of sense and corporeal individuation:

a. Between internal and external space: the labyrinth of the hotel in the labyrinth of the city.
b. Between vertical and horizontal, collective and personal: the dark, exposed city in which the naked, handcuffed body lies prostrate on the iron bed.
c. Between sense experience, noise and eyesight: the sirens, the defense artillery in the streets, which surround the supplicant suffering of the torture scene staged in the secret room.
d. Between cover and uncovering: the exposure to danger by hiding in the oblivion of sexual desire.
e. Between diverse temporalities: the medieval poetic imagery of pleasure that both collaborates with and betrays the hollowness of contemporary reality.
f. Between somatic traumas: war injuries and mutilations are confounded with the bruises and wounds of desire.

All these junctions are summarized in two systems of reference: Paris-Pompeii-Sodom on the one hand and Charlus-Prometheus-catacombs on the other. The first system presents different circumstances of catastrophe; the contiguity of Sodom's fire from the sky, Pompeii's volcanic eruption, and the bombing of Paris by German Gothas renders the violent strikes as moral or divine punishment. By contrast, the recourse to the heroic myth of Prometheus and the free debauchery in the Paris metro, compared to the catacombs of early Christianity, points both to Charlus's sacrifice and his equals' obligation to pay for devoting themselves to the immanent message of the joy and desire of the body. The cynical transgression and the moral perversion not only signal the triumph of corruption and decadence in the old continent but simultaneously reinforce the call for a new illness of love, for the pleasure caused by the pain that belongs to the obscure underground or to the burning fire, to the conflagration.

Insofar as the becoming of the event is actualized in the non-presence of the violation, in the timeless violation, the violated body divides itself into the twofold force of both anguish and joyfulness, "both as 'vice' ('sin') and as punishment," as Genette similarly remarks.[12] Each corporeal striking accomplishes itself as a split: as differentiation and mutation. As I noted earlier, the event as such is the productive modality of being in the making: it happens for the very sake of the happening, "il se produit pour se produire" (Romano). Between the striking down of Sodom and the striking down of Prometheus, between this unhinged substitution and alternation, the punishment of fire from the sky becomes deliverance; the last avatar of the Titan's heroic audacity becomes the prison of "pure matter," like a cursed poet condemned to seek love in shameful squalor.[13] In other words, each flogging of the whip redoubles not only Charlus/Prometheus but also the gigolo-pseudo Morel/soldier, the narrator/voyeur, the real city into a legendary vision, all these internal splits express the characters' feigning of true joy, and their own recognition of being visibly-invisibly chained in the situation.

In addition, when juxtaposed to the other series, this paradigmatic redoubling becomes a syntagmatic sequence, or in Jakobson's terms, metaphorical selection redistributes itself (without order) through metonymic succession and combination. Each falling bomb is incontrovertible proof of the condemnation that paradoxically releases the human condition from the aristocracy's sham decency: both downward to the animalistic celebration in the underground metro tunnel and upward to the radiant exaltation of the consuming fire: to the instinctual occult bacchanalia and to the deadly splendor of enthusiasm.

As these two series of throbbing strikes are brought into synchrony, finally, we cross the "fictive distance" of the literary event. Here the corporeal movement of the happening acts on the linguistic work, involving singular efforts regarding discursive levels and stylistic deformations. It is here that the work of writing may incessantly accomplish what does not happen in the happening itself. One of the final sequences in this scene sheds light on Proust's writing, concisely and easily. Using a condensed, brisk rhythm—a musical score would indicate *vivace* or *presto*—Proust succeeds in combining almost all the elements we encountered in the above analysis:

> It was the same sentiment that made him [i.e., Charlus], every time he arrived, say to Jupien: "I hope there will be no alert this evening, for already I see myself consumed by this fire from heaven like an inhabitant of Sodom." And he affected to be nervous of the Gothas, not that they caused him the slightest shadow of fear, but so as to have a pretext, as soon as the sirens sounded, to rush into the shelters in the Métro, where he hoped for pleasure from brief contact with unseen figures, accompanied by vague dreams of mediaeval dungeons and oubliettes.

> C'est dans le même sentiment que, chaque fois qu'il arrivait, il disait à Jupien: "Il n'y aura pas d'alerte ce soir au moins, car je me vois d'ici calciné par ce feu du ciel comme un habitant de Sodome." Et il affectait de redouter les gothas, non qu'il en éprouvât l'ombre de peur, mais pour avoir le prétexte, dès que les sirènes retentissaient, de se précipiter dans les abris du métropolitain où il espérait quelque plaisir des frôlements dans la nuit, avec de vagues rêves de souterrains moyenâgeux et d'*in pace*.[14]

One can observe the temporal modality of the imperfect tense: Proust's predilection for undefined iteration here interlaces with the unique occurrence described. One can also notice the temporal deictic of "every time" ("chaque fois") in comparison with "this evening" ("ce soir au moins") and, obviously, the alternation between general indirect speech and the specificity of direct speech. These first observations reflect the rhythmic accomplishment of the strikes, their instant determination as well as their indeterminate repetition.

The oscillation between desired repetition and unpredictable attack is succinctly expressed in Charlus's phrase, where the becoming of the strikes is almost noticeable *underneath* the logical appearance of negation "there will be no" ("il n'y aura pas"); of causality "for" ("car"); and of the simile "like an inhabitant of Sodom" ("comme habitant de Sodome"). At first glance, Charlus's remarks seem to be all too paradoxical; to paraphrase them: The air-raid alarms will not be going off tonight because I will be consumed by the fire of Sodom. There will be no air raid tonight, but nevertheless the fire will find me unready. Yet the text suggests that Charlus's remark is a kind of wishful thinking in which "there won't be any alarm this evening" means more likely that the bombing will come as a surprise, without his having the time to escape and to find shelter. More interesting is the fact that Proust inverts the logical relation between cause and effect. Instead of saying, There will be no alarm tonight, *therefore* the fire bombs will take me by surprise, he vaguely subordinates the objective fact of the air raid on Paris to the subjective delirium of Charlus's sexual desire. In other words, he says, There will be no alarm *because* tonight I am becoming a Sodomite, *for* tonight I will undergo a metamorphosis as I am already being beaten on the iron bed.

Here Proust specifically writes that Charlus is "like an inhabitant of Sodom." Use of this declarative metaphor, "like," ironically dissimulates what is truly going on in the brothel. The Sodomite simile veils the violent pulse of the whip lashings in the same manner that the negative statement "there will be no" ("Il n'y aura pas") veils the about-to-drop bomb. One might say that the sign of Sodom is an accumulation: the war becomes a state of mind, a free-floating desire, in the same way as Charlus and his equals are distracted from the imminent physical danger, but because the destructive fire of desire rules, war reappears in a totally new meaning (mythical fascination, theological sin, possibility of pagan fusion, prophetic sign on the wall of the approaching catastrophe, etc.). As if Charlus had said, There is no war outside, for I cover myself in Sodom; I am not in here tonight, because the fire has struck me, like a Sodomite, and if it hasn't, it will hopefully strike me by and by, so that the metamorphosis may finally be completed.

In another passage, Proust literally observes this distraction: "But what mattered sirens and Gothas to the men who had come to seek their pleasure? . . . The siren with its warning of bombs troubled Jupien's visitors no more than an iceberg would have done. Indeed, the threat of physical danger delivered them from the fear which for long had morbidly harassed them. . . . For a few hours now the police would have their hands full looking after something as trivial as the lives of the city's inhabitants and their reputations were temporarily in no danger."[15]

The second part of the passage analyzed earlier, of Charlus's words to Jupien, complicates the reader's understanding even further. The narrator's impersonal indirect speech returns to comment on Charlus's statement: "I hope there will be no alert this evening, for already I see myself consumed by this fire from heaven like an inhabitant of Sodom." However, instead of simply clarifying or supplying additional information, the text now reverses all perspectives as if they were reflecting an inverted mirror: "And he affected to be nervous of the Gothas, not that they caused him the slightest shadow of fear, but so as to have a pretext, as soon as the sirens sounded, to rush into the shelters in the Métro, where he hoped for pleasure from brief contact with unseen figures, accompanied by vague dreams of mediaeval dungeons and oubliettes."

One might say, according to this simple passage, that the literary event unfolds by folding and wrapping itself around itself (*déroule par s'enrouler*), around the same undefined axis. For each one of Charlus's appearances seems to connote elusive signs and unrevealed sensations, due to the ambiguous expressions in this passage: "he affected to be" and "to have a pretext." Thus, the negative declaration "There will be no alert this evening" ("Il n'y aura pas d'alerte ce soir") turns into a waiting for the sound of the sirens, "as soon as the sirens sounded" ("dès que les sirènes retentissaient"); the exposure to the air raid changes into the closed shelter of the Métro. Charlus's vision of being "consumed by this fire from heaven" ("calciné par ce feu du ciel") appears to be the hope to get "pleasure from brief contact with unseen figures" ("plaisir des frôlements dans la nuit"), ashes become "vague dreams," lashings are replaced by caresses and frictions, the Gothas' menace ends in sensual hallucination (in virile sensual torture) of underground "mediaeval dungeons" ("souterrains moyenâgeux"), and, at last but not least, the inhabitants of Sodom transform into a persecuted religious sect hidden in catacombs and, like martyrs, scarifying their lives (*"in pace"*).

Proust's equivocal *logos* no longer dissimulates the twofold striking of the whip and of the air raid: their present synchronization appears complete at last. Now the burning refraction named "Sodom" finds a lawful dwelling place by reversing itself in the dark descent into Hell. This subterranean abode is where the multiple consequences of whip and bomb finally fuse into an original night. The shelter of night offers total deliverance from both physical danger and moral persecution, cleansing both war and Sodomites, as they celebrate the absolute corporeal magma, their corporeal gift and social acceptance, in the dark sanctification and oblivion of mediaeval oubliettes.[16]

> But if some, their fears allayed, remained in Jupien's establishment, others were tempted not so much by the thought of recovering their moral liberty as by the darkness which had suddenly settled upon the streets. Some of these, like the Pompeians upon whom the fire from heaven was already raining, descended into the passages of the Metro, black as catacombs. They knew that they would not be alone there. And darkness, which envelops all things like a new element, has the effect, irresistibly tempting for certain people, of suppressing the first halt on the road to pleasure—it permits us to enter without impediment into a region of caresses to which normally we gain access only after a certain delay.... In the darkness this time-honoured ritual is instantly abolished—hands, lips, bodies may go into action at once.... [This] adds an extra pleasure to the happiness of having bitten straight into the fruit without first converting it with our eyes and without asking permission. Meanwhile the darkness persisted; Plunged into the new element, imagining that they had travelled to a distant country and were witnessing a natural phenomenon like a tidal wave or an eclipse, that they were enjoying not an artificially prepared, sedentary pleasure

but a chance encounter in the unknown, the men who had come away from Jupien's house celebrated, while the bombs mimicked the rumbling of a volcano, deep in the earth as in a Pompeian house or ill fame, their secret rites in the shadows of the catacombs.[17]

Proust's air raid is a brilliant aggregate combining different eyewitnesses and diverse points of view: the transcendent judgment of the superego and the immanent necessity of the libido; the narrator who is personally involved in his passionate voyeurism and the impersonal narrative voice that sometimes comes to tell the happening and at other times comments and gropes for more meanings and consequences. However, according to the present approach, these decisions regarding the writing and composition are necessarily linked to the unsolved problem created by the literary event, that is, the qualitative dimension that keeps the intersection between the real and words in a continual state of potentiality by again and again accomplishing itself through non-accomplishment.

In effect, I suggest that this state of potentiality can be vividly expressed through the violent synchronization between the beating of the whip and the falling of the bombs. Following this formula, both literally and symbolically, each throb and each strike inserts into the event an excess and a lack, creating a type of undefined moment that implies an immeasurable motion: it is as if an alarmed exposure to death marks the text.

Yet the spiritual achievement of the literary event is not guaranteed by the incorporeal distance that the composition of the artistic work imposes beyond the seal of death. On the contrary, what matters is the corporeal proximity of the linguistic work that introduces a chaotic vivacity into fiction. In order to undo words' incorporeal distance, their performative independence or their constative representation, the writing must infuse them with the immediacy and non-sense of living corporeality that produce the event. Traversing this distance consists in embodying the word's image, or the image between the words, not only by appropriating it as an instance of the historical forms of human imagery, as a fictional illusion or as a system of knowledge produced by the literary codes, but also as the experience of an impersonal field of forces, motions, and sensations that constantly evolving and go beyond the focus of human perspective and *telos*.

The poetic production of language must then evoke the conditions of the real within the fictive imaginary—not to separate the real from the image, but to reaffirm the real *of* the image. It consists of being captured by the very distance of the most proximate presence that the event of the work projects: the non-sense of the raw corporeality that bursts forth in each lashing of the whip and each crashing bomb; the undefined call for sense that each strike sounds and tears down into the non-present abyss of the violence: wound more than definitive death, the oblivion within the wounded memory.[18]

9

Writing Corporeally
A Vital Move

Defining the event of literature as *the un-happening within the happening* brings us to a main intersection between a transcendent understanding of the event and an immanent approach to it. The transcendent approach emphasizes the absolute other that engenders the happening: essentially the impossible horizon of the happening or the ungraspable which is always about to occur. The immanent approach insists, instead, that the event is graspable as it takes place, that it is a fact unfolding among or between its declared historical elements, a real undetermined movement of flight, what Nancy calls "the *that* itself of the '*that-it-happens*.'"[1]

To clarify the differences between these two approaches, we will have to schematize further: first in relation to Blanchot and Derrida, and second in relation to the work of Deleuze.[2] Concerning the ideas and images these thinkers employ when they deal with the question of the event, we can say in general that Blanchot-Derrida's way highlights the power and image of death, while Deleuze focuses on the power and image of life. The first two perceive art as a living dead-body, while the latter perceives art as a dying living-body. The former way constructs the problem of the event through the present-absent terminology of different states of death: the corpse, survival, loss, grief, the phantom (*revenant*) and vampires, resemblance or simulacrum. The latter, in contrast, speaks of the event in the terminology of life decomposing: flesh, meat, bones, sensations, intensities, "affects" and "percepts," joy and suffering, illness and the project of health—all these accompany the affirmation of a dazzling becoming.

This difference is remarkably manifest in Deleuze's comment on Blanchot's concept of *dying*. Although Deleuze explicitly avows to develop his own conception of *event* from Blanchot's *dying*, he delivers an interpretation that relates the anonymous effacement of this unaccomplished death to the accomplished naked magma of life, to the joyful and resistant forces of a creative process that is both pre-individual and impersonal becoming.[3] Deleuze finds a constitutive example of the event in Blanchot's concept of dying. Dying is not one event among others, Deleuze writes: "Every event is like death," because dying is a double occurrence.[4] On the one hand, it possesses an aspect that is effectively present and singularly real, a possible aspect. On the other hand, dying, in itself, is impossible, because it is the "non-place" and the "non-identity" that are incessantly *un-happening* and therefore impersonally *unaccomplished*.

Deleuze adds the Stoic distinction between *corporeal* and *incorporeal* to this dual conception of the *possible* and the *impossible*. This new conception allows him a clearer perception of dying in relation to the real state of things and particularly to the living body. Dying acts on the body or grows in the body, not as an obscure state of mind like in Blanchot's novel *Thomas l'Obscure*, but in extreme proximity to a concrete wound or illness. The body concretely personifies the seal of death by showing its devastating power. At the same time, death becomes real as the most distant, the incorporeal par excellence that has no name and no ground. "Yes, dying is engendered in our bodies, comes about in our bodies, but it comes from the Outside, singularly incorporeal, falling upon us like the battle which skims over the combatants."[5]

Sensible of living corporeality and its surplus signification, Deleuze hastily passes over the abstract *eventum tantum* of dying toward the concrete arrangement of battle or war: "The battle which skims over the combatants." Related to a different line of thinking (Heraclitus, Nietzsche, Foucault) from that of the concept of *dying*, the reasons for this new paradigm are easy to observe: the battlefield offers an extensive visible spatiality in which multiple actors take part simultaneously in one greater entity. The war explodes as an absolute historical present:

each soldier empirically participates in it and as such directly contributes to producing it. But the *eventness* of war is nowhere to be found; it remains a neutral, incorporeal, anonymous entity that produces unlimited combinations of personal and collective consequences. A multiplicity of past significations and future actions already exist undefined within the corporeal, present instant of war, in the "will of anonymity" that war inspires in the present of the mortal wound, without ever being simply reproduced or anticipated.

> If the battle is not an example of an event among others, but rather the Event in its essence, it is no doubt because it is actualized in diverse manners at once, and because each participant may grasp it at a different level of actualization within its variable present. . . . [But] the battle is graspable only by the will of anonymity which it itself inspires. This will, which we must call will "of indifference," is present in the mortally wounded soldier who is no longer brave or cowardly, no longer victor or vanquished, but rather so much beyond, at the place where the Event is present, participating therefore in its terrible impassibility. "Where" is the battle?[6]

In addition to the incessant dissimulation of unaccomplished dying, the battlefield unfolds a strategy of eventness that is spatially and temporally perceived, based on accomplished series of occurrences that include repressive violence, wounds, and death. More than to dying's fictitious temporality and the destitution of the self's certainty and truth, war relates the event to the idea of multiplicity, according to which every singular case is necessarily collective and each historical fact applies to productive new aggregates of happenings from other times and other places. Deleuze recognizes the neutrality of war in death, in the lethal wound beyond winner or loser: war rather disperses and extends the neutrality of dying beyond any form of individualization or personification, like a storm or earthquake striking indifferently, beyond good and evil. Yet, with the counter-paradigm of combat, Deleuze's living interpretation of dying leans on two focal points of accomplishment: "There are thus two accomplishments, which are like actualization and counter-actualization."[7]

According to Deleuze, every event accomplishes corporeal actualization (*effectuation*) as well as virtually accomplishing creative counter-actualization (*contre-effectuation*). The actualization of the event is corporeal by definition: an event occurs when there is an encounter between bodies. The qualities and organization of the bodies, their vulnerability and rawness, bring the actual traits of happening to the surface. The latter are reduced to their primitive and tangible condition: when the blade cuts the meat, when the flesh is touched by the fire's heat, or when two eyes meet, a physical process wraps itself in a visual or in sound effects that call for a counter-actualization, for a somatic language and ethical concerns. The substantive notation of the fissure, fusion or friction, attraction and rejection of particles, the conduction and insulation of heat, are the language of the generative corporeal motif, attitude, and relation. Thus the pure energy of life is involved in the event; a supreme sensibility exists in the impersonal entity that emerges from the bodies' incommensurable shock and confrontation.

The creative counter-actualization consists in following this energetic material effect, that is, this physics of abstract action, looking for the linguistic and ethical project of vitality that is suggested by the corporeal actualization of the event. Deleuze does not search for the internal law or the spiritual logic of the actual corporeal actualization. He does not wish to muster the event to the image of human being (Hegelianism). Neither does he leave the impersonality of the event absolutely separate from the real experience, as that which disappeared while appearing, as in the state of grief or promise (Blanchot). Instead, Deleuze suggests that counter-actualization is the process in which the bodies accept the impersonality of the event, as if it were their singular most productive individuation. In other words, the violence of corporeal war, the negation of wound or death, is also the precise point where the forces of life most aggressively assert themselves. The war, which in actuality either occurs on the bodies or happens because of them, becomes vitally productive only when the bodies create themselves in new language and new will through the war's counter-effort. The counter-actualization of war happens only when the bodies reach out to expose themselves to the point of reversal at which war turns into the undefined desiring flow of life that moves through the work of art and resists all atrocity and suffering. This is a point of reversal at which "the wound would be the living trace and the scar of all wounds, and death turned on itself would be willed against all deaths."[8]

What exactly does this reversal mean? It is one of Deleuze's most fervent expressions of an eternal return: the foundation for a philosophy that expounds health from disaster and encourages enthusiastic resistance from self-subversion or deformation. According to Deleuze, any historical event that takes place encloses a non-historical becoming which is in itself the generative movement of happening: a virtual movement of multiplicity, differentiation, or deviation. It is a substantive, undefined movement of proliferation and ramification, though real and unique enough to impose an eruption of life without form, without self and without sense, on the bodies: "It is life which overwhelms me, scattering its singularities all about, in no relation to me, nor to a moment determinable as the present."[9] As long as the bodies can bear this great impersonal force, they can take part in the birth of the event's singular offspring, offering their will and language to the new opportunity of this event. Thus, the counter-actualization of the event indicates the power of the bodies' vivacity beyond the concrete happening in history. Now, inversely, the bodies' intensive will and creative language appear to be the source itself of the event. Their cultural involvement and their productive discourse translate virtual becoming into a new expressive corporeality, a new concrete assemblage of living practices and modes of thinking.

Thus, Deleuze's insistence on the incorporeal corporeality of becoming displaces Blanchot's *dying* into a living de-figuration to come; Deleuze's great interest in hybridization and animality, conceiving as he does of immanent meshes of *bodies without organs*, as in the tearing of Dionysus or Hercules's poisoned robe, is already implicit in this commentary on Blanchot: "This is the point at which death turns against death; where dying is the negation of death, and the impersonality of dying no longer indicates only the moment when I disappear outside of myself, but rather the moment when death loses itself in itself, and also *the figure which the most singular life takes on in order to substitute itself for me*."[10]

Returning to our own concern with the theory of literary events, we can deduce from this last assumption that the happenings in a given work are part of the event's creating for a language and forces to come.

In this sense, the traditional notion of the author as the "father" of the work must be put aside; the author is not even the son of the work, as Bergson or Valéry would have it, because here the work is the production of the event. This is why the work can be essentially qualified as the bodies' struggle to break through historical fact and personal biography to reach the point of reversal at which the surging motion of becoming extends a singular but necessarily syntactic vision along with verbal images, as for example in Claude Simon's *La Route des Flandres*. Thus, one has to perceive the text as a new composition of corporeal forces, sensations and rhythms, intensities and temperaments. One must diagnose the text as if it were a clinical case, a psychosis, in which the mental anomaly creates itself through impersonal language that conveys dying as a unique and groundless promise by turning it into a exigency of will.

Of course, the examination of textual events can be related to the representation of a particular experience; for example, what can we learn from Proust's oeuvre about his personal experience of World War I? The textual event can also testify to how the particular rediscovers its general motifs and themes by the idealistic sublimation of the experience into the images of words and ideas, for example, Proust's new definition of sexuality in the European crisis of World War I. Deleuze teaches us that the inimitable combination between the artistic material (*matériau*) and the forces of life unfolds a source of energy of which both the particular and the general remain ignorant. This is why the work of art creates an "insolvable problem" that continues to impose its urgent difficulties, as we observed in Proust's synchronization between two different series of violation (see the previous chapter).

This is the vital move that the theory of literary events devotes itself to following. First, one has to convert the discursive signs that appear to constitute the activity of man's reading and writing into a map of corporeal entities and relations. Second, through these quantitative corporeal measures, one has to take the risk of approaching the work's qualitative becoming (the virtual of the actual, the incorporeal of the corporeal). Finally, one has to experience the immense stream of life through the text, with the purpose of recognizing the work's law of transformation, the work's engagement in the future offspring of the event.

Such a reading promises a mythology of happenings, events that have already occurred and yet are still to come, a mythology of artistic happenings that extricate the coherent and acknowledgeable historical course from itself and take it toward a different threshold.

If this method follows Deleuze's aspiration to analyze the work of art in the manner of an ethological study of a singular living corporeality, we must always keep in mind the other direction of the intersection, the road not taken, namely, that of Blanchot's and Derrida's fictional writing, which defines itself through the pure death of the body. Already on the question of auto*bio*graphy, Derrida suggests that any "truthful attestation" of a life-happening necessarily implies a fictional effort to make it possible. The testimonial speech regarding my life, *of* my life and *from* my life, seems to enfold another speech, that of auto*thanato*graphy: "*from* my death, *from* the place and *from* the taking-place, better yet, from the *having-taken-place*, already, of my death."[11] This is not a capricious statement. Blanchot's chapters "The Two Versions of the Imaginary" in *The Space of Literature* and "Literature and the Right to Death" in *The Work of Fire* provide solid ground for this argument by developing one of the most important insights on the notion of fiction during the postwar years.

One can summarize Blanchot's thought as follows: Naming is replacing the actual thing with a word. Naming does not simply designate the presence of the thing: it defines the presence of the thing in its absence. The word evolves out of its distance from the thing: first, it is the thing's symbolic substitute; second, it is the cancellation of the thing's existence itself. From Hegel and Heidegger, Blanchot assumes that any act of language witnesses the negation of man's condition of finitude. Language demonstrates the threat of death in a living manner, allows for the spoken things to appear nonexistent and for the speaker to disappear from his or her present reality. Blanchot considers this idealistic negation in the light of different significations attributed to it by these thinkers. Hegel sees negation as *Aufhebung*, the transmutation of matter into the spiritual, as part of the self-incorporation of the conceptual process; it is the way humans control things, that provides the latter refuge in their unchanging idea and essence, beyond the world. Heidegger, and later Sartre, demonstrate that the distance imposed by language is the condition of all understanding, the power of negativity to brings things into the light of day and as a result keeping us attached to the world, not only to things in their functions, but also to the intimate Being of their existence.

But Blanchot goes much further than Hegel, Heidegger, or Sartre. Relying on the poetic inheritance of Mallarmé and the modern perspective of the literary exigency, Blanchot believes that the negative force of a word relates first and foremost to the being of language itself. Literary language is where the being of language affirms itself as an essence; it is where the image necessarily appears as an act of fiction that puts the world into question—the very concept of world, in contrast to Hegel's spiritual *idea* of the world or to Heidegger's genuine openness to the *being* of the world. In this respect, the image of words is not a secondary projection of the substance of the things themselves. It is not a substitute that recompenses the loss of the thing, that which allows of conceiving the thing beyond its present appearance, beyond its immediate use or in its total disappearance. According to Blanchot, the image has no direct concern with the world; on the contrary, it questions "what things and beings would be if there were no world."[12] The image is the fictional possibility of an *other-world*, not simply as an unrealistic universe that will replace the real one, nor as a higher sphere beyond us, but rather as the affirmation of a space that is either a *before-world* or an *after-world*. It is the affirmation of the presence of absence in itself: an absolute negativity that deposits at the heart of being the deceptive principle of the image's dissimulation. According to Blanchot, the negation of the linguistic image is not a definitive death; it is not the dramatic trial of life's end, the nothing that dialectally opposes being. Nor does it concern the possibility of *Dasein* as an authentic figure of subjectivity. Writing leads the writer and reader to the restless power of the impossibility of a dying that is neither the achievement of life nor the coming to rest of death.

How can this conception be more clearly illustrated? Blanchot compares the emergence of the imaginary to being in the presence of a dying acquaintance: at the moment of death the beloved face remains the same, though the anonymity of the corpse is already reflected from the eyes. When the moment of death occurs, the same intimately known room and bed on which the beloved lies also contain the "nowhere," the void, as the suspension of all temporal and spatial markers. With this state of the recently deceased, between sameness and strangeness, between the unique, recognizable person and the corpse which is no-body's, between this man here beside you and the fact that he is no longer here with you—it is with this mise-en-scène that Blanchot describes the mode of being of the image. The image is the unfamiliar that lives at the very heart of the familiar; it is the nowhere at the core of everywhere, the ghostly double, the *Doppelgänger* who exposes the unreality of all that is real, something between Freud's *das Unheimliche* and Husserl's *noema*, but without corresponding to a psychological subjectivity, transcendental intentionality or perceptual givenness of the real world.[13]

The imaginary does not come after the perceived reality: rather, it is the torturous *resemblance*[14] that coexists alongside and within every perception. Blanchot's conception of *resemblance* negates the identical reflection of reality in favor of a *dissemblance* that inhabits the same, like Gide's counterfeit coin and novel. In this sense, the image effaces the real, but animates this obliteration itself. The image is therefore the pure alteration appearing with the double itself, like the vacant and subversive existence of phantoms that haunts the enlightened. Blanchot calls this effect "a language addressing itself to the shadows of events" ("langage qui s'adresse aussi à l'ombre des événements"), "[to] belong to the shadow of events" ("appartenir à l'ombre des événements"), "To live an event as an image" ("vivre un événement en image"):[15]

> To live an event as an image is not to see an image of this event, nor is it to attribute to the event the gratuitous character of the imaginary. The event really takes place—and yet does it "really" take place? The occurrence commands us, as we would command the image. That is, it releases us, from it and from ourselves. It keeps us outside; it makes of this outside a presence where "I" does not recognize "itself." ... Here *meaning* does not escape into another meaning, but into the *other* of all meaning. Because of ambiguity nothing has meaning, but everything *seems* infinitely meaningful. Meaning is no longer anything but semblance; semblance makes

meaning become infinitely rich. It makes this infinitude of meaning have no need of development—it makes meaning immediate, which is also to say incapable of being developed, only immediately void.[16]

However, the appearance of the image as the other of any sense or as the void whose sense resides only in its instantaneous self may problematically lead to a culture of images that is completely detached from the vulnerability of the real body. The image poses the ethical danger of an aesthetic model in which what effectively governs is the distractingly simple fantasy of the "gratuitous character of the imaginary." From a same concern, Barthes writes in *Camera Lucida*:

> One of the marks of our world is perhaps this reversal: we live according to a generalized image-repertoire. Consider the United States, where everything is transformed into images: only images exist and are produced and are consumed. . . . [P]leasure passes through the image: here is the great mutation . . . because, when generalized, it completely de-realizes the human world of conflicts and desires, under cover of illustrating it. What characterizes the so-called advanced societies is that they today consume images and no longer, like those of the past, beliefs.[17]

As shallow and deceptive as it seems, the value of Blanchot's conception of the image, compared to Barthes's observation regarding virtual consumption, is that it is necessarily embedded in a corporeal state, even if it is at the price of the death of the body or the already dead body. In this vein, Genette shows a similar tendency in which the writing of hyperrealism, the "objective literature" of Robbe-Grillet, eventually results in a troubling hallucination. Beyond all human symbols and signification, the insistence on a surface description of things' geometric figures and bodies' gestures, he says, produces a series of repetitive variations, like a musical *reverie* on a painting: "nothing has changed, everything stays the same, but what a vertigo" ("rien n'a bougé, tout en place, et pourtant, quel vértige").[18] Genette comes to the same conclusion: however vigorously the writer examines the presence of the thing, his firm observation is penetrated by the incessant circulation of the same within the other, of difference within the identical, as if the thing were haunted by a different eye or followed by an undefined power of vision. What matters here is not the objectivity of the thing but rather the objective complex of mirrors, the refractive domain of projections, where the different rays fuse and become indistinct: the remembered past with the hypothetical future, sensory perception and delirious phantoms, daytime and nighttime, midday and midnight. The irreducible presence of the thing thus announces the repetition of the imaginary, which, then, grows as an intensive difference. "While searching for . . . a fantasy of integral realism," Genette writes, "Robbe-Grillet makes an involuntary leap to the unreal. . . . [T]his work ends by a strict objective spectacle, and this very objectivity is the reason of its absolute unreality."[19]

Derrida's concepts of *spectrality* or *phantomality* further expand the ambiguity of the image. The neutrality of Blanchot's image as corpse becomes, for Derrida, the image as a returning specter, a phantom (derived from the Greek *phainesthai*, "to appear"; an image more broadly related to the production of art, as a living dead-body, and to the "appearing to vision" of a spectacle). Derrida specifies that once there are techniques of image production, that is to say in our case, techniques of literary image, a visibility not present in flesh and blood appears. The image yielded by such techniques is a type of night vision, says Derrida, incarnated in a "night body" and radiating night-life.

Night vision, in this sense, does not negate sight by day. The specter's appearance is in fact essentially paradoxical: it is neither visible nor invisible. It exceeds all oppositions: between sensible and insensible, alive and dead, being and being-not, in such a way that the figure of the specter takes part in a larger project of *Living-On* (*sur-vivance*) and of *hauntology* which questions the very ontology of presence. The specter is paradoxical insofar as it records and projects a different presence, which is neither already present nor possesses any presence at all. Not only because the image produced in language detaches itself from our corporeal and historical presence, but because the image also takes into account our possible absence in the future. From this Derrida concludes that the image brings the other time of our disappearance into the present of writing. It is not our identical and spiritual reflection, but rather the production of a *dissembling resemblance*, something Derrida names, among other things, a "visor effect,"[20] whose singular apparition, since it contains our not being present in flesh and blood, is essentially a repetition, a *re*-apparition that strikes us as an absolutely new horizon. "Repetition *and* first time," writes Derrida in *Specters of Marx*, "this is perhaps the question of the event as question of the ghost. . . . Repetition *and* first time, but also repetition *and* last time, since the singularity of any *first time*, makes of it also a *last time*. Each time it is the event itself, a first time is a last time. Altogether other."[21]

In general, Derrida conceives of the image as the return from the afterlife, the return of what has already survived our death: our *dissembling-resemblance* which continues to reproduce itself as the distance of our not-being-present within the most intimate experience. From this perspective, the specter is one of the names of the irreducible other—in the Levinasian sense—which is always before us, an anterior injunction that haunts us as the invisible law of any visible act of writing. Thus spectrality displays the way the other inhabits us or the way we expropriate ourselves in the face of this ghostly other—a way that connotes host, guest (*hôte*), and hostage. This is also how Derrida understands the process whereby language affirms itself as the technical trace of inheritance (Hölderlin, Heidegger), not simply as the blind reception of the other's legacy but rather as the translation of an open initiative that is still to come (*un relancement*), bearing witness to the other's language while, deconstructively, being already implicated in a different creative inscription (*iterability*).[22]

This is how Derrida offers us writing-the-image as the invisible that re-appears in every act of vision. The haunting effect cannot critically operate unless language asymmetrically reduplicates itself between the return of the no-longer-alive and the arrival of the not-yet-alive. Caught between life and death, the specter is "dead insofar as immortal."[23] It transcends any act of mourning, of identifying the dead, as well as any eternal and unforgettable proof of life. Thus haunting, as a living abyssal "thing" and as ghostly survival, continues to re-appear insofar as it appears, to re-occur insofar as it occurs, already non-present and urgently to come: "In order for there to be event and history, there must be a 'come' that opens and addresses itself to someone, to someone else that I cannot and must not determine in advance.... Perhaps there is something of the ghost [*revenant*] and of the 'come back' [*reviens*] at the origin or end of every 'come' [*viens*]."[24]

In complete opposition to a Deleuzian theory of literary events based on living corporeality, Derrida and Blanchot open the horizon to a theory of literary events based on a dying corporeality: the work of fiction is a spectral speech, of a body that is the other of any body and hence of an image that is the other of any image. This is how Blanchot and Derrida define literature as the historicity of a discourse that keeps itself always unstable, undefined, since it remains suspended (*demeure*) in the face of "impossible necessary death" (Blanchot). A discourse whose rule is transgression and whose law is the absolute other, it abides (*demeurer*) at the suspended instant of death and at the imminence of being suspended by death (*mourir*).[25]

With this dying corporeality, Blanchot's corpse and Derrida's specter both suggest a model of textual event that can be summarized by the formula of "X without X": an event without event. What does not happen in the happening will be, from this perspective, the passionate passivity of the un-experienced experience and of the *événement en image*.[26] It is the passion of a *dying move* that takes the opposite direction from Deleuze's vital move.[27] "Is not the force that comes from outside a certain idea of Life, a certain vitalism?" Deleuze writes in response, "Is not Life this capacity to resist force? . . . the set of forces and functions which resist the death of man."[28]

Through Nietzsche and Foucault, Deleuze conveys the idea of "vitalism" to Blanchot's and Derrida's concept of dying bodies. Deleuze succeeds to transform the aporia of "unexperienced-experience" into an impersonal stream of life that generates and defines bodies as singular living beings. In this way, actual living bodies, their incoherent divisions and incommensurable assemblages, constitute the real possibility to conceive of the virtual stream of life that passes between or through them as a type of intensive struggle. Blanchot's dying and *événement en image* becomes in Deleuze an energetic event of living affirmation. The event is thus a point of accumulation, an active boundary around which are struggling multiple flows of desire and sensation, different forces and faculties that affirm the qualitative power of the participating bodies.

In this respect, the creation of literature becomes one of the favorite realizations of intensive life events. For Deleuze, literature is an art of language that inscribes, with its sensitive technique and imagery, the most intimate experience of living bodies and the release of the virtual flow of life that forces these bodies to become decentered and deformed. Literature is a counter-actualization in which the eternal return of what differs triumphs with all its multiple forces of alteration and transformation to come. In Deleuze's own words in "Literature and Life":

> Syntax is the set of necessary detours that are created in each case to reveal the life in things. To write is not to recount one's memories and travels, one's loves and griefs, one's dreams and fantasies. . . . But literature takes the opposite path, and exists only when it discovers beneath apparent persons the power of an impersonal—which is not a generality but a singularity at the highest point: a man, a woman, a beast, a stomach, a child. . . . [L]iterature begins only when a third person is born in us that strips us of the power to say "I" (Blanchot's "neuter"). Of course, literary characters are perfectly individuated and are neither vague nor general; but all their individual traits elevate them to a vision that carries them off in an indefinite, like a becoming that is too powerful for them.[29]

A Vital Move

Following Deleuze's thought, I suggest a vital move for literature. I call a *vital move* the process whereby critical reading exposes the unknown factor within the corporeality of the literary event—the process, that is, through which the corporeal becomes a principle of vitality, a living corporeality that conditions and singularizes the event in literature. This is in contrast to any other approach to the event: historical, narrative, clinical, or judicial. The following points describe the vital move:

I consider a move "vital" when it reveals the speed and power of the event's energy of life, focusing on the way this energy unfolds through the participants of the event, inscribes itself on their bodies, and transforms their actions and passions.

The vital move is neither historicist nor essentialist. It is neither a purely historical approach that defines literature with regard to a specific place and time nor an essential one that strives to yield a universal definition of literature. It is true that the singular energy of the textual event is necessarily rooted in history. Written language is, by definition, a historical practice that allows us to configure the meaning of the event with regard to a real reference. Yet as much as the course of happening indefinitely proceeds, the event seems to uproot all existing rules, beyond all present reference and historical understanding. In other words, the deviation from the knowable facts of history defines the event's essentialism. On the one hand, the sense of the vital move is rooted in history. On the other hand, it is its madness and zeal, its ahistorical metamorphosis, through which the vital move's essentialism is achieved.

The corporeal dimension of the event is the content of the vital move. I name "corporeal" the variable factor that characterizes the singularity of the literary event. The corporeal is the unknown element that does not happen in the happening. Similar to the "negative" of a non-digital photograph or the blurred colors in a thermal image, the corporeal testifies to the real and primitive condition of the event and simultaneously remains undefined and irreducible because of its meaningless language. In this respect, the examination of the historical and judicial consequences of the event, its clinical symptoms or narrative evidence, serves only to designate the corporeal while it remains silent as an immanent abyss: the corporeal supplies sense only as the raw material of the event and as its senseless happening.

Reducing the event to its corporeal condition defines the "body of the event." The vital move consists in exposing the "body of the event" in order to reveal the creativity and necessity of literature. Only when literature shows its state of corporeality does the urgent voice of needs and desires reverberate within the distance of the written text as an impersonal creation of life. Writing, then, becomes the vehicle of a real and senseless energy detached from any living experience or narrative protagonist, from any social identity or historical destiny.

What exactly is the "body of the event"? One can distinguish three types of entities that are necessarily active in the body of the event: (1) corporeal substances that participate in the event as its actual cause or result; (2) relations of forces that define the nature of the encounter between these substances, as well as the spatial and temporal relations of the event; and (3) impersonal life energy that agitates in and between the substances as the signature of the event's being of becoming, thus imposing a unique production of writing.

The body of the event is an unpredictable composition of corporeal substances, a violent encounter between incommensurable substances that produces an ongoing state of affairs. Tristan and Yseult's potion in Thomas of Britain's romance, Golaud's murder of Pelléas, Lord Chandos and the agonizing rats, Aschenbach and Tadzio in Venice, and the turbulent duplication between Witold and Frederic in Gombrowicz's *Pornography* are all good examples. Thus, the enforced contiguity of the substances, their complex attraction and repulsion, their dissymmetrical resistance and change create a complex and multiple force field. The vibration of the substances in the text, as language stretches its limits and is charged by this force field, increases the creative speed and power of the event. This is where the undefined energy of life becomes perceptible in the body of the event. This is also how the speech of the being of becoming traverses the corporeal dimension of the event. In this case, the vital move affirms the singularity of the event in its impersonality (1) as the violent "outside" that inscribes itself on the corporeal, (2) as the trial or injunction that the corporeal must bear or confront, or (3) as the call for a metamorphosis that will involve a different production of language and a generative will for life.[30]

The modality of the body of the event is ambiguous: it is both actual and virtual at once. Any actual embodiment of what does happen within the force field of the encounter between the substances testifies to the virtual becoming of what does not happen in the happening. One reaches the virtual becoming only by first considering the actual corporeal situation. Yet the actual situation is already the effect of virtualization that renders the actualization different. For example, the story of Tristan and Yseult takes place in an actual culture consisting of practices and meanings. According to this textual construction, the singular flow of their prohibited desire, its embodiment of love and death, is exactly the virtualization that entails the medieval actualization of the happening in Beroul or Thomas of Britain. At the same time, this virtualization allows for the differentiation of the happening in other acts of reading and writing, such as Bedier's version and Wagner's, among others. In other words, the virtual is first the necessary condition of the event's accomplishment in history, the way the being of becoming acquires a finite configuration in the textual event; second, it is the impersonal stream of life that manifests in the text as a-historical and unaccomplished, as the internal difference that overflows all graspable impression, recognition, or judgment. One can conceive of the corporeal writing of literature, the "glorious body" of literature, as Deleuze calls Klossowski's work, by reference to the process of iterability, in which outside violence inscribes itself in the textual event, as long as the event's law of transformation continues to act in other places and at other times. Virtual inexhaustibility does not occur without the exhaustion of the actual realization.

The ambiguous modality of the body of the event suggests that literature is the creation of a "corporeal language." In contrast with Blanchot, who conceives of the written image with regard to the transmutation of the bodily event of death, the vital move continues Deleuze's effort to situate the image within the living body as the very principle of life. The image made by words is the virtual becoming that passes through the corporeal actualization of happening. This is why the image is necessarily real, dynamic, and alive. It is not the absent phantom of corporeal presence, the anxiety and fascination in face of fiction's vanishing. Neither is the image the symbolic force of the Idea, the threat and chance of the eternal truth of the temporary. In the vital move, the concept of image features as the dissimilar reflection between the actualization and the virtualization of the "body of the event." In this sense, the image of the corporeal is also the translation of its living inexhaustibility. Any determined translation of the corporeal is by definition a senseless movement toward sense that remains a mistranslation because of the in-appropriability of the corporeal.

This ambiguous refraction of the image is at work mainly in the production of literary technique (e.g., in the discontinuous-continuity of the long sentences of Mallarmé's prose, Proust, and Claude Simon).

Insofar as the linguistic image intervenes in the corporeal bifurcation between actual and virtual, any literary act necessarily creates a "corporeal language." As a matter of fact, the vital move seeks literary performance as "writing corporeally." This means that writing becomes not only the vehicle of the undeniable, living corporeality of the actual realization of the event but also constitutes the stimulus that introduces to the real "body of the event" a project of health: the virtual counter-realization that promises a new creation of language and will.

In this sense, the work of writing exceeds the question of the unrepresentability of representation or that of the presentation of the speechless witness (Celan's "Niemand zeugt für den Zeugen"). It is a poetic-fictional effort that indirectly translates the living image of the body of the event. As such, "writing corporeally" has the vital vocation to create distortions of language and fictional detours to penetrate the namelessness and nonlinguistic being of the corporeal through language. The intimate approach of the corporeal is expressed in the reemergence of the distance that marks the virtual image. The pure idea of the corporeal, which can be defined as the immanent abyss of autism or animality, becomes, through the bifurcation of the linguistic image, the impersonal expression of life: the being of the sensible.

This is where literature becomes the productive work of vital energy. The refraction between the real image and the real body shows how the work of literature emerges from the unknown element of *the unhappening within the happening*. The creation of language dis-covers the "body of the event" via the covering of the textual image while simultaneously indestructible, real corporeality gives itself without giving. Both accumulate in the literary event as a vital intensiveness in which the *being of becoming* affirms its a-historical creativity and resistance.

10

AIR RAID TWO

Louis-Ferdinand Céline's *Fable for Another Time*

An uncanny scene of sexual seduction takes place under the menace of an air raid at the end of Céline's novel *Féerie pour une autre fois* (*Fable for Another Time*).¹ Locked in a prison cell, Ferdinand, the character of the writer in this novel, attaches his memories of the Allies' invasion of Paris in the spring of 1944 to his betrayal by his best friend and his wife.² This scene begins by a sudden, brief eruption of the narrative tone, a violent textual crack, and what appears to be present of the writing is flooded by anger and shame. The text seems to be torn apart under the pressure of an ineluctable certainty, as if an unacceptable image has come to mind, already signified and yet still floating without signifier. This is how Céline's music sounds:

> Oh, the brute! Wait! the worst! I'm getting all worked up about it, sitting here on my scabs thinking about it again! when you think about it again! the worst! the very worst! the camel's back! the straw! the dirty low-down trick! Lili! Ole Arlette! Ah, when you think about these dastardly deeds! it was an ambush! the vice of the man! but I have to face it!

> Ah, brute! Attendez! le pire! Je m'encolère là sur mes croûtes de repenser! d'y repenser! Je repense! le pire! le pire! la coupe! la goutte! le turbin! Lili! l'Arlette! Ah! remémorer ces forfaits! quel traquenard! le vice de l'être! il faut! il faut!³

What exactly happens here? What is this unnamed "worst" ("le pire") that must be faced? What is this "vice of the man" ("vice de l'être") that emerges suddenly and pushes the writer's monologue to the foreground? What is this living voice, instantaneous beyond the narrative present, that exposes the writer's rumination and his biographical situation between the walls of the Danish prison cell in 1946? Is this discontinuous writing gesture so unusual because we realize that the writer constantly traverses the distance between the recent past in Paris and the postwar monologue during his imprisonment?

It seems, nevertheless, that an unpredictable force intrudes here reversing Céline's monotony of insults and accusations and radically tormenting the writer's position itself. The writing, in a way, imposes a delay, a respite, a waiting: "wait!" ("attendez!"). Céline orders a stop, whether to alert his imagined interlocutors, to draw the reader's attention, or perhaps to suspend the incessant chatter and rustle he hears in his solitude. "Oh, the brute! Wait! the worst! I'm getting all worked up about it . . . the worst! the very worst!" This sentence acts as a disruption that recharges the text—an extremely fragmented movement on the one hand, an insistently repeated exclamation on the other—that effects a sense of growing astonishment, an accumulation of delirious anger, which with the advent of the "worst" briefly loses all bearings.

This imposed halt seems to promptly offer a new threshold. The temporary confusion must be reactively restrained in order to tell what is precisely at stake here, what exactly troubles the narrator's mind: "Honesty above all! the facts! just the facts! and with Arlette, of all people! Maybe you think I'm being unfair! [. . .] all of a sudden! too bad, I'll tell the whole story!" ("Probe avant tout! les faits! les faits! Arlette pensez! Je pourrais être injuste! [. . .] soudain! tant pis! je dis! toute l'histoire!").[4] It is as if the writer is saying that there is more to tell, more of which even he is unaware; there is a hidden detail that must be clarified, that will change everything. Wait until you hear the facts, and I myself, the writer, will try to suspend my own prejudices. The reader will have to hear the facts before judging who is the real traitor, who is the "vice of the man," who has to languish and die in the dark cell.

Now, it seems, the writer can evoke the happening that returns to befall him; now he tries to let the event speak, even if this event brings about what is most horrible. In 1944, just before the liberation of Paris, why was he banished from his country, and why did he lose his reputation and property and, even worse, lose his wife to his friend, as she, Arlette, also known as Lili "ma femme," offered herself naked to the handicapped artist, Jules?[5]

Once the curtain rises a page later, a painfully grotesque dance appears on the stage. In one or two paragraphs there is a gathering of bodies around a single point: Lili, who descends to Jules's artistic basement to bring back her undisciplined dance students, offers herself as a model for the artist. Down in the street she sees Jules sitting in his wheelchair. Jules approaches her, grasps her thighs, sticks his nose under her skirt, and begs her to pose for him. As he declares his passion, a crowd of people emerging from the metro or descending from the Sacré-Coeur gathers around them, among them Ferdinand, the narrator-character, and if that were not enough, an "aerial combat was going on just then" ("il y avait juste un combat aux nuages"), the Allied airplanes at this same instant appear in the sky and start their bombardment of Paris.[6]

Five corporeal substances feature in this scene: Lili, Jules, the Parisian crowd, Ferdinand, and the airplanes. Céline assembles them in a confrontational relationship and defines the presence of each through their interwovenness. Each of the corporeal substances is bound to the other in a delirious vertical construction. Jules is under Lili's skirt, and above them the stream of people goes up and down the hill, "hordes contre hordes," in a rush either to have a better view of the bomber planes or to take shelter in the metro. The planes surprise the crowd, people are staring upward, "all of them with their schnoz in the air!" ("tous le tarin en l'air!"), shouting and scrambling one on top of the other.[7] Ferdinand cannot see clearly what happens between Jules and Lili, cannot cross through or pass over the multitude, since the couple is covered under the crowd, "packed in by the crowd."

> I look up in the sky . . . I look down on the ground . . . I look under the people . . . I see ole Jules hanging on for dear life under Arlette's skirt . . . Still stuck to her! [. . .] I wanted to get to Arlette! I move three people aside . . . twelve come piling back in! . . . twenty! . . . a hundred! . . . I have look from down below . . . still at it! . . . I see ole Jules! in Lili's crotch! clutching on between her thighs! Jules and Lili, they're packed in I said by the crowd, compact! . . . Her standing straight up . . . him in his gondola . . .

> Je regarde en l'air . . . je regarde par terre . . . je regarde sous les gens . . . je vois le Jules agrippé sous Arlette . . . Ah, toujours accroché! [. . .] Je voulais arriver à Arlette! J'écarte trois gens . . . s'en recompressent douze! . . . vingt! . . . cent! . . . Je regarde par en dessous . . . encore! . . . je le vois le Jules! dans le sexe à Lili! agrippé dans son entrecuisse! Ils sont Jules Lili enserrés j'ai dit par les gens, compacts! . . . Elle tout debout . . . lui dans sa gondole . . .[8]

This sense of a whirlwind, chaos, that begins by rotating in the sky, circling with the planes above Montmartre and down into Lili's sexual organ, runs counter to any realistic aspiration of mise-en-scène. However, more than through visual assemblage, this dreamlike corporeal superposition oddly works by way of auditory hallucination. It is strange to find that in the situation of an air raid, where "the windows screeching louder! louder than the throng!" ("les fenêtres qui hurlent plus fort! plus fort que la foule!"),[9] among all this screaming, howling and bellowing (*beugles*), the voice of Jules resounds above all. Jules's repeated avowals of love are unmistakably articulate as they rise from the pit of the whirlwind and become perceptible in a meaningful way, as if they were not only subjective utterances but constituted an already more primitive echo issuing from Lili's *sexual cave*:

> I worship you! I worship the ground you dance on! clutching Arlette's thighs! under her skirt! I can hear him! . . . Me! I hear him! I get down . . . I see him! He's clutching on under the surge of pilgrims . . . his head under Arlette's skirt. [. . .] I adore you! Do you hear? ole Jules is crying . . . under the skirt . . . between her thighs . . . he was all worked up! kissing her all over! all over the place! I see this!

> Je t'adore! je t'adore! en plein sous le ventre à Arlette! sous sa jupe! Ah je l'entends . . . Moi! je l'entends! Je me baisse . . . Je le vois! Il est agrippé sous la houle . . . sous les pèlerins . . . la tête sous la jupe à Arlette. [. . .]—Je t'adore! je t'adore! que crie le Jules . . . sous la jupe . . . dans l'entrecuisse . . . crispé qu'il était . . . embrassant plein! plein! je vois![10]

Amid the chaotic tremor that starts up between planes and rabble, between the message of the planes on high and the frenetic faces of the crowd below, Jules's voice seems to act as a mythical voice of desire. His voice is like a vibration, a sound wave rumbling from below the earth, rising from the lowest and most invisible ground as if indirectly responsible for the mess above and directly taking advantage of it. But, Jules's calls accompany a gesture: the reason his voice has such an impact is that it is continually bound to the persistent corporeal disposition of Jules's nose stuck between Lili's thighs. The vocal tossing and turning, together with the protruding organs, grotesquely points to a fundamental tendency: the wish that masculine penetration of *the feminine cave* should firmly pronounce, there and then, the law of the event, *the command* of Céline's expulsion: Get out! Ferdinand! Beat it! Move it!

This event in Céline's *Fable* produces the image-sensation of a whirlwind that rolls around a black hole. It is a whirlwind that hides an open cave or that blows from a cave. All excluded creatures are destined to turn and tremble out of the cave in the whirlwind. However, the whirlwind is controlled by the cave. The whirlwind originates in the center of the Earth, not in the sky. The one who succeeds in penetrating the cave gains the power to speak the law and is entitled to restart the whirlwind and make it spread outward. This is a matter of a movement of simultaneous exclusion and inclusion. The storm issues from the booming cave; the *included* one enounces the whirlwind. But, inversely, the storm causes those who are *excluded* to fall back and enter into a reduplicated cave, into the "other cave" which turns out to be the terrible shelter of the outlaw.

What does it mean, here, to penetrate into a cave or to be carried away by the whirlwind, to be excluded from one cave and to fall back into another? What exactly is this cave? Is it a female sex organ, an urban sewer, or a prison cell? Who enters the cave: Jules or Ferdinand; the filthy artist or the pro-Nazi writer, the Kraut (*Boche*)? What is the relation of forces? What happens in the whirlwind that conveys one into the cave and another out of it? Is it the threatened air raid, the manifest betrayal, or the secret collaboration; is it the power of pronouncing the cave's law or, inversely, the profound revulsion (*dégoût profond*) of the one who remains an outlaw?

If Proust's air raid sets into motion a disjunctive synthesis of two series of violations between war and sadomasochism, Céline's creates two distinct series that redistribute their singularities in the respective efforts of exclusion and inclusion. One floating entity traverses the two on the same level as corporeal desire and artistic destination, universal disaster and political fault.

Jules's series is the foreground happening that paradigmatically inverts and syntagmatically ends up in Ferdinand's background series. Jules presents a stubborn movement from outside in: he pulls Lili into his studio and does not allow anyone to disturb his courtship. The more feasible the penetration of the feminine cave becomes, the more control Jules gains, and he commands: "Now beat it! hit the road!" ("Maintenant carre grand enflé! la rue!"),[11] thus provoking Ferdinand's jealousy and the crowd's lust and asserting his artistic authority over Lili: "Go to the back! The back! Lie down!" ("Allez dans le fond! Dans le fond! Couche-toi!"). "I've got to model her" ("Faut que je la modèle"), "I'll do her for you in the oven! And he starts pawing at her again, lifts her behind up, on purpose, so I can see! that he's got rights!" ("Je te la ferai au four! et il la retripote, lui rehausse les fesses, exprès, que je regard! qu'il a des droits!").[12]

Jules transgresses the intimacy of the married couple. Lili, the dancer, becomes inanimate, and Ferdinand, the writer, loses his power to speak, swaying hesitantly now that he has lost his solid position. The narrator's weak attempts to physically separate Lili from Jules, or even to violently attack the handicapped artist, are only the first step before he is finally expelled: "Four times he kicked me out! I couldn't make up my mind . . ." ("Quatre fois qu'il me foutait à la porte! Je me décidais pas . . .").[13] As Jules gets inside and Lili gets undressed, Ferdinand moves away. This is the visible course of events. Ferdinand may be a political traitor, but his friend and wife betray him artistically and personally. Ferdinand moves away not only from Lili's body and out of Jules's studio: he moves *out* in the fullest sense of the word (from "the other door").¹⁴ He falls prey to the chaotic whirlwind, out of joint, out of place and civilization, out of his human body, without any right of existence, remaining a sort of hunted animal, left to rot in the Danish prison cave.

Jules's intervention at the very instant Céline's living situation becomes precarious due to the Allied approach complicates the historical position of the writer. A phantasmatic disorientation subverts the writer's voluntary actions and opinions. Jules takes the political contrast between Ferdinand's treason and guilt and his claim that he is being innocently persecuted to a carnal level. The personal threat of losing Lili to Jules completely blurs the distinct values of Ferdinand's political alternative: the fact that he is either guilty or innocent for having collaborated with the occupying regime. Now, the twofold movement of exclusion and inclusion, which seems to organize the event, eventually questions both the origin of exclusion and the aim of inclusion. Rather, the movement of exclusion returns as inclusion: Jules's inclusion entertains a secret and strong agreement with Ferdinand's exclusion. This scene introduces a primitive conflict and adds a fictitious dimension to Ferdinand's destiny.

Let us read this textual event more carefully. One can distinguish three recurrent expressions of Jules's movement of penetration: the diverse insinuations of masculine force, the gradual discovery of feminine nakedness, and, more generally, Jules and Lili's search for a secluded place that will protect their encounter. First, the protruding organs, long and pointed instruments, evoke, initially figuratively and later literally, the phallus. We have already witnessed Jules's nose inserted between Lili's thighs in the opening scene: "le nez profond entre ses cuisses."¹⁵ In the studio, Jules asserts his force with his iron crutches or sticks, which he uses to threaten the eager crowd if they do not get lost.¹⁶ A similar struggle, this time with a fire poker, takes place between Ferdinand and Jules; Ferdinand does not wound Jules, while Jules comically threatens to gouge out Ferdinand's eyes.

> I get hold of his poker! I grab it good! his iron bar! . . . for poking the fire! [. . .] I don't want his goddamn poker! So he grabs it!

And he starts to threaten me! He makes believe he's gauging [*sic*] my eyes out!

J'attrape son tisonnier! je l'empoigne! son fer . . . son pique-feu [. . .] J'en veux pas de son fer! C'est lui qui l'empoigne alors! Et il me menace! Il fait semblant qu'il me crève les yeux!¹⁷

Finally, the confrontation resolves when Jules raises his hands to unmistakably suggest a "rigid pecker" ("Braquemart tendu") while seeming to indicate the projected size of Lili's sculpture at the end of the craft process. Though ludicrous, the rhetoric leaves no doubt. Henceforth, the symbolic possibility of Jules fornicating with Lili haunts Ferdinand, already as evidence:

And I'm not jealous! and he made Arlette come on me, I wasn't there but I'm sure of it! . . . I'd rather not look into it! [. . .] they would have come, all right, the pair of them . . . They were asking for it . . . they wanted to finish off . . . they'd provoked me enough! . . . [. . .] It's the way he fondled her I can't get over . . . That's what it was . . . the way he fondled her! . . . I was really worked up! . . . Yup . . . really excited! . . . a regular John!

Et je suis pas jaloux! et il m'a fait pâmer Arlette, j'étais pas là mais je suis sûr! . . . J'aime mieux pas approfondir! [. . .] [I]ls auraient joui tous les deux . . . Ils demandaient . . . ils voulaient finir . . . ils m'avaient assez provoqué! . . . [. . .] Je suis resté sur les caresses . . . Voilà . . . voila! . . . sur les caresses! . . . J'étais excité comme tout! . . . C'est tout . . . excité! client!¹⁸

This is not merely symbolic mistrust. The louder and more decisive Jules's orders become, the more wantonly Lili abandons her body to the artist's hands. And thus the corporeal detail becomes linguistically exposed and the walls of the cave reveal themselves as naked, spread legs. If initially Lili seems hesitant to take her clothes off,¹⁹ Jules insists: "Come on! take off your clothes!"; then: "Lie down Arlette! Nice and long!"; and soon after: "Spread them! Spread them wide! [. . .] There you go, kid! So I can do this modeling right!"²⁰ Once the touching begins: grabbing, pawing, rubbing (*à plein bras*), with Lili cheerfully laughing like a "flopping fish" caught on the folding bed, Ferdinand grows convinced this is not only a question of aesthetic beauty but of admiration, even of love ("so it was love").[21] Silently, he admits that Jules "got rights" ("qu'il a des droits") on Lili and leaves the room, and as he watches them together through the window, he remarks that they must have plotted together or "have an understanding" ("ils sont d'accord"). At this point Lili is naked, but it is no longer her proper body, the pure dancer's body, but rather an artistic and sexual object, fleshy colors, lights in the darkening studio that expose the unbearable shame of prostitution: "there she is again under the gaslight . . . thighs open . . . the tits . . . throat . . . shoulders . . . it's all green . . . blue . . . and a little pink . . . flesh."[22] "[H]e got her all worked up! she caved in! [. . .] Ole Arlette posing starkers, thrown on her back on the folding bed! pussy wide open!" ("[I]l la émue! elle a fondu! [. . .] L'Arlette à poil posante renversée sur le lit-cage! la chatte ouverte!").[23]

This is what remains of this scene ("the "remainder"). This is what, ghostly, revisits Ferdinand's mind in the other dark hole of prison. What troubles him is not what he has witnessed but rather what he has not seen, the possible facts that begin to proliferate after his departure, the happening of his absence. Thus, the evolving seclusion of the happening, the couple's enclosure behind the locked door, in the old kitchen where "no one could see from the street," constitutes, paradoxically, the visibility that obsessively enlightens. "I wasn't there but I'm sure of it!" Ferdinand confesses. "I'd rather not look into it" ("J'aime mieux pas approfondir").[24] The *never seen before* (*le jamais vu*) is always the *déjà vu*. This is the no-body of the body, the *black hole* of these bodies, that re-creates them differently from Jules's studio to the prison cell, from one cave to another. This is Lili's statuette, incompletely modeled in Jules's kiln, infinitely molded in the dark fire of the artistic oven.[25] That is to say, it is the confabulated, lucid presence of Lili's nudity, "thrown on her back on the folding bed," suggesting the presence of someone else.

"I rehash memories in my head [. . .] I keep thinking about that . . . they were in it together" ("Je remémore [. . .] j'y pense . . . j'y pense . . . ils était complices").[26] Beyond the evident psychological elements of jealousy, involuntary memory, and the active force of the imagination, the problem that concerns the theory of literary events in this literary text is, Precisely what happens between the studio and the prison?

How does the invisible, reclining feminine nudity finally unfold in the animality of the sexual organ (*la chatte*, pussy)? Why does the openness of the vagina resonate between the walls of the prison cell? Why do this vivid animality and fiery artistic oven redouble or burst out in another cave?[27]

Gazing and hearing play an important role in this different-repetition between caves. Céline's senses do not only passively receive and control impressions. The senses are always irritated; they are persistently fascinated by noises and frenetic excitations. They are constantly overloaded, always too full, yet this does not lead to synthetic understanding and decisive, active experience. This mere reactivity of Ferdinand's usually amounts to a repetitive, carnivalesque inventory of insults or of unaccomplished cruel wishes. At times he even forces himself to act against his own reason. It can only be due to fear and uncertainty that Ferdinand has been reacting like this. This fear and uncertainty in the face of violence, this mistranslation of practical judgment, only makes things worse. One could say that the noise and commotion continue reverberating through Ferdinand's body, taking advantage of his perplexity, attacking the senses, as if gazing and hearing were still at work, as if their fullness were showing right through their deficiency.

By locating this gazing in the text, we can observe how the narrator's violent awareness goes hand in hand with the helplessness of his literary character. Ferdinand always considers the destructive trap with a sort of passive fascination. For example: "He was ordering her! I *watched* him [. . .] She hesitated . . . and I could *see* that [. . .] he was hoping it would all turn nasty!"[28] Jules's authority only grows stronger as a result of Ferdinand's silent staring.[29] This is perhaps why the gaze itself, not only the image of betrayal, is rendered in writing years later in the prison cell.

The gaze is, however, limited: the furthest Ferdinand's eyes are able to see is the understanding between Jules and Lili at the very moment of his exclusion and departure. "[Jules] didn't want me to leave until I saw that they were in cahoots" ("que je parte pas avant de regarder qu'ils étaient d'accord").[30] More than the testimonial gaze, it is hearing that conveys a stronger sensation of *what does not happen in the happening*.[31] Jules's deliberate orders in the studio continue spinning in Ferdinand's ears and set the event's whirlwind into motion. Ferdinand confesses, "I reflect with my ear always cocked, glued against the marble, I hear everything! I rehash memories in my head" ("je réfléchis l'oreille à l'écoute, collé contre le marbre, j'entends tout! je remémore"): he has glued his ear to the prison wall to recollect how Jules gained Lili.[32] The sense of hearing is more abstract and primitive than vision, and Ferdinand "hears everything": not only Lili's laughter, Jules's insults and orders, and Ferdinand's own humiliation, but also the way he himself abandoned Lili, the way he made her suffer later on. He hears the air-raid sirens, their troubled whistle, ringing in his head; he hears the other prison inmates screaming and the accusations and verdict at the French court of law. All these voices that ambiguously suggest what actually happened after Ferdinand left Lili and Jules alone.

In this event, sense perception is always bound to ethical doubt. Ruminating gazes and resonating voices engage in a systematic act of judgment, of collective values. Ferdinand's sense of being betrayed combines with contradictory streams of sensation dominated by guilt and innocence, persecution and rage. Céline passes through Jules's betrayal to reach Ferdinand's own political and personal guilt. Is Ferdinand a "nasty pimp" encouraging Lili to model for Jules "in payment for her thighs and her hole"?[33] Is he an anti-Semitic "killer" and a collaborating "Kraut"? The arrival of the bombers and the threat of lynching by the hostile mob confirms the narrator's treason. "He [Jules] knew what he'd said! that he'd pointed me out as a traitor! handed me over! [. . .] [T]ell it like it is . . . let's have a rethink . . . I was the one whose blood they were out for! not him! . . . I was the one to blame for everything!" ("Il s'avait ce qu'il avait dit! qu'il m'avait désigné traître! traité! [. . .] [D]isons les choses . . . repensons . . . c'était moi, la curée! pas lui! . . . tous les torts moi!").[34]

At the same time, it is Jules, the one who cheated Ferdinand out of his dearest, who handed him over. The cheat denounces the traitor; the opportunist takes advantage of Ferdinand's "idiotic and patriotic escapades [frasques]." These are not extenuating circumstances, though; on the contrary, Jules only increases Ferdinand's guilt and helplessness as he faces this private pillage. Exposure of Ferdinand's treason blends with the giving up or handing over of Lili to another. From that moment, what is left is only the suffering of an approaching massacre, a flight like that of a hounded animal: "[T]hat we were hounded, I can safely say so wretchedly hounded, worse than animals! . . . not for a month! . . . ten months! . . . ten years!" ("qu'on a été de ces traqués, je peux dire traqués si malheureux pires que bêtes! . . . pas pendant un mois! . . . dix mois . . . dix ans!").[35]

There is no clear distinction here between collective treason and personal shame, between declared political engagement and undeclared self-ruination. All these conflicting languages issue from Ferdinand's flesh and blood, as if he is simultaneously fleeing from his own state of horror and caught up in his own trap. This is the whirlwind in which he is spinning: "the tornado is launched."[36] An intermeshing of appellations signals his coming individuation: he is the "Judas-in-Chief," the "Shame of Montmartre," the "Exterminator of Paris," along with "haunted quarry" ("curée") and "hounded prey" ("hallali"). He is the "natural-born pimp" ("broche"), a "big dope" ("nave"), "the unspeakable" ("l'immonde"), "the worst kind of dunghill Kraut you can dream up!" ("le plus fumier numéro boche rêvable croyable!"). Ho! He is lamenting his "turpitudes" ("turpides") and "escapades" ("frasques"); the suffering he causes Lili without being deserved.[37] And still: "Me, they took everything from! my shirt! my hide! my years! . . . my manhood!" I can't get it up anymore!" ("Ils m'ont tout pris moi! ma chemise! ma peau! mes années! . . . ma virilité! je bande plus!");[38] "my body's shot! . . . the soul, too, almost . . . The world has been too cruel" ("j'ai plus de corps! . . . presque plus d'âme . . . Le monde a été trop cruel").[39]

This is the whirlwind in which Ferdinand gets caught up: torture, vertigo, collapse, until he falls into the other cave of the prison hole. Jules gradually enters between Lili's thighs, while inversely Ferdinand is being expelled from the cave, cast out into the storm. "Get out!" Jules shouts to Ferdinand: "Go on! Scram! Beat it!" ("Allez! Allez! Carrez! Carrez!"); "Fuck away off with you!" ("Fous le camp! Fous le camp!"); "Trot yourself off!" ("Poulope! Poulope!"), "move your ass, you schnook! Move it!" ("Grouille! Grouille! Chnok! Grouille!"). The virulent rhythm of commands urges upon the reader that exclusion does not amount to a mere, local exit into the street but is a type of mythical expulsion, like that of Cain. Ferdinand's deep shame, aware that his treason was denounced and his wife seduced; the effect of Jules's voice as though it was pronouncing a death sentence; the menace of the airplanes from the sky; the evacuation of the streets—all these elements present a solitude and a desolation that are ready for the eruption of the outside.

> [T]he avenue was empty, that's for sure . . . no more cops! . . . Absolutely nobody! . . . Maybe it was an alert after all? . . . but there were alerts all the time! . . . sirens . . . cat screechings in the sky! . . . I had my own noises! my own high-flying meowings! . . . blasting in both ears at once sometimes! high-pitched mewlings! . . . not only just sometimes . . . it could be four hours on end! . . . right in my ears! . . . All the same . . . all the same . . . "To the Metro! Get to the shelter!"

> l'Avenue était vide c'est certain . . . plus des flics! . . . Ah, absolument plus personne! . . . C'était tout de même peut-être l'alerte? . . . mais tout le temps y avait des alertes! . . . des sirènes! . . . des miauleries hautes! . . . j'en avais aussi des bruits moi! à moi! des miauleries hautes! . . . plein les deux oreilles des moments! des miauleries hautes . . . pas que des moments . . . des heures des fois! . . . de mes propres oreilles! . . . Tout de même . . . tout de même . . . "Au métro! Au métro!"[40]

At this moment, *the becoming of the event* strikes, namely, where the event inscribes itself on the body as an impersonal figure, as a violent attack, as an injunction and corporeal metamorphosis to come. This is the moment when "death loses itself in itself," Deleuze says, "the figure which the most singular life takes on in order to substitute itself for me."[41] Céline's mythical tone does not seek the transcendent moral of the storm; the punishment that hits the excluded one holds no interest at all. What fascinates Céline is the way the storm breaks: the chaotic entrails of the storm, its visceral inversion that swells up and pours down in streams of dirt and nausea, sewage and blood, in a violent osmosis between inside and outside. According to Céline's mythical law, Earth is not punished from heaven; heaven does not redeem Earth with the approaching destruction wreaked by the bombs. Ferdinand himself also avows that he does not hear the air-raid alerts. The alerts are confounded, in his mind, with an internal disruption; he confesses that he cannot distinguish the alerts from the vertiginous buzzing in his ears.⁴² This confusion suggests that the storm does not necessarily come from above; that the alerts may involve something else. They render Ferdinand's *state of alert* perceptible and become moreover the impact of Jules's shouted command: "Au métro! Au métro!"

One might say that the sirens in this war event do not warn against the bombers; the warnings point to a different danger. When Ferdinand declares, "I don't see any airplane," he suggests that the danger is elsewhere, that the sky is clear. The war scene, then, is penetrated by another logic: explosion will well up from underground, from the calamity of the cave, not from the sky. This is the first reversal that occurs here: the sirens become the speech of the cave, announcing the explosion of the cave, and thereby affirming the inhuman horror in it. Ferdinand does not simply flee his historical situation at the end of the war; the sirens signal the trajectory of his expulsion, his *danse macabre*, the becoming of a cosmic disaster in which all things subterranean turn upside down, overflowing the surface, carrying Ferdinand away with the immense power of the flooding gutter or dragging him down into the chasm.

> [T]he gutter! . . . A gutter can be enormous sometimes! . . . It's a chasm . . . a chasm that swells up . . . and recedes . . . that swells up and calms down again! . . . it makes you dizzy! . . . . the Eiffel Tower that you'd think was a gutter! . . . way in the distance a little hole, it's a sewer! . . . and then huge, gigantic! . . . the immensity of it! . . . all of Paris . . . the sewer . . . at the bottom of the sewer!

> [L]e ruisseau! . . . C'est énorme un ruisseau des coups! . . . c'est un gouffre! . . . un gouffre qui remonte . . . et qui renforce! . . . qui remonte et qui rabaisse! . . . le vertige! . . . la tour Eiffel que vous diriez un ruisseau! . . . tout au fond un petit trou, l'égout! . . . et puis immense et puis géant! . . . l'immensité! . . . tout Paris! . . . l'égout . . . au fond de l'égout!⁴³

This cosmic inversion is accompanied by a corporeal explosion. The delirium of the overflowing sewer is attended by a profound revulsion (*dégoût*). Céline's body, Richard says, must be understood as a figure of the world itself: "the great illness of the Célinian body [. . .] is clearly its internal incertitude, the lack of grip" ("la grande maladie du corps celinien [...] c'est, on le voit, l'incertitude interne, la manque de *tenue*").⁴⁴ In the case of Ferdinand's expulsion, "la manque de *tenue*," the lack of grip, is first moral and then becomes corporeal decline (*déchéance*) and dehiscence. The expelled one cannot digest his own condition: he has become the victim of his own power to betray; he was profoundly cheated and yet he finds himself out in the streets, hounded as the epitome of the worst enemy. Exalted by guilt and shame, surrounded by hate and horror, the *content* of moral complexity cannot be resolved unless the *container* itself blows up. The internal ferment finds a way out only through a corporeal convulsion, through a violent dizziness, nausea, and vomiting. Yet this nausea is more than the perceptible symptom of uncontrolled anxiety and excitement; it is the involuntary ambience of self-destitution's "centrifugal force." The impulsive discharge of vomiting translates the ecstasy of impersonal becoming, the complete banishment from identity and self.

> I reel...one step...another...I get a hold of myself! and *bleuuu*! I puke!...It comes over me right there...not twenty meters from his door...the sidewalk's all I see...and then nothing at all... I'm puking all over the sidewalk...on all fours!...crawling... it's the gutter I want to get to...because it's the alert! Am I buzzing or am I sirening?...it's an air raid!...I'm vomiting like a drunk, me! I know it! and I don't drink! Never! Never anything! It's the dizziness!

> Je vacille...un pas...un autre...je me rattrape!...et *wouaf*! je dégueule!...Ça me prend là...pas loin...vingt mètres de sa porte...je vois le trottoir, c'est tout...et plus rien...je dégueule plein le trottoir...à quatre pattes alors!...quatre pattes...au ruisseau je veux...parce que c'est l'alerte! Je bourdonne ou je sirène?...C'est l'alerte!...Je vomis en ivrogne, moi! Je sais! et je bois pas! Jamais! Jamais rien! C'est les vertiges!⁴⁵

If the cosmic explosion (above/below) shows how the storm breaks out with all its might from the expulsion command issued by Jules rather than from the aerial bombardment, the corporeal explosion (inside/outside) shows how the radical distress of the one expelled becomes the fascination of the storm or even the apocalyptic crusade of the tempestuous power itself. This is the second reversal of the event: the one who is expelled from the law and from the object of his desire seems to suffer physical breakdown; he spews himself, so to speak, out of himself, thus breaking out of any local expulsion. The vomiting happens to occur "right there," only twenty meters from Jules's studio. *It* comes over Ferdinand just when he "gets hold of himself," as a kind of infinite leap or epiphany, Richard argues, that purifies him both of the feminine cave and of the political prison hole. For a moment it transports him into the wide-open cave of being, into infinity. At this point, deliriously, Céline goes beyond human corporeality and beyond human language. His vomiting in the storm appeals on one hand to a material utopia of animality and on the other to an abstract utopia of music.

In *Powers of Horror*, Kristeva perceives the link between Céline's scenes of vomiting and the exploration of animality: "Human beings caught flush with their animality, wallowing in their vomit, as if to come closer to what is essential for Céline, beyond all 'fancies': violence, blood, and death."[46] In this fragment of *Fable*, vomiting leads to a corporeal metamorphosis in which Ferdinand falls on his "quatre pattes" then starts crawling like a large insect or a rat, holding onto the sidewalk so as not to be sucked into the great sewer:

> I clutch on, hold fast . . . a thousand little lights! seeing stars! . . . the sewer's edge! . . . bravo! . . . I haven't been sucked into the sewer! . . . no, I haven't! I haven't been sucked into the precipice! Bravo! . . . I'm puking . . . I'm puking into it! I'm buzzing! . . . I'm so dizzy! But I won't give in to it! Menière's syndrome, it's called!
>
> je me cramponne! . . . mille petites lumières! . . . chandelles! . . . le rebord! . . . bravo! . . . Il m'a pas l'égout! . . . il m'a pas! le précipice m'a pas! bravo! . . . je dégueule . . . je dégueule dedans! je bourdonne! . . . le vertige! il m'a pas le vertige! vertige de Ménière ça s'appelle![47]

Like an animal, the only testimony of the excluded is his flesh and blood. The only substantive body of the expelled is the material stream of sewage and body waste, of blood and vomit. Céline finds the direct inscription of the storm itself in the animality. The unprotected, savage, and senseless corporeality of the animal exposes the violent testimony of the expelled, either in the form of worthless garbage (*déchet*) removed through the sewer or in the form of entrails spilling from their corporeal envelope; *either as the violent forces that act on him or as the pure aggression that acts in itself.* The corporeal sign of the animal is always the primitive vision of abjection and fascination in the face of what culture attempts to repress, between exaltation and repulsion; as Kristeva writes, "an apocalypse without god [. . .] without morality, without judgment, without hope."[48] It is an apocalyptic utopia that is profoundly present in the last pages of the novel as a kind of testament: dying for the animals not for men:

> When I finish myself off I'm gonna say to you: it's for the animals, that's why, not men! like Cabbage Head and Nana and Sarah, my cat that left one night and that we never saw again, like the farm horses, and our friends the animals who have suffered a thousand times just like men! rabbits, owls, blackbirds! who spent so many winters with us! in the back of beyond! . . . death will be a blessing to me . . . I will have given my heart to everyone . . . It'll be over and done with, no more you, or your attachments, or yours lies! . . . [. . .] I do not want my death to be caused by men, they lie too much! not from them would I get eternal rest!

> Quand je me finirai je vais vous dire: c'est en pensant aux animaux, pas aux hommes! à "Tête de Chou," à "Nana," à "Sarah" ma chatte qu'est partie un soir, qu'on n'a jamais revue, aux chevaux de la ferme, aux animaux compagnons qu'ont souffert mille fois comme des hommes! lapins, hiboux, merles! passé tant d'hivers avec nous! au bout du monde! . . . la mort me sera douce . . . j'aurai donné mon cœur à tous . . . je serai débarrassé de vos personnes, de vos affections, de vos mensonges! . . . [. . .] Je veux pas que la mort me vienne des hommes, ils mentent trop! ils me donneraient pas l'Infini![49]

Finally, the pure living animal body corresponds to the pure linguistic abstraction of music. For curiously, at this moment of emergency Céline's writing is interrupted by an inscription of musical notes. For the first time in the novel, the cosmic and corporeal explosion inscribes itself with a type of melancholy song—"Be gone with the wind! / Farewell, dead leaves!"—words accompanied by a graphic representation of musical notes. Kristeva writes: "Beyond the narrative, dizziness finds its language: music."[50] Beyond the vocal intonation of Céline's discourse, beyond Céline's stylistic pattern of ellipsis, broken lines, onomatopoeia, and exclamation, the universal disaster inaugurates the writer's swan song and the music of the "universal organ." The last narrative images—"The houses are spinning . . . Holy smoke! the buildings in the air!"—are penetrated by the other language of nostalgia and a farewell melody, reminiscent of Mahler's *Song of the Earth*: "[L]ife goes on . . . blood flows . . . you get carried away . . ." ("[L]a vie passe . . . le sang passe . . . il emmène . . .").[51]

11

AIR RAID THREE

T. S. Eliot's "Little Gidding" from *Four Quartets*

Under the German Blitz on London, during the World War II, the meditative poetry of Eliot's *Four Quartets* is suddenly breached by an urgent sense that an inevitable ordeal is under way.[1] A key moment erupts from the long sequences of this poetic texture, throwing into disarray the all-embracing spiritual experience as well as the previous questioning of its truthful sources and achievements. What occurs here is not only the devastation wreaked by the air raid but a dramatic encounter of the poet with a ghost—the reappearance of a dead author walking through the dark streets of London, a dead author whose guidance seems indispensable in this present situation. If the poet generally succeeds in translating the lesson of the dead to the living as the way of humility and forgiveness, what matters more is the nature of the beginning of this encounter, namely, with a shout of unsure recognition that comes to dominate this event: it is not a scream of horror at the aircraft flying over the city, but the ambiguity marking the interval: once the bombs have fallen and before the all-clear sirens, as the flames still consume and the smoke still spirals: "What! are *you* here?"[2]

When read apart from the metrical pattern in which it is embedded, this question in "Little Gidding II" can be understood merely as it is: a shout of surprise resonating in the desolate urban labyrinth just before dawn, the first "direct speech" in the poem. "What! are *you* here?" We will have to recite this astonishment again and again, adopting the poet's—or his persona's—voice, perhaps even rehearsing an anonymous voice, so as to gradually grasp what pierces and wounds us in this cry.

A brief examination of the critical readings of "Little Gidding" shows that an essential preoccupation in this context is to answer the question: What is the name of this "dead master"? Who is this "*you*" passing by the poet at this dreadful moment? To which works does the poem refer by quoting, imitating, or insinuating with the aim of synthesizing this "familiar compound ghost" ("Little Gidding II")? Is it Yeats, Shelley, or Hamlet's father? Is it Dante, Swift, Milton, Pound, or Mallarmé?[3] What are the thematic and prosodic effects of intertexuality, and hence the poetic tradition that is called upon to reinforce the existential resistance in this place and point of time?[4]

Indeed, these erudite overlays provide keys to comprehending the poem and emphasize its place in the history of the spirit by reaffirming the poet's gifted speech and radical experience. It is well known that Eliot intentionally included these referential elements, and later on he even suggested illuminating some of them,[5] opening this sequence of the poem to a sort of encyclopedic interrogation that the literary research on Eliot enjoys continuing from one article to another by suggesting diverse possibilities. It is certainly important to know who addresses this exclamation—"What! are *you* here?"—and to whom it is addressed, whether this "*you*" is a singular or plural pronoun or whether eventually the dead author is simultaneously "both one and many."

However, what is left untouched in these observations is the function of this statement itself: these striking words have a raison d'être of their own that precedes the presence of the speakers in the poem by putting into question not only their identity but mainly their very experience of "being there." To be precise, one has to insist upon hearing in this perplexed formulation a whole, resounding series of questions: "What! are *you* here?" also means "Is it you?" "Are you here too?" "What are you doing here?" "Are you aware of this?" and "Where exactly are we?" This vertiginous questioning means, first of all, that the first direct speech in the poem does not simply establish the presence of the interlocutors, but amplifies the wonder of their gaze, directs it forward and backward, this way and that, to expose a more primary process of *becoming aware* of the other and of oneself and *being found* by the other and by oneself. Although this process begins before the shout of surprise and continues to develop after it, it is at this point of accumulation that the real seems to penetrate the poem, the corporeal gesture breaks free from the words, as if it translates the poem's tearing of itself, its becoming present to itself, present to the poet's situation and to its encounter with other times, other persons, and other poems.

> So I assumed a double part, and cried
> And heard another's voice cry: "What! are *you* here?"
> Although we were not. I was still the same,
> Knowing myself yet being someone other—
> And he a face still forming; yet the words sufficed
> To compel the recognition they preceded.[6]

What is the meaning of this accumulation point? What is the scale of its impact, and how does it then proceed, in the middle of "Little Gidding II"? Let us revert to the stanza's beginning. Eliot's air raid starts with an effort to establish the location of the scene: "In the uncertain hour before the morning / Near the ending of interminable night." These first lines use a conventional narrative beginning by introducing a new dramatic landscape, and in doing so they emphasize the trustworthiness of the poetic testimony by effectively giving it an empirical grounding. The first sequence of lines, indeed, insists on temporal and spatial markers: "*Near* the ending," "*at* the recurrent end," "*After* the dark dove," "*While* the dead leaves," "*Over* the asphalt," "*Between* three districts"—all of these signs render the event from the internal position of the one who experienced it. The recurrent use of the definite article is also noteworthy: writing thus disposes of the already acknowledgeable surrounding elements; "*the* dark dove," "*the* dead leaves"—they all receive a determinate presence, as they are being dynamically evaluated by the personal witness of the poet's persona who perceives them in passing.

This sensation of precipitated movement at the beginning of this stanza unsettles the actual surroundings by infusing immeasurability into the measurable details. This is how Eliot describes the exact time of timelessness: it is the "*waning dusk*" of dawn, the edge of "*interminable* night," or "the recurrent end of the *unending*."[7] Even more so, the real impression blends with mental images and symbols: "the dark dove with the flickering tongue" is a metaphor of the bombarding airplane, as if it were both a religious vision of an evil god and an expressionist painting of a monstrous animal. The fallen metal leaves designate the ruin caused by modern weapons; the leaves still "rattled on like tin / Over the asphalt" as if they were burnt objects or damaged parts of objects blown about after the attack and the fire.

This tension between contemporary urban descriptions and dreamlike or mythic representations is better observed in Eliot's use of the word *wind*. The first mention of "wind" refers to an atmospheric phenomenon: it is a sudden gust that blows the fallen leaves across the asphalt, its cold stinging unprotected faces and causing strangers, the passersby, to bump into each other. The second mention is after the appearance of the ghost. Now, it is not a matter of "dead leaves" but rather of a "dead master"; it is no longer an irresistible wind but a "common wind" to which both the living poet and the dead one are "compliant." With this move, the real shadowy street transforms into a part of hell or of a purgatorial limbo in which all and everyone is afloat. All of London turns into a Dantesque scene to the extent that those who are present in the poem enter a third realm ("between two worlds") in which they are both dead and alive, a kind of presence without present that gradually evolves from the concretization of the singular moment of 1940.

> And so, compliant to the common wind,
>   Too strange to each other for misunderstanding,
> In concord at this intersection time
>   Of meeting nowhere, no before and after,
>   We trod the pavement in a dead patrol.[8]

Indeed, the air raid only constitutes the background to a different drama. It is not the catastrophe of war that engraves the event on the text, but its transformation and its substitution by another foreign appearance. Soon after the fascination or fright in the flickering face of the "dark dove" gives rise to an uncanny visit of a dead author, the vertical menace of the Blitz becomes a horizontal encounter; the appearance of the revenant marks the astonishing invasion that occurs in the poem, the coming of the absolute other. Therefore, it is only by following these ghostly imprints that one can say something about Eliot's air raid. Of course, the ghost carries an important message that affects both the content and style of the poem. Eliot disclosed elsewhere that his intention here was to transpose Dante's thought into contemporary English by writing in a parallel terza rima.[9] While such data have a general significance that must be taken into account, it is necessary to examine this encounter, first of all, in the limited context of the event itself. The question, more precisely, is, In what sense does this foreign appearance change the structure of the event itself by offering the key to the singularity of Eliot's air raid, that is, to the change that happens as we move from "Little Gidding II" to "Little Gidding IV"?

In this sense, the exclamation with which this analysis began—"What! are *you* here?"—is a revealing intersection: the shout of surprise first marks the essence of the gradual process of recognition that replaces the external description of the situation. It translates a movement of withdrawal from the manifest historical moment toward a sensorial and perceptual analysis. I have said already that through this direct call, the real imposes its grip on the poem by affirming the rudimentary astonishment of becoming aware of other and self and of being found by other and self. But this exclamation promotes something additional; we know that these words are an exact quote from canto 15 of Dante's *Inferno*. Therefore, it also opens the threshold to another poem, reverting to Dante's writing but also rewriting Eliot's own passage in *The Waste Land* (1922): "Unreal city . . . over London Bridge." The various folds of intertext that constitute this line precede the long monologue that covers the continuation of this stanza in "Little Gidding II" by announcing the passage from empirical time to the time of writing itself.

Viewed from this angle, this first manifestation of direct speech testifies to the radical change the ghost brings into the poem: The menace of bombs vanishes under the "dead master's" monologue. Eliot covers the timebound reality by a long reflection on a lifetime's poetic work: now, the ephemeral becomes a retrospective summary of old age, the historical apocalypse becomes an epic invocation, the danger, no longer military-political, is moral, and therefore the speech about the destiny of poetry—hence, the speech about the meaning of speech itself—suggests a spiritual effort to endure the dire situation. These are the words of the dead author to the poem's narrator:

> Since our concern was speech, and speech impelled us
>> To purify the dialect of the tribe
>> And urge the mind to aftersight and foresight,
> Let me disclose the gifts reserved for age
>> To set a crown upon your lifetime's effort.[10]

At this stage, one can observe that the poem pits the "dark dove" and the "dead master" against one another. Both bring a certain speech to the world, but the artillery tongue of the dark dove is an inverted part of the dead man's tongue: "the communication / Of the dead is *tongued with fire* beyond the language of the living" (emphasis added), Eliot writes at the end of "Little Gidding I."[11] While the German aircraft appears as a deceptive demon, the dead author carries a secret "annunciation" from the Holy Spirit. Hence the dark dove's fire tongue imposes a dreadful crisis, the precarious historical situation of war, but in Eliot's work, this terrible experience of being reduced to flesh and blood must induce an opening up to the promise of the white dove's Word, to the work of creation and the symbol of wholeness.

> The dove descending breaks the air
> With flame of incandescent terror
> Of which the tongues declare
> The one discharge from sin and error.[12]

This spiritual asceticism (whose sources I will here ignore) traverses all of *Four Quartets*: at the end of "Little Gidding II," the ghost asserts that one must fall "From wrong to wrong" to be restored by a "refining fire"; one must suffer a painful death in order to be reborn as redeemed. "Descend lower, descend only / Into the world of perpetual solitude, / World not world, but that which is not world," writes Eliot in "Burnt Norton III," already having in mind that "the way up and down is one and the same,"[13] as the epigraph from Heraclitus at the beginning of his entire project suggests.[14]

However, this observation requires more caution. Eliot's opposition between the speech of the dead author and that of the war machine, between the messenger of the Holy Spirit and that of the god of evil, implies neither dualism nor pluralism, but must be understood in the metaphysical context of monism. Throughout *Four Quartets*, Eliot moves around an Heraclitean unity of opposites, if not a Christian-Hegelian coexistence of opposed elements: time past and time future, stillness and perpetual motion, past and present, "in my beginning is my end," "Midwinter spring is its own season," and so on.

The same thing happens in the air raid in "Little Gidding": the dark dove's and the white dove's speech are one and the same. They are changing aspects, expressions, or qualities of the same fundamental fire: destruction and creation coincide within the "ever-living Fire," in Heraclitus's language, that "was ever and is and shall be . . . kindled in measure and quenched in measure."[15] In this respect, fire is not one of the four physical and moral elements, as in Anaximander of Miletus's fragment in which the opposites "give to each other justice and recompense for their injustice."[16] Here, fire itself is the infinite motion of transformation into other elements: the death of air, the death of earth, the death of water—these are all interchangeable in the living strife of fire.[17]

Yet the cyclical or dialectical unity between the contradictory elements in "Little Gidding" remains enigmatic. What is obvious is only the secret passage from one fire to another: as said, the real fire carried by the aircraft is covered by the verbal fire of the dead author. Empirical time progressively becomes the time of writing. The path through the streets of London becomes the ghost's discursive path. The "dead patrol" at what seems to be the unending-end of history changes into a sober *oraison funèbre* that pleads to let things be so that, retrospectively, the beginning can be perceived from the end, whether this beginning happened long ago or must find itself again.

This narrow boundary between experience and *logos*, where urban itineraries and steps of thought blend together, already occurs in the first stanza of Eliot's "Love Song of J. Alfred Prufrock" (1917): "Let us go, through certain half-deserted streets, / The muttering retreats . . . Streets that follow like a tedious argument / Of insidious intent / To lead you to an overwhelming question . . ."[18] Yet here, in "Little Gidding II," the actual road is wholly dissolved by the virtual road of language. Even if the ghost's message indicates that his words are relevant only to the present experience, to the challenge of the destructive fire, they lead to an *elsewhere*, to a sort of mythic transformation of the present and within the present. Indeed, the ghost declares that the *logos* evolves from incessant, ongoing experience and depends on time, when he says:

> For last year's words belong to last year's language
> And next year's words await another voice.
> [...]
> So I find words I never thought to speak
> In streets I never thought I should revisit.[19]

But the spiritual path of his eloquence eventually purges the present from itself by reaching the "refining fire" and the "mov[ing] in measure" of the dancer. These are other names for the pure moment where human folly, shame, and honor appeal beyond and out of history toward "the word without a word."[20]

Here is where "becoming" traverses Eliot's literary event. Similarly to Deleuze's argument that becoming originates in its historical conditions even though it manifests itself in the course of history as indefinite rupture and transformation, Eliot believes that the purification from history is based on its being first and foremost situated in history. Real attachment to "our own field of action" is a necessary condition for finding the principle of detachment, that is, how everything is destined to vanish "The faces and places, with the self which, as it could, loved them, / To become renewed, transfigured, in another pattern."[21]

I am not saying that Eliot is a Deleuzian poet, not at all. Unlike Deleuze, Eliot adheres to a theological or metaphysical ethics: the triumph of freedom within servitude and the appeal for restoration within inevitable sin. But exposing the becoming in Eliot's poem is necessary not to underline the moral (re)solutions between the opposites that it offers; instead, becoming marks the uncertain move and the indecisive passage between them, namely, the fact that in this literary event all opposites appear in one move, to the degree that they become wholly the same. Here lies the splendor of Eliot's monism: the one and same constantly acts on itself; the one and the same forces itself on itself as if to extract from itself the unknown motion of difference. Yet this difference is identical to itself, it strives for itself and with itself, as if all things had entered the ancient furnace in which everything folds up on itself, covers itself, repeating the selfsame as different from itself.

This is what motivates Eliot's air raid: The need to understand how the fire simultaneously destroys and purifies itself in a scarifying process that resembles *Aufhebung*, a form of negation that also preserves and elevates, elevating as it descends and annihilates. In this sense, the fire as the force of unity and identity surely does not act as a reconciliation of opposites, or as a harmonious wholeness that transcends them, or even as an immanent dialectic between them. The fire remains an enigmatic boundary between the opposites; it constitutes the relation of "non-relation," that which attracts the opposites into an endless combat; it is, in Eliot's language, an enigmatic boundary between "being redeemed" and "being consumed," between mortality and immortality.[22]

Perhaps it is possible to say that the fire in this literary event constitutes a dynamic conception of fate. It is the intensely dissymmetrical boundary between "chance and non-chance," as Gombrowicz writes in *Cosmos*.[23] It is the Shakespearean "to be or not to be," the thin line that joins and dis-joins "yes" and "no," as Georg Büchner puts it in *Woyzeck*.[24] And here, the fire tongue of the dead author, that is, the white dove, illuminates the way toward the redemption of the living, but this salvation from the dark dove's fire also exposes us to the danger, strips off our skin as we face this one-and-the-same consuming disaster.

Finally, Eliot reveals in "Little Gidding IV," as a direct continuation of "Little Gidding II," that one must suffer one's terrible nakedness, accepting the fire's burning as the only way of being refined. The spiritual guidance of the dead author after the night attack in "Little Gidding II" leads to the reappearance of the dove in "Little Gidding IV." Now the dove "breaks the air" above the city in *vivo*; now it is both black and white, imposing on the one hand a "flame of incandescent terror" while on the other hand their "tongues declare / The one discharge from sin and error." In the gap between "Little Gidding II" and "Little Gidding IV," an ethical principle affirms itself: the bombardment is also the new chance of the *vita nova*, precisely because "The only hope" in the face of the dove "Lies in the choice of pyre or pyre," namely, in the demand to choose to experience the unavoidable fire.

In other words, the only tenable ethical principle is that of accepting the "poisoned shirt" of *amor fati*, of the love of fate that purifies by devouring one's body. For Eliot defines *amor fati* as "The intolerable shirt of flame / Which human power cannot remove." Intolerable but unremovable, the love of fate is this devoted acceptance of Nessus's shirt: to accept the inevitable fire, the explosion, that is, to will unresistingly the moment when the event strikes, the point that is ruled by the unstable boundary between happening and un-happening.

> Who then devised the torment? Love.
> Love is the unfamiliar Name
> Behind the hands that wove
> The intolerable shirt of flame
> Which human power cannot remove.
>   We only live, only suspire
>   Consumed by either fire or fire.[25]

Accepting the disaster of war as an ethical attitude to what happens means to perceive war neither as unfortunate determinism nor as blind escape, neither in total resignation nor in confidence nor in resentment. Eliot recognizes that although London's citizens are hidden (or trapped) in their houses and shelters, their situation does not differ from that of the soldiers confronting the enemy frontline. "We die with the dying," he writes in "Little Gidding V": all must be prepared to sacrifice their lives. However, unlike the English soldiers, the city dwellers are in a state of suspense, seized by an impatient patience; their passivity during the nights of the Blitz internalizes the violence. Although the event fatally imposes death and injury, wearing "the intolerable shirt of flame" also means bringing about, inversely, a transformation of the event by the event: masochistically embodying the event in order to modify the horror by passion, the anxiety by love, and thus miraculously to change the nature of fire by means of fire itself.

To resist and to maintain dignity in the face of the event that befalls us, it is implied here, is to reflectively lighten the passion that marks our intimate, passive state. As Deleuze might have put it, one must extricate oneself from the actual situation and engage oneself in the becoming of the event by bearing the power of fire to the point at which it reverses and opposes fire itself. To accept the fire will be to create the fire anew as if it originated in one's self. This does not merely mean overcoming death by retaining fear and pain, but more precisely, Eliot suggests, by entering into the one and same furnace of fate where redemption and consumption are interchangeable: "To be redeemed from fire by fire.... Consumed by either fire or fire."

In some ways this existential route resonates with the romantic virtue according to which life's dignity depends on the moment of death; it is also in dialogue with the classic moral of controlling the passions and thus sublating them into a spiritual sublime. Yet the center here is not formed by the triumph of the living but by their fascination in the face of the blinding moment of the event: it is the love of fate that renders the living humble and dignifies them, as they yield to the "tongues of flame" ("Little Gidding V"), after which there remain either pale ashes or "the purification of the motive" ("Little Gidding III").

What matters in this vision is that both the "fortunate" and the "defeated" are engulfed by the same raging fire; together they blend into a symbol "united in the strife which divided them" ("Little Gidding III").[26] This symbol perfected in time further bears out how Eliot builds a bridge between the realm of the living and that of the dead: no longer separate, in "Little Gidding V" they interlace to form one single metaphysical knot:

> See, they depart, and we go with them.
> We are born with the dead:
> See, they return, and bring us with them.
> The moment of the rose and the moment of the yew-tree
> Are of equal duration ...[27]

Perhaps the communication between the living and the dead is realized by the passage through this surge of flames. The two spheres converge in the conflagration. At this moment, it is not only the living who recognize their mortality—"[F]or the scene to be changed ... / [W]ith a movement of darkness on darkness" ("East Coker III")—it is also where the dead return as a present figure of absence by conveying an immortal sign.[28] To quote once more from Heraclitus: "Immortals are mortal, mortals are immortal: [*each*] lives the death of the other, and dies their life."[29] Derrida's *hauntology* opens a meaningful horizon to this: "Beyond the opposition between presence and non-presence, actuality and in-actuality, life and non-life, . . . thinking the possibility of the specter, the specter as possibility." And a little before this: "[T]his is perhaps the question of the event as question of the ghost."[30]

And thus we are back at the beginning, and hear again the poet's wonder and astonishment—"What! are *you* here?"—which now seems to express the timeless moment that is ruled by the surge of flames. The shout of surprise is the spectral speech that passes through the living and the dead; it translates the way the living and the dead are roaming lost in their timeless fate. At the same time, this is where they find one another in their need to confine the unknown to a traceable history.

"[F]or history is a pattern / Of timeless moments," Eliot writes in "Little Gidding V," suggesting neither a cyclic temporality nor an eternal present stretching between the dead and the living, but the indefinite time of *Aion* in which a present instant is divided infinitely between end and beginning, a single instant opens itself to the haunted encounter of the dead and the living, between which whirls the fire of the event. This, finally, is how the eternal return proceeds as the different untimeliness that constantly returns by engraving itself on the historical moment.

12

Conclusion

Being Is in the Hands of the Event

Walking through Washington Square in New York City, I discovered this inscription cut into a monument: "The event is in the hand of God." Though poetically articulated, this is of course an imprecise statement, because God, rather, is always in the hands of the event. That is to say, God is something other than the omnipresent demiurge who pronounced the words "fiat lux." Perhaps what we call God is only the blink of an eye at the instant the voice resounded: Let there be light. It may well have been the combined and undefined vibration of matter and perception, of a luminous radiation that affirms itself through language as the virtual necessity of Being.

Let us be cautious, however, in tying Being to language. Perhaps, at first, we are inclined to reconfirm our historical finitude in the face of the transcendent and to integrate ontological fore-understanding with the transmission of the voice. Intuitively we hear the logos of "fiat lux" as the voice of Being, as "the logos *of* Being." Derrida cites Heidegger, "Thought Obeying the Voice of Being."[1] But we also know that we should attend to that voice in other ways. One might say that language existed before the symbolic unit of the word, that language did not have to wait for the thought of man. The performative appeal, "fiat lux," may be the Immaculate Conception in which Being is entirely surrendered into the hands of the event.

In the beginning there was not the Word; neither was the Word with God, nor was the Word God, and so on. This call for the origin in John's gospel should be amended according to Louis-Ferdinand Céline's suggestion: "In the beginning was the emotion,"[2] and the emotion was with the event, and the emotion was the event.

The theory of the literary event is only at its beginnings, though it is evident that from the outset the objective of literature has been twofold: both to hold the knife firmly and to suffer the cut. From as far back as Homer and Hesiod, the event has been the generative act of creating: the impossible trials of myth simultaneously resonate the violent emotion that generates and breaks the laws of language, of gods and of time.

As a creative stimulus, the event is critically irreducible to any horizon of expectation; it is the coming forth of emotion or the violence of a signal. What comes about is not the force of the law as it resides in the word, but the savage violence that traverses the word insofar as it splits and transforms what there is. Refractions of light pass through the words' cracks, making them shine and dazzle with a living corporeality that is senseless: language that is beyond any experienced presence.

Here we no longer speak of Being or of God, but rather of violence as such. We know that the stillness of Being dissolves to reveal, instead, the joy of movement and disintegration. We know that God neither died nor was he dramatically murdered; he has only surrendered himself to the sleepy twilight of his fatigue: glorious hallucinations, imaginary incidents, and nightmarish stupor of a bleary-eyed God, while at his side a chaotic profusion of colors and sounds is giving birth to a world.

"Minuit sonne!" The stroke of midnight sounds! In this hiatus between what is already gone and what is still to come, we yearn for the emotion of the dice falling. At this moment it may happen that the real is what is mimed without model, or again the wounded incarnation of the fictitious. Thus, this accumulating imbroglio of the event enwraps us: an ongoing encounter initiated by the tacit, surprising element, by the powers and speeds of uncontainable entities, a variable relation through which unfolds our molecular cartography.

Notes

PREFACE

1. Hofmannsthal, "A Letter."
2. Hofmannsthal, "A Letter," 118, 121.
3. Hofmannsthal, "A Letter," 122.
4. Hofmannsthal, "A Letter," 123.
5. Hofmannsthal, "A Letter," 124.
6. Hofmannsthal, "A Letter," 125.
7. Deleuze, *Francis Bacon*, 20–21.

1. INTRODUCTION

1. The etymology of the word *event* already suggests the semantic strata of our definition. The word *événement* in modern French derives from two Latin verbs: *evenire* (to come out) and *advenire* (to arrive). Each of these relates to a different semantic field: *evenire* refers to the accomplished result of a process that testifies to past experience; *advenire*, on the contrary, indicates a rupture in the time sequence that points to the unaccomplished future, to what is still approaching or about to come. From the roots of *evenire* (*eventum, eventus*) stems *événement* in French: result, achievement, successful end, and denouement after confronting a problem or difficulties. *Advenire* (*venio, advenire, adventura*) becomes *avènement*: unexpected emergence, becoming, encounter with the marvelous, transformation. In the seventeenth century a first shift occurs at the level of the signifier in which the sign *événement* refers also to the semantic field of *avènement*. In the eighteenth and nineteenth centuries a shift at the level of the signified can be observed: the meaning of *unpredictable and unknown emergence* conceals the meaning of *a remarkable adventure*, receiving the evident lexeme of *événement*, as we make use of it today. See Emannuel Boisset, "Aperçu historique sur le mot *événement*," in Boisset and Corno, *Que*

m'arrive-t-il?, 17–30; Françoise Daviet-Taylor, "L'événement: Une globalité saisie," in Daviet-Taylor, *L'événement*, 13–23; *Le Robert dictionnaire historique de la langue francaise*, ed. Alain Rey (Paris: Le Robert, 1992).
2. Deleuze, *The Logic of Sense*, 150.
3. Deleuze, *The Logic of Sense*, 149.
4. Eliot, *Collected Poems*, 194.
5. Ricoeur, "Événement et sens."
6. Lyotard, *Political Writings*, 24.
7. Ricoeur, *Time and Narrative I*, 96–97.
8. Bensa and Fassin, "Les sciences sociales face à l'événement"; see also Manfred Gangel, "Evénement, structure et histoire," in Daviet-Taylor, *L'événement*, 25–38.
9. Ricoeur quotes Braudel in *Time and Narrative I*, 103–4.
10. Veyne quoted in Ricoeur, *Time and Narrative I*, 169–70. See Veyne, *Writing History*.
11. Ricoeur, *Time and Narrative I*, 229–30; see also Boisset, "L'événement est inadmissible, d'ailleurs il n'existe pas," 59.
12. Ricoeur, *Time and Narrative I*, 52–71; see also Ricoeur, "Événement et sens."
13. Ricoeur, *Time and Narrative I*, 98–99.
14. Ricoeur, *Time and Narrative I*, 171, quoting Veyne, *Writing History*.
15. Gadamer, *Truth and Method*, 341–71.
16. Gadamer, *Truth and Method*, 351.
17. For Gadamer's concept of "temporal distance" see *Truth and Method*, 297–98: "Hence temporal distance is not something that must be overcome. This was, rather, the naïve assumption of historicism, namely that we must transpose ourselves into the spirit of the age, think with its ideas and its thoughts, not with our own, and thus advance towards historical objectivity. In fact the important thing is to recognize temporal distance as a positive and productive condition enabling understanding. . . . Everyone is familiar with the curious impotence of our judgment where temporal distance has not given us sure criteria. Thus the judgment of contemporary works of art is desperately uncertain for the scholarly consciousness. Obviously we approach such creations with the unverifiable prejudices, presuppositions that have too great an influence over us for us to know about them; these can give to contemporary creations an extra resonance that does not correspond to their true content and significance. Only when all their relations to the present time have faded away can their real nature appear, so that the understanding of what is said in them can claim to be authoritative and universal. . . . [T]emporal distance obviously means something other

than the extinction of our interest in the object. It lets the true meaning of the object emerge fully. But the discovery of the true meaning of a text or a work of art is never finished; it is in fact an infinite process. Not only are fresh sources of errors constantly excluded, so that all kind of things are filtered out that obscure the true meaning; but new sources of understanding are continually emerging that reveal unsuspected elements of meaning."

18. Dilthey, "Formation of the Historical World."
19. Ricoeur, *Time and Narrative I*, 207–8.
20. Blanchot, *The Space of Literature*, 204–7.
21. Blanchot, *The Book to Come*, 6.
22. Following Ricoeur's point of view, I use the term *plot* (*intrigue*) in order to differentiate it both from the term *history*, which I used in the previous section regarding the problem of historiography, and from the term *narrative* (*récit*), which, according to Genette, *Narrative Discourse*, corresponds to the way the plot is being particularly written and poetically manipulated in a singular text.
23. Tomashevsky, "Thematics," 67.
24. Lotman, *The Structure of the Artistic Text*, 232.
25. Genette, *Narrative Discourse*, 25.
26. Ricoeur, *Time and Narrative I*, 66; see also 65: "First it [plot] is a mediation between the individual events or incidents and a story taken as a whole. In this respect, we may say equivalently that it draws a meaningful story from a diversity of events or incidents (Aristotle's *pragmata*) or that it transforms the events or incidents into a story. The two reciprocal relations expressed by from and into characterize the plot as mediating between events and a narrated story."
27. Lotman, *The Structure of the Artistic Text*, 234–37.
28. Barthes, "Introduction to the Structural Analysis of Narratives," 256; see also Ricoeur, *Time and Narrative II*, 29–32; Todorov, *The Poetics of Prose*, 108–20.
29. Bonnefoy, *La présence et l'image*, 11.
30. Genette, *Narrative Discourse*; Tzvetan Todorov, "Les catégories du récit littéraire," in *Communications 8* (Paris: Seuil, 1981), 132–33.
31. Ricoeur, *Time and Narrative I*, 32–42.
32. Aristotle, *Poetics*, 11–12.
33. Aristotle, *Poetics*, 28. Narrative semiotics continues to affirm the primacy of the action over the protagonist. Vladimir Prop reconstructs the narrative logic by distinguishing narrative "functions," that is, abstract segments of action (Ricoeur): "Les événements constants, permanent du conte sont les fonctions du personnage, quelque soient ces personnages et que soit

la manière dont ces fonctions sont remplies. Ces fonctions sont les parties constitutives du conte" (*see Morphologie du conte* [Paris: Seuil, 1965], 80). Later on, Greimas names the protagonists *actants* and *acteurs* those who make progress the action. Barthes agrees that the actant is the only entrance to the narrative. See also, e.g., Greimas's introduction to *Du Sens II*.

34. Aristotle, *Poetics*, 15.
35. Aristotle, *Poetics*, 15.
36. The simple chronological succession of the action is being condemned as improbable when compared to the causality that constitutes the probable (Ricoeur, *Time and Narrative I*, 38–41).
37. Ricoeur, *Time and Narrative I*, 41.
38. Aristotle, *Poetics*, 17.
39. Ricoeur, *Time and Narrative I*, 43–44.
40. In a long note in *Time and Narrative II* (167 n. 45), Ricoeur invites us to read Lotman in this manner.
41. Lotman, *The Structure of the Artistic Text*, 236; Ricoeur similarly asks in *Time and Narrative I*, 44: "Is not our perplexity greatest where reversals of fortune were most unexpected?"
42. Lotman, *The Structure of the Artistic Text*, 237.
43. Lotman's position suggests a regulated negation of the event that creates a plot from the plot-less state of affairs. Inversely, I would argue that the irregular negation of the event creates a plot-less image from the regulated structure of the plot. In a similar intersection, Romano distinguishes two phenomenological concepts of event: an *événementiel* and an *événemential*. The former cannot be comprehended unless it refers to a contextual unity of world, or to the *topos* in Lotman's terms, while the latter, *l'événemential*, the revolutionary element in itself, "is necessarily an-archic, since it eludes any antecedent causality and is announced, freed from any relation to preexisting possibility, as its own origin." Romano, *Event and World*, 38.
44. Ricoeur, *Time and Narrative II*, 24–26; Blanchot offers the opposite conception: "He [the writer] feels within himself, vital and demanding, the role of the reader still to be born. And very often, through a usurpation which he barely escapes, it is the reader, prematurely and falsely engendered, who begins to write in him. (Hence, to give only a simplistic example, those choice passages, those fine phrases which come to the surface and which cannot be said to have been written, but only to be readable.)" *The Space of Literature*, 200.
45. See Barthes, "Introduction to the Structural Analysis of Narratives" and "The Reality Effect."
46. Maingueneau, *Elements de linguistique pour le texte littéraire*.

47. Deleuze and Guattari, "Introduction: Rhizome," in *A Thousand Plateaus*. See also Barthes, *On Racine*, 165–70.
48. Blanchot, *The Space of Literature*, 125.
49. See Barthes quoting from Nietzsche in *The Pleasure of the Text*, 60–61: "We are not *subtle* enough to perceive that probably *absolute flow of becoming*; the *permanent* exists only thanks to our coarse organs which reduce and lead things to shared premises of vulgarity, whereas nothing exists *in this form*. A tree is a new thing at every instant; we affirm the *form* because we do not seize the subtlety of an absolute moment."
50. Nancy, "The Surprise of the Event," in *Being Singular Plural*, 164–67.
51. See Kristeva, *Revolution in Poetic Language*.
52. Bataille, Avant-propos; my translation.
53. Roland Barthes, "La chronique," in *Oeuvres completes,* vol. 3 (Paris: Seuil, 1995), 991 (*Le Nouvel Observateur*, 1979): "Non, ce ne sont pas des 'Mythologies'; plutôt le relevé de quelques incidents qui marquent, à la semaine, ma sensibilité, telle qu'elle reçoit le monde des incitations ou des coups: mes *scoops* à moi, qui ne sont pas directement ceux de l'actualité. Pourquoi alors les donner? Pourquoi donner le ténu, le futile, l'insignifiant, pourquoi risquer l'accusation de dire des 'riens'? La pensée de cette tentative est la suivante: l'événement dont s'occupe la presse paraît une chose toute simple; je veux dire: il apparaît toujours à l'évidence que c'est un 'événement,' et cet événement est fort. Mais, s'il y avait aussi des événements 'faibles' dont la ténuité ne laisse pas cependant d'agiter du sens, de désigner ce qui dans le monde 'ne va pas bien'? Bref, si l'on s'occupait peu à peu, patiemment, de remanier la grille des intensités? . . . Peut-être faut-il, et dans la presse même, tenter de résister au prestige des grandes proportions, de façon à freiner l'emportement des médias à créer eux-mêmes l'événement. Je sais que mon langage est petit mais cette petitesse est peut-être utile; car c'est à partir d'elle que je sens à mon tour, parfois, les limites de l'autre monde, du monde des autres, du 'grand' monde, et c'est pour dire cette gêne, peut-être cette souffrance que j'écris: ne devons-nous pas aujourd'hui faire entendre le plus nombre de 'petits mondes'?"
54. Genette, *Fiction and Diction*, 139: "Style thus defines in some sense a *minimal degree of literariness* . . . since it consists in the text's *being* [*l'être du texte*], as inseparable but distinct from its *saying*. . . . The most common state is the intermediate or rather the mixed state in which language simultaneously effaces itself as sign and allows itself to be perceived as form. Language is neither totally conductive nor totally resistant; it is always semiconductive, or semiopaque, and thus always at once intelligible, as denotative, and perceptible, as exemplificatory."

55. Borges, *The Aleph and Other Stories*, 47.
56. Gombrowicz, *Cosmos*, 91–92, 97–98.
57. Duras, *The Ravishing of Lol Stein*, 38.
58. Musil, *The Man without Qualities*, 81, 214.
59. James, "The Beast in the Jungle," 372.
60. Döblin, *Berlin Alexanderplatz*, 1.
61. See, e.g., Lyotard, *Political Writings*, 24: "The modern is a feeling for the event as such, impromptu, imminent, urgent, disarming knowledge and even consciousness. The event is an absolute performative: it happens. Fashion [la mode] is affirmed by the desire to be the event."
62. See Barthes, "The Two Criticisms," in *Critical Essays*, 249–54; and Barthes, *Criticism and Truth*.
63. See, e.g., Alexandre et al., *Que se passe-t-il?*; Boisset and Corno, *Que m'arrive-t-il?*; Glaudes and Meter, *Le sens de l'événement*.
64. Heidegger, *Identity and Difference*; Heidegger, *On Time and Being*.
65. Heidegger, *On Time and Being*, 19.
66. Cf. Romano, *Event and World*, 50: "If a fundamental requirement of phenomenology is that it takes appearance as being the source for description by right, without presuming in advance about the meaning of these appearances, then the first phenomenon, the one that is primary by right is precisely the one that is the source of all meaning and right for itself, (and hence also for us), the one that illuminates itself and is brought about in light of its own manifestation: the pure *montrance* of events." The events are the first phenomenon to manifest itself by right, because "in their radical unpreparedness, they are the sole condition (without conditions) of their own advent . . . their arising is its own measure; it reaches us *outside of any measure from ourselves*, and is not subjected to any prior condition, any ontological *a priori*."
67. Heidegger, *Poetry, Language, Thought*, 192.
68. Heidegger, *Poetry, Language, Thought*, 227.
69. Heidegger, *Poetry, Language, Thought*, 228.
70. Blanchot, *The Space of Literature*, 43.
71. Blanchot, *The Book to Come*, 208.
72. Levinas, *Proper Names*, 134.
73. Blanchot, *The Space of Literature*, 125.
74. Derrida, *Specters of Marx*, 17; see also 29: "Not to maintain together the disparate, but to put ourselves there where the disparate itself *holds together*, without wounding the dis-jointure, the dispersion, or the difference, without effacing the heterogeneity of the other."
75. Derrida in Borradori, *Philosophy in a Time of Terror*, 90.

76. See also Juranville in *L'événement*, 39: "ce qu'on appelle événement est ainsi fondamentalement, pour l'existant, ce qui, venant de l'Autre et, avant tout, de l'Autre absolu." Romano, *Event and World*, 114: "others always become evident as such for an *advenant* starting from *events*."
77. Derrida, "A Certain Impossible Possibility," 451.
78. Derrida, "No Apocalypse, Not Now," 27.
79. Derrida, *Demeure*, 28–29: "its passion consists in this—that it receives its determination from something other than itself. Even when it harbors the unconditional right to say anything, including the most savage antinomies, disobedience itself, its status is never assured or guaranteed permanently [à demeure], at home, in the inside of an 'at home.'"
80. Derrida, "A Certain Impossible Possibility," 453.
81. Deleuze and Guattari, *What Is Philosophy?* 38.
82. Deleuze, *Difference and Repetition*, 36.
83. Deleuze, *Essays Critical and Clinical*, 134.
84. Deleuze, *The Logic of Sense*, 22: "The event belongs essentially to language; it has an essential relationship to language. But language is what is said of things." And 94–95: "The event is subject to double causality, referring on one hand to mixtures of bodies which are its cause and, on the other, to other events which are its quasi-cause. . . . The events of a liquid surface refer to the inter-molecular modifications on which they depend as their real cause, but also to the variations of a surface tension on which they depend as their (ideational or 'fictive') quasi-cause."
85. Deleuze, *The Logic of Sense*, 148–53.
86. Juranville, *L'événement*, 44, my translation. The French reads: "l'événement historique terminal vers lequel elle [la philosophie] dirige (justice, Révolution), rien, *a fortiori*, de l'événement historique primordial pour elle qu'est le Sacrifice du Christ."
87. Romano, *Event and World*.
88. Romano, *Event and World*, 52.
89. Romano, *Event and World*, 52.
90. Romano, *Event and World*, 16–19; Romano opposes, however, the event of birth of the *advenant* (*le sens d'Être*) in contrast to *Dasein*'s possible impossibility of death (*le sens de l'Être*).
91. Derrida, "Typewriter Ribbon: Limited Ink (2)," 72.
92. On Badiou and Deleuze, see Deleuze and Guattari, *What Is Philosophy?* 151–52; Badiou, *Deleuze: La clameur de l'Être*, 81, 88, 97, 126, 132; Badiou, "L'événement selon Deleuze"; Williams, "If Not Here, Then Where?"; Badiou, *Being and Event*; see also Boisset, "L'événement est inadmissible, d'ailleurs il n'existe pas."

93. Badiou, *Deleuze: La clameur de l'Être*, 97.
94. Nancy, "The Surprise of the Event," in *Being Singular Plural*.
95. Deleuze, *The Logic of Sense*, 152.
96. Derrida, *Demeure*, 45.
97. Deleuze, *Essays Critical and Clinical*, 2.

2. INTERMEZZO

1. N. Austin, "Name Magic in the *Odyssey*"; N. Austin, *Archery at the Dark of the Moon*, 147–49; Podlecki, "Guest-Gifts and Nobodies in *Odyssey*"; Heubeck and Hoekstra, *Commentary on Homer's* Odyssey, 33–35.
2. Homer, *The Odyssey*, Book 20, lines 21–24.
3. Homer, *The Odyssey*, Book 9, lines 325–28.
4. Homer, *The Odyssey*, Book 9, lines 435–37.
5. Duras, *Moderato Cantabile*, 15; p. 12 in the French edition. Hereafter, pages in the French edition are given in brackets.
6. Duras, *Moderato Cantabile*, 44 [43–44].
7. Duras, *Moderato Cantabile*, 47–8 [47–48].
8. Duras, *Moderato Cantabile*, 58, 89, 93[56, 91, 95]; ellipsis in the source.
9. Duras, *Moderato Cantabile*, 102–5 [105–9]; my ellipses.

3. HEIDEGGER

1. Pöggeler, "Being as Appropriation," 101–2: "Being as the event of appropriation: with this definition Heidegger's thinking has arrived at its goal." Agamben, *Potentialities*, 117: "The term Ereignis, 'event,' with which Heidegger designates the supreme problem of his thought after *Being and Time*."
2. Heidegger, *Identity and Difference*, 32.
3. Heidegger, *Poetry, Language, Thought*, 218–19: "The same is the belonging together of what differs, through a gathering by way of difference."
4. Heidegger, *Identity and Difference*, 36, emphasis added.
5. Heidegger, *On Time and Being*, 21.
6. Heidegger, *On Time and Being*, 23.
7. Heidegger, *On Time and Being*, 23–24.
8. Heidegger, *Being and Time*, 23.
9. Verstraeten, "Le sens de l'Ereignis."
10. Heidegger, *On Time and Being*, 5,17–18; see, e.g., 24: "thinking that explicitly enters Appropriation in order to say It in terms of It about It." Also see Kisiel, "The Language of the Event."
11. Heidegger, *On Time and Being*, 24; Biemel, "Poetry and Language in Heidegger," 104.

12. Heidegger, *Poetry, Language, Thought*, 140–41: "The more venturesome will more strongly in that they will in a different way from the purposeful self-assertion of the objectifying of the world. Their willing wills nothing of this kind. If willing remains mere self-assertion, they will nothing. They will nothing, in this sense, because they are more willing. They answer sooner to the will which, as the venture itself, draws all pure forces to itself as the pure whole draft of the Open. The willing of the more venturesome is the willing of those who say more sayingly."
13. Bruns, *Heidegger's Estrangements*, 169.
14. Heidegger, *Identity and Difference*, 36; Heidegger, *On Time and Being*, 19.
15. Romano, *Event and World*, 15.
16. Romano, *Event and World*, 15; cf. Fédier, *Regarder voir*, 116–17.
17. Heidegger, "A Dialogue on Language," in *On the Way to Language*, 1-56.
18. Heidegger, *On Time and Being*, 11, 13.
19. Heidegger, *On Time and Being*, 18.
20. Heidegger, *On Time and Being*, 14.
21. Heidegger, *On Time and Being*, 13.
22. Heidegger, *On Time and Being*, 15.
23. Heidegger, *On Time and Being*, 15–16, 17, 22.
24. Heidegger, *Identity and Difference*, 37; Heidegger, *Poetry, Language, Thought*, 190; Heidegger, *On the Way to Language*, 126–27.
25. Eliot, *Collected Poems*, 222.
26. Heidegger, *On the Way to Language*, 10; Heidegger, *Acheminement vers la parole*, 95: "Provenance est toujours avenir."
27. Heidegger, *Identity and Difference*, 41: "Whatever and however we may try to think, we think within the sphere of tradition. Tradition prevails when it frees us from thinking back to a thinking forward, which is no longer a planning. Only when we turn thoughtfully toward what has already been thought, will we be turned to use for what must still be thought."
28. Heidegger, *Poetry, Language, Thought*, 95; Agamben, *Potentialities*, 129–30.
29. Heidegger, *On Time and Being*, 7; see also Kockelmans, *On the Truth of Being*, 60–61; and cf. Derrida, *Positions*, 80–81: "Il faut non seulement se demander quelle est l' 'essence' de l'histoire, l'historicité de l'histoire, mais l' 'histoire' de l' 'essence' en général . . . l'histoire du sens de l'être."
30. Staumbaugh, introduction to Heidegger, *On Time and Being*, ix; see also 7–8, 17.
31. Heidegger, *On the Way to Language,* 31.
32. Agamben, *Potentialities*, 134, 123–24, 131–32.
33. Bruns, *Heidegger's Estrangements*, 166.
34. Heidegger, *Identity and Difference*, 25–26.

35. Heidegger, *Identity and Difference*, 37–39.
36. Bruns, *Heidegger's Estrangements*, 166.
37. Heidegger, *Identity and Difference*, 38, 31.
38. On the etymological link between *Sagen* and *Zeigen*, see, e.g., Heidegger, *On the Way to Language*, 47, 121–23; cf. Deleuze, *Foucault*, 111: "[In Heidegger], [l]ight opens up a speaking no less than a seeing, as if signification haunted the visible which in turn murmured meaning."
39. See also Rueff, *Différence et identité*, 17: "comprendre comment le pronominal qui définit la condition de la réflexion (*je me vois me voir*) peut s'appliquer au champ impersonnel du monde: le *se déclarer des choses elles-mêmes qui révèlent sous nos yeux*."
40. Heidegger, *On the Truth of Being*, 62: "It is the appropriating event which in each case lets man come into what he most properly is; it is what first launches man into his essence. At the same time, it constitutes his destiny. Out of this destiny history grows, in the sense that history is shaped from the way Being presents itself and all beings to man in each case. The appropriation event, thus, in each case 'determines' the way and form in which Being and beings arise for man or are closed off to him." See also de Man, *Aesthetic Ideology*, 133: "History is therefore not a temporal notion, it has nothing to do with temporality but it is the emergence of a language of power out of a language of cognition."
41. Heidegger, *Poetry, Language, Thought*, 192.
42. Heidegger, *On the Way to Language*, 123–24.
43. Heidegger quoted in Kockelmans, *On the Truth of Being*, 64; see also Agamben, *Potentialities*, 132–33: "the unsayable is precisely what remains unsaid in human speech but can be experienced in human speech as such . . . insofar as all human language is necessarily historical and destined, only by un-speaking."
44. Heidegger, *On the Way to Language*, 112: "language . . . is the foundation of human being."
45. Samuel Beckett, "What Is the Word," *Grand Street* 9, no. 2 (Winter 1990): 17–18.
46. Heidegger, *On the Way to Language*, 128–30; Heidegger, *Poetry, Language, Thought*, 206.
47. Heidegger, *Poetry, Language, Thought*, 194.
48. Heidegger, *Poetry, Language, Thought*, 206–7: "language speaks as the peal of stillness."
49. Heidegger, *On the Way to Languge*, 147. See also Blanchot, *Le livre à venir* (Paris: Gallimard, Folio, 1959), 320; and cf. with Barthes, "Le degré zero

de l'écriture," in *Oeuvres complètes*, vol. 1 (Paris: Seuil, 2002), 164: "C'est le mot qui est 'la demeure.'"

50. Heidegger, *Poetry, Language, Thought*, 91, quoting Hölderlin's elegy "Bread and Wine."
51. Heidegger, *On the Way to Language*, 154: "[language is] capable of bestowing, capable of offering, of allowing to attain and reach. But this is the word's essential [deployment] richness that in Saying, that is, in showing, it brings the thing as thing to radiance."
52. Heidegger, "The Origin of the Work of Art," 197–99; Biemel, "Poetry and Language in Heidegger," 76–82; Heidegger, *Approche de Hölderlin*, 48: "là seulement où il y a langage, il y a un monde, c'est-à-dire un cercle continuellement changeant de décision et d'entreprise, d'action et de responsabilité, mais aussi d'arbitraire et de tumulte, de déchéance et d'égarement. Et là seulement où il y a un monde, il y a Histoire. Le langage est un bien en un sens plus originel. Qu'il soit le bien, caution de ce monde et de cette histoire, cela veut dire qu'il garantit que l'homme peut être en tant qu'historial."
53. Heidegger, *Poetry, Language, Thought*, 218.
54. Heidegger, *Poetry, Language, Thought*, 227, 228.
55. Heidegger, *On the Way to Language*, 135.
56. Heidegger, *Poetry, Language, Thought*, 208; see also 228: "Man is capable of poetry at any time only to the degree to which his being is appropriate to that which itself has liking for man and therefore needs his presence."
57. Heidegger, *On the Way to Language*, 135.
58. It is possible that Heidegger refers to Dilthey's conception of analogy as a series of differences; see Dilthey, "Formation of the Historical World," 240–41. Similarly, Blanchot writes on H. Broch in *The Book to Come*, 122: "to express, at once and as if in one single sentence, all opposing movements, to maintain them in their opposition while at the same time opening them up to unity."
59. Janicaud, *Heidegger en France II*, 116.
60. Janicaud, *Heidegger en France II*, 116–18.

4. BLANCHOT

1. Foucault, "Maurice Blanchot," 12.
2. Blanchot, *The Space of Literature*, 239.
3. Blanchot, *The Space of Literature*, 43. See also Blanchot, *The Book to Come*, 232, 237–38. "Does something like literature exist? In what way does it exist? What relationship is there between literature and the assertion of being?" (230).

4. See, e.g., Blanchot, *The Space of Literature*, the chapter "The Essential Solitude," 19–34.
5. Blanchot, *The Space of Literature*, 282–311; Blanchot, *The Book to Come*, 195–202.
6. Blanchot, *The Space of Literature*, 220.
7. Blanchot, *The Space of Literature*, 230.
8. Blanchot, *The Space of Literature*, 217.
9. Blanchot, *The Space of Literature*, 220.
10. Blanchot, *The Space of Literature*, 234.
11. Blanchot, *The Space of Literature*, 227.
12. See Blanchot, *The Space of Literature*, 30–31; also see Heidegger, *Acheminement vers la parole*, 237, in which the translator, Fédier, notes: "En français, les mots qui commencent par im-ou in-ne disent pas quelque chose du simplement négative. L'inconscient est bien plus que le non-conscient; l'impatience, tout autre chose que le fait de ne pas être patient"; see also Foucault, "Maurice Blanchot," 21–23: "That is why Blanchot's language does not use negation dialectically."
13. Blanchot, *The Space of Literature*, 51, 263–64 n. 1.
14. See Blanchot, *The Space of Literature*, 224–25, 231–33; see also Heidegger, "What Are Poets For?" in *Poetry, Language, Thought*, 91–93.
15. Blanchot, *The Book to Come*, 235; Blanchot, *The Space of literature*, 232–33.
16. Blanchot, *The Book to Come*, 238: "Because there is poetry, not only is something changed in the universe, but there is an essential change of the universe."
17. Blanchot, *The Space of Literature*, 238.
18. Blanchot, *The Space of Literature*, 247.
19. See Michel, *Blanchot et le déplacement d'Orphée*, 57–58; Foucault, "Maurice Blanchot," 44.
20. Blanchot, *The Space of Literature*, 224–25; Blanchot, *The Book to Come*, 3–11.
21. The event of literature is bound up with the emotional experience of the myth as opposed to the conceptual truth of logic. In *The Space of Literature*, 239, Blanchot joyfully quotes Nietzsche, "We have art so as not to go under [touch the bottom] on account of truth." He comments: "We have art in order that what makes us go all the way to the bottom not belong to the domain of truth . . . and that is why all work of art and all literary works seem to leave comprehension behind and yet seem never to reach it, so that it must be said of them that they always understood too much and always too little." This illusory movement becomes characteristic; see, e.g., Derrida about Blanchot's *Pace not(s)* in *Parages*.

22. Returning to the myth in this way is a methodological example of a different repetition that runs counter to the cyclic model, where the historical time is only a variation on the origin. It is possible that Blanchot—like other great modern writers (Proust, Joyce, Kafka, Eliot)—not only creates an equivalent analogy between the modern condition and the classical but offers a different adaptation of the myth, without ironically reducing it to parody. Blanchot thus creates an irreducible gap in which the myth provides the meaningful condition of nonsense for modernism, whereas the classical myth receives the excessive power of modern desire and deliriousness.
23. Blanchot, *The Space of Literature*, 175.
24. Turning to Hölderlin's poetry, Heidegger, in contrast to Blanchot, constitutes the poetic night as the holy night. See Heidegger, *Poetry, Language, Thought*, 94.
25. Blanchot, *The Space of Literature*, 174.
26. Blanchot, *The Space of Literature*, 176; Blanchot, *The Book to Come*, 208: "The 'leap' is immediate, but the immediate escapes all verification. We know that we write only when the leap is accomplished, but in order to accomplish it we must first write, write without end, write straight from the infinite."
27. Blanchot, *The Book to Come*, 229.
28. Blanchot, *The Space of Literature*, 43. Cf., e.g., Heidegger's "The Origin of the Work of Art," 161–62, 165: "If there occurs in the work a disclosure of a particular being, disclosing what and how it is, then there is here an occurring, a happening of truth at work. In the work of art the truth of beings has set itself to work. . . . The artwork opens up in its own way Being of beings. This opening up, i.e., this revealing, i.e., the truth of beings, happens in the work. In the artwork, the truth of beings has set itself to work."
29. Blanchot, *The Book to Come*, 237–38. On Blanchot and Heidegger, see Levinas, *Proper Names*, 134. For Blanchot on Mallarmé, see *The Space of Literature*, the chapter "Mallarmé's Experience," *The Book to Come*, the chapter "The Book to Come," and in particular 265–66 n. 9.
30. Blanchot, *The Book to Come*, 232; 203: "That speech can stop being indispensable for understanding . . ."
31. Foucault, "Maurice Blanchot," 54: "We know now that the being of language is the visible effacement of the one who speaks." See also Foucault, *The Order of Things*, 304–6, 327–28.
32. Blanchot, *The Space of Literature*, 43. Blanchot quotes, e.g., from "*Crise de Vers*" and from the letter to Viélé-Griffin, August 18, 1891; see also *The Book to Come*, 225, 240–41. About the importance of Mallarmé to Derrida,

see "The Double Session," in *Dissemination;* to Deleuze, in *The Logic of Sense*, 59–64, and Deleuze and Guattari, *What Is Philosophy?* 159–60; and to Foucault, in "Man and His Doubles," in *The Order of Things*, 303–6.

33. Blanchot, *The Space of Literature*, 109. See, e.g., Mallarmé's sonnet from 1887: "Une dentelle s'abolit / Dans le doute du Jeu suprême / A n'entr'ouvrire comme un blasphème / Qu'absence éternelle du lit" (Mallarmé, *Selected Poetry and Prose*, 58).

34. Blanchot, *The Book to Come*, 229–30; see also 227–28 for the essential difference with mysticism, occultism, and German romantics (Novalis's belief that the work is the path toward the dream) as well as the philosophy of Nature; or *The Space of Literature*, 42, about the difference with the "poem-thing" of Rilke and Ponge. See also Foucault, "Maurice Blanchot," 53, 55.

35. Blanchot, *The Book to Come*, 235.

36. Blanchot, *The Book to Come*, 233.

37. Blanchot, *The Book to Come*, 221.

38. Blanchot, *The Book to Come*, 208.

39. Foucault, "Maurice Blanchot," 12: "the reason it is now so necessary to think through fiction—while in the past it was a matter of thinking the truth"; Blanchot, *The Book to Come*, 239: "doubt belongs to poetic certainty, just as the impossibility of affirming the work brings us close to its own affirmation."

40. Blanchot, *The Book to Come*, 220, 221.

41. In what way does the work raise specters, or is it indeed a space of phantoms? See, e.g., Blanchot, "The Two Versions of the Imaginary," in *The Space of Literature*, 254–64; and the use of "shadow" in "The Essential Solitude," in *The Space of Literature*, 29: "a gaze becomes the ghost of an eternal vision."

42. Blanchot, *The Space of Literature*, 25–26.

43. About Blanchot's concept of "inspiration," see *The Space of Literature*, 176, 182–87; in the same way, the "narrative" approaches the event in *The Book to Come*, 6–7.

44. Barthes, *Journal de deuil*.

45. About Blanchot's concept of "impersonality," see, e.g., Blanchot, *The Infinite Conversation*, chapter 14, "The narrative voice (the 'he,' the neutral)," 556–67; *The Space of Literature*, 28; and *The Book to Come*, 202: "How is it that in us and outside us something anonymous keeps appearing while concealing itself? Prodigious mutation, dangerous and essential, new and infinitely old. We speak, and the words, precise, rigorous do not care about us and are ours only thanks to this strangeness that we have become to ourselves."

46. Foucault, "Maurice Blanchot," 21–24: "To be deprived of the very ability to speak"; Blanchot, *The Space of Literature*, 26–28.
47. Blanchot, *The Step Not-Beyond*, 89–90; Blanchot, *The Space of Literature*, 90–92, 94–95.
48. See also *The Space of Literature*, 25, where Blanchot refuses to consider the biographical death of the writer as the point at which the work is concluded, in favor of an unaccomplished dying which is bound up with the making of the work itself.
49. Blanchot, *The Space of Literature*, 104.
50. Blanchot, *The Space of Literature*, 94–95; see also *The Book to Come*, 195.
51. Blanchot, *The Space of Literature*, 112–13: "From such a perspective the event could never happen (death could never become an event).... This contradiction expresses everything that makes both death and the work difficult. One and the other are somehow unapproachable."
52. Blanchot, "The Instant of My Death," 10–11.
53. Blanchot, *The Space of Literature*, 106.
54. Blanchot, *The Space of Literature*, 106: "It is the fact of dying that includes a radical reversal, through which the death that was the extreme form of my power not only becomes what loosens my hold upon myself by casting me out of my power to begin and even to finish, but also becomes that which is without any relation to me, without power over me—that which is stripped of all possibility—the unreality of the indefinite."
55. Blanchot, *The Book to Come*, 219, and *The Step Not-Beyond*, 94–96: "The work of mourning: the inverse of dying." Dying is not the dialectical movement in which death is the ultimate trial of the writer, regaining by appropriating the negation: "writing to be able to die"; see Hegel, Freud, and Kristeva. Instead, the writer must intensify the crisis without possible opening, to disappear into the neutral voice of origin. Death vs. Dying: Death is the writing region of lamentation or deception, the loss of the past or the unrealized promise of the future; both are possible expressions in the present. However, Dying begins where we forget our losses and we keep waiting for what cannot come about: "It is in forgetting that the wait remains a waiting: an acute attention to what is radically new" (Foucault, "Maurice Blanchot," 56, 22). There is neither before nor after, no lamentation nor hope but the eternal wandering of a kind of Cain who is "always in abeyance."
56. Blanchot, *The Space of Literature*, 155.
57. Blanchot, *The Space of Literature*, 32–33, about the "void": it is no real object, no real figure, but "the limitless depth behind the image, a lifeless profundity, unmanipulable ... where objects sink away when they depart from their sense, when they collapse into their image"; see also 26, 154, 156.

58. Blanchot, *The Book to Come*, 33.
59. Blanchot, *The Book to Come*, 3.
60. Blanchot, *The Book to Come*, 5.
61. Narration, like the movement that leads up to its beginning, thus progresses by coming back: what is happening in the narrative points to the condition of telling what is happening. The happening does not exist outside the way it is being told. In this manner the telling becomes the very happening: the event of the work of literature and the "step-not beyond." See also *The Book to Come*, 6–7, and also see 236: "Profundity of meaning consists of the step backwards-in retreat—that meaning makes us take in relation to it."
62. Blanchot, *The Book to Come*, 7.
63. Blanchot, *The Book to Come*, 9, 230, 240–41.
64. Blanchot, *The Book to Come*, 8–10, 225, 239, and see also 207–8: "That the world, where we have only things to use, first of all collapsed, that things have become infinitely distanced from themselves, have recovered the inalienable distance of the image—that is why I'm no longer myself and can no longer say 'I.' A formidable transformation."
65. Blanchot, *The Book to Come*, 239, 241, 242–44, 19–21; see also Derrida, "The Book to Come," in *Paper Machine*, 4–18.
66. Barthes, *Criticism and Truth*, 51.

5. DERRIDA

1. Derrida, "A Certain Impossible Possibility."
2. Derrida, "A Certain Impossible Possibility," 454.
3. See Derrida, *Paper Machine*, 131–32. And Derrida, "Typewriter Ribbon": "an impossible event, and therefore the only possible event" (279). "For what threatens is also what makes possible the expectation or the promise . . . the condition of possibility *is* the condition of impossibility" (335–36). "It is that which, within desire, constitutes it as possible and insists there while resisting it, as the impossible . . . the becoming possible of the impossible as im-possible" (358).
4. Derrida, "A Certain Impossible Possibility," 451: "The event's eventfulness depends on this experience of the impossible."
5. Borradori, *Philosophy in a Time of Terror*.
6. Derrida, "A Certain Impossible Possibility," 446.
7. See Derrida, "No Apocalypse, Not Now."
8. Derrida, "A Certain Impossible Possibility," 451–52.
9. Borradori, *Philosophy in a Time of Terror*, 90.
10. Derrida, *Signéponge/Signsponge*, 16; Derrida and Stiegler, *Echographies of Television*, 10–12.

11. Derrida, "A Certain Impossible Possibility," 452.
12. Derrida, "A Certain Impossible Possibility," 453.
13. About the concept of "iterability," see, e.g., Derrida, *Margins of Philosophy*, 315: "This iterability—(*iter*, once again, comes from *itara*, other in Sanskrit, and everything that follows may be read as the exploitation of the logic which links repetition to alterity)." See also Derrida, *Limited Inc.*, 53: "Iterability supposes a minimal remainder (as well as a minimum idealization) in order that the identity of the *self-same* be repeatable and identifiable *in, through*, and even *in view of* its alteration." On "spectrality" see Derrida and Stiegler, *Echographies of Television*, 115–16: "A specter is both visible and invisible, both phenomenal and nonphenomenal: a trace that marks the present with its absence in advance."
14. Derrida, "A Certain Impossible Possibility," 451–54.
15. Derrida, "Typewriter Ribbon: Limited Ink (2)," 72–74.
16. Derrida, *Parages*, 155–56.
17. Kronick, "Between Act and Archive," 75 n. 25: "It is the condition of something being recognized in different times and places, *and* it deconstitutes the 'thing,' as eidos or essence (that is, as self-identical). Iterability is an impure 'idea,'" quoting Derrida, Limited Ink, 53: "a differential structure escaping the logic of presence or the (simple and dialectical) opposition of presence and absence, upon which the idea of permanence depends."
18. Borradori, *Philosophy in a Time of Terror*, 85–86.
19. Borradori, *Philosophy in a Time of Terror*, 87–88.
20. Borradori, *Philosophy in a Time of Terror*, 87–88.
21. Derrida and Stiegler, *Echographies of Television*, 36.
22. Derrida, *Specters of Marx*, 17.
23. Derrida, *Parages*, 156.
24. Derrida, *Parages*, 33.
25. Derrida, *Parages*, 155. This is precisely the coming of the event: the "Pas" of Derrida-Blanchot, the "dying" of Blanchot, the "self-concealment" of Heidegger.
26. Derrida and Stiegler, *Echographies of Television*, 76–77; Derrida, "A Certain Impossible Possibility," 460; Borradori, *Philosophy in a Time of Terror*, 89.
27. See Bataille, "A propos de récits d'habitants d'Hiroshima," for the same distinction between the "animal" experience of the victims and the political experience and discourse. Another example is Derrida's discussion on 9/11 in *Philosophy in a Time of Terror* dealing especially with the media's artificially producing a "major event" while ignoring other catastrophes that pass "unnoticed."
28. Derrida, "A Certain Impossible Possibility," 460.

29. Derrida, *Demeure*, 65.
30. On Blanchot's and Derrida's understanding of the event as a "dying move" see chapter 9, "Writing Corporeally."
31. These two directions are everywhere in the work of Derrida: "Viens" and "récit" in *Parages*; "confession and guilty" and "textual event (machine)" in "Typewriter Ribbon"; "the instant of death" and "testimony" in *Demeure*; "things" and "event of signature" in *Signéponge/Signeponge*; and "date" and "poetry" in "Shibboleth."
32. Borradori, *Philosophy in a Time of Terror*, 189 n. 9; see also Derrida and Stiegler, *Echographies of Television*, 129.
33. Derrida, *Demeure*, 31–32.
34. See: Derrida, *The Gift of Death*.
35. Derrida, *Signéponge/Signsponge*, 14.
36. Janicaud, *Heidegger en France II*, 116–18, my translation: "Dans ce que je dit de l'événement, quelque chose ne se laisse pas facilement heideggérianiser. Je suis du côté de la dislocation, de la dispersion, de la dissémination.... le conflit, il [Heidegger] le pense comme ce qui rassemble les adversaires, ce qui tient ensemble les deux pôles opposés; moi je pense à une différence qui ne tiendrait même pas ensemble les différents.... J'essaie de penser une différence qui ne se laisse pas rassembler." And later on, "J'y résiste du côté de ce qui ne se laisse plus rassembler—hélas ! Hélas et non, d'ailleurs, parce que le fait de résister au rassemblement peut être ressenti comme une détresse, un malheur, une perte-la dislocation, la dissémination, le ne-pas-être-chez-soi, etc.—mais c'est aussi une chance. La chance de la rencontre, de la justice, de l'altérité absolue.... Et, inversement [chez Heidegger], du côté du rassemblent ou du logos ou de l'être, il y a, bien sûr, la chance du rassemblement, mais aussi certainement une certaine non-rencontre, un certain aveuglement à l'autre, une certaine annulation de l'événement, une certaine non-événmentialité pure. Tel serait le débat."
37. Borradori, *Philosophy in a Time of Terror*, 90. Derrida affirms that the movement of "ex-appropriation" is already found in the appropriation event of *Ereignis*. Between appropriation and expropriation, the question is thus where to put the accent. Janicaud, *Heidegger en France II*, 118.
38. Derrida and Stiegler, *Echographies of Television*, 37.
39. Derrida, *Signéponge/Signsponge*, 102.
40. On Heidegger's abyss, see Derrida and Stiegler, *Echographies of Television*, 134.
41. Derrida, *Signéponge/Signsponge*, 30: "some hand to hand conflict with the impossible, with something which, within the proper, within the very

structure of the proper, is produced only by shifting into its opposite, by being set in abyss, by being inverted, contaminated, and divided. And one has to suspect that the grand affair of the signature is to be found there."

42. Derrida, *Signéponge/Signsponge*, 26, 30, 52, 54, 102.
43. Blanchot, *Parages*, 25–26.
44. Heidegger, *On Time and Being*, 19.
45. Derrida, *Demeure*, 91: "the experience of what arrives must be passion"; see also Derrida and Stiegler, *Echographies of Television*, 105–6, where Derrida presents the paradox of anticipation: the calling for the coming event also nullifies the future.
46. Blanchot, *Death Sentence*, 30; see also Derrida, *Parages*, e.g., 52: "The event does not manage to happen [n'arrive pas à arriver], but that is because he himself gets by rather well: because he is not himself disabled enough. He does not manage to let the event come. The best that could happen to him himself is to be disabled enough, on the brink of wrecking, no longer getting by at all, for the chance (the failure and the due date) of the event: something (other) that would happen (to him) finally, the best and the worst. His mastery is put in check for what is called to come: *come*."
47. Derrida, "Shibboleth," 10.
48. Derrida, *Signéponge/Signsponge*, 42–44, 54.
49. See Derrida, "Typewriter Ribbon," 331–32: "singularity, semelfactivity (that is, the concept of what happens just once), the 'one time only' of the event." Derrida, *Papier Machine*, 108–9: "Le 'une seule fois,' le 'une fois pour toutes' de l'événement." Derrida, "No Apocalypse, Not Now," 30: "Thinking the event, the coming or the venue of the first time which is also to be the last time."
50. Derrida, *Demeure*, 94.
51. See also Merleau-Ponty, "The Specter of a Pure Language," in *The Prose of the World*, 3–8. For "transcendental signified" see, e.g., Derrida, *Of Grammatology*, 20.
52. Derrida, *Margins of Philosophy*, 316.
53. Derrida, "A Certain Impossible Possibility," 460.
54. Derrida, *Demeure*, 91–94; Derrida and Stiegler, *Echographies of Television*, 81; Derrida, "Shibboleth," 40.
55. Derrida, *Paper Machine*, 336: "It would be a matter of thinking an event that is undeniable but without pure presence." See already in "Qual Quelle, Valéry's Source" in *Margins of Philosophy*, 290–91: "Can one conceive of an initial event without presence, the value of a first time that cannot be thought in the form of category of presence?"; 297: "a paradoxical logic of the event as a source which cannot present itself, happen to itself. The

value of the event is perhaps indissociable from that of presence; it remains rigourously incompatible with that of self-presence."

56. Derrida, "A Certain Impossible Possibility," 456–58; Derrida, "Typewriter Ribbon," 336, 358; Borradori, *Philosophy in a Time of Terror*, 96–98.
57. See, e.g., Freud, "Beyond the Pleasure Principle," 29: "We describe as 'traumatic' any excitations from outside which are powerful enough to break through the protective shield. It seems to me that the concept of trauma necessarily implies a connection of this kind with a breach in an otherwise efficacious barrier against stimuli. Such an event as an external trauma is bound to provoke a disturbance of a large scale in the functioning of the organism's energy and to set in motion every possible defensive measure." See also Laplanche and Pontalis, *The Language of Psychoanalysis*, 465–69: "[T]he traumatic event triggers the setting up by the ego of a 'pathological defence' operating in accordance with the primary process, instead of the normal defences generally used against an unpleasurable event . . . the idea that external events derive their effectiveness from the phantasies they activate and from the influx of instinctual excitations they provoke . . . a kind of diametrical opposition between the external danger and the internal one: the ego is attacked from within—that is to say, by instinctual excitations—just as it is from without." For an example of the literary criticism and the event as trauma, see Dominque Rabaté, "Evénement et traumatisme: Modalités de l'après coup dans le roman du XXe siècle," in Glaudes and Meter, *Le sens de l'événément*, 169–80.
58. Borradori, *Philosophy in a Time of Terror*, 91, 96; Derrida, "Typewriter Ribbon," 358.
59. Derrida, *Specters of Marx*, 25.
60. Borradori, *Philosophy in Time of Terror*, 97.
61. Barthes, *Journal de deuil*, 216–17.
62. On the tense of "futur antérieur" see Derrida, "Shibboleth," 24–25; Derrida, *Demeure*, 49–50; Borradori, *Philosophy in a Time of Terror*, 97; and Derrida and Stiegler, *Echographies of Television*, 123. This tense is also studied by Deleuze, *The Logic of Sense*, 349 n. 5 (from Sartre and Stern); Blanchot, *The Book to Come*, 9, 241; Baudrillard, *The Spirit of Terrorism*; and Lyotard, *The Postmodern Explained*.
63. According to Freud, repetition (compulsive repetition) is an act of the subject's self-protection, self-control, discharge, and resistance also when it relates to the death drive and the traumatic event. For Deleuze, by contrast, repetition is what ruins the subjective formation of coherence and identity. See Deleuze on Freud in *Difference and Repetition*, 16–19.

64. In *Demeure*, Derrida shows in what way fiction is an integral part of the truth conditions of the judicial testimony and inversely constitutes its threat. For example, the translation of perception into words is a faculty of fiction. Fiction is therefore an important factor in the reconstruction of judicial proof, although it is based on conventional conversions that necessarily apply perjury and deception.
65. See J. L. Austin, *How to Do Things with Words*.
66. Derrida, "A Certain Impossible Possibility," 446.
67. Derrida, "A Certain Impossible Possibility," 446.
68. The difference between the constative and the performative can be further studied in literature in terms of different stages: omnipresent narrator and subjective narrator; indirect discourse and direct discourse; Valéry's difference between "faire" and "dire"; etc.
69. Austin's definition of the performative utterance joins the understanding of the "Word event" in the hermeneutical tradition; this approach conceives of literary transmission (reading, interpretation, performance) as a ceremony that reactualizes and presents the continuity of a language and a culture. See Palmer, *Hermeneutics*, 18–20.
70. Derrida, "Typewriter Ribbon: Limited Ink (2)," 158: "But then this arbitrariness undoes the power and the force of a performative which, as I was suggesting earlier, tends always to neutralize the event it seems to produce."
71. Derrida, "Typewriter Ribbon: Limited Ink (2)," 146.
72. Derrida, *Margins of Philosophy*, 314–20.
73. Derrida, "Shibboleth," 32.
74. See, e.g., Derrida, "No Apocalypse, Not Now," 27: "Literature belongs to this nuclear epoch . . . at least if we mean by this the historical and ahistorical horizon of an absolute self-destructibility without apocalypse, without revelation of its own truth, without absolute knowledge. . . . [O]n the one hand we have the principle of reason (interpreted since the seventeenth century according to the order of representation, the domination of the subject/object structure, the metaphysics of will, modern techno-science, and so on . . .) and on the other hand, we have the project of literature in the strict sense, the project which cannot be shown to antedate the seventeenth and eighteenth centuries. . . . In what I am here calling in another sense an absolute epoch, literature comes to life and can only experience its own precariousness its death menace and its essential finitude. The movement of its inscription is the very possibility of its effacement."
75. Derrida, *Demeure*, 73: "absolute interruption."
76. Derrida, *Parages*, 165; and Blanchot's narrative in *The Book to Come*, 9–10.
77. Foucault, "Maurice Blanchot," 25.

6. DELEUZE

1. See Deleuze and Guattari, *What Is Philosophy?* 38; Deleuze, *The Logic of Sense*, 128.
2. For Deleuze's critique of transcendence (Neoplatonism, Christianity) and later on of the transcendental—"la manière moderne de sauver la transcendence" (Kant, Husserl)—see Deleuze and Guattari, *What Is Philosophy?* 46–49; Deleuze, *The Logic of Sense*, "15th Series of Singularities." See also Badiou, *Deleuze: The Clamor of Being*, 21–22.
3. Deleuze and Guattari, *What Is Philosophy?* 47.
4. Deleuze and Guattari, *What Is Philosophy?* 49–50; they quote Nietzsche, who defines four great errors of philosophy: the illusion of transcendence, the universal concepts, the eternal, and the discursive aspirations.
5. Deleuze and Guattari, *What Is Philosophy?* 60.
6. Deleuze, *The Logic of Sense*, "12th Series of the Paradox"; and in regard to Husserl, 97–98, 102; see also *Difference and Repetition*, "The Image of Thought."
7. Deleuze, *The Logic of Sense*, 78.
8. Deleuze, *The Logic of Sense*, appendix 1.
9. Deleuze, *The Logic of Sense*, 265: "Thus, the eternal return is, in fact, the Same and Similar, but only insofar as they are simulated, produced by the simulation, through the functioning of the simulacrum.... It does not presuppose the Same and the Similar; on the contrary, it constitutes the only Same—the Same of that which differs, and the only resemblance—the resemblance of the unmatched. It is the unique phantasm of all simulacra (the Being of all beings). It is the power to affirm divergence and decentering and makes this power the object of a superior affirmation." Contrary to Aristotle's belief that Being has many senses, Deleuze's Being is said in a unique sense as the very act of differentiation: "Being is said in a single and same sense of everything of which it is said, but that of which it is said differs; it is said of difference itself" (*Difference and Repetition*, 36). Badiou devotes much attention to this problem in his book on Deleuze, showing that the originality of Deleuze is in the movement between the multiplicity of singular cases and the univocity of Being, a movement that can be found throughout his entire work, taking different names and regarding different questions: nonsense and sense, virtual and actual, inorganic life and states of things, chaos and "chaosmos," soil (*terre*) and territory.
10. *Pluralism* = *monism* means that Being divides itself into multiple dimensions only if the nature of the one simultaneously transmutes. See, e.g., Deleuze and Guattari, *A Thousand Plateaus*, 23, 275.

11. Deleuze, *The Logic of Sense*, 72.
12. Deleuze, *Difference and Repetition*, 154.
13. Deleuze, *The Logic of Sense,* 4–11; Deleuze and Parnet, *Dialogues II,* 62–65; Deleuze and Guattari, *A Thousand Plateaus*, 96–98.
14. According to Deleuze, the terms "incorporeal" and "sense" do not directly refer to the realm of linguistic expression but to what makes language converge with the corporeal by affirming its difference. However, to keep the description of the problem as simple as possible, I find it useful to oppose "incorporeal" and "corporeal" in order then to define the event that agitates between the words and the bodies. For further detail Deleuze cites Bréhier, *La théorie des incorporels dans l'ancien Stoïcisme*.
15. This is what Deleuze refers to with "phantom" (*The Logic of Sense*, 20), "phantasmes," "simulacra" (7–8), and even Husserl's "perceptual noema" (20).
16. Deleuze and Guattari, *A Thousand Plateaus*, 96: "What incorporeal transformation is expressed by these dates, incorporeal yet attributed to bodies, inserted into them? . . . [A] parceling of the two, a manner in which expressions are inserted into contents, in which we ceaselessly jump from one register to another, in which signs are at work in things themselves just as things extend into or are deployed through signs." See also Deleuze, *The Logic of Sense*, 166–67, 95.
17. Deleuze, *The Logic of Sense*, 40: "it guarantees, therefore, the convergence of the two series which it traverses, but precisely on the condition that it makes them endlessly diverge."
18. Deleuze, *The Logic of Sense*, 22.
19. Deleuze, *The Logic of Sense*, 8.
20. Deleuze, *The Logic of Sense*, 182.
21. Deleuze, *The Logic of Sense*, 128.
22. Deleuze, *The Logic of Sense*, 107.
23. Deleuze, *The Logic of Sense*, 173–75.
24. Deleuze, *The Logic of Sense*, "Eighth Series of Structure"; see also Deleuze, "À quoi reconnaît-on le structuralisme"; Badiou, *Deleuze: The Clamor of Being*, 37–38.
25. On structuralism and poststructuralism, see, e.g., Blanchot, "Michel Foucault as I Imagine Him," 69; Derrida, "Structure, Sign, and Play in the Discourse of the Human Sciences," in *Writing and Difference*, 351–70; Ricoeur, "Structure, Word, Event," in *The Conflict of Interpretations*, 79–98; and Deleuze and Guattari, introduction, *A Thousand Plateaus*.
26. Deleuze, *The Logic of Sense*, 51.
27. Deleuze, *The Logic of Sense*, 8.
28. Deleuze, *The Logic of Sense*, 71, 35.

29. In *The Logic of Sense*, 22, Deleuze distinguishes between Carroll's *logical work* and his *fantastic work*.
30. Leskly, *Collected Poems*, 151 (in Hebrew); translated by I. Rowner and M. Hadar.
31. Badiou, *Deleuze: The Clamor of Being*, 44. For the moral confrontation with war, wounds, and death see Deleuze, *The Logic of Sense*, 148–53. Beyond all negative or positive lived experience, the affirmation of Life is where the deformation of the corporeal and of the imaginary meet the limit of its creation. From here see also the place Deleuze grants to the non-philosophical creations of thinking particularly in *What Is Philosophy?*
32. Barbaras, *Le tournant de l'expérience*, 7–8, my translation.
33. Deleuze, *The Logic of Sense*, 66; see also 40–47.
34. Deleuze, *The Logic of Sense*, 107.
35. Deleuze, *The Logic of Sense*, 106. See the discussion of "foundation" and "abyss" in Badiou, *Deleuze: The Clamor of Being*, 43–45.
36. Deleuze, *The Logic of Sense*, 40, 176; Deleuze and Guattari, *A Thousand Plateaus*, 7.
37. Deleuze, *The Logic of Sense*, 71; Deleuze, *Difference and Repetition*, 154–56.
38. Deleuze, *The Logic of Sense*, 105, where Deleuze criticizes Husserl and Kant: "But we do not, for all this, escape the vicious circle which makes the condition refer to the conditioned as it reproduces its image"; see also 123: "We cannot think of the condition in the image of conditioned.... We must have something unconditioned which would be the heterogeneous synthesis of the condition in an autonomous figure binding to itself neutrality and generic power."
39. Yet there is a fundamental difficulty between the neutrality and the productivity of nonsense; after all, how does nonsense produce differentiation if it does not have any sense at all? Deleuze formulates this problem explicitly in *The Logic of Sense*, 96. He argues that neutrality (transcendental impersonality) is the only condition to conceive of a "heterogeneous synthesis" between two or more incompatible series. In this way language for example, does not represent the real, language does never coincide with the real. This incommensurability between the series generates their perpetual dissymmetrical productivity.
40. In this light Deleuze suggests, with Guattari, replacing the concept of *Être* (Being) with *Et . . . Et . . . Et* (and . . . and . . . and). See Deleuze and Parnet, *Dialogues II*, 56–59; Deleuze and Guattari, *A Thousand Plateaus*, 27. Deleuze and Guattari, *What Is Philosophy?* 152: "The multiplicity is precisely what happens between the two."
41. See, e.g., Heidegger, *On the Way to Language*, 121–23.

42. Badiou, *Deleuze: The Clamor of Being*, 22, 21. For Deleuze about Heidegger, see in particular Deleuze, *Foucault*, 108–14: "The Visible or the Open does not give us something to see without also providing something to speak" (111).
43. It is true that Heidegger's *Ereignis* is very close to Deleuze's event in the sense that *Ereignis* can be determined only from "elements" that are appropriated. Hence, *Ereignis* is studied in the context of different relationships in *The Essence of Identity* (1957), *On Time and Being* (1962), and *On the Way to Language* (1959), but Heidegger is more preoccupied by the same ideal mechanism that makes the elements belong to one another in their own nature than he is by studying their new production of real singular situations. Heidegger less accentuates the differentiation of the internal elements of *Ereignis* than the fact that the identity of these elements themselves depends on the condition of their belonging together. The event of appropriation, the belonging together of what differs, is what allows the essence of identity through differentiation. To summarize, the disagreements between Heidegger and Deleuze focus on the following: (1) removing the emphasis from the ideal production of sense to the real differentiation of sense produced (actual and virtual); (2) the belonging together of what differs becomes the process of actual differentiation; and (3) the expressions of the dimensions of Being, language and vision, do not converge by analogical relation, but are in an incessant struggle of "no-relation." See also Deleuze, *Difference and Repetition*, 321 n. 11.
44. Merleau-Ponty, *Phenomenology of Perception*, 177; Barbaras, *Le tournant de l'expérience*, chapter 8. Although he is specifying the work of the sensible rather than of reason, it seems that Merleau-Ponty does not break completely with the tradition that confronts the actual with the potential. Generally speaking, he remains attached to the consequences of this reversal, which privileges the activity of the actual rather than that of the potential. He discards the hierarchical logic of cause and effect in favor of a horizontal oscillation in which every actual accomplishment stretches and develops the new horizons of the potential; the actual transforms the potential by transcending its sources. In this Merleau-Ponty does still epistemologically chime in with the hermeneutical circle beginning in Schleiermacher and with the linguistic distinction between "langue" and "parole" used since de Saussure's *Course*.
45. About the "virtual" and the "actual," see Deleuze, *Difference and Repetition*, 208–14; Deleuze and Partnet, *Dialogues II*, 148–52; Deleuze and Guattari, *What Is Philosophy?* 151–62.

46. Deleuze, *Difference and Repetition*, 212: "it [actualisation] does not result from any limitation of a pre-existing possibility. It is contradictory to speak of 'potential' . . . and to define differentiation by the simple limitatition of a global power"; "The subordination of difference to identity and that of difference to similitude must be overtuned in the same movement."
47. Deleuze, *Difference and Repetition*, 212.
48. Deleuze and Guattari, *What Is Philsophy?* 160. Deleuze and Parnet, *Dialogues II*, 149–50: "The plane of immanence includes both the virtual and its actualization simultaneously, without there being any an assignable limit between the two. The actual is the complement or the product, the object of actualization, which has nothing but the virtual as it subject."
49. Deleuze and Guattari, *What Is Philosophy?* 96, 112–13, 151–62.
50. Deleuze and Guattari, *What Is Philosophy?* 158.
51. Deleuze and Guattari, *What Is Philosophy?* 156.
52. See Deleuze, *The Logic of Sense*, "20th Series on the Moral Problem in Stoic Philosophy" and "21st Series of the Event."
53. Deleuze, *Proust and Signs*, 97: "It is precisely the contingency of the encounter that guarantees the necessity of what it leads us to think."
54. Deleuze, *The Logic of Sense*, 148; see also Bousquet, Oeuvre romanesque complète; in *What Is Philosophy?* 159, Deleuze and Guattari add on behalf of Bousquet: "I was born to embody it as event because I was able to disembody it as state of affairs or lived situation."
55. Deleuze, *The Logic of Sense*, 151; for *Amor fati* see, e.g., Nietzsche *The Gay Science*, section 267; Nietzsche, *Ecce Homo*, section 1; Magnus, *Heidegger's Metahistory of Philosophy*, 43–46, 53–54.
56. Deleuze and Guattari, *What Is Philosophy?* 160; Deleuze and Parnet, *Dialogues II*, 65: "The wound is something that I receive in my body, in a particular place, at a particular moment, but there is also an eternal truth of the wound as impassive, incorporeal event"; Deleuze, *The Logic of Sense*, 152: "Only the free man, therefore, can comprehend all violence in a single act of violence, and every mortal event in a *single Event*." See also the event as impersonal "mime," as becoming the actor of your own wound (evoking Mallarmé), in *The Logic of Sense* and *What Is Philosophy?*
57. Deleuze and Guattari, *What Is Philosophy?* 113. In *Being Singular Plural*, 159, Nancy finds in Hegel a similar description of the task of philosophy, quoting the philosopher: "Philosophy is not meant to be a narration of happenings but a cognition of what is *true* in them, and further, on the basis of this cognition, to *comprehend* that which, in the narrative, appears as a mere happening [pure event—trans.]" Hegel, however, strives to reveal the truth of the concept beneath the appearance of the event's narrative representation.

The progress of Hegel's truth depends therefore on historical occurrences, in opposition to Deleuze's becoming which is non-historical and truthless.
58. Deleuze, *Essays Critical and Clinical*, 134–35. See also chapters 2 and 15.
59. The uncontainable becoming could misleadingly carry the face of the eternal, but its infinite truth has the non-image of Dionysian agony and joy and not the absolute symbolic message of Zeus; it is the pantheism (natural, vital, corporeal) of deformation and creation in opposition to the generative word of the monotheism: hinting without being spectacular, immanent, real and not abstract, violent and intensive without assurance and confirmation. The becoming is always now, always in the surface of present as the turbulence of dissimilarity that divides the present. This is why it expresses no authentic hope or melancholic nostalgia, for it does not break into the real like the miracle revelation of the eternal.
60. See Deleuze, *Essays Critical and Clinical*, 154.
61. Deleuze and Guattari, *A Thousand Plateaus*, 10th plateau: "1730: Becoming Intense, Becoming-Animal, Becoming-Imperceptible."
62. Deleuze and Guattari, *What Is Philosophy?* 172–74; see also Deleuze, *Essays Critical and Clinical*, 4; Deleuze, *The Logic of Sense*, 172–73; Deleuze, *Foucault*, 92–93.
63. Deleuze and Guattari, *What Is Philosophy?* 108–10; Charles Peguy already writes in *Note conjointe sur M. Descartes* (1914): ouvrir "une race mental nouvelle, une race nouvelle de la pensée."
64. Deleuze and Guattari, *A Thousand Plateaus*, 235.
65. Deleuze, *The Logic of Sense*, 22.
66. See Deleuze, *The Logic of Sense*, 298–99: "That *I* may be an other, that something else thinks in us in an aggression which is the aggression of thought, in a multiplication which is the multiplication of the body, or in a violence which is the violence of language—this is the joyful message. . . . At the same time that bodies lose their unity and the self its identity, language loses its denoting function (its distinct sort of integrity) in order to discover a value that is purely expressive."
67. See, e.g., Derrida on Heidegger in Derrida and Stiegler, *Echographies of Television*, 131–32: "We inherit language in order to be able to bear witness to the fact that we are inheritors. That is to say, we inherit the possibility of inheriting, the fact that we inherit is not an attribute or an accident; it is our essence, and this essence, we inherit."
68. Deleuze and Guattari, *What Is Philosophy?* 160: "Philosophy's sole aim is to become worthy of the event, and it is precisely the conceptual persona who counter-effectuates the event"; see also Jean Sarocchi, "L'événement Socrate," in Glaudes and Meter, *Le sens de l'événement*, 71–104.

69. Deleuze, "The Exhausted," in *Essays Critical and Clinical*, 152–74.
70. Rancière, *The Flesh of Words*, 154.
71. See Deleuze and Parnet, *Dialogues II*, chapter 1 and chapter 2; page 4: "We must be bilingual even in a single language, we must have a minor language inside our own language." Deleuze, *Essays Critical and Clinical*, lv: "When another language is created within language, it is language in its entirety that tends towards an 'asyntactic,' 'agrammatical' limit, or that communicates with its own outside." See also Deleuze and Guattari, *A Thousand Plateaus*, 108–9.
72. On the *Aion* see Deleuze, *The Logic of Sense*, 61–64, 77–78, 162–68; Deleuze and Parnet, *Dialogues II*, 148–52.
73. Heidegger, *On Time and Being*, 13.
74. Gadamer, *Truth and Method*.
75. Heidegger, *On Time and Being*, 17.
76. Deleuze and Parnet, *Dialogues II*, 151.
77. Émile Benveniste, "Expression Indo-européene de l'"éternité,"" *Bulletin de la Société de Linguistique de Paris* 38 (1937): 103–12.
78. Deleuze and Guattari, *What Is Philosophy?* 158.
79. Barthes, *S/Z*, 3–4.
80. See Deleuze and Guattari, *A Thousand Plateaus*, 8th plateau: "1874—Three novellas or 'What Happened,'" 212–28. Asking, What can I see or say today? Deleuze writes about Foucault: "We will then think the past against the present and resist the latter, not in favor of a return, but 'in favor, I hope, of a time to come' (Nietzsche)" (Deleuze, *Foucault*, 119): the troubled continuation of "what has happened" brings about the past as the new in the present, as if this novelty consisted in the discontinuity of the unexpected, the exception and the chance of "what is going to happen," the future creation of the event.
81. Deleuze, *Essays Critical and Clinical*, lv.
82. See Foucault, "Maurice Blanchot," 69; Deleuze, *Foucault*, 70–123 (outside and forces); Deleuze and Guattari, *A Thousand Plateaus*, "Introduction: Rhizome" (ouside and book); Deleuze and Guattari, *What Is Philosophy?* 185–86, 192 ("chaos" as synonym); Deleuze, *Essays Critical and Clinical* (outside and writing).
83. Foucault, "Maurice Blanchot," 22: "Not reflection, but forgetting; not contradiction, but contestation that effaces; not reconciliation, but droning on and on; not mind in laborious conquest of its unity, but the endless erosion of the outside; not truth finally shedding light on itself, but the streaming and distress of a language that has always already begun." Perhaps, in Blanchot's view, this void is full (Foucault, "Maurice Blanchot,"

23) because it is everywhere, everywhere there is sound and speech. But it offers itself only as the attraction of infinite absence, the fascination of indifference or as an ambiguous silence, "the threshold of all positivity . . . the void serving as its site" (Foucault, "Maurice Blanchot," 16).

84. Deleuze, *Foucault*, 87: "In Foucault's work the article on Nietzsche and the one on Blanchot join up, or rejoin." In *Deleuze: The Clamor of Being*, 86–87, Badiou notes that for Deleuze, Foucault offers the only chance to clarify Nietzsche's "play of forces."
85. Deleuze, *Foucault*, 113.
86. Deleuze, *Foucault*, 86–87, 111–12.
87. Deleuze, *Foucault*, 72.
88. Blanchot, *The Book to Come*, 235: "The space . . . not actually existing anywhere it is"; 236: "Like that place where nothing took place . . . an indefinite stirring of absence"; 242: "That outwardness [le dehors] where it [the book] will be in contact with its own distance."
89. About the fold, see, e.g., Badiou, in *Deleuze: The Clamor of Being*, the chapter "The Outside and the Fold," 79–94.
90. Deleuze, *Foucault*, 91–92, 122–23; see also Deleuze's commentary on Blanchot's concept of dying in Deleuze, *The Logic of Sense*, 148–53; see also Deleuze and Parnet, *Dialogues II*, 62–65; and Deleuze and Guattari, *What Is Philosophy?* 156.
91. Deleuze, *The Logic of Sense*, 173.
92. Deleuze and Guattari, "Percept, Affect, and Concept," in *What Is Philosophy?*
93. Deleuze and Parnet, *Dialogues II*, 30: "to make writing an act of thought"; and see p. 38; Deleuze, *Proust and Signs*, 97–98.
94. Deleuze, *Foucault*, 118.

7. TOWARD A THEORY OF LITERARY EVENTS

1. Genette, *Fiction and Diction*, vii.
2. Genette, *Fiction and Diction*, 6–16.
3. Flaubert, *Letters*, 175, 159, 154.
4. Flaubert, *Letters*, 154.
5. Flaubert, *Letters*, 230.
6. Paul Celan, "The Méridien," in *Collected Prose*, trans. Rosmarie Waldrop (Manchester: Carcanet Press, 1983), 37.
7. Paul Valéry, *Monsieur Teste*, in *Collected Works*, vol. 6.
8. Merleau-Ponty, *Notes de Cours*, 211–15 (my translation); see Merleau-Ponty, "Eye and Mind," in *The Primacy of Perception*, 159–92; *The Prose of the World*; *The Visible and the Invisible*, 138–39: "The world seen is not 'in' my body and my body is not 'in' the visible world ultimately, as a flesh

applied to a flesh, the world neither surrounds it nor is surrounded by it.... [T]here is a reciprocal insertion and interwining the one in the other ... so that the seer and the visible reciprocate one another and we no longer know which sees and which seen. It is this visibility, this generality of the Sensible in itself, this anonymity innate to Myself that we have previously called flesh, and one knows there is no name in traditional philosophy to designate it.... We should need the old term 'element,' in the sense it was use to speak of water, air, earth, and fire ... midway between the the spatio-temporal individual and the idea, a sort of incarnate principle that brings a style of being wherever there is a fragment of being. The flesh is in this sense an 'element' of Being." On Merleau-Ponty and Proust, see Kristeva, *Time and Sense*, 246–47, 269–75.

9. Kristeva, *Colette*, 3: "Colette found a language to express a strange osmosis between her sensations, her desires, her anxieties ... and the infiniteness of the world.... Writing, therefore, has no autonomous existence; it is part of the monogram of the world.... The alphabet writes the world, and the world comes to pass through the alphabet: writing and world coexist as the two aspects of a single experience, for this woman who writes in a state of feverish rapture that defies language" (1–2); "an alphabet written as part of the world's flesh" (6); Kristeva, *Time and Sense*, 208: "Proust sensory exuberance, while struck by the osmosis between the self and the felt object, ceaselessly questions the fleeting nature of sensation. In this way, memory is both the agent that restores sensation to us and the veil that separates it from us. Memory, the equivalent of language, assigns language the role of a filter that signifies what is felt (in abstentia) while also mariking it (in presentia)."

10. Foucault, *The Order of Things*, 9.

11. See, e.g., Deleuze quoting from Proust in *Dialogues II*, 5: "Great literature is written in a sort of foreign language. To each sentence we attach a meaning, or at any rate a mental image, which is often a *mistranslation*. But in great literature all our mistranslations result in beauty" (emphasis added).

12. Derrida and Stiegler, *Echographies of Television*, 131–32, 26–27.

13. Deleuze might disagree with this suggestion regarding the non-inheritance of our body. It is possible that the problem simply lies in the difference between "heredity" and "inheritance." Commenting on Zola's novel *The Human Beast*, Deleuze argues that heredity is essentially biological and that one body transmits its very instincts to another; the transmitted instincts, moreover, are concentrated in the wounds or cracks of the body, reappearing as arbitrary signs in various cultural spheres: "Heredity is not that which passes through the crack, it is the crack itself—the imperceptible rift or

the hole. In its true sense, the crack is not a crossing for morbid heredity; it alone is the heredity and the morbid in its entirety." Deleuze, *The Logic of Sense*, 360.
14. Rueff (following the German historical hermeneutists) invites us not to neglect the historical situation of the work examined; see *Différence et identité*, 10–12, 20 n. 5. While the corporeal does not deny its being bound to a historical situation, it also flees from any attempt to establish its historical sense. Since the corporeal is inexhaustible, it is by definition an internal deviation in history and of history, so that the body extricates itself from history, so to speak, as the heart of the *non-place of the taking place*. See also Blanchot, *The Space of Literature*, 228: "the work is not history's business . . . and yet the work is history; it is an event, *the* event of history itself." Blanchot's concept of the work could be seen as a new understanding of the myth.
15. Deleuze, *The Logic of Sense*, 281: "Being no longer a question of speaking of bodies such as they are prior to, or outside of, language, they [bodies] form, on the contrary, with words a 'glorious body' for pure minds. . . . The obscene is not the intrusion of bodies into language, but rather their mutual reflection and the act of language which fabricates a body for the mind. This is the act by which language transcends itself as it reflects a body."
16. Kafka quoted in Wagenbach, *Kafka*, 42. In this sense, Cixous makes a remarkable call to be "wounded by the coming of the text." See "Difficult Joys," 25.
17. Blanchot, *The Space of Literature*, 194: "But the book which has its origin in art has no guarantee in the world, and when it is read, it has never been read before. It does not come into its presence as a work except in the space opened by this unique reading, each time the first and each time the only."
18. Barthes, *Criticism and Truth*, 71 (see part 2, "Plural Language," 67–73).
19. Barthes, *Camera Lucida*, 47–49; another example is Arasse, *Le détail*: "Cette expérience est au cœur de ce livre, nourri de ces 'surprises' qui suscitent tels ou tels détails, vus inopinément ou progressivement découverts. Les étonnements éprouvés étaient d'autant plus forts que le détail se manifestait alors comme un écart ou une résistance par rapport à l'ensemble du tableau; il semblait avoir pour fonction de transmettre une information parcellaire, différente de message global de l'œuvre—ou indifférente à celui-ci" (6–7); "le détail est un moment qui fait événement dans le tableau, qui tend irrésistiblement à arrêter le regard, à troubler l'économie de son parcours . . . c'est aussi un moment privilégié où le plaisir du tableau tend à devenir jouissance de la peinture" (12).

20. Blanchot, *The Space of Literature*, 193.
21. Blanchot, *The Space of Literature*, 227: "Author and reader ... neither has any existence except through this work and based upon it."
22. Jakobson, *Language in Literature*, 41–42.
23. See Paul Valéry, "Questions de la poésie," in *Oeuvres*, vol. 1.
24. Derrida, "Shibboleth," 40. On the question of the "perceptible secret" see Deleuze and Guattari, *A Thousand Plateaus*, 318–19. Derrida, "Shibboleth," 26: "The poem unveils a secret only to confirm that there is something secret there, withdrawn, forever beyond the reach of hermeneutic exhaustion, a non-hermetic secret, it remains, and the date with it, heterogeneous to all interpretative totalization." Blanchot, *The Space of Literature*, 155: "the *doubleness* within which such an event withdraws as if to preserve the void of its secret." Heidegger, *Acheminement vers la parole*, 136: "un secret n'est secret que si n'apparaît pas même le fait que, là, existe un secret. . . . il est nécessaire que tout semble comme si nulle part il n'y avait de secret."
25. Paul Valéry, *Oeuvres*, 2:562, my translation; Jean Paulhan quoted by Maurice-Jean Lefebve in "Cet homme de confiance," *La Nouvelle Revue Française*, no. 197 (May 1969): 688.
26. Blanchot, *The Book to Come*, 6.
27. Derrida, *Margins of Philosophy*, 302–3.

8. AIR RAID ONE: PROUST

1. Proust, *In Search of Lost Time VI, Time Regained*. Hereafter cited as *Time Regained*.
2. Proust, *Time Regained*, 202.
3. Proust, *Time Regained*, 215–17; see also Kristeva, *Time and Sense*, 93.
4. Derrida, "A Certain Impossible Possibility," 451.
5. Proust, *Time Regained*, 207.
6. The sign of "Sodom" is not the simple repetition of the biblical myth that reimposes its truth on the present; it is the already-taken-place disaster that is arising from the not-yet-happening future. This impression grows stronger when Proust blends together Sodom's fire from the sky, Pompeii's volcanic eruption, and Paris's German Gothas. By the way, Charlus is the first to evoke this series of analogies.
7. The complicity between the narrator and Charlus must be closely observed. Charlus brings to light the extreme madness and autism of the corporeal, while the writer's recognition affirms the poetic destination of bringing the inhabitants of Sodom back from underworld. On Charlus see, e.g., Deleuze, *Proust and Signs*, the chapter "Presence and Function of Mad-

ness: The Spider"; and Kristeva, *Time and Sense*, part 1, "Charlus: All Sex and Beyond Sex."
8. Proust, *Time Regained*, 204. From this perspective, Rancière's chapter on Proust in *The Flesh of Words*, 154, suggests analyzing this event in the brothel at Jupien's house not only through the obvious presence of the Baron de Charlus but also with reference to another protagonist, Robert de Saint-Loup, who loses his *croix de guerre* in the brothel. The narrator does not describe Saint-Loup's presence in the brothel, but he mentions this trace. See also *Time Regained*, 174–75, 189, 218, 236.
9. Deleuze, *The Logic of Sense*, 40.
10. Proust, *A la recherche du temps perdu IV*, 468: "On peut faire se succéder indéfiniment dans une description les objets qui figuraient dans le lieu décrit, la vérité ne commencera qu'au moment où l'écrivain prendra deux objets différents, posera leur rapport, analogue dans le monde de l'art à celui qu'est le rapport unique de la causale dans le monde de la science, et les enfermera dans les anneaux nécessaires d'un beau style." See also Kristeva's commentary in *Time and Sense*, part 2, 212–13: "The connection described here draws together the objects whose similarities are discovered by the narrator. He superimposes them onto one another, condenses their differences, and creates linked 'rings.' As a continuous chain of circles, analogy serves to guide the surface of signs towards depth. As a creator of figures, the maker of metaphors is similar to geometrician." Deleuze, *Proust and Signs*, 48: "style is essentially metaphor. But metaphor is essentially metamorphosis and indicates how the two objects exchange their determinations, exchange even the names that designate them, in the new medium that confers the common quality upon them."
11. Stylistically speaking, this effect is perhaps what Kristeva means when she talks about Proust's "breathless phrase," a state of incessant arrival (*arrivance*) that cannot produce a statement unless additional corrections and different iteration are already implied. See Kristeva, *Time and Sense*, part 3, "The Proustian Sentence," and 307: "Proust's style outlines this other temporality, which transcends measurement, space, and duration by telescoping two events, signs, or sensations in order to present a metaphor as an index of truth, by hollowing out syntax through multiple and diverse embeddings, and by targeting polyphonic regions of understanding at the limit of language. Finally, this second temporality challenges the notion of identity by superimposing one character onto another."
12. Genette, *Narrative Discourse*, 61n.
13. Proust, *Time Regained*, 215.
14. Proust, *Time Regained*, 217–18; *A la recherche du temps perdu IV*, 419.

15. Proust, *Time Regained*, 208.
16. Andreas Mayor and Terence Kilmartin translate the Latin expression *in pace* used by Proust in the French text with *oubliettes* (i.e., a secret dungeon, medieval tomb and tunnel). *Oubliettes* derives from the French verb *oublier*, "to forget," "to be oblivious." This may be intended to resonate with the insinuated meaning of early Christian epitaphs in the catacombs, such as REQVIESCIT IN PACE, "rest in peace." Stephen Hudson translates by means of the word *prostrations* (*Time Regained, Remembrance of Things Past*, vol. 12 [London: Chatto & Windus, 1957], 175), perhaps to render the religious humiliation, sufferance, or asceticism of this context.
17. Proust, *Time Regained*, 209–10.
18. In a very relevant chapter on Proust's *Time Regained*, Rancière (*The Flesh of Words*) opposes the principle of the real to that of the fictional in Proust's oeuvre. The unexpected introduction of the episode of the 1914 war momentarily suspends the fictional truth and infuses the real as the instant in which there "is an identity-truth of the word made flesh." For Rancière, the scene in the brothel is where Proust succeeds in confronting this "incarnate truth" of the real, its epic characteristics and Christian sources. It is where Proust "wages its own war on war" by reimposing the lies of the "fictional truth," that is, the aspiration and frustration of the aesthetic illusory which bases itself on the distance between word and flesh: "If literature exists as such, it exists from that knowledge, from the knowledge that the word is not made of flesh. It exists, at the same time, from the invention of these quasi-bodies, from these fictional devices that construct their truth as the truth of this abandonment" (123).

9. WRITING CORPOREALLY

1. Nancy, "The Surprise of the Event," in *Being Singular Plural*, 164–67.
2. In the history of Continental philosophy, this difference was made explicit by Agamben's diagram that distinguishes the line of immanence from the line of transcendence; see the chapter "Absolute Immanence" in Agamben, *Potentialities*, 239.
3. Deleuze, *The Logic of Sense*, 148–53; Deleuze and Parnet, *Dialogues II*, 62–65; Delueze and Guttari, *What Is Philosophy?* 156–57.
4. Deleuze, *The Logic of Sense*, 152.
5. Deleuze and Parnet, *Dialogues II*, 65.
6. Deleuze, *The Logic of Sense*, 100–101. Cf. an image of the battlefield in Aristotle, who compares the multiple senses of Being to a fleeing army that is controlled and unified by the universal scientific truth (see Gadamer, *Truth and Method*, 346). Deleuze's concept of battle is not the general unity

made up by all particular soldiers but rather the virtual anonymity that acts on each soldier of the army as differentiation: "This is why the soldier . . . [is] determined to consider each temporal actualization from the height of the eternal truth of the event which incarnates itself in it and, alas, incarnates itself in his own flesh" (*The Logic of Sense*, 101). The soldier wears the anonymous mask of death and mimes the war which has no model.

7. Deleuze, *The Logic of Sense*, 152.
8. Deleuze, *The Logic of Sense*, 149.
9. Deleuze, *The Logic of Sense*, 151.
10. Deleuze, *The Logic of Sense*, 153, emphasis added.
11. Derrida, *Demeure*, 45; see also 50–56; Derrida quotes Blanchot, *The Writing of Disaster*, 64: "To write one's autobiography . . . *in the manner of a work of art*, is perhaps to seek to survive, but through a perpetual suicide—*total insofar as fragmentary death*." See also Cixous, "Difficult Joys," 19–20: "That's why Virgil as a metaphor is so important for poets . . . because Virgil is the poet who decided that the poet should go into the realm of the dead—and come back . . . actually you write thanks to death, against death, beginning with death, and at the price of death."
12. Blanchot, *The Work of Fire*, 333.
13. This conception of the image can be perceived as parallel to the modern revolution of painting, from impressionism to cubism and toward abstract painting where the image engenders itself from itself.
14. Collin, *Maurice Blanchot*, 173: "La ressemblance est la contestation de tout modèle, que celui-ci soit un objet empirique ou une essence. L'œuvre est l'épreuve du dédoublement. C'est pourquoi il a pu être vrai de dire de l'œuvre, tout à la fois, qu'elle renvoie toujours à quelque chose qui n'est pas elle, mais en même temps ne renvoie jamais qu'à elle-même." See also Lilti, "L'image du mort-vivant chez Blanchot et Kafka."
15. Blanchot, *The Space of Literature*, 24, 34, 261–62.
16. Blanchot, *The Space of Literature*, 262–63.
17. Barthes, *Camera Lucida*, 118.
18. Genette, "Vertige fixé," 304, my translation.
19. Genette, "Vertige fixé," 292–93.
20. Derrida, *Specters of Marx*, 7–9.
21. Derrida, *Specters of Marx*, 10.
22. Derrida and Stiegler, *Echographies of Television*, 25–26.
23. Derrida, *Demeure*, 67.
24. Derrida and Stiegler, *Echographies of Television*, 12; 123: "It is not simply because there is something real that is undecomposable, or not synthesizable, some 'thing' that was there. It is because there is something other that

watches or concerns me. This Thing is the other insofar as it was already there—before me—ahead of me, beating me to it, I who am before it, I who am because of it, owing to it. My law. . . . The 'reality effect' stems here from the irreducible alterity of another origin of the world. . . . [T]he word 'real,' in this context, signifies the irreducible singularity of the other insofar as she opens a world."

25. One may call this *la de-meurt* of literature; to say that literature *de-meurt* (or even *dé-meurt*) is *la demeure de mourir* and *le demeurer de la mort*: *le demeurance* or *le demourir*. See Derrida, *Demeure*, 77–78; see also 28–29: "There is no essence or substance of literature: literature is not. It does not exist. It does not remain at home, *abidingly* [*à demeure*] in the identity of a nature or even of a historical being identical with itself. It does not maintain itself abidingly [*à demeure*], at least if 'abode' [*demeure*] designates the essential stability of a place; it only remains [*demeure*] *where* and *if* 'to be abidingly' [*être à demeure*] in some 'abiding order' [*mise en demeure*] means something else." "[I]ts passion consists in this—that it receives its determination from something other than itself. Even when it harbors the unconditional right to say anything, including the most savage antinomies, disobedience itself, its *status* is never assured or guaranteed permanently [*à demeure*], at home, in the inside of an 'at home.'"

26. Derrida, *Demeure*, 89–94.

27. Though it arrives at a similar conclusion of a virtuality that does not oppose actuality; see Derrida, "The Eyes of Language"; and Derrida, "Qual Quelle," in *Margins of Philosophy*.

28. Deleuze, *Foucault*, 92–93. Deleuze quotes Foucault: "Bichat relativized the concept of death, bringing it down from that absolute in which it appeared as an indivisible, decisive and irrecoverable event."

29. Deleuze, *Essays Critical and Clinical*, 2–3.

30. This can be analogically compared with the basic terms of thermodynamics: heat, energy, transfer, and movement.

10. AIR RAID TWO: CÉLINE

1. Céline, *Féerie pour une autre fois I*, 146–76; Céline, *Fable for Another Time*, 181–218. Hereafter cited as Céline, *Féerie*, with pages in the English translation given in brackets.

2. For a brief summary of other analyses of this scene see Hainge, *Capitalism and Schizophrenia*, 234–35 nn. 43, 46.

3. Céline, *Féerie*, 146 [181].

4. Céline, *Féerie*, 146 [181]. Céline frequently uses ellipses in his writing. Hereafter my own ellipses will be marked by square brackets.

5. Céline, *Féerie*, 155 [193]: "Eh bien, c'est de ce moment [...] que les horreurs ont commencé [...] pas pendant un mois!... dix mois... dix ans!"
6. Céline, *Féerie*, 147 [182].
7. Céline, *Féerie*, 148 [183].
8. Céline, *Féerie*, 148–49 [183–84].
9. Céline, *Féerie*, 148 [184].
10. Céline, *Féerie*, 147–48 [183].
11. Céline, *Féerie*, 155 [193].
12. Céline, *Féerie*, 156 [194], 153 [190], 154 [191].
13. Céline, *Féerie*, 155 [193].
14. Céline, *Féerie*, 157 [195].
15. Céline, *Féerie*, 148 [184].
16. Céline, *Féerie*, 152 [189].
17. Céline, *Féerie*, 154–55 [192].
18. Céline, *Féerie*, 174–76 [216–18].
19. Céline, *Féerie*, 150 [186].
20. Céline, *Féerie*, 152–54 [186–91].
21. Céline, *Féerie*, 154–55 [191–92].
22. Céline, *Féerie*, 156 [194].
23. Céline, *Féerie*, 165 [205].
24. Céline, *Féerie*, 174 [216].
25. Céline, *Féerie*, 165 [205].
26. Céline, *Féerie*, 165 [205], 172 [213].
27. See also Hainge, *Capitalism and Schizophrenia*, 83–85, 96–97.
28. Céline, *Féerie*, 152 [189], emphasis added: "Il commendait! Je le regardais."
29. "[Q]ue je regard! qu'il a des droits" ("[S]o I can see! that he's got rights!"): Céline, *Féerie*, 154 [191]; "He haunts me from the window"; "He wants me to watch her pose" 156 [194–95]; "and was pawing at her on me so that I should watch everything!" 172 [213].
30. Céline, *Féerie*, 172 [213].
31. "Ce que je regrette là à plat au sol écoutant la pierre c'est de pas avoir vu assez!... j'aurais insisté assez il y aurait tout fait devant moi, je l'aurais étranglé après!" ("What I regret here flat out on the floor listening to the stone is not to have seen enough!... if I'd really insisted he'd have done it all in front of me, I'd strangled him afterward!"). Céline, *Féerie*, 175 [218].
32. Céline, *Féerie*, 165 [205].
33. Céline, *Féerie*, 165 [205].
34. Céline, *Féerie*, 151–52 [187–88].
35. Céline, *Féerie*, 155 [193].
36. Céline, *Féerie*, 108 [129].

37. Céline, *Féerie*, 165–66 [205–6], 174 [216–17].
38. Céline, *Féerie*, 160 [199].
39. Céline, *Féerie*, 163 [203].
40. Céline, *Féerie*, 157–58 [196].
41. Deleuze, *The Logic of Sense*, 153.
42. Godard, préface, in Céline, *Romans IV*, xxv: "des bruits qu'il a 'dans l'oreille,' mais dans une oreille cette fois intérieure, une mémoire d'oreille."
43. Céline, *Féerie*, 158 [196].
44. Richard, *Nausée de Céline*, 8; my translation.
45. Céline, *Féerie*, 158 [196].
46. Kristeva, *Powers of Horror*, 147.
47. Céline, *Féerie*, 158 [196–97].
48. Kristeva, *Powers of Horror*, 206.
49. Céline, *Féerie*, 166 [206–7].
50. Kristeva, *Powers of Horror*, 146.
51. Céline, *Féerie*, 176 [218].

11. AIR RAID THREE: ELIOT

1. Eliot, *Collected Poems*.
2. Eliot, *Collected Poems*, 217.
3. See, e.g., Bergonzi, *T. S. Eliot*; Smith, *T. S. Eliot's Poetry and Plays*, 289–91; Kenner, *The Invisible Poet*, 320–21; Traversi, *T. S. Eliot*, 190–91; Gish, *Time in the Poetry of T. S. Eliot*, 113–14; Litz "The Allusive Poet," 145–50; Harding, *T. S. Eliot in Context*, 167, 205–6.
4. Gardner, *The Art of T. S. Eliot*, 44: "We might begin a description of *Four Quartets* by saying it presents a series of meditations upon existence in time, which, beginning from a place and a point in time, and coming back to another place and another point, attempts to discover in these points and places what is the meaning and content of an experience, what leads to it, and what follows from it, what we bring to it and what it brings to us."
5. See T. S. Eliot, "What Dante Means to Me," 128–29; and Eliot's letter to Professor Maurice Johnson dated June 27, 1947, in Gish, *Time in the Poetry of T. S. Eliot*, 114.
6. Eliot, *Collected Poems*, "Little Gidding II," 217. Hereafter, quotations from "Little Gidding" and other sections of *Four Quartets* will be cited by section and page.
7. See "Little Gidding I," 215: "Here, the intersection of the timeless moment / Is England and nowhere. Never and always"; and Gish "'A Pattern of Timeless Moments': Four Quartets," in *Time in the Poetry of T. S. Eliot*, 91–120.

8. "Little Gidding II," 217.
9. Eliot, "What Dante Means to Me," 128–30.
10. "Little Gidding II," 218.
11. "Little Gidding I," 215.
12. "Little Gidding IV," 221.
13. Heraclitus of Ephesus, fragment 60, in Freeman, *Ancilla to the Pre-Socratic Philosophers*, 29.
14. For more on Eliot and Heraclitus see Blissett, "T. S. Eliot and Heraclitus."
15. Heraclitus of Ephesus, fragment 30, in Freeman, *Ancilla to the Pre-Socratic Philosophers*, 26.
16. Freeman, *Ancilla to the Pre-Socratic Philosophers*, 19.
17. See also Eliot's stanzas that precedes the air raid in "Little Gidding II." Indeed, Heraclitus's fragment 76 defines fire as one of the four elements, "Fire lives the death of earth, and air lives the death of fire; waters lives the death of air, earth that of water," but Heraclitus chooses fire as the *arche*, the fundamental principle: "There is an exchange: all things for Fire and Fire for all things" (fragment 90). Freeman, *Ancilla to the Pre-Socratic Philosophers*, 31. Namely, fire is the physical and ethical condition of death and birth of the world's eternal change.
18. Eliot, "The Love Song of J. Alfred Prufrock," *Collected Poems*, 13.
19. "Little Gidding II," 218.
20. Eliot, "Ash Wednesday V" (1930), in *Collected Poems*, 102. See, e.g., Wolosky, "Linguistic Asceticism in 'Four Quartets.'"
21. "Little Gidding III," 219; see also "East Coker III," 119–20.
22. "Little Gidding IV," 221.
23. Gombrowicz, *Cosmos*, 97–98.
24. Büchner, *Woyzeck*, 56. Cf. John Mackendrick's translation in Büchner, *The Complete Plays*, 196–97.
25. "Little Gidding IV," 221.
26. "Little Gidding III," 220.
27. "Little Gidding V," 222.
28. "East Coker III," 200.
29. Heraclitus of Ephesus, fragment 62, in Freeman, *Ancilla to the Pre-Socratic Philosophers*, 29.
30. Derrida, *Specters of Marx*, 12, 10.

12. CONCLUSION

1. Derrida, *Of Grammatology*, 20.
2. Céline, "Louis Ferdinand Céline vous parle," 933.

Bibliography

Agamben, Giorgio. *Potentialities: Collected Essays in Philosophy.* Trans. Daniel Heller-Roazen. Stanford: Stanford University Press, 1999.

Alexandre, Didier, Madeline Frédéric, Sabrina Parent, and Michèle Touret, eds.*Que se passe-t-il? Événements, sciences humaines et littérature.* Rennes: Presses universitaires de Rennes, 2004.

Arasse, Daniel. *Le détail: Pour une histoire rapprochée de la peinture.* Paris: Champs flammarion, 1993.

Aristotle. *Poetics.* Trans. Malcolm Heath. London: Penguin, 1996.

———. *Poétique.* Trans. Michel Magnien. Paris: Le livre de poche classique, 1990.

Austin, J. L. *How to Do Things with Words.* Oxford: Oxford University Press, 1986.

Austin, Norman. *Archery at the Dark of the Moon: Poetic Problems in Homer's Odyssey.* Berkeley: University of California Press, 1975.

———. "Name Magic in the *Odyssey.*" *California Studies in Classical Antiquity* 5 (1972): 1–19.

Bachelard, Gaston. *L'intuition de l'instant.* Paris: Stock, 1931.

———. *La poétique de la rêverie.* Paris: Presses universitaires de France, 1960.

———. *La poétique de l'espace.* Paris: Presses universitaires de France, 1957.

Badiou, Alain. "The Adventure of French Philosophy." *New Left Review* 35 (September–October 2005): 67–77.

———. *Being and Event.* Trans. Oliver Feltham. New York: Continuum, 2005.

———. *Deleuze: La clameur de l'Être.* Paris: Hachette Littératures, 1997.

———. *Deleuze: The Clamor of Being.* Trans. Louise Burchill. Minneapolis: University of Minnesota Press, 2000.

———. "L'événement selon Deleuze." In *Logiques des mondes,* vol. 2 of *L'être et l'événement,* 403–10. Paris: Seuil, 2006.

Barbaras, Renaud. *Le tournant de l'expérience: Recherches sur la philosophie de Merleau-Ponty.* Paris: Vrin, 1998.

Barbaras, Renaud, Camille de Belloy, and Arnaud Bouaniche, eds. *Annales Bergsoniennes II: Bergson, Deleuze, la phénoménologie.* Paris: Presses universitaires de France, 2004.

Barthes, Roland, ed. *L'analyse structurale du récit (Communications, n° 8).* Paris: Seuil, 1981.

———. *Camera Lucida: Reflections on Photography.* Trans. Richard Howard. London: Vintage, 2000.

———. *Critical Essays.* Trans. Richard Howard. Evanston: Northwestern University Press, 1972.

———. *Criticism and Truth.* Trans. Katrine Pilcher Keuneman. Minneapolis: University of Minnesota Press, 1987.

———. *Elements of Semiology.* Trans. Annette Lavers and Colin Smith. New York: Hill and Wang, 1967.

———. "Introduction to the Structural Analysis of Narratives." In *A Barthes Reader*, ed. Susan Sontag, 251–95. New York: Hill and Wang, 1982.

———. *Journal de deuil.* Paris: Seuil, 2011.

———. *Mourning Diary.* Trans. Richard Howard. New York: Hill & Wang, 2010.

———. *On Racine.* Trans. Richard Howard. New York: Performing Arts Journals Publications, 1983.

———. *The Pleasure of the Text.* Trans. Richard Miller. New York: Hill and Wang, 1975.

———. *The Preparation of the Novel: Lecture Courses and Seminars at the Collège de France, (1978–1979 and 1979–1980).* Trans. Kate Briggs. New York: Columbia University Press, 2010.

———. "The Reality Effect." In *French Literary Theory Today: A Reader*, ed. Tzvetan Todorov, trans. R. Carter, 11–17. Cambridge: Cambridge University Press, 1982.

———. *S/Z.* Trans. Richard Miller. New York: Hill and Wang, 1974.

———. *Writing Degree Zero.* Trans. Annette Lavers and Colin Smith. New York: Hill and Wang, 1968.

Bataille, Georges. "A propos de récits d'habitants d'Hiroshima." In *Oeuvres complètes*, 11:172–87. Paris: Gallimard, 1988.

———. Avant-propos. In *Le bleu du ciel.* Paris: l'Imaginaire, Gallimard, 1957.

———. *Inner Experience.* Trans. Leslie Anne Boldt. Albany: State University of New York Press, 1988.

———. *Literature and Evil.* Trans. Alastair Hamilton. London: Calder & Boyars, 1973.

———. *Theory of Religion*. Trans. Robert Hurley. New York: Zone Books, 1989.
Baudrillard, Jean. *Simulacra and Simulation*. Trans. Sheila Faria Glaser. Ann Arbor: University of Michigan Press, 1994.
———. *The Spirit of Terrorism*. Trans. Chris Turner. London: Verso, 2002.
Bensa, Alban, and Eric Fassin. "Les sciences sociales face à l'événement." *Terrain* 38 (2002): 5–20.
Benveniste, Émile. *Problems in General Linguistics*. Trans. Mary Elizabeth Meek. Coral Gables: University of Miami Press, 1971.
Bergonzi, Bernard, ed. *T. S. Eliot: Four Quartets: A Casebook*. London: Macmillan, 1969.
Bergson, Henri. *Creative Evolution*. Trans. Arthur Mitchell. New York: Modern Library, 1944.
Biemel, Walter. "Poetry and Language in Heidegger." In *On Heidegger and Language*, ed. Joseph J. Kockelmans, 65–106. Evanston: Northwestern University Press, 1972.
Blanchot, Maurice. *The Book to Come*. Trans. Charlotte Mandell. Stanford: Stanford University Press, 2003.
———. *Death Sentence*. Trans. Lydia Davis. Tarrytown NY: Station Hill Press, 1978.
———. *The Infinite Conversation*. Trans. Susan Hanson. Minneapolis: University of Minnesota Press, 1993.
———. "The Instant of My Death." In Jacques Derrida, *Demeure: Fiction and Testimony*, trans. Elizabeth Rottenberg, 1–11. Stanford: Stanford University Press, 2000.
———. "Michel Foucault as I Imagine Him." In *Foucault, Blanchot*, trans. Jeffrey Mehlman and Brian Massumi, 63–109. New York: Zone Books, 1990.
———. *The Space of Literature*. Trans. Ann Smock. Lincoln: University of Nebraska Press, 1989.
———. *The Step Not-Beyond*. Trans. Lycette Nelson. Albany: State University of New York Press, 1992.
———. *Thomas the Obscure*. Trans. Robert Lamberton. New York: D. Lewis, 1973.
———. *The Unavowable Community*. Trans. Pierre Joris. Barrytown NY: Station Hill Press, 1988.
———. *The Work of Fire*. Trans. Charlotte Mandell. Stanford: Stanford University Press, 1995.
———. *The Writing of the Disaster*. Trans. Ann Smock. Lincoln: University of Nebraska Press, 1986.

Blissett, William. "T. S. Eliot and Heraclitus." In *T. S. Eliot and Our Turning World*, ed. J. S. Brooker, 29–46. New York: St. Martin's Press, 2001.

Boisset, Emmanuel. "L'événement est inadmissible, d'ailleurs il n'existe pas." In *Que se passe-t-il? Événements, sciences humaines et littérature*, ed. Didier Alexandre, Madeline Frédéric, Sabrina Parent, and Michèle Touret, 57–77. Rennes: Presses universitaires de Rennes, 2004.

Boisset, Emmanuel, and Philippe Corno, eds. *Que m'arrive-t-il? Littérature et événement*. Rennes: Presses universitaires de Rennes, 2006.

Bonnefoy, Yves. *La présence et l'image*. Paris: Mercure du France, 1983.

Borges, Jorge L. *The Aleph and Other Stories*. Trans. Andrew Hurley. New York: Penguin Classics, 1998.

Borradori, Giovanna. *Philosophy in a Time of Terror*. Chicago: University of Chicago Press, 2003.

Bousquet, Joë. *Oeuvre romanesque complète*. 3 vols. Paris: Albin Michel, 1979–82.

Bréhier, Emile. *La théorie des incorporels dans l'ancien Stoïcisme*. Paris: Vrin, 1970.

Bruns, Gerald L. *Heidegger's Estrangements: Language, Truth, and Poetry in the Later Writings*. New Haven: Yale University Press, 1989.

———. *Hermeneutics, Ancient and Modern*. New Haven: Yale University Press, 1992.

Büchner, Georg. *The Complete Plays*. Ed. M. Patterson. London: Methuen, 1987.

———. *Woyzeck*. Trans. Michael Ewans. New York: Peter Lang, 1989.

Céline, Louis-Ferdinand. *Conversations with Professor Y*. Trans. Stanford Luce. Bilingual ed. Hanover: Published for Brandeis University Press by University Press of New England, 1986.

———. *Death on Credit*. Trans. Ralph Manheim. London: John Calder, 1989.

———. *Fable for Another Time*. Trans. Mary Hudson. Lincoln: University of Nebraska Press, 2003.

———. *Féerie pour une autre fois I*. In Céline, *Romans IV*, 1–176. Paris: Gallimard, 1993.

———. *Journey to the End of the Night*. Trans. Ralph Manheim. New York: New Directions, 1983.

———. "Louis Ferdinand Céline vous parle." In Céline, *Romans II*, 931–36. Paris: Gallimard, 1974.

Cixous, Hélène. "Difficult Joys." In *The Body and the Text: Helene Cixous, Reading and Teaching*, ed. Helen Wilcox, Keith McWatters, Ann Thompson, and Linda Williams. New York: St. Martin Press, 1990.

———. "The Laugh of the Medusa." *Signs* 1, no. 4 (Summer 1976): 875–93.

Clark, Timothy. *Derrida, Heidegger, Blanchot: Sources of Derrida's Notion and Practice of Literature*. Cambridge: Cambridge University Press, 1992.
Collin, Françoise. *Maurice Blanchot et la question de l'ecriture*. Paris: Gallimard, 1986.
Compagnon, Antoine. *Le démon de la théorie: Littérature et sens commun*. Paris: Editions du Seuil, 1998.
Daviet-Taylor, Françoise, ed. *L'événement: Forme et figure*. Angers: Presses universitaires d'Angers, 2006.
Deleuze, Gilles. "À quoi reconnaît-on le structuralisme?" In *Histoire de la philosophie: Idées, doctrines*, vol. 8, *Le XXe siècle*, ed. F. Châtelet, 299–335. Paris: Editions Hachette, 1973.
———. *Bergsonism*. Trans. Hugh Tomlinson and Barbara Habberjam. New York: Zone Books, 1991.
———. *Difference and Repetition*. Trans. Paul Patton. New York: Columbia University Press, 1994.
———. *Essays Critical and Clinical*. Trans. Daniel W. Smith and Michael A. Greco. Minneapolis: University of Minnesota Press, 1997.
———. *Foucault*. Trans. Sean Hand. Minneapolis: University of Minnesota Press, 1988.
———. *Francis Bacon: The Logic of Sensation*. Trans. Daniel W. Smith. New York: Continuum, 2003.
———. *The Logic of Sense*. Trans. Mark Lester and Charles Stivale. New York: Columbia University Press, 1994.
———. *Nietzsche and Philosophy*. Trans. Hugh Tomlinson. New York: Columbia University Press, 1983.
———. *Proust and Signs*. Trans. Richard Howard. London: Athlone Press, 2000.
Deleuze, Gilles, and Felix Guattari. *Anti-Oedipus: Capitalism and Schizophrenia*. Trans. Robert Hurley, Mark Seem, and Helen R. Lane. Minneapolis: University of Minnesota Press, 1983.
———. *Kafka: Toward a Minor Literature*. Trans. Dana Polan. Minneapolis: University of Minnesota Press, 1986.
———. *A Thousand Plateaus: Capitalism and Schizophrenia*. Trans. Brian Massumi. New York: Continuum, 2004.
———. *What Is Philosophy?* Trans. Hugh Tomlinson and Graham Burchell. New York: Columbia University Press, 1994.
Deleuze, Gilles, and Claire Parnet. *Dialogues II*. Trans. Hugh Tomlison and Barbara Habberjam. NewYork: Columbia University Press, 2007.
De Man, Paul. *Aesthetic Ideology*. Ed. Andrzej Warminski. Minneapolis: University of Minnesota Press, 1996.

Derrida, Jacques. *Acts of Literature*. Ed. Derek Attridge. New York: Routledge 1992.
———. "A Certain Impossible Possibility of Saying the Event." Trans. Gila Walker. *Critical Inquiry* 33, no. 2 (2007): 441–61.
———. *Demeure: Fiction and Testimony*. Trans. Elizabeth Rottenberg. Stanford: Stanford University Press, 2000.
———. *Dissemination*. Trans. Barbara Johnson. Chicago: University of Chicago Press, 1981.
———. "The Eyes of Language: The Abyss and the Volcano." Trans. Gil Anidjar. In *Acts of Religion*, ed. Gil Anidjar, 189–227. London: Routledge, 2002.
———. *The Gift of Death*. Trans. David Wills. Chicago: University of Chicago Press, 1995.
———. *Limited Inc*. Trans. Samuel Weber and Jeffrey Mehlman. Evanston: Northwestern University Press, 1988.
———. *Margins of Philosophy*. Trans. Alan Bass. Chicago: University of Chicago Press, 1982.
———. "No Apocalypse, Not Now (Full Speed Ahead, Seven Missiles, Seven Missives)." Trans. Catherine Porter and Philip Lewis. *Diacritics* 14, no. 2 (Summer 1984): 20–31.
———. *Of Grammatology*. Trans. Garyatri Chakravorty Spivak. Baltimore: John Hopkins University Press, 1976.
———. *Paper Machine*. Trans. Rachel Bowlby. Stanford: Stanford University Press, 2005.
———. *Papier Machine*. Paris: Galilée, 2001.
———. *Parages*. Ed. John P. Leavey. Stanford: Stanford University Press, 2011.
———. *Positions*. Paris: Editions de Minuit, 1972.
———. "Shibboleth: For Paul Celan." In *Sovereignties in Question: The Poetics of Paul Celan*, ed. Thomas Dutoit and Outi Pasanen, 1–64. New York: Fordham University Press, 2005.
———. *Signéponge/Signsponge*. Trans. Richard Rand. New York: Columbia University Press, 1984.
———. *Specters of Marx: The State of the Debt, the Work of Mourning, and the New International*. Trans. Peggy Kamuf. New York: Routledge, 1994.
———. "Typewriter Ribbon." Trans. Peggy Kamuf. In *Material Events: Paul de Man and the Afterlife of Theory*, ed. Tom Cohen, Barbara Cohen, J. Hillis Miller, and Andrzej Warminski, 277–360. Minneapolis: University of Minnesota Press, 2001.
———. "Typewriter Ribbon: Limited Ink (2)." In *Without Alibi*, trans. and ed. Peggy Kamuf, 71–160. Stanford: Stanford University Press, 2002.

———. *Writing and Difference*. London: Routledge, 2001.
Derrida, Jacques, and Bernard Stiegler. *Echographies of Television: Filmed Interviews*. Trans. Jennifer Bajorek. Cambridge: Polity Press, 2002.
Dilthey, Wilhelm. "The Formation of the Historical World in the Human Sciences." In *Selected Works*, ed. Rudolf A. Makkreel and Frithjof Rodi, 3:226–41. Princeton: Princeton University Press, 2002.
Döblin, Alfred. *Berlin Alexanderplatz: The Story of Franz Biberkopf*. Trans. Eugene Jolas. New York: Continuum, 2003.
Duras, Marguerite. *La douleur*. Trans. Barbara Bray. London: Collins, 1986.
———. *Hiroshima mon amour*. Trans. Richard Seaver. New York: Grove Press, 1961.
———. *The Lover*. Trans. Barbara Bray. New York: Harper Perennial, 1985.
———. *Moderato Cantabile*. Paris: Minuit, "double," 1958.
———. *Moderato Cantabile*. Trans. Richard Seaver. London: Calder and Boyars, 1960.
———. *The Ravishing of Lol Stein*. Trans. Richard Seaver. New York: Grove Press, 1968.
Eliot, T. S. *Collected Poems, 1909–1962*. London: Faber and Faber, 1963.
———. *The Sacred Wood: Essays on Poetry and Criticism*. London: Faber and Faber, 1920.
———. "What Dante Means to Me." In *To Criticize the Critic and Other Writings*, 125–35. London: Faber and Faber, 1965.
Fédier, François. *Regarder voir*. Paris: Belles lettres, 1995.
Flaubert, Gustave. *The Letters, 1830–1857*. Trans. Francis Steegmuller. London: Faber and Faber, 1980.
Foucault, Michel. *Discipline and Punish: The Birth of the Prison*. Trans. Alan Sheridan. New York: Vintage Books, 1995.
———. "Maurice Blanchot: The Thought from Outside." In *Foucault, Blanchot*, trans. Jeffrey Mehlman and Brian Massumi, 7–60. New York: Zone Books, 1990.
———. *The Order of Things: An Archaeology of the Human Sciences*. New York: Vintage Books, 1994.
Freeman, Kathleen. *Ancilla to the Pre-Socratic Philosophers*. Cambridge: Harvard University Press, 1983.
Freud, Sigmund. "Beyond the Pleasure Principle." In *The Standard Edition of the Complete Psychological Works of Sigmund Freud*, vol. 18, ed. James Strachey, 1–64. London: Hogarth Press, 1955.
———. "The Negation." In *The Standard Edition of the Complete Psychological Works of Sigmund Freud*, vol. 19, ed. James Strachey, 235–40. London: Hogarth Press, 1961.

Gadamer, Hans-Georg. *Truth and Method.* Trans. Joel Weinsheimer and Donald G.Marshall. New York: Continuum, 2004.
Gardner, Helen. *The Art of T. S. Eliot.* London: The Cresset Press, 1949.
Genette, Gerard. *Fiction and Diction.* Trans. Catherine Porter. Ithaca: Cornell University Press, 1993.
———. *Narrative Discourse.* Trans. Jane E. Lewin, Oxford: Basil Blackwell, 1980.
———. "Vertige fixé." In Alain Robbe-Grillet, *Dans le labyrinthe,* 273–306. Paris: 10/18,1962.
Girard, René. *Violence and the Sacred.* Trans. Patrick Gregory. Baltimore: John Hopkins University Press, 1977.
Gish, Nancy K. *Time in the Poetry of T. S. Eliot: A Study in Structure and Theme.* London: Macmillan, 1981.
Glaudes, Pierre, and Helmut Meter, eds. *Le sens de l'événement dans la littérature française des XIXe et XXe siècle.* Bern: Peter Lang, 2008.
Godard, Henri. Preface. In Louis-Ferdinand Céline, *Romans IV*, ix–xl. Paris: Gallimard, 1993.
Gombrowicz, Witold. *Cosmos.* Trans. D. Borchardt. New Haven: Yale University Press, 2005.
———. *Pornografia.* Trans. Alastair Hamilton. London: Calder and Boyars, 1966.
Greimas, Algirdas Julien. *Du sens II: Essais sémiotiques.* Paris: Seuil, 1983.
Hainge, Greg. *Capitalism and Schizophrenia in the Later Novels of Louis-Ferdinand Céline.* New York: Peter Lang, 2001.
Harding, Jason, ed. *T. S. Eliot in Context.* Cambridge: Cambridge University Press, 2011.
Haughton, Hugh. "Allusion: The Case of Shakespeare." In *T. S. Eliot in Context*, ed. Jason Harding, 157–68. Cambridge: Cambridge University Press, 2011
Heidegger, Martin. *Acheminement vers la parole.* Trans. Jean Beaufret, Wolfgang Brokmeier, and François Fédier. Paris: Gallimard, 1976.
———. *Approche de Hölderlin.* Trans. Henry Corbin, Michel Deguy, François Fédier, and Jean Launay. Paris: Gallimard, 1973.
———. *Being and Time.* Trans. John Macquarrie and Edward Robinson. Oxford: Blackwell, 1962.
———. *Elucidations of Hölderlin's Poetry.* Trans. Keith Hoeller. Amherst NY: Humanity Books, 2000.
———. *Identity and Difference.* Trans. Joan Stambaugh. New York: Harper and Row, 1969.
———. *On the Way to Language.* Trans. Peter D. Hertz. San Francisco: Harper and Row, 1971.

———. *On Time and Being.* Trans. Joan Stambaugh. New York: Harper and Row, 1972.

———. "The Origin of the Work of Art." In *Basic Writings: From Being and Time (1927) to The Task of Thinking (1964),* ed. David Farrell Krell, 139–212. New York: HarperCollins, 1993.

———. *Poetry, Language, Thought.* Trans. Albert Hofstadterm. New York: Harper and Row, 1975.

Heubeck, Alfred, and Arie Hoekstra. *A Commentary on Homer's Odyssey.* Vol. 2. Oxford: Clarendon Press, 1989.

Hofmannsthal, Hugo Von. "A Letter." In *The Lord Chandos Letter and Other Writings,* sel. and trans. Joel Rotenberg, 117–28. New York: NewYork Review of Books, 2005.

Homer. *The Odyssey.* Trans. Robert Fagles. London: Penguin, 1996.

Jakobson. Roman. *Language in Literature.* Ed. Krystyna Pomorska and Stephen Rudy. Cambridge: Belknap Press of Harvard University Press, 1987.

James, Henry. "The Beast in the Jungle." In *Complete Tales 11,* 351–402. London: Rupert Hart-Davis, 1964.

Janicaud, Dominique. *Heidegger en France.* Vol. 2, *Entretiens.* Paris: Albin Michel, 2001.

Jensen, Alexander S. "The Influence of Schleiermacher's Second Speech on Religion on Heidegger's Concept of Ereignis." *Review of Metaphysics* 61, no. 4 (June 2008): 815–26.

Juranville, Alain. *L'évènement: Nouveau traité théologico-politique.* Paris: Presses universitaires de France, 2007.

Kenner, Hugh. *The Invisible Poet: T. S. Eliot.* New York: Ivan Obolensky, 1959.

Kisiel, Theodore. "The Language of the Event: The Event of the Language." In *Heidegger and the Path of Thinking,* ed. John Sallis, 85–104. Pittsburgh: Duquesne University Press, 1970.

Kockelmans, Joseph. *On the Truth of Being: Reflections on Heidegger's Later Philosophy.* Bloomington: Indiana University Press, 1984.

Kristeva, Julia. *Black Sun: Depression and Melancholia.* Trans. Leon S. Roudiez. New York: Columbia University Press, 1989.

———. *Colette: or The World's Flesh.* Trans. Jane Marie Todd. New York: Columbia University Press, 2004.

———. *Powers of Horror: An Essay on Abjection.* Trans. Leon S. Roudiez. New York: Columbia University Press, 1982.

———. *Revolution in Poetic Language.* Trans. Margaret Waller. New York: Columbia University Press, 1984.

———. *The Sense and Non-sense of Revolt: The Powers and Limits of Psychoanalysis*. Trans. Jeanine Herman. New York Columbia University Press, 2000.

———. *Tales of Love*. Trans. Leon S. Roudiez. New York: Columbia University Press, 1987.

———. *Time and Sense: Proust and the Experience of Literature*. Trans. Ross Guberman. New York: Columbia University Press, 1996.

Kronick, Joseph. "Between Act and Archive: Literature and the Nuclear Age." In *Future Crossings: Literature between Philosophy and Cultural Studies*, ed. Krzysztof Ziarek and Seamus Deane, 52–75. Evanston: Northwestern University Press, 2000.

Laplanche, Jean, and Jean-Bertrand Pontalis. *The Language of Psychoanalysis*. London: Karnac, 1988.

Levinas, Emmanuel. *Proper Names*. Trans. Michael B. Smith. Stanford: Stanford University Press, 1996.

Leskly, Hezy. *Collected Poems* [in Hebrew]. Tel Aviv: Am Oved, 2009.

Lilti, Ayelet. "L'image du mort-vivant chez Blanchot et Kafka." *Revue Europe n° 940–941* (August–September 2007): 154–66.

Litz, A. Walton. "The Allusive Poet: Eliot and His Sources." In *T. S. Eliot: The Modernist in History*, ed. Ronald Bush, 137–52. Cambridge: Cambridge University Press, 1991.

Lotman, Jurij. *The Structure of the Artistic Text*. Trans. Ronald Vroon. Ann Arbor: University of Michigan Press, 1977.

Lyotard, Jean François. *Political Writings*. Trans. Bill Readings and Kevin Paul Geiman. Minneapolis: University of Minnesota Press, 1993.

———. *The Postmodern Condition: A Report on Knowledge*. Trans. Geoffrey Bennington and Brian Massumi. Minneapolis: University of Minnesota Press, 1984.

———. *The Postmodern Explained: Correspondence, 1982–1985*. Trans. Don Barry. Minneapolis: University of Minnesota Press, 1993.

Magnus, Bernd. *Heidegger's Metahistory of Philosophy: Amor Fati, Being and Truth*. The Hague: Martinus Nijhoff, 1970.

Maingueneau, Dominique. *Elements de linguistique pour le texte littéraire*. Paris: Bordas, 1986.

Mallarmé, Stéphane. "Ballets." In *What Is Dance?* ed. Roger Copeland and Marshall Cohen, 111–14. New York: Oxford University Press, 1983.

———. *Selected Poetry and Prose*. Ed. Mary Ann Caws. New York: New Directions Books, 1982.

Merleau-Ponty, Maurice. *Notes de Cours, 1959–1961*. Ed. Stéphanie Ménasé. Paris: NRF, Gallimard, 1996.

———. *Phenomenology of Perception*. Trans. C. Smith. London: Routledge and Kegan Paul, 1962.
———. *The Primacy of Perception: And Other Essays on Phenomenological Psychology, the Philosophy of Art, History, and Politics*. Ed. James M. Edie. Evanston: Northwestern University Press, 1964.
———. *The Prose of the World*. Trans. John O'Neill. Evanston: Northwestern University Press. 1973.
———. *The Visible and the Invisible*. Trans. Alphonso Lingis. Evanston: Northwestern University Press, 1968.
Meschonnic, Henri. *Critique de rythme: Anthropologie historique du langage*. Lagrasse: Verdier, 1982.
Michel, Chantal. *Maurice Blanchot et le déplacement d'Orphée*. Saint Genouph: Librarie Nizet, 1997.
Musil, Robert. *The Man without Qualities*. Vol. 1. Trans. Eithne Wilkins and Ernst Keiser. London: Secker and Warburg, 1979.
Nancy, Jean-Luc. *Being Singular Plural*. Trans. Robert D. Richardson and Anne E. O'Byrne. Stanford: Stanford University Press, 2000.
Nietzsche, Friedrich. *The Complete Works of Friedrich Nietzsche*. Ed. Oscar Levy. New York: Russell and Russell, 1964.
Ophir, Adi. *The Order of Evils: Toward an Ontology of Morals*. Trans. Rela Mazali and Havi Carel. New York: Zone Books, 2005.
Palmer, Richard E. *Hermeneutics*. Evanston: Northwestern University Press,1969.
Podlecki, A. J. "Guest-Gifts and Nobodies in *Odyssey*." *Phoenix* 15 (1961): 125–33.
Pöggeler, Otto. "Being as Appropriation." In *Heidegger and Modern Philosophy: Critical Essays*, ed. Michael Murray, 85–115. New Haven: Yale University Press, 1978.
Proust, Marcel. *A la recherche du temps perdu IV*. Paris: Gallimard, 1989.
———. *In Search of Lost Time VI, Time Regained*. Trans. Andreas Mayor and Terence Kilmartin. New York: Modern Library, 2003.
Rancière, Jacques. *The Flesh of Words: The Politics of Writing*. Trans. Charlotte Mandell. Stanford: Stanford University Press, 2004.
Richard, Jean-Pierre. *Nausée de Céline*. Montpellier: Fata Morgana, 1980.
———. *L'univers imaginaire de Mallarmé*. Paris: Seuil, 1961.
Ricoeur, Paul. *The Conflict of Interpretations*. Evanston: Northwestern University Press, 1974.
———. "Événement et sens." In *L'événement en perspective*, ed. J. L. Petit, 41–57. Paris: École des hautes études en sciences sociales, 1991.
———. *Time and Narrative I*. Trans. Kathleen McLaughlin and David Pellauer. Chicago: University of Chicago Press, 1984.

———. *Time and Narrative II.* Trans. Kathleen McLaughlin and David Pellauer. Chicago: University of Chicago Press, 1985.

Rimmon-Kenan, Shlomith. *Narrative Fiction: Contemporary Poetics.* London: Methuen, 1983.

Robbe-Grillet, Alain. *Snapshots and Towards a New Novel.* Trans. Barbara Wright. London: Calder and Boyars, 1965.

Romano, Claude. *Event and World.* Trans. Shane Mackinlay. New York: Fordham University Press, 2009.

Ronell, Avital. *Stupidity.* Urbana: University of Illinois Press, 2002.

Rueff, Martin. *Différence et identité: Michel Deguy, situation d'un poète lyrique à l'apogée du capitalisme culturel.* Paris: Hermann, 2009.

Sarraute, Nathalie. *Tropisms and The Age of Suspicion.* Trans. Maria Jolas. London: John Calder, 1963.

Sebald, W. G. *On the Natural History of Destruction.* Trans. Anthea Bell. New York: The Modern Library, 2003.

Sheehan, Thomas. "On the Way to Ereignis: Heidegger's Interpretation of Physis." In *Continental Philosophy in America,* ed. Hugh J. Silverman, John Sallis, and Thomas M. Seebohm, 131–64. Pittsburgh: Duquesne University Press, 1983.

Smith, Grover. *T. S. Eliot's Poetry and Plays: A Study in Sources and Meaning.* Chicago: University of Chicago Press, 1956.

Sollers, Philippe. *Writing and the Experience of Limits.* Trans. Philip Barnard and David Hayman. New York: Columbia University Press, 1983.

Spitzer, Leo. *Linguistics and Literary History: Essays in Stylistics.* Princeton: Princeton University Press, 1948.

Stiegler, Barbara, *Nietzsche et la biologie*, Paris: Presses universitaires de France, 2001.

Todorov, Tsvetan. *The Poetics of Prose.* Trans. Richard Howard. New York: Cornell University Press, 1977.

Tomashevsky, Boris. "Thematics." In *Russian Formalist Criticism: Four Essays,* trans. Lee T. Lemon and Marion J. Reis, 61–98. Lincoln: University of Nebraska Press, 1965.

Traversi, Derek. *T. S. Eliot: The Longer Poems.* London: The Bodley Head, 1976.

Valéry, Paul. *The Collected Works of Paul Valéry.* Ed. Jackson Mathews. 15 vols. London: Routledge and Kegan Paul, 1957–75.

———. *Oeuvres.* Ed. Jean Hytier. 2 vols. Paris: Gallimard, Pléiade, 1960.

Verstraeten, Philippe. "Le sens de l'Ereignis dans temps et être." *Les Etudes Philosophiques* 1 (1986): 113–33.

Veyne, Paul. *Writing History: Essay on Epistemology.* Trans. Mina Moore-Rinvolucri. Middletown CT: Wesleyan University Press, 1984.

Wagenbach, Klaus. *Kafka.* Trans. Ewald Osers. London: Haus, 2003.

Williams, James. "If Not Here, Then Where? On the Location and Individuation of Events in Badiou and Deleuze." *Deleuze Studies* 3, no. 1 (2009): 97–203.

Wolosky, Shira. "Linguistic Asceticism in 'Four Quartets.'" In *Language Mysticism: The Negative Way of Language in Eliot, Beckett, and Celan,* 10–50. Stanford: Stanford University Press, 1995.

Zourabichvilli, François. *Deleuze: Une philosophie de l'événement.* Paris: Presses universitaires de France, 1994.

Index

absence: activity of, in presence, 151–52; in *Ereignis*'s new conception of presence, 61, 62, 63; literature and evocation of things from, 80; of sense, 135; and trace of difference, 120

abyssal encounter, Derrida on, 109–11

abyss of indetermination, *Ereignis* and leaping into, 59–60

accidental, and "willing the event," 143–44

action: imitated by *muthos*, 17; unity of, 17–18

actual: in Derrida's conception of event, 137–41; and embodiment of event, 206; and event in *Time Regained*, 180; Merleau-Ponty on potential and, 265n44; and plane of immanence, 266n48; and temporality as aspect of becoming, 152–53; virtual as inseparable from, 34

actualities, extricating virtualities from, 141, 142–43

actualization: body of the event and, 206–7; corporeal, 193–94; in Deleuze's conception of event, 34; literature as ground for exposing, of event, 35; plane of immanence and, 266n48; of virtual, 140

advenire, 241n1

Agamben, Giorgio, 64, 248n1, 250n43, 274n2

Aion, 150–51, 153, 238

alterity: absolute, 31, 108, 109, 130; indecipherable secret of, 106; in literary text, 112–13; and logic of iterability or spectrality, 105; repetition and, 257n13; trauma and, 115. *See also* other

amor fati, 144, 235–36

analogy, 70, 182, 251n58, 273n10

animality: Deleuze on, 41, 195; in *Fable for Another Time*, 44, 218, 224–25; in Lord Chandos letter, xi–xii; writing and, 208

Annales School, 5–6

"anonymity, will of," 193

Anti-Oedipus (Deleuze and Guattari), 137

aporia, 32, 34, 103, 203

appropriation, event of. See *Ereignis*

Arasse, Daniel, 171, 271n19

Aristotle: on character, 17–18; defines *poiesis*, 161; narrative theory of, 19–20; on roles of poet and historian, 12

295

art: being of work of, 80; Blanchot and Derrida on, 191; Blanchot on purpose of, 73–74, 252n21; Blanchot on work of, 72–73; Deleuze on, 191; as dying-living physical gesture, 164; as essential inessential, 75–76; modern invention of corporeal in, 166; work of, in Orpheus myth, 79

Austin, J. L., 117–19, 261n69

author, as father or son of text, 163, 167, 196

autobiography, Derrida on, 197, 275n11

avènement, 241n1

Badiou, Alain, 28, 36, 37, 132, 137–38, 262n9, 269n84

Barbaras, Renaud, 133

Barthes, Roland: on actant, 244n33; on ambiguity of work, 170; on application of pre-understanding to text, 23; Aristotle's narrative theory compared to, 19; defense of "Nouvelle Critique," 27; on *événement faible*, 245n53; grief of, 83; on narrative grammar, 15; on nature of detail, 171; on ontological time revealing new artistic understanding, 154; on permanent and absolute flow of becoming, 245n49; on process of writing, 95; semiological analysis of fashion or cooking, 138; and structural explanation of narrative analysis, 16; on style, 24; and terror of future, 116; on virtual consumption, 200

battle, Deleuze on corporeality and, 192–93, 194, 274n6. *See also* war

Beckett, Samuel, 67, 84, 103, 145, 148, 149, 164

becoming: appearance yielded through, 62–63; being of, 23; Deleuze and incorporeal corporeality of, 195; Deleuze on aspects of, 144–57; Deleuze's concept of, 266n57; ethical order of, 144–45; and event in *Time Regained*, 180–81; "Little Gidding" and engaging in, of event, 236–38; secret of being of, 174; traversing literary event in "Little Gidding," 234–35; uncontainable, 267n59

"becoming minor" of body and writing, 146

becoming of event: Deleuze on, 34–35, 141–44; in *Fable for Another Time*, 221–22; in Lord Chandos letter, ix–xii

Being: chaos and, 135; Deleuze on, 33; in Deleuze's conception of event, 124, 167, 262n9; Deleuze's question of, 134; and Heidegger's study of pre-Socratic sources of metaphysics, 63–64; indefinability of, 158–59; language and, 65–67, 239; literature and, 71–76, 79–80; ontological difference between beings and, 28–29; and ontology of event, 133; and production of sense, 138; question of, linked to *Ereignis*, 57–58, 59, 61

being: of becoming, 23; Deleuze on series of, 126–27, 129; of image, 199; of language, 148, 198, 253n31; secret of, of becoming, 174. *See also* series of being

being of the work: Blanchot's conception of, 79–81; death and

296 | Index

confrontation of, 86; event as affirmation of, 31; negation as concealed affirmation of, 74
beings: ontological difference between Being and, 28–29; truth of, 253n28
Bensa, Alban, 4–5
Bergson, Henri, 139, 154
betrayal, in *Fable for Another Time*, 219–21
Blanchot, Maurice: on autobiography, 275n11; on being of language, 253n31; on biographical death of writer, 255n48; on collapse of world and recovery of inalienable distance of image, 256n64; conception of, of event, 30–31, 191, 271n14; concept of, of outside, 155–56; corporeality and fictional writing of, 197–200; on death as event, 255n51; and Deleuze's redefinition of structuralism, 130; Derrida and, 102–3; on doubt, 254n39; dying in conception of event of, 82–89, 192, 195, 255nn54–55; and event's effect on possibility of narrative as principle of literary writing, 89–95; on existence of author and reader, 272n21; on expressing opposing movements, 251n58; on extraordinary, 111; Foucault on, 121; and free indirect discourse, 148; and ignorance in intelligent creativity, 24; on impersonality, 254n45; on language, 198; on language of literature versus language of history, 12; on literature, 38; on literature and Being, 71–76, 251n3; on naming, 197; on nature of narrative, 13; on *neuter*, 24; offers different adaptation of myth, 253n22; on outside, 269n88; on perceptible secret, 272n24; on poetry, 71, 252n16; on purpose of art, 252n21; on reading, 171, 271n17; on resemblance, 199–200; on secret of event, 174; on speech and understanding, 253n30; study of, of event, 76–77; and temporality as aspect of becoming, 152; and theory of literary events based on dying corporeality, 203–4; transcendence of, 41; use of negation, 252n12; on void, 255n57, 268n83; on writing, 244n44, 253n26. See also *The Book to Come* (Blanchot); *The Space of Literature* (Blanchot)
body. *See* corporeality
body of the event, 42, 46, 47, 51–52, 205–8
Bonnefoy, Yves, 16
The Book to Come (Blanchot), 76, 89–93
Borges, Jorge L., 26
Bousquet, Joë, 143–44, 266n54
Bruns, Gerald L., 60, 65
Büchner, Georg, 235

cave: calamity of, in *Fable for Another Time*, 222; in Homer's *Odyssey*, 45–49, 53; and whirlwind in *Fable for Another Time*, 212–14
Celan, Paul, 112, 164, 175, 208
Céline, Louis-Ferdinand, 239. See also *Fable for Another Time* (Céline)
chance: Gombrowicz on boundary of, and non-chance, 26, 235; plane of immanence and, 136; in plot, 14, 20

chaos: Being and, 135; and plane of immanence, 123; sense of, in *Fable for Another Time*, 211–12
character, Aristotle on, 17–18
Chronos, 150–51, 153
Chrysippus, paradox of, 131
circulation, 129–31
Cixous, Hélène, 271n16, 275n11
classicism, Blanchot on, 82–83
classic moment, 162
Colette, 166, 270n9
Collin, Françoise, 275n14
"common sense," Deleuze's critique of, 123–24
configuration, in Ricoeur's theory of narrative intelligence, 6–7
consciousness, historically effected, 9
constative utterances, 117–18, 261n68
corporeal explosion, in *Fable for Another Time*, 222–24
corporeality: of actualization, 193–94; and Deleuze on Blanchot's conception of dying, 192; Deleuze on war and, 192–93; and emergence of event in *Odyssey*, 45–47; of event in *Time Regained*, 181–85; and fictional writing of Blanchot, 197–200; figure and language of text's becoming forged from, of happening, 181; history and, 271n14; versus impression of war, 103–5; incorporeal, of becoming, 195; literary creation and, xii–xiii, 40–41; in Lord Chandos letter, xi–xii; and modern articulation of poetic fiction, 164–68; of no-body in *Odyssey*, 47–49; of nonsense, 145; as principle of vitality, 41–44; and spiritual achievement of literary event in *Time Regained*, 189–90; theory of literary event based on dying, 203–4; trauma and, 114–16; and vital move, 204–8
corporeal series of being, Deleuze on, 126, 129
corporeal substances, in *Fable for Another Time*, 211–12
counter-actualization, creative, 35, 41, 153, 193–94, 195, 204
countersignature, 108
creation: aim of artistic, 3; corporeality and literary, xii–xiii
crisis, importance of literature as compound of, viii
crisis of naming, in Derrida's conception of event, 102

dead: communication between living and, 237–38; corporeal experience of, 114; and impression versus corporeal war, 103–5. *See also* death; dying
death: Blanchot on, of writer, 255n48; Blanchot on, versus dying, 255n55; Deleuze on Bichat's relativization of concept of, 276n28; as event, 255n51; event constructed through terminology of, 191; fictional writing of Blanchot and Derrida defined through pure, 197. *See also* dead; dying
Deleuze, Gilles: on actualization and counter-actualization in living interpretation of dying, 192–93; and aspects of becoming, 144–57; and Badiou's concep-

tion of event, 37; and becoming of event, 141–44, 221; on Being, 262n9; on Bichat's relativization of concept of death, 276n28; on Blanchot's concept of dying, 192, 195; on book as image of world, 23; conception of, of battle, 274n6; conception of, of becoming, 266n57; conception of, of event, 33–34, 122–26, 191, 263n16, 265n43; on condition, 264n38; on contingency of encounter, 266n53; on corporeality and war, 192–93; on differentiation, 266n46; Eliot versus, 234; on embodiment of wound, 266n54; on errors of philosophy, 262n4; on eternal return, 262n9; on event and language, 247n84; and event in *Time Regained*, 180; on Foucault, 268n80, 269n84; on heredity, 270n13; on *I* as other, 267n66; and impossibility of event, 178; on incorporeal and sense, 263n14; on language and body, 271n15; on language within language, 268n71; on literature, 204, 270n11; on living corporeality of literature, 41; model of disjunctive synthesis of, 181–82; on non-inheritance of body, 270n13; on nonsense, 264n39; on past and present, 268n80; on philosophy, 267n68; on plane of immanence, 266n48; psychoanalysis and phenomenology in ontology of, 166–67; on reality of becoming, xii; on relation between emergence of sense and becoming of real, 126–29; on repetition, 260n63; on replacing concept of *Être*, 264n40; and sense and nonsense, 135–37; structuralism in concept of event of, 129–35; on style, 273n10; on style and metaphor, 273n10; and theory of literary events based on living corporeality, 203–4; on un-accomplished, 41; and virtual and actual, 137–41; on Visible or Open, 265n42; vital move and, 204–5; on wounds and violence, 266n56; on writing and creation of literature, 35–36, 38

Derrida, Jacques: and ambiguity of image, 201–3; on autobiography, 197, 275n11; conception of, of event, 31–33, 96–97, 191, 247n79, 259n46; on conflict with impossible, 258n41; corporeality and fictional writing of, 197; and Deleuze's redefinition of structuralism, 130; discussion on 9/11, 257n27; on disparate, 246n74; on dying corporeality of literature, 41; and emergence of event as other, 106–11; on event and presence, 259n55; and event as Thing, 101–6; on eventfulness of event, 256n4; and fiction as factor in reconstruction of judicial proof, 261n64; on gathering, 70; on implex, 176; and impossibility of event, 97–101; on impossible event, 256n3; on inheritance of language, 168, 267n67; on iterability, 257n13, 257n17; Juranville on, 36; on literature, 38, 261n74, 276n25; on movement of "ex-appropriation" in *Ereignis*, 258n37; and other in literary text,

Derrida, Jacques (*continued*) 111–14; on passion and anticipation, 259n45; on perceptible secret, 272n24; on possibility of event, 178; on real, 275n24; Romano and, 37; on singularity of event, 259n49; on specter, 257n13; and temporality as aspect of becoming, 152; and theory of literary events based on dying corporeality, 203–4; transcendence of, 41; on trauma, 114–17; on unreadable, 174; and writing of event, 117–21

destiny: emergency of Being as foundation of, 29; *Ereignis* and, 64, 250n40

detail, scrutiny of, as fourth principle of theory of literary event, 170–71

diction, 161, 162

difference: in Derrida's conception of event, 96, 108, 109; as mode of articulation between creation of sense and becoming of real, 126; structuralism and, 130, 131

differentiation: and actualization of virtual, 140; becoming and, 181; Deleuze on, 266n46; nonsense and, 136; as principle of Deleuze's ontology, 33, 135; and virtual and actual, 139

Dilthey, Wilhelm, 10, 251n58

direct speech: in "Little Gidding," 227, 228, 231; free direct speech in *Moderato Cantabile*, 50–51

disjunctive synthesis, 42, 127, 129, 136, 138, 181–82

dissembling resemblance, 201–2

Döblin, Alfred, 26

doubt: Blanchot on, 254n39; bound to sense perception in *Fable for Another Time*, 219–20

Duras, Marguerite, xiv, 26, 49–53, 84, 128, 162

dying: in Blanchot's conception of event, 30–31, 34, 82–89, 255nn54–55; Deleuze on Blanchot's concept of, 192, 195; Deleuze's interpretation of, 193–94. *See also* dead; death

élan vital, 134

Eliot, T. S., 3, 44, 63, 233. *See also* "Little Gidding" (Eliot)

"Emma Zunz" (Borges), 26

emplotment, 22–23, 25

Enteignis, 109–10

Ereignis: and comparison of Being-as-event to internal laboratory of production, 137; defined, 57–59; and Deleuze's event, 265n43; Derrida on, 109; as event rather than ground, 59–60; Heidegger on, 250n40; and Heidegger's conception of event, 28–29, 57; and question of language, 65–69; and question of time, 61–64

eternal return, 35, 117, 153–54, 195, 238, 262n9

ethics, difference between poetics and, in regard to praxis, 17

événement, etymology of term, 241n1

événementiel, *événementielle* 244n43

evenire, 241n1

event: body of the, 42, 46, 47, 51–52, 205–8; defined, 1; Derrida's definitions of, 97–99; etymology of term, 241n1; examination of conventional use of, 3–4; God in hands of, 239; historical, 4–13; impossible, 30, 31–32, 92, 97–101, 178–79, 256n3; improbable, 20–21; literature as making of, 2; narrative, 14–26; negation of, 21, 244n43; non-advent of, 102, 111, 121; nucleus, 16, 19; questioning concept of, vii–viii; saying, 118–20; threshold of, 178; transcendent approach to, 191; unpredictability of, 10, 98. *See also* becoming of event; literary event; theory of the literary event; "willing the event"

event analysis, 25

eventness, eventfulness, 1–2, 11, 25, 31–32, 39, 49, 97.102, 104, 109, 115, 119, 175, 193

event of appropriation. See *Ereignis*

ex-appropriation, 31, 98, 109–10, 115, 258n37

exclusion, struggle between inclusion and, in *Fable for Another Time*, 43–44, 213, 214–15

exemplarity, 104, 112–14

exhausted, 149

"The Exhausted" (Deleuze), 149

existence, possibility and concept of, 139–40

experience: boundary between *logos* and, in "Little Gidding," 233–34; examination of textual events related to representation of, 196; in Gadamer's hermeneutics, 8–10

expropriation: Derrida on, 109–10, 258n37; event as encounter of, 31

extraordinary, Blanchot on, 111

Fable for Another Time (Céline): animality and vomiting in, 224–25; becoming of event in, 221–22; betrayal and guilt in, 219–21; corporeal explosion in, 222–24; corporeality and music in, 225–26; gaze and hearing in, 218–19; haunting of Ferdinand in, 216–18; recurrent expressions of Jules's movement of penetration in, 215–16; scene of sexual seduction in, 209–14; struggle between inclusion and exclusion in, 214–15; and theory of literary events as vital move, 42, 43–44

facts, contrary to event, vii, xii, 2–3, 12, 17, 22, 48, 139, 205

Fassin, Eric, 4–5

fate, fire in "Little Gidding" as dynamic conception of, 235

Fédier, François, 61, 252n12

fiction: Blanchot on literature as, 72; Blanchot on unreality of, 80; corporeality and, 164, 165; as criteria for literary work, 161; Deleuze and, 197; Derrida on history and, 117, 118; doubt of unhappening through work of, 48; Foucault on thinking through, 71, 254n39; image and, 198; as important factor in reconstruction of judicial proof, 261n64; nonsense and, 132; Rancière on real versus, in *Time Regained*, 274n18

fictional writing, corporeality and, of Blanchot, 197–200

fictive distance, 11–13, 185–87

fire: Heraclitus on, 279n17; in "Little Gidding," 44, 232, 233, 235–38; sky pouring, 42; in *Time Regained*, 184–87

Flaubert, Gustave, 81, 148, 163

forces, and temporality as aspect of becoming, 156–57

Foucault, Michel: on being of language, 253n31; on Bichat's relativization of concept of death, 276n28; on Blanchot, 121; concept of, of outside, 155–56; Deleuze on, 268n80, 269n84; and Deleuze on productions of Being, 138; on dying, 255n55; and idea of "vitalism," 203; on language of Blanchot, 252n12; order of discourse of, 148; on struggle between saying and perceiving, 166–67; on thinking through fiction, 71, 254n39; on void, 268n83; on writing, 80

free indirect discourse, 147, 148

Freud, Lucian, 175

Freud, Sigmund, 260n57, 260n63

Gadamer, Hans-Georg: on historical distance, 11; on locating absent elements in presence, 151; and methodological conflict between historical doubt and trust, 8–10; on temporal distance, 242n17

Gardner, Helen, 278n4

gathering, 70, 108–10

gaze, in *Fable for Another Time*, 218–19

Genette, Gérard: on being of the text, 25; defines narrative, 14; on literature, 161–62; on narrative, 16; narrative axes of, 172; on plot, 243n22; on style, 245n54; on violated body in *Time Regained*, 184; on writing of hyperrealisim, 200–201

George, Stefan, 68, 108

God: death of, 240; "good sense" and "common sense" and notion of, 123–24; in hands of event, 239

Gombrowicz, Witold, 26, 206, 235

"good sense," Deleuze's critique of, 123–24

grammar, narrative, 15

Guattari, Felix: on book as image of world, 23; conception of, of becoming, 266n57; conception of, of event, 263n16; on construction of immanent substance, 122–23; on four errors of philosophy, 262n4; on philosophy, 267n68; on production of sense, 137; on replacing concept of Être, 264n40; on untimely, 153; on wounds and violence, 266n56

guilt, in *Fable for Another Time*, 219–21

happening: corporeality and, 40–41; and corporeality of no-body in *Odyssey*, 48–49; evoking, in *Fable for Another Time*, 210–11; and fictive distance in *Time Regained*, 185; figure and language of text's becoming forged from corporeality of, 181; un-happening within, 3, 23, 27, 39, 40, 48, 176, 208. *See also* mythology of happenings

hauntology, 32, 34, 152, 201, 237–38

health, creation as, 145–146, 191, 195, 208,

hearing, in *Fable for Another Time*, 218–19

"Hebrew Lesson" (Leskly), 132

Hegel, Georg Wilhelm Friedrich: becoming of being of, 24; Deleuze and, 194; Gadamer and,

8; on historical appearance, 64; on negation, 197–98; progress of truth of, 266n57

Heidegger, Martin: Deleuze on, 250n38; Derrida on, 108–9; on difference, 248n3; on distance imposed by language, 198; and *Ereignis* in study of event, 57; essay of, on George's "Words," 108; and free indirect discourse, 148; on language, 250n44, 251nn51–52; Levinas on Blanchot and, 30; and meaning of *Ereignis*, 57–59, 250n40; on perceptible secret, 272n24; on poetic night, 253n24; on poetry, 38, 251n56; Pöggler on, 248n1; on question of language and poetry, 29; self-concealment of, 257n25; study of, of pre-Socratic sources of metaphysics, 63–64; on tradition, 249n27; on truth of beings in artwork, 253n28; and virtual and actual, 137–38; on willing, 249n12; writings of, establish conditions for ontological priority of event, 28–29. See also *Ereignis*

Heraclitus, 232, 233, 237, 279n17

heredity, 270n13. *See also* inheritance

hermeneutic circle, in *Ereignis*'s new conception of presence, 63, 136

historical distance, 9, 11–12

historical event, 4–13

historically effected consciousness, 9

historicity: Derrida's concept of, 32; Heidegger on, 63–64; hermeneutical, 9–10; Ricoeur split between historical positivism and, 5

historiography: and emergence of event, 3–5; and ethical suspension of past, 10; and neutrality of event, 11; and understanding of past, 7–8

history: corporeality and, 271n14; differences between literature and, 12–13; Eliot on, 234, 238; Heidegger on, 250n40; sense of vital move rooted in, 205; and temporality as aspect of becoming, 152; traditional positivist, 5

Hofmannsthal, Hugo Von, Lord Chandos letter, ix–xii

Homer, *Odyssey*, 18, 45–49, 53, 89–95

identity: challenged by temporality, 273n11; Deleuze and principle of, 123–24; essence of, through differentiation, 265n43; event deprives subject of stable, 147; Heidegger on, 65; resemblance and, 140; subordination of difference to, 266n46

ignorance, in intelligent creativity, 24

image: Barthes on consumption of, 200; Blanchot on world and, 198; Derrida's concepts of spectrality and phantomality and, 201–3; living event as, 199–200; mode of being of, 199; and vital move, 207–8; word and, 74, 164-168, 189

immanence: nonsense and, 136; as principle of Deleuze's ontology, 33, 135; of sense and real, 126. *See also* plane of immanence

immanent approach to event, 191

impersonality: Blanchot and, 83–84; of event, 147, 194, 206

impersonal singularities, 146–48
implex, Derrida on, 176
impossible: Deleuze's conception of possible and, 192; event as mourning of and call for, 111
impossible event, 30, 31–32, 92, 97–101, 178–79, 256n3
impressions, production of, in Derrida's conception of event, 103–5
improbable event, 20–21
inappropriability, event as phenomenon of, 98
inclusion, struggle between exclusion and, in *Fable for Another Time*, 43–44, 213, 214–15
incorporeal series of being, Deleuze on, 126–27, 129, 263n14
indifference, will of, 193
infinite, and confirmation and justification of philosophical system, 123
infinitive-form verbs, 147–48
inheritance: of body and language, 168, 267n67; versus heredity, 270n13
injury, and "willing the event," 143–44
inspiration, Blanchot and, 83
intelligent creativity, ignorance in, 24
"it," neutrality of, 147
iterability, 32, 99–100, 105–6, 113, 207, 257n13, 257n17

James, Henry, 26
Janicaud, Dominique, 258n36
Jesus Christ, and Juranville's conception of event, 36
judgment, suspension of, in theory of literary events, 38–39

Juranville, Alain, 36, 247n76, 247n86

Kafka, Franz, 30, 83, 106, 121, 149, 164, 170
knowledge: historical, 7–8, 9, 10; suspension of, in theory of literary events, 38–39; true, of historical existence, 36
Kristeva, Julia: on Colette, 270n9; on corporeal sign of animal, 225; on exploration of animality and scenes of vomiting, 224; on music, 226; poetic and linguistic psychoanalysis of, 166; on prelinguistic semiotic impulses, 24; on Proust, 273nn10–11

language: as aspect of becoming, 146–50; being of, 148, 198, 253n31; Blanchot on, 71, 198; of corporeal, 165; corporeal as impossibility of all, 168; creativity of, 145; Deleuze on body and, 271n15; Deleuze on event and, 247n84; Derrida on, of literature, 111–12; in Derrida's conception of event, 99; disappearance of real in, 80–81; distance imposed by, 197–98; *Ereignis* and question of, 60, 65–69; Genette and idea of pure, 162; Heidegger and question of, 29; Heidegger on, 251n51; inheritance of, 168, 267n67; within language, 268n71; limit of, 155; of literature and history, 12; literature as creation of corporeal, 207; poetic production of, 190; spectrality and, 202; tying Being to, 239
Laplanche, Jean, 260n57
Leskly, Hezy, 132
Levinas, Emmanuel, 30, 96

limit, event's spatial activity as internal, 154–55
literary event: defined, 3, 173–74; illustrated in Lord Chandos letter, ix–xii; questioning, 26–37; singularity of, 37–44; studying and understanding, viii–ix. *See also* theory of the literary event
literature: aim of, 1–2; approach of, to event, 1; Being and, 71–76, 79–80; being of, 80; Blanchot and Derrida on, 38, 203; Blanchot on, 251n3; Blanchot's conception of, 94; and ceaseless movement of dying, 88; and corporeality of ontological event, 167–68; as creation of corporeal language, 207; defined, 161–62; Deleuze on, 35–36, 204, 270n11; and Deleuze's conception of event, 157–58; Derrida on, 261n74, 276n25; in Derrida's conception of event, 32–33; differences between history and, 12–13; as dying corporeality, 41; as dying-living physical gesture, 164; essences of poetic-fiction articulated by history of, 162–64; event of, bound up with emotional experience of myth, 252n21; event questions understanding of, 173; exposes temporality of event, 152; image of, as affirmation in modality of suggestion, 94–95; importance of, as compound of crisis, viii; as making of event, 2; modern invention of corporeal in, 166; modern work of, 81–82; objective of, 240; political engagement of, 146; reading and writing of, 13; and structural explanation of narrative analysis, 16; and temporality as aspect of becoming, 157; vital move for, 204–8
"Little Gidding" (Eliot), 44; and acceptance of *amor fati*, 235–36; becoming traversing literary event in, 234–35; boundary between experience and *logos* in, 233–34; cyclical or dialectical unity between contradictory elements in, 231–33; dramatic landscape of, 229–30; and engagement in becoming of event, 236–38; examination of encounter with ghost in context of event in, 230–31; shout dominating event in, 227–29
living, communication between dead and, 237–38
logos: boundary between experience and, in "Little Gidding," 233–34; event questions foundations of, 101–2
Lord Chandos letter, ix–xii
Lotman, Jurij, 14, 15, 20–22, 244n43
"Love Song of J. Alfred Prufrock" (Eliot), 233
Lyotard, Jean François, 3, 246n61

Mallarmé, Stéphane, 30, 79–81, 148, 154, 164, 198, 254n33, 266n56
Merleau-Ponty, Maurice, 138–39, 166, 265n44, 269n8
Meschonnic, Henri, 24
metaphor, Deleuze on, 273n10
metaphysics: Heidegger and dismantling of foundations of, 59; Heidegger's study of pre-Socratic sources of, 63–64
microanalysis, as fourth principle of theory of literary event, 170–71

mimesis, 17, 18, 27, 118
mimetic-cultural explanation of narrative analysis, 15
Moderato Cantabile (Duras), 49–53
mistranslation, 42, 49, 113, 167, 207, 270n11
modernity, 81–82
modern moment, 162–68
moments, irregular, attention given to, in theory of literary events, 38
Monsieur Teste (Valéry), 165–66
moral judgment, Deleuze on, 144
multiplicity: becoming as, 34; Deleuze and Guattari on, 264n40; nonsense and, 135–36; plane of immanence as pure, 122, 137; as principle of Deleuze's ontology, 33, 124, 135; as role of event developed by Deleuze, 126; war relates event to idea of, 193; "willing the event" and, 35
music, 81, 90, 171, 209, 225–26
Musil, Robert, 26, 88
muthos, 6–7, 17–19, 22
mythology of happenings, 175–76, 197
myth(s): Blanchot offers different adaptation of, 253n22; event of literature bound up with emotional experience of, 252n21; used in Blanchot works, 76–77

naming: Blanchot on, 197; crisis of, in Derrida's conception of event, 102; as type of poetic work, 68
Nancy, Jean-Luc, 24, 40, 191, 266n57
narrative: event's effect on possibility of, as principle of literary writing, 89–95; Ricoeur on time and, 4

narrative analysis, lines of explanation of, 15–18
narrative event, 14–26
narrative grammar, 15
narrative intelligence, Ricoeur's theory of, 4, 6–7
narrative semiotics, 243n33
narrativity, 14
narratology, 14, 15, 22
negation: defining art through, 73–74; language and, of man's condition of finitude, 197–98; in *Time Regained*, 186
negation of event, 21, 244n43
neutrality: of death and dying, 193; of historical event, 11; of "it," 147; and productivity of nonsense, 135, 264n39
neutral third-person, asserting priority of, 147
Nietzsche, Friedrich: conception of, of becoming, 34; conception of, of eternal return, 35, 153–54; Deleuze and, 128; Foucault and, 292n84; on four errors of philosophy, 262n4; on outside, 156; on permanent and absolute flow of becoming, 245n49; on philosopher, 145; on purpose of art, 252n21
"Nobody," as embodiment of struggle in *Odyssey*, 47–49
non-advent of event, 102, 111, 121
non-chronological nature of plot, 14
"non-relation," 138, 156, 181, 235
nonsense: Deleuze and, 132; immanent corporeality of, 145; neutrality and productivity of, 264n39; sense and, 135–37
non-writer, Charlus as, in *Time Regained*, 179–80

Nora, Pierre, 5
no-thing, terrible thing as, 102–3, 104, 179
novel, versus narrative, 91–92
nucleus event, 16, 19

Odyssey (Homer), 18, 45–49, 53, 89–95
on, neutrality of, 147
onto-poetic, x, 167, 175, 182
the open, *Ereignis* and leaping into, 59–60
opposites, unity of, in "Little Gidding," 231–33, 235
originality of self, 163–64
Orpheus, event of work in myth of, 76–82, 89
other: awareness of and being found by, in "Little Gidding," 228, 231; Charlus as, in *Time Regained*, 180; defined, 106; Deleuze on *I* as, 267n66; in Derrida's conception of event, 98–99, 106–11; in literary text, 111–14; literature and quest for, 81–82; spectrality and, 202
outside, 155–58, 269n88

paradoxical act, Deleuze and comparison of action of event to, 131–33
Parnet, Claire: on embodiment of wound, 266n54; on language within language, 268n71; on plane of immanence, 266n48
past: Deleuze on, 268n80; Gadamer's approach to, 8–10; historiography and ethical suspension of, 10; historiography and understanding of, 7–8
pathos, issued from *peripeteia*, 19–20
Péguy, Charles, 141, 267n63

performative utterances, 117–19, 261nn68–69
peripeteia, 19–20
phantomality, and ambiguity of image, 201–3
philosopher, Deleuze on weakness of, 145
philosophy: Deleuze and Guattari on, 267n68; four great errors of, 262n4; Nancy on, 266n57; political engagement of, 146
plane of immanence: Being as, 33; conception of, 125; Deleuze on, 122–24; difference and, 131; fundamentally aggregated nature of, 157; multiplicity and chance and, 136, 137; rooted in groundless chaos, 135; structure transcends, 129; virtual and actual dwell together in, 141, 266n48
plot: Aristotle's construction of mimetic, 17; chance in, 20; emplotment and, 22–23; event as fundamentally bound to concept of, 13–14; logic of, 19; narrative structure of, 13–14; nucleus event and, 16; plot-less image of, 20–21; Ricoeur on, 18, 243n26
plot-less deviation, plot-less image: 20–22, 39, 170, 244n43
poetic-fiction: corporeality and modern articulation of, 164–68; essences of, articulated by history of literature, 162–64
Poetics (Aristotle), 17
poetics, difference between ethics and, in regard to praxis, 17
poetry: as art, 73; Blanchot on, 71, 252n16; *Ereignis* and, 60; and event as other, 107–8; Heidegger

poetry (*continued*)
  and question of, 29; Heidegger on, 38, 251n56; and language of Being, 68–69; Mallarmé's conception of, 81
poiesis, 17, 161
Ponge, Francis, 107, 112
Pontalis, Jean-Bertrand, 260n57
possible: and concept of existence, 139–40; Deleuze's conception of impossible and, 192
potentiality, in *Time Regained*, 189
praxis, 17
prefiguration, 6–7, 23
prejudices, and accessibility of junctions between present and past, 151, 242n17
presence, metaphysical link between present and, 151, 259n55
presencing, 62, 151, 152
present: Deleuze and Guattari on, 268n80; and Deleuze's becoming, 141; *Ereignis* and coming into view of, 60–64; metaphysical link between presence and, 151; and temporality as aspect of becoming, 153
Prop, Vladimir, 243n33
Proust, Marcel: conception of, of analogy, 182, 273n10; and examination of textual events, 196; fictive distance and, 12; and focusing on fragment of work, 171; on great literature, 270n11; Kristeva on, 270n9, 273n11; Rancière on, 273n8, 274n18; and theory of literary events as vital move, 42, 43, 44; use of term *in pace*, 274n16. See also *Time Regained* (Proust)

psychoanalysis: of Deleuze, 166–67; of Kristeva, 166

Rancière, Jacques, 149, 273n8, 274n18
reading: Blanchot on, 171, 271n17; Derrida's strategy of, 32
real: Derrida on, 275n24; disappearance of, in language, 80–81; emergence of sense and becoming of, 126–29; versus fictional in *Time Regained*, 274n18; and giving of sense, 125; possible and, 140
redoubling, in *Time Regained*, 184
refiguration, 6–7, 23
religious ceremonies, art's relation to, 72
repetition: appearance yielded through, 62–63; Deleuze on, 260n63; Freud on, 260n63; oscillation between unpredictable attack and desired, in *Time Regained*, 186; singularity of event emerges within impression of, 99–100; spectrality and, 202
resemblance: Blanchot's conception of, 199–200; Derrida and production of dissembling, 201–2
"The Return of the Event" (Nora), 5
Revolution, and Juranville's conception of event, 36
rhythm, 24
Richard, Jean-Pierre, 222–23, 224
Ricoeur, Paul: on action and character, 17; on application of pre-understanding to text, 23; on chronological and non-chronological natures of plot, 14; on composition, 20; on difference between poetics and ethics in

regard to praxis, 17; and historical event, 4, 5–7, 10; on plot, 18, 243n26; on reversals of fortune, 244n41
Robbe-Grillet, Alain, 84, 154, 200–201
Romano, Claude: on *advenant*, 247n76, 247n90; conception of, of event, 36–37, 244n43; on *Ereignis*, 61; and event as productive modality of being in the making, 184; influences on, 28; on phenomenology, 246n66
romanticism, Genette on literature and, 161–62
romantic moment, 162
romantic subjectivity, 82–83, 163

saying event, 118–20
secret: of being of becoming, 174; literary event as perceptible, 174–75, 272n24; testifying to, 106
self, pure originality of, 163–64
sense: becoming of real and emergence of, 126–29; Deleuze and giving of, 125; Deleuze on, 263n14; event exposes striving for, 134; of historical event, 10; nonsense and, 135–37; paradoxical construction of, 131–33; production of, 138, 172–73
sensible, expression of, 138–39
September 11, 2001 terrorist attacks, 96–97, 102, 103, 257n27
series of being: Deleuze on, 126–27, 129; event as inherent to both, 133; as incessant compositions that produce singular, 134; violence and, 136
shame, in *Fable for Another Time*, 219–21

Simon, Claude, 162, 166, 196, 207, signature, event of, 108
singularities, 134; impersonal, 146–48
Sirens, Ulysses's encounter with, in *The Book to Come*, 89–93
The Space of Literature (Blanchot), 71–76
spatiality, as aspect of becoming, 146, 154–57
spectrality, 99–100, 105–6, 113, 201–3, 257n13
speech: direct, in "Little Gidding," 227, 228, 231; direct, in *Moderato Cantabile*, 50–51
speech acts, 117–19, 253n30
Stiegler, Bernard: on inheritance of language, 267n67; on real, 275n24; on specter, 257n13
structural explanation of narrative analysis, 17
structuralism, 129–35
structural narratology, 15–16
style: Barthes on, 24; creativity of, 145; Deleuze's concept of, 149–50, 273n10; as deviation from norm, 163; Genette on, 245n54
subjectivity, romantic, 82–83, 163
surprise: event as, 3, 24, 32, 98, 104, 271n19; shout of, 227, 228, 231, 238
symptom, corporeal, 96, 116
syntax: Deleuze on, 41, 204; materiality of, 167

temporal distance, 9–10, 11, 242n17
temporality: as aspect of becoming, 150–54; narrative and, 93–94; trauma and, 115–17. *See also* time
temperature, temporament: 170

Index | 309

theory of the literary event: based on dying corporeality, 203–4; mission of, 181; as mythology of happenings displaying new configurations of becoming, 175–76; versus narratology, 22; and past theorizations, 25–26; principles of, 169–76; and variables affecting text, 23–24

Thing, event as, in Derrida's conception of event, 101–6

thinking, in Deleuze's conception of event, 122–23, 124

A Thousand Plateaus (Deleuze and Guattari), 137

threshold of event, 178

time: *Ereignis* and question of, 60–64; event of dying and, 88; events as outside of, 26; Ricoeur on narrative and, 4; trauma and modality of, 115–16; writing produces breach in ordinary observation of, 94. *See also* temporality

Time and Narrative I (Ricoeur), 4

Time Regained (Proust): accessing event in, 178; becoming in, 180–81; corporeality of event in, 181–85; event in, 177–78; fictive distance of literary event in, 185–87; formulation of literary demand of event in, 179–80; poetic production of language in, 190; Rancière on real versus fictional in, 274n18; spiritual achievement of literary event in, 189–90; state of potentiality in, 189; subterranean abode in, 188–89; and theory of literary events as vital move, 42, 43, 44; unfolding of literary event in, 187–88

Todorov, Tzvetan, 15–16, 19

Tomashevsky, Boris, 14

trace: conception of, as difference, 120; written, 113

tradition, Heidegger on, 63, 64, 249n27

transcendent approach to event, 191

translation: of corporeal, 207; pure, 113

trauma: defined, 260n57; Derrida on, 114–17

truth: in Badiou's conception of event, 37; of beings set to work, 253n28; in literary event, 175; progress of Hegel's, 266n57

Ulysses, in *The Book to Come*, 89–93

uncontainable becoming, 267n59

un-happening within happening, 3, 23, 27, 39, 40, 48, 176, 208

unpredictability of event, 10, 98

unreal: image and, 94; as movement of work of art and literature, 80–81; Robbe-Grillet's leap to, 201

unsaid, *Ereignis* and question of language and, 67, 68

untimely, 153

Valéry, Paul, 164, 165–66, 173, 174, 176, 259n55, 261n68

verbs, impersonality of event expressed by infinitive, 147–48

Verstraeten, Philippe, 59

Veyne, Paul, 5–6, 7

victims: corporeal experience of, 114; distinction between political experience and that of, 257n27; and impression versus corporeal war, 103–5

violence: of Being, 136, 138; of being of becoming, 24; of corporeal war, 194; Deleuze on, 266n56, 267n66; of event, 32, 240; structure of, in *Time Regained*, 181, 182–84

Virgil, 275n11

virtual: in Derrida's conception of event, 137–41; and embodiment of event, 206; and event in *Time Regained*, 180; as inseparable from actual, 34; and plane of immanence, 266n48; plane of immanence and, 266n48; and temporality as aspect of becoming, 152–53

virtual consumption, Barthes on, 200

virtualities, extricating, from actualities, 141, 142–43

virtualization: body of the event and, 206–7; in Deleuze's conception of event, 34

visor effect, 202

vitality, historicism of, 165–66

vital move, 41–44, 165, 196, 203, 204–8

void: appearance of image as, 200; Blanchot on, 255n57, 268n83; event as un-presented, 37; outside and, 155

vomiting, and animality in *Fable for Another Time*, 43, 223–25

war: acceptance of, as ethical attitude to what happens, 236; corporeal and impression of, 103–5; Deleuze on corporeality and, 192–93, 194, 274n6

"What Is the Word" (Beckett), 67

whirlwind, in *Fable for Another Time*, 211–14

"willing the event," 35–36, 44, 143–44

"will of anonymity," 193

will to power, 134, 156

wind, use of word in "Little Gidding," 230

"Words" (George), 68, 108

words, and language of Being, 68–69

world: Barthes on image and, 200; Being and, 60; Blanchot on image and, 198, 256n64; book as image of, 23–24; event of appropriation and, 65; Kristeva on writing and, 270n9; letting, speak as it is, 132–33; Merleau-Ponty's concept of flesh of, 166, 269n8; and Proust's conception of analogy, 182

writing: Blanchot and new image of, 83; Blanchot on, 244n44, 253n26; corporeal as constructed through resistance of, 167; Deleuze on, 35–36, 38; Derrida and, of event, 117–21; Derrida on, 111–12; as event, 13; event's effect on possibility of narrative as principle of literary, 89–95; impersonal, 84; imposition of other on, 112; Kristeva on, 166, 270n9; Mallarmé on, 80; performance of, in Derrida's conception of event, 96; as singular act of thinking, 158; vital move and, 208; as work of ceaseless death, 85–88

writing corporeally, 42–43, 207, 208

writing-event, 117, 119, 121